SPENSER STUDIES

XXVII

SPENSER
STUDIES
A Renaissance
Poetry Annual
XXVII

EDITED BY

Anne Lake Prescott
William A. Oram
Andrew Escobedo

AMS PRESS, INC.
New York

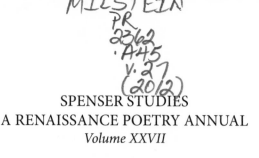

SPENSER STUDIES
A RENAISSANCE POETRY ANNUAL
Volume XXVII

Edited by
Anne Lake Prescott, William A. Oram, and Andrew Escobedo

Spenser Studies is published annually by AMS Press, Inc. as a forum for Spenser scholarship and criticism and related Renaissance subjects. Manuscripts must be double-spaced, including notes, which should be grouped at the end and should be prepared according to *The Chicago Manual of Style*. Authors of essay-length manuscripts should include an abstract of 100–150 words and send it (preferably in a Windows-compatible format) by email attachment to Anne Lake Prescott, William A. Oram, and Andrew Escobedo at the following email addresses: aprescot@barnard.edu, woram@smith.edu, and escobedo@ohio.edu.

Please send inquiries concerning subscriptions or the availability of earlier volumes to AMS Press, Inc., Brooklyn Navy Yard, 63 Flushing Avenue – Unit #221, Brooklyn, NY 11205-1073, USA.

ISSN 0195–9468
e-ISSN 2167-8529

International Standard Book Numbers
Set ISBN-13: 978-0-404-19200-6

Vol. XXVII Cloth ISBN-13: 978-0-404-19227-3
Vol. XXVII e-ISBN-13: 978-0-404-90227-8

AMS PRESS, INC.
Brooklyn Navy Yard, 63 Flushing Avenue – Unit #221
Brooklyn, NY 11205-1073, USA
www.amspressinc.com

MANUFACTURED IN THE UNITED STATES OF AMERICA

Contents

Gleanings
313

Illustrations

Index

CAROL KASKE

Chivalric Idealism versus Pragmatism in Spenser and Malory: Taking up Arms in a Wrongful Quarrel (The Kathleen Williams Lecture, 2010)

Spenser and Malory both tell stories in which admirable people contradict themselves, acting in ways that they condemn else-where—not because of human weakness, but because of a nec-essary pragmatism. Particular situations force them to descend from their earlier idealistic pronouncements about chivalric conduct in order to deal with the actual world. After Malory has his Arthur require in the Pentecostal Oath that his knights fight only in just quarrels, he puts him in a position that forces him to break his own rule. Spenser, too, puts his Arthur in a position in which, speaking to Sir Turpine, he contradicts his earlier prescription against fighting in wrongful quarrels in stating that fighting in a wrongful quarrel is less bad than cow-ardly behavior (VI.vi.35). In a related case, Spenser's Artegall harangues the turncoat Sir Burbon (V.xi) that to relinquish the shield bearing his personal device as he has done is unjustifi-able under any circumstances; this tenacity illustrates another chivalric rule: "come home either with your shield or on it." But then Artegall abandons his own shield for a good strategic rea-son and the poet applauds him for it. Artegall further silently helps the turncoat to win the Lady Flourdelis, giving aid to the

Spenser Studies: A Renaissance Poetry Annual, Volume XXVII, Copyright © 2012 AMS Press, Inc. All rights reserved.   DOI: 10.7756/spst.027.001.1-22

man whose lack of secure principle he has criticized—an action based on a necessary pragmatism in late sixteenth-century religious politics. All three heroes must accommodate their ideals to the demands of the actual world.

> Be not thou just overmuch, neither make thy selfe overwise: wherefore shouldest thou bee desolate?
>
> *Ecclesiastes* 7:18 (Geneva translation)

*I*WILL CONCERN MYSELF HERE with several moments in which we see Malory and Spenser contradicting themselves, insisting absolutely on a chivalric code only to suggest that it is possible in some cases to violate it blamelessly. We see them thinking through, and forcing the reader to think through, what happens when the ideal values of chivalry meet the demands of the actual world, or where competing values conflict.[1] I will argue that both writers are idealistic pragmatists, committed to the values of chivalry but aware that in the actual world it is sometimes necessary to choose the lesser of two evils. Malory's *Morte Darthur* and Spenser's *Faerie Queene* rarely call direct attention to these violations of chivalry. Instead they work in two stages. Initially they shock their readers when a speech or an act contradicts chivalric principles articulated earlier, and that shock forces the reader to understand the rationale for the action and, with it, the necessity of acting imperfectly in an imperfect world. While the evidence suggests that Spenser refers at times to particular moments in Malory's text, the writers also share a temperamental similarity, an idealistic pragmatism. I will focus mainly on the way both writers treat taking up arms in a wrongful quarrel, but I will consider as well other problematic episodes in which Spenser's pragmatism appears, notably the Sir Burbon episode in *FQ* V.

I. CHIVALRIC CONTRADICTION IN MALORY

When Malory describes the founding of the Round Table on Pentecost, in the beginning of the *Morte Darthur*, he adds to his French source a Pentecostal Oath administered by Arthur himself at his coronation, and prescribed for recitation on each annual recurrence of this festal day (Caxton III.15,

Winchester folio 49ʳ). This annual event is not recounted again, but knights frequently mention swearing to uphold the Oath, which follows:[2]

> The Kynge . . . charged them never to do outerage nothir mourthir, and allwayes to fle treson, and to gyff mercy unto hym that askith mercy, uppon payne of forfiture of their worship and lordship of Kynge Arthure for evirmore; and allwayes to do ladyes, damesels, and jantilwomen and wydowes [socour], strenghthe hem in hir ryghtes, and never to enforce them [that is, rape them], uppon payne of dethe. Also, that no man take no batayles in a *wrongefull quarell,* for no love [emphasis mine; Caxton, the only version which Spenser is likely to have known, reads "for no *lawe*"]—ne for no worldis goodis.[3]

The Oath in general sets certain standards for the knights' behavior if they want to retain Arthur's royal favor. The Oath is not Malory's last word on ethics, but it constitutes a list of fundamentals. It is just idealistic enough and not too much. In explicitly forbidding rape, the Oath's standard may seem pretty low. But it is not too low for the dramatis personae, in that before the Oath, in Caxton III.iii, we learn that Pellinore once took a farm-girl's maidenhead "halfe by force." Malory's Arthur admonishes his knights in terms of their moral characters as he finds them to be at the time. As Robert L. Kelly puts it, "King Arthur . . . knows that his military order cannot yet be [an] idealistic, truly chivalric fraternity."[4]

Arthur's limiting his strictures to what auditors such as Pellenore can understand at the moment has what I call a dialogical relativity. In a literary work that is truly dialogic in form—not a treatise chopped up into the mechanical question-and-answer of Magister and Discipulus, but a form like that which Plato predicts he would use when questioning a friend[5]— the magister or spokesman for the author does not declare his entire belief-system at once, but proposes an initial part of it. Pellenore shows only a small respect for the woman's right to refuse sex, but he could perhaps be persuaded by the Oath to respect it entirely and to forswear force altogether. So what is said is relative to the depicted audience and the circumstances.[6] To take a much larger example, if, as could be argued from the Grail-Quest, Christianity is the norm for the whole book, then the previous, more worldly and martial, ethics of combat such as that contained in the Oath represents not precisely evil but a good only in a dialogically relative sense: it is only part of the whole duty of man; it needs to be supplemented by other values, such as some greater good.[7]

The most significant part of the Oath for our purpose is Malory's last sentence: "Also, that no man take no batayles in a wrongefull quarrel, for no law ne for no worldis goodis." In the real world, the oath of the Order of the Bath resembled the Oath in forbidding a knight to dignify by his presence a trial in which a judgment is handed down that to the best of his knowledge is wrongful. A *fortiori*, fighting in a trial-by-combat for such a cause would presumably be prohibited as well. Government officials also swore not to allow wrongful quarrels; naturally, since such discernment was their job and physical fighting was not.[8] Malory's wrongful-quarrel clause, like its counterpart in the Order of the Bath, sets a high standard for the ethics of individual knights.

Aside from Malory, Lydgate's Fall of Princes and Hardyng's rhymed Chronicle are the only other contemporary belletristic works to decree that the knights of the Round Table "are to fight only in just, true, and well-examined causes" (Kelly, 54); as such they constitute probable sources. Malory brings in this particular prohibition for several reasons, one of which is to promote what has long been regarded as the redeeming social value of chivalry—harnessing in the cause of justice, or at least within some rules, the restlessness and blood-lust of young gentlemen who are bored with long peace. It is part of Malory's concern to clarify and emphasize ethics.

Another precedent for Malory's emphasis, although from a religious perspective, was a chivalric handbook, *The Tree of Battles*, by Honoré Bonet, a middle-level cleric born in the 1340s whose works were known in England. Here chivalric idealism reaches its apogee as Bonet decides that a man who dies in the heat of battle is almost certainly "in the way of damnation" unless the man is not otherwise in mortal sin and unless he is sure—for example, if the Church has told him so—that the cause is just.[9] The implication is that for the sake of his soul, a knight should avoid not only personal sin but also social sin: that is, wrongful quarrels.

Nonetheless, later on in the *Morte*, Arthur violates his own oath. In the section which Vinaver entitles "Arthur and Accolon" and Shepherd "After Thes Questis," Arthur and two of his knights are snatched away by Morgan le Faye's enchantment. Arthur is transported into the prison of Sir Damas, who is heartily despised by his people because he is cowardly, deceitful, and merciless. Damas has also tried to dispossess his younger brother Sir Outlake, whom everyone respects, of the manor that constitutes his "livelode," his sole support. In the source, Outlake has other property and so does not need the manor so desperately (Asher, 257). Malory makes

Damas's cause more wrongful by making Outlake both more impoverished and more popular. Damas asks Arthur, who does not reveal his identity, to fight a trial by combat with Sir Outlake on Damas's behalf to prove or establish Damas's ownership of the manor. Damas has successively captured and importuned thirty-eight knights in an attempt to persuade one of them to fight this trial by combat on his behalf. All have refused because of Damas's disgrace—deserved because of his deceitfulness, his cruelty, and the cowardice that prevents his fighting Outlake on his own behalf. According to Bonet's tradition, the thirty-eight knights who are or were held in Damas's prison should not do battle for him, lest, being killed on the battlefield, they should go to hell. These knights have clear consciences, but eighteen of them have already died from lack of food and other harsh prison conditions, and the twenty that remain are in poor health. Arthur, when invited, replies pragmatically that although the choice is "harde" he would rather "fyght with a knyght than to dey in prison" (Winchester 50^v, Caxton 4.7). As Kenneth Hodges alone recognizes, in undertaking to fight on Damas's behalf, Arthur is taking up arms in a wrongful quarrel.[10] Arthur apparently makes light of Bonet's views about the fate of his soul, though he later takes the precaution of hearing Mass before he starts out for the battlefield (51^v). Arthur here sees the necessity of taking arms in a wrongful quarrel and living to see another day—perhaps in the hope that he might ultimately undo the wrong that he has done.

This is just what Arthur does. Malory's adaptation of the source in the end of the episode highlights the moral issues and corrects the unjust social situation, for he adds that Arthur crafts a just resolution of the dispute that originally motivated the trial by combat. First, in a risky battle Arthur wins the manor for Damas as he promised to do. But after he identifies himself as the king, he then turns around and tells Damas to give the disputed manor back to his disinherited brother, implying that what Arthur and Damas had previously done was wrong. Malory's Arthur placates Sir Damas a bit by decreeing that Outlake, as the younger brother (so stated in the source), will hold the manor from Damas and pay him a yearly tribute. But in a jibe at Damas's cowardice, Arthur specifies that the tribute be a palfrey, a horse ridden mostly by women (fo 55^r, Caxton IV.11–12). By contrast, in the source Arthur merely tells both brothers to stop fighting, as if they were equally culpable, and we never hear who got the disputed manor: indeed, we presume Damas had his way since it was his champion, Arthur, who eventually won the battle and no one reversed its outcome (Asher, chapter 38, 264).

Thus, although Arthur rights the wrong he has done by fighting in a wrongful quarrel, he flouts the legal outcome of his victory—namely the verdict rendered through a trial by combat. Here is a second moment in which Arthur seems to stray from the straight and narrow. How are we to account for his act? I propose that Malory made Arthur's new decree in this episode into an example of equity as distinct from the letter of the law. The law is exemplified here in the authority a of trial by combat. By awarding the disputed manor to the wrong man, namely, Sir Damas, the law as represented by the trial failed to bring about justice. Changing a verdict to what the lawgiver would presumably have decided had he himself witnessed a miscarriage of justice, says Aristotle, is called equity—an overriding of the law that is permitted only to a ruler.[11] (Arthur can thus set aside the trial by combat when his kingship is revealed.) Yet Arthur, in restoring the manor to Outlake, has broken the legal rule of trial by combat and shocked his readers once again only to rise above rules as his social status rises. By this second reversal of rules, a palinode of a palinode, as Patricia Phillippy would say, Arthur realigns himself with the Oath. In this episode, fighting in a wrongful quarrel is good only in a dialogically relative sense. Malory among others is interested in what Armstrong calls "the tensions, shortcomings, and blind spots of the chivalric project" (29). This may be one of the things that attracted Spenser to him.

By portraying his Arthur fighting on behalf of the contemptible Sir Damas, Malory afforded Spenser a model of the principled breaking of the wrongful-quarrel clause; then, by having Arthur reverse the outcome of his wrongful quarrel to a righteous one, Malory models for Spenser the principled breaking of a law of trial by combat.

In reading this passage I have treated its contradictions by chronicling in order the two phases that may be presumed to take place in the responses of the reader—from an initial shock to dialogic resolution or understanding. In this, my critical method somewhat resembles that of the early Stanley Fish.[12] An initial idealistic statement is enunciated only to be contradicted by the later action of a hero, an action shocking the reader into consideration of its rationale. We must give the moral shock its real weight because it is part of the intended aesthetic and moral response, not something to be quickly explained away and forgotten. Each shock provokes the reader to consider more deeply both the original ideal and the action that contradicts it, and the result is a finer and more nuanced understanding of the way in which ideals need to work in the world. The new view of events usually leaves something still standing that is of value; it does not cancel out and supplant all of the original ideal. The reader can take home a message containing an adversative. A judicious reconciliation of the wrongful-quarrel clause with the subsequent behavior of Malory's Arthur, in "Arthur and Accolon," and of Spenser's Arthur too, as we shall see, would be something to the effect that one should usually avoid taking up arms in wrongful quarrels, but sometimes for a greater good this precept needs to be violated to fit the messy circumstances of life.

II. SPENSER ON WRONGFUL QUARRELS

Spenser knew and used Malory. Besides the well-known parallels of *Faerie Queene* Book I to Malory's Tale of Gareth in Book VI,[13] other parallels are constituted by both the antagonist the Blattant Beast, based on Malory's Beast Glatissant, and the Malorian knights Pelleas and Lamoracke.[14] More importantly for my purposes, A. C. Hamilton in his edition has already signaled in an episode we will be dealing with—Arthur's encounter with Turpine—an allusion to a different clause of the Oath, the command to give mercy when asked. I believe it is thus likely that Spenser not only borrows from but alludes to Malory, and we need to consider what the poet made of him on the topic of how far it is necessary and permissible to compromise with evil.

Spenser's view on this would at first seem unequivocal. He repeats four times in the course of his epic that good knights fight for just causes and the very insistence shows his earnestness. In Book I, a reliable judge commends a knight because he has never "throwne to ground the unregarded right" (this is Una's recommendation of Red Crosse, I.vii.47).[15] In Book III, when Spenser's Arthur and the Palmer persuade Britomart and Guyon to cease fighting and pledge eternal friendship and when Red Crosse takes the defeated Guyon to ride with him on his own horse, the poet-speaker exults, without the irony of Ariosto's original:

> Oh goodly usage of those antique times
> In which the sword was servaunt unto right; . . .
>   (III.i .13)

Two statements appear in Book V of chivalry's need for a moral purpose: The poet-speaker himself comments admiringly about Arthur:

> But the brave Prince for honour and for right,
> Gainst tortious power and lawlesse regiment,
> In the behalfe of wronged weake did fight:
> More in his causes truth he trusted then in might.
>
> (V viii.30)

And in V.xi.17, just a few cantos farther on, Arthur deflects praise from himself, demurring that it was not his prowess but "the causes right: / That same is it, which fought for you this day." These are four unanimous assertions of chivalric idealism, four counterparts to the wrongful-quarrel clause in the Oath. The last two, those in Book V, establish Spenser's Arthur as both subject to and spokesman for chivalric idealism. These also assert that if the cause is just, the knight will get extra help either from Providence or from his own conscience.

Yet six cantos later, Arthur contradicts his own repeated injunction. He is addressing Sir Turpine, who has played the part, as his name suggests, of a thoroughly base creature. When Calepine and the wounded Serena ask his help, first in fording a stream and then in giving them a night's lodging, he taunts them and later attacks them. To punish this mistreatment of Calepine and Serena, Arthur pursues this discourteous knight to his castle. Turpine, at his wife Blandina's invitation, hides from Arthur under her "garment." When Blandina intercedes for him, Arthur allows him to emerge from his hiding place and arise, giving him mercy in contrast to Turpine's own refusal of mercy to his suppliants.

Arthur then castigates the pusillanimous villain, regretting that he had spared his life at their last encounter (VI.vi.33–5). Turpine has committed crimes in harming others, and has shamed himself and "all knights" (33) by hiding, as he has just done, under his lady's garments. Moreover, in the past he has directly and physically harmed some people. But as he continues to point out Turpine's weaknesses, Arthur also returns to the issue of wrongful quarrels:

> Yet further hast thou heaped shame to shame,
> And crime to crime, by this thy cowheard feare.
> For first it was to thee reprochfull blame,
> To erect this wicked custome, which I heare,

Gainst errant Knights and Ladies thou dost reare;
Whom when thou mayst, thou dost of arms despoile,
Or of their upper garment, which they weare:
Yet doest thou not with manhood, but with guile
Maintaine this evill use, thy foes thereby to foile.

And lastly in approvance of thy wrong,
To shew such faintnesse and fowle cowardize,
Is greatest shame: for oft it falles, that strong
And valiant knights doe rashly enterprize,
Either for fame, or else for exercize,
A *wrongfull quarrel* to maintaine by fight;
Yet have, through prowesse and their brave emprise,
Gotten great worship in this worldes sight,
For greater force there needs to maintaine wrong, then right.

(*FQ* VI.vi.34–35; my emphasis)

It is in lines 3–9 of the second stanza (35) that Arthur casually by-passes the wrongful-quarrel edict. Tonkin and Hamilton are struck by his contradiction of chivalric idealism in general.[16] Arthur thus makes what Humphrey Tonkin calls an "interesting" and a "somewhat surprising declaration";[17] and A. C. Hamilton, in his note, an "extraordinary claim." I agree with both.[18]

Several points are surprising. Arthur says the unprincipled knights are still honored by this world for their physical courage and knightly ability. Because Arthur's praise, though tempered, is not ironic, Spenser seems to agree that the unprincipled knights deserve some credit. (Arthur can sometimes be ironic, as in his comment on the two mercenaries in VI.vii.13.2, but when he is, his tone differs.) The four affirmations of chivalric idealism are no longer definitive, all-inclusive descriptions of knighthood but only of what happens under ideal circumstances; there are other ways to earn fame and to win battles. Although the words "lastly" and "rashly" and the phrase "in this worldes sight" diminish Arthur's approval, the phrase "strong / And valiant knights" is tolerant, as is the overall tone of lines 3–9. Through Arthur, Spenser says that manly aggression armed with physical courage does not always need a righteous pretext but can constitute an intrinsic, freestanding value in itself. He could have mentioned that courage is one of the four cardinal virtues. Conversely, a wrongful quarrel is no longer viewed as an absolute evil to be avoided at all costs, as in Malory's Oath or in Bonet; it is just another circumstance in which to gain fame or "worship." In fact, Spenser's Arthur praises wrongful quarrels as exhibiting the knights' "force" to the world better than do righteous quarrels. This is to privilege athletics over ethics.

The last three lines of our stanza read,

> And have, for prowesse and their brave emprise,
> Gotten great worship in this worldes sight,
> For greater force there needs to maintain wrong, then right.

These lines are theologically problematic. The unprincipled knights can "often" eventually defeat the less powerful upholders of the right, provided that they have sufficient prowess and courage; and they can survive to enjoy not only still more prowess from their "exercize" but also enhanced fame. This statement renders moot the Providential control and revelatory nature of trial by combat. It assumes what Spenser as well as Malory often state, that Providence reinforces the cause of right. But Arthur announces that many knights, for the sake of a greater challenge, decline that Providential assistance and fight wrongful quarrels anyway; and sometimes they win. Honoré Bonet would condemn the knights and deny their major premise. Only in this "extraordinary" stanza—and that is what makes it extraordinary—is divine aid seen as undesirable because a hindrance to honor. Normally in *The Faerie Queene*, as in other chivalric romances, supernatural aid is a credit to the hero who receives it, as is Arthur's miraculous shield in I.vii. Here it is glorious to do without God's aid.

I think that in his approach to Turpine, Arthur is being pedagogical, following a Platonic strategy. Appeals to shame and fame, prowess and courage have a chance of imparting to Turpine some backbone, whereas an exhortation appealing to chivalric idealism, Christian charity, getting to Heaven, or virtue for virtue's sake would not. Arthur's scolding is relative to the outlook of his addressee at the present time, and pitched, in the manner of Plato, just a little above it. Arthur tolerates taking up arms in a wrongful quarrel as the next stage in the process of Turpine's development; it is a minimalist morality. Turpine will be a little nobler (though more destructive) if he becomes like the unprincipled knights; they have the virtue of physical courage—classical, chivalric, and respected even by theologians as one of the Four Cardinal Virtues. This lowering of standards is an example of Spenser's and Arthur's pedagogical and pragmatic thinking, and hence a version of dialogic relativity. Arthur here pares down chivalry's requirements to the minimum of courage. Thus he plans to contain one unknightly impulse, cowardice, within bounds, even if he cannot move Turpine to fight only for the right. Bravery is a minimum qualification for a knight—a virtue that often proves useful in time of war. The preservation of community through the institutionalization of violence exemplifies the traditionally recognized social utility of chivalry. To value social utility above personal ethics is to focus on the practical.

An outrageous statement like VI.vi.35.3–9 becomes more palatable if it is seen as a part of a "thread" on the same topic. Besides Arthur's unprincipled knights, another example of a person breaking a rule, wrongfully taking up arms, and winning both his battle and the commendation of an authority-figure is Tristram at the beginning of Book VI (ii.8–39). At issue is the generally known rule that a civilian should not attack and above all not kill a knight. The as yet unknighted Tristram kills a knight who is physically and verbally abusing his own "lady"—his own wife or mistress (VI.ii.7–8). When Calidore questions his behavior, Tristram replies, ". . . loth were I to have broken/ The law of armes: yet breake it should againe,/ Rather then let my selfe of wight be stroken."

Calidore, the authority-figure in this episode, adds the main justification for Tristram's transgression, which is to help someone in distress: "What he spake, for you he spake it, dame" (VI.ii.14). Thus Tristram and his defender Calidore bend one chivalric rule for a greater good, as Malory's Arthur bends the wrongful-quarrel clause to benefit the twenty imprisoned knights. This instance differs from the wrongful-quarrel issue because it hinges on the contradiction between two different chivalric rules, the imperative against a civilian killing a knight and the imperative that a knight (in Malory's Oath) "strengthe" women "in hir ryghtes." Tristram flouts one rule to obey a greater one. The Tristram episode is about the principled breaking of a rule in order to defend a wife or mistress in her rights. Thus Tristram's quarrel is wrongful only in a technical sense. Like Malory's Arthur, he illustrates placing equity over the letter of the law because he does what the lawgiver would have decreed had he himself been present and seen the circumstances.

III. SIR BURBON'S SHIELD

My final example, a rich one, concerns a good knight who, while he does not fight in a wrongful quarrel, nonetheless bends or breaks several chivalric rules for a good cause. This is Artegall who, in the last cantos of Book V, changes his attitudes toward the abandonment of a shield between his encounter with Sir Burbon (V.xi.44–65) and his battle with Grantorto (VI.xii.13–26). Artegall's explicit comments on shields appear in the first episode, and it is seemingly contradicted by his attitude toward his own shield in the later one—an episode on which the narrator comments (V.xii.18–19).

In the first episode, Sir Burbon has just abandoned his shield because it has been badly battered in his ongoing struggle to win his beloved back from Grantorto and his army. Burbon offers the justification of "necessity" but Artegall rebukes him, insisting that nothing, not even self-preservation, could justify such a deed (V.xi.55–56). Artegall's chivalric attitude toward shields obeys the militaristic admonition attributed to Spartan mothers: "Come back either holding your shield or upon it," that is, dead. Heroes of Books I and V dramatize this tenacity. As Borris and others point out, a knight's shield symbolizes his principles.[19] Because of its provenance, and the allegory which equates Sir Burbon with Henri IV of France, I would add that Burbon's shield stands for Henri's Protestant faith (I.i.2; II.i.27; V.xi.53): Artegall's rebuke of Sir Burbon insists, allegorically, that one must hold onto one's religious principles at all costs. But despite his reproof, Artegall suddenly consents to help the man who threw away his religious faith and to win Flourdelis (i.e., France), back for him.

Yet after Artegall's rescue of Burbon, he seems to contradict the rule by which he has condemned him. When he resumes his quest and sails to Irena's land to help her against her persecutor, Grantorto, the subsequent battle is a trial by combat. Grantorto's axe sticks in Artegall's shield and when he tries to hang onto it, the giant uses it to drag him "all about": the fight degenerates into a tug-of-war (V.xii.22). Artegall is symbolically replaying (and perhaps Spenser makes him unconsciously parody) his earlier verbal praise of tenacity, as well as the tenacity of Redcrosse in Book I (xi.38–43) and of Arthur in his conquest of Geryoneo's monster in Book V (xi.27). But here holding on to the shield does not work. Accordingly Artegall relinquishes his shield, leaving Grantorto "cumbred" with it and manages in the giant's discomfiture to win (V.xii.21–23).

The move is undignified and breaks a chivalric rule. But we can tell that Spenser nevertheless approves of the strategy not only because of the favorable outcome, but also because he comments on it. Four stanzas earlier, when Artegall performs an undignified maneuver and stoops to avoid Grantorto's blows, the poet-speaker applauds:

> No shame to stoupe, ones head more high to reare,
> And much to gaine, a little for to yield;
> So stoutest knights doen oftentimes in field.
>
> (V.xii.19)

Spenser bestows such praise on this trivial maneuver because the praise also applies to the later, and more serious, of Artegall's apparently shameful actions, his relinquishing his own shield. But, of course, the allegorical meaning of this shield differs: it is not religious and it is therefore expendable. Abandoning it is not an apostasy. Here Spenser distinguishes between secular and religious principles: as I have argued in *Spenser and Biblical Poetics*, Artegall's abandonment of his shield suggests the replacement of English Common Law (the ideal of justice), with the autocratic but in Spenser's view necessary martial law (73–80). There I further argued (78–80) that in the contrast between the two episodes Spenser gives us a pattern of relinquishing one's shield first in a bad sense as Burbon does, then in a good one, as Artegall does, or *in malo* and *in bono*, as medieval biblical exegetes phrase it. The moral of the action in these two seemingly contradictory passages is that while one must hold to one's religious principles through thick and thin (Arthur reproves Burbon for his weakness), other principles, such as English Common Law, may sometimes be sacrificed for a greater good (V.xii.2–27). Hanging onto all one's principles manifests integrity, but it may also allow one's enemies to drag one "all about." The episode thus distinguishes when one should or should not relinquish one's principles.

It does not, however, explain Arthur's rescue of Burbon. In the historical allegory, as critics have long recognized, Artegall's actions parallel the reluctant decision of Queen Elizabeth and her advisers to send troops in order to help Henri of Navarre take his place on the throne of France, even though he had become a turncoat and changed his religion from Protestant to Catholic. Together, Arthur and Burbon with the help of Talus, successfully "rescue" the sullen maiden Flourdelis, who seems not to know which suitor she wants, Burbon or Grantorto. Thus, while Artegall's rescue of Burbon allegorizes the English support of the rightful heir to the French throne, it also embodies the compromising support of a man who has abandoned his Protestant faith. If this is not a wrongful quarrel, it is hardly a shining example of principled action.

As critics realize, Artegall's own actions (and the poet's comments on them) sometimes disturbingly fulfill or echo the statements of Burbon. One distinction between the two can be explained. The argument (erroneously prefixed to xii instead of xi) accuses Burbon of "changing shield." When Burbon claims that "my former shield I may resume again" (V.xi.56.2) his statement is unconvincing because, allegorically, Henri's abandonment of his religion was almost certainly permanent. On the other hand, when Artegall relinquishes his shield, he can claim that he will resume it again because his only purpose was to kill Grantorto and, that done, he will be able to resume it. Artegall obviously does not mean to give up even his expendable shield for any length of time, let alone exchange it for another (cf. V.xi.54, 56 with V.xii.19). Allegorically, Spenser sees the loss of the common law as temporary; after Ireland has been Anglicized, it can resume the English legal system.

Artegall and his real-life counterparts Essex and Elizabeth condescended to help the disgraced apostate Sir Burbon because they hoped to gain something from him and those he led. I suggest that while Spenser was pondering whether Elizabeth's action was right or wrong, he saw that life was imitating art—that those contemporary historical events recalled Malory's palinodic episode of "Arthur and Accolon." He must have thought of Malory's Arthur's general prohibition against taking up arms in a wrongful quarrel and of the same character's nevertheless helping the wicked and cowardly Sir Damas. Such parallels between Elizabeth's behavior and that of Malory's Arthur could thus have spawned Spenser's whole string of episodes of rule-breakers rewarded—V.xi, V.xii, VI.ii, and VI.vi.35.

Borris (p. 62) and others have shown that the obvious historical allegory has determined, from outside, the story of Artegall's rule-breaking on behalf of Sir Burbon. As Anne Lake Prescott has explained, while Henri probably did not in fact say "Paris is worth a mass," he did quip "to a fellow convert 'Oh, I see—you have some crown to win.'"[20] Prescott documents both Elizabeth's disappointment in Henri and her reasons for nevertheless continuing to help him. The good achieved by Elizabeth's pragmatic advocacy included retaining France as an ally, under whatever regime or religion, as a bulwark against Spain's attempts to conquer and to Romanize England. In helping Henri to gain his throne Elizabeth and her counselors also put Henri in a position to promulgate the Edict of Nantes (1598), also called the Edict of Toleration (Prescott, 208), which he enacted in order to protect the Huguenots whom he had deserted. Spenser published the second installment of *The Faerie Queene* in 1596, before this important event;

but he may well have favored helping Henri in this poem in hopes that he would take some such step to help the Protestants.

The containment of Spain would from an English viewpoint have fallen under the heading of a "necessity," as in Burbon's line, "whenas necessity doth it constrain," after the attempted attack of the Spanish Armada in 1588 and the actual Spanish and papal invasion of Ireland in 1580. As Prescott argues, Henri was also constrained by political "necessity," given that France sorely needed a king, and that with this one exception—his Protestantism—he was admirably suited and positioned for the post (and indeed, according to Salic law, had already held it since 1589).[21] In order to secure possession of the throne, however, Henri became a turncoat, distrusted by many of his new Catholic coreligionists who both endorsed the tradition that the king of France must be Catholic and distrusted the sincerity of his conversion. Yet he apparently represents another type of rule-breaker who, although stigmatized as an apostate, should be granted some leeway because he might improve or at any rate can understand both sides of the religious conflict and perhaps act as a mediator. These hopes for Henri's kingship could fall under the heading of a greater good—a very practical one. Kenneth Borris comments: "The Burbon episode emphatically marks a transition from the . . . plane of ideal resolutions to the compromises of human history" (62–63; Borris insulates Arthur from this pragmatism, but in VI.vi.35, as I have shown, he exemplifies it).

In considering these compromises it is important to notice that the Bible itself contains a deliberately startling command promoting moral and legal leniency if not laxity: "Noli esse justus multum"—"Do not be overly just" (Ecclesiastes 7:16, sometimes numbered 7:17). In defense of Artegall's willingness to help Burbon, Lowell Gallagher perceptively cites the verse from Ecclesiastes as it is quoted and translated by William Perkins, 'And herein is the proverbe true: *summa ius, summa injuria*: that is, the extremitie of the law is extreme injury. And of this doth the Holy Ghost meane, Eccles. 7:7 [*sic*], Bee not over just, that is, presse not justice too far, nor urge it too extremely in all cases, lest sometimes you make the name of justice, a cover for cruelty.'[22]

What Gallagher does not mention is that the verse, in some versions, also appends to the Hebrew text a down-to-earth practical motive: the Preacher goes on to say, in the King James Version: "Why shouldest thou destroy thyself?" or, in the Geneva translation, "Why shouldest thou be desolate?" These strictures apply to the wrongful quarrel of Malory's Arthur, since he consents to fight in Damas's quarrel partly to avoid dying in Damas's prison. Both Malory's and Spenser's critiques of chivalric single-mindedness have as a background—whether remote or immediate—Jesus' campaign against legalism; see, for example, "The Sabbath was made for man, not man for the Sabbath" (Mark 2:27). Jesus himself actually endorses one of David's transgressions while fleeing from Saul—eating the consecrated show-bread when he and his men had no food (I Sam. 21:6, cited in all three synoptics, namely Matth. 12:4; Mark 2:26; and Luke 6:4; for similar examples, see Matth. 12:2, 5, 8,10–12). The motive is clearly practical. Worse still (and Jesus did not mention this) David also gained support in his exile by joining in the wrongful campaigns of one of Israel's enemies—King Achish. David is imitated in this compromising of principles by Malory's Arthur working for the evil Sir Damas and by Spenser's Artegall assisting the turncoat Sir Burbon, and none of the three heroes seems to be punished for it.

In the opening of his commentary on Ecclesiastes 7:17 (without citations and thus apparently expressing his own opinions) a judicious and circumspect commentator, the Belgian Jesuit Cornelius à Lapide, debates with himself whether justice can ever be excessive, thus registering his shock at the statement.[23] Cornelius is one of those who add the threat, "Why shouldest thou destroy thyself?/ become desolate?" This threat marks the prohibition as a practical one, though we cannot tell from Spenser's text alone what would have happened to Artegall had he refused Burbon's request. Cajetan's interpretation of the threat of desolation and destruction explains the threat to Artegall: "those who are overly wise or overly just, being little suited for practical affairs (*praxis*) and everyday social life, are often shunned by businessmen and those who deliberate and seek counsel" (translation mine).[24] This Scripture tells us what Spenser probably surmised was going through the minds of Elizabeth and Essex when they "rescued" France for Henri IV. Elizabeth and Essex feared that if they clung to their Protestant convictions and alienated *politiques* like Henri, the Guise faction, which formed the French alternative, would hand England over to Catholic Spain, leaving her free to drag England "all about." Artegall could have been deserted and dragged all about, we infer from both Cornelius and Cajetan, had he refused absolutely to fight on Burbon's behalf: that would constitute being overly just (V.xi). The same threat hangs over Artegall's second temptation—holding on to his shield of principles at all costs. After years of fighting the Catholic League and deliberating with himself and his advisers, Protestant as well as Catholic (Wolfe, 135), Henri IV probably saw the same threat to himself. Borris suggests vaguely but correctly that Artegall's temporary, strategic abandonment of his shield in V.xii for the sake of self-preservation "may well express the pragmatic value of religious tolerance for Protestants . . . and perhaps also that of some political flexibility" (66).

IV. Conclusion

In Malory, King Arthur breaks his own rule and participates in a wrongful quarrel, and in Spenser we have four incidents of rule-breaking. The most general is Arthur's "extraordinary claim" in VI.vi.35.3–9 that wrongful quarrels can sometimes be won without divine aid and thus can provide a knight with a much-needed challenge: the gravest specific incident being Artegall's consenting to fight on behalf of a turncoat; another being Artegall's strategic release of his shield to Grantorto; and the fourth being Tristram's breaking of the law of arms to save an abused wife or mistress.

The placement of the four episodes of rule-breaking and the three endorsements of wrongful quarrels in both the books of justice and of courtesy stitches the books together. As has often been remarked, the books constitute a pair, as do Books I and II. Both V and VI concern public virtues, virtues involving society as a whole more than the protagonists' spiritual states and inner conflicts. Yet wrongful quarrels seem to be contrary to each virtue. They are introduced in the Book of Justice, as in the Oath, partly in order to introduce the not contrary but supplemental principle of equity. Both, as Hadfield suggests, contradict certain features of Books I and II. The word "grace" reappears but in a secular sense; and Calidore's self-defense "Bloud is no blemish; for it is no blame / To punish those, that doe deserve the same" (VI.i.26) not only speaks in the voice of justice, but contradicts the Hermit Contemplation in Book One: "Bloud can nought but sin, and wars but sorrowes yield" (x.60). Book One's hermit accommodates the request of Redcrosse only reluctantly and because he is sponsored by Mercy, who has a theological dimension. The parallel and contrasting hermit of Book VI accommodates Timias and Serena, on general principles, through the knightly experience he shares with Timias and by the vulnerability to circumstance which he shares with both of them: "What haps to me today, tomorrow may to you" (VI.i.41). The fact that the theme of wrongful quarrels continues in Book VI after the political point has been made, shows that tolerance of them is more than political; it is also social and esthetic, areas which constitute the province of Book VI.

Many Spenserians used to think that the contradictions between Spenser's idealism and the practice of his heroes and their real-life counterparts constituted flaws in his imagination—that Spenser descended to dirty politics in order to make a living. It has now become increasingly clear that Spenser was grimly announcing the necessity for concessions on his part and on that of the nation to social and political practicality.[25] Even the Knight of Justice figures the need to lend troops to a turncoat; even the seemingly ideal Prince Arthur needs to retain the service of unprincipled knights. The implied motto, "Be not overly just; why shouldest thou destroy thyself?" renders the poem less beautiful and inspiring but also less quixotic, more worldly-wise, endowed with an air of authenticity.

This debate as to what justifies engaging in a wrongful quarrel illustrates how fruitful it is to read Spenser and Malory against each other, because they treat some of the same legal and ethical problems and solutions and because it is interesting to see how Spenser adapted Malory to the topical question about helping Henri IV. Spenser's Arthur breaks the Oath (represented by its four counterparts) verbally in order to contain unprincipled knights within at least some rules, if not within the prohibition against wrongful quarrels. Spenser's Artegall breaks it in practice by fighting on behalf of the apostate Sir Burbon, but his real-life counterparts Elizabeth and Essex do so, the allegory implies, to induce Henri to protect England against Spain. These discoveries and others prove that for Spenser, Malory's work was not just raw material but a quarry of thematic allusions in his debate—both with Malory and with himself and his own characters—about chivalric idealism.

Cornell University

NOTES

1.   My thanks are due to the following people: first, to the members of the Program Committee for inviting me to deliver a version of the present study at the annual meeting of Spenser at Kalamazoo in May of 2010; then to Joseph B.

Dallett, Anne Lake Prescott, William A. Oram, Michael Twomey, Thomas D. Hill, Carol B. Tucker, Paul R. Hyams, and Alice Colby-Hall for their friendly suggestions and corrections.

A number of critics approach these texts through their contradictions. Catherine Brown in her book *Contrary Things: Exegesis, Dialectic, and the Poetics of Didacticism* (Stanford, CA: Stanford University Press, 1998), 7–11, argues that the most important thing in any medieval text is the reader's process of looking for and reconciling planned contradictions. Dorsey Armstrong argues that analyzing these in connection with chivalry is "what is interesting and important about the *Morte*" (29). Kenneth Hodges avers that Malory progresses from one to another and contradictory definition of chivalry—definitions signaled by changes in style (*Forging Chivalric Communities in Malory's Morte Darthur* [New York: Palgrave Macmillan, 2005]). Both Hodges on Malory and also Patricia Phillippy on Spenser construct Bakhtinian frameworks for such contradictions, applying to their chosen authors Bakhtin's concern with the dialogical nature of the modern novel. For Hodges differences of style dramatize differences of ideology. Phillippy focuses on Spenser's dialogism as recantation of one work or section in another. See *Love's Remedies: Recantation and Renaissance Lyric Poetry* (Lewisburg, PA: Bucknell University Press, 1995), 16–31 (esp. 16 and 28), and 191–95, where she argues that "This 'retractation'. . . . reiterates, rather than cancels, the primary ode" (195).

2.   Dorsey Armstrong, *Gender and the Chivalric Community in Malory's* "Morte d'Arthur" (Gainesville: University of Florida Press, 2003), 30–31.

3.   My emphasis; Caxton 3.15, MS fo 44v. Except for using the Caxton chapter and verse numbers, I quote the Winchester MS from *Le Morte Darthur, Sir Thomas Malory*, essentially reproduced in Stephen H. A. Shepherd, ed. (New York, W. W. Norton, 2004), which in turn is based on *The Winchester Malory, a Facsimile*, Introduced by N. R. Ker, Early English Text Society, Supplementary Series 4 (London, 1976). Shepherd promotes his own edition, I think justly, by quoting advice from P. J. C. Field: "prefer Winchester to Caxton but in a thorough modern edition." Shepherd performs the usual modernizations of u and v, i and j, and so do I. "For no love" (fo 49ʳ) is undoubtedly correct because it precisely foreshadows Lancelot's trial by combat with Meleagaunt in defence of Guinevere's alleged innocence of adultery (Caxton XIX,6–9; MS folio 441ᵛ–444ᵛ), whereas Caxton's "for no law" bears little relevance except to the general skepticism about laws that I will be pointing out and represents a type of error—*aw* for *oue*—that was facilitated by the orthography of the day. But in such an important yet minutely philological dispute as this, I must quote also Caxton's version—the only version available in Spenser's day.

4.   "Royal Policy and Malory's Round Table," *Arthuriana* 14:1 [2004]: 60.

5.   Meno 75b, in *The Dialogues of Plato*, trans. Benjamin Jowett, 3rd edition, (New York: Random House, 1937), 354.

6.   I owe the concept of dialogic relativity to a private communication from Carol B. Tucker, an independent scholar of Plato.

7.   Malory also wants the general standard to be low in the Oath for a literary reason—so that he can correct it later, in the Grail-Quest. There he abruptly raises the bar for sexual behavior and changes the status of women (cf. Armstrong, 26). The Oath commands knights always to succor damsels and gentlewomen, but in the Grail-Quest some damsels are seductive devils in disguise, casting suspicion on all women. For this and other reasons, knights are forbidden to take their ladies along when they quest for the Grail (Caxton 13.8). Thus, *Le Morte Darthur* becomes genuinely contradictory about physical lovemaking when it shifts from a courtly and chivalric discourse to that of monastic asceticism (Books 13–17). One could interpret this shift of attitude toward physical lovemaking as another instance of dialogic relativity.

8.   This is the oath taken by, for example, barons of the Exchequer, sheriffs, and justices of the peace (Kelly, 60–62). While I rely upon Kelly's vast research into primary documents, I cannot agree with Kelly's basic thesis, as announced in his Abstract, denying that Malory's Oath is chivalric just because it contains statutes that were also upheld by civilians such as these.

9.   *The Tree of Battles of Honoré Bonet: An English Version with Introduction*, by G. W. Coopland (Liverpool: Liverpool University Press, 1949), chapter 52, "If a knight happen to die in battle, do we say that his soul is saved?" 156. How the average soldier is supposed to discern the justness or injustice of the war he finds himself in, or if it is unjust, how he can extricate himself from it, is not explained. Bonet's standard seems too high: perhaps it is so intended in order to increase the power of the knight's priest and of the Church.

10.   *Forging Chivalric Communities in Malory's* Le Morte Darthur (New York: Palgrave, McMillan, 2005), 52.

11.   Equity is necessary because "all law is universal, but about some things it is not possible to make a universal statement which shall be correct. . . . When the legislator . . . has erred by over-simplicity . . . it is necessary to . . . say what the legislator himself would have said had he been present," Aristotle, *Nicomachean Ethics*, trans. W. David Ross, book 5, chap. 10 (London: Oxford University Press, 1963), 132–34. For an application of the concept of equity to Spenser, see Joel Altman, "Justice and Equity," *Spenser Encyclopedia*, ed. A. C. Hamilton et al. (Toronto: University of Toronto Press, 1990), 414; *Spenser Encyclopedia* hereafter cited in text by author and title of article.

12.   *Self-Consuming Artifacts: The Experience of Seventeenth-Century Literature* (Berkeley, University of California Press, 1972), "Literature in the Reader," 383–93.

13.   *Refashioning "Knights and Ladies Noble Deedes": The Intertexuality of Spenser's Faerie Queene and Malory's Morte Darthur* (Cranbury, NJ: Associated University Presses, 1996); Andrew King, The Faerie Queene *and Middle English* Romance: *The Matter of Just Memory* (Oxford: Clarendon, 2000); C. Kaske, "How Spenser Really Used Stephen Hawes," in *Unfolded Tales*: *Essays on Renaissance Romance*, ed. George Logan and Gordon Teskey (Ithaca: Cornell University Press, 1989), 119–36.

14. VI.xii.39. Spenser brings these knights into a new context in that, in Malory, these particular knights have no connection with the Beast Glatissant.

15. Quotations from *The Faerie Queene* follow A. C. Hamilton and Hiroshi Yamashita, eds., *The Faerie Queene*, by Edmund Spenser (New York: Pearson Publishing, 2001).

16. While Tonkin was prescient, Hamilton's thought on this stanza developed slowly; this observation was not in his original 1977 edition of *The Faerie Queene*. Indeed, in 1977, Hamilton hardly commented on this stanza at all; he noticed its oddity only in his second edition of 2001. The seventies were the tail-end of the age of celebratory criticism; in the eighties began the age of negative criticism, with its love of contradictions and other self-contestatory moves, which called forth Hamilton's observation in 2001, and which by and large still sets the tone today.

17. *Spenser's Courteous Pastoral* (London: Oxford University Press, 1972), 83. Tonkin is referring to VI.vi.35, but he says no more about the surprise sparked by its contradiction of chivalric idealism, swerving off onto a different point. My next quotation from Tonkin, which came out in *The Spenser Encyclopedia* eighteen years later, does not mention this stanza explicitly but the general skepticism of his entry implies it.

18. I cannot agree with what Hamilton says next, however, that the claim is fulfilled, even "to a degree," neither in the mercenaries—Sir Enias and his unnamed companion—whom Turpine hires at VI.vii 3–5 to attack Arthur, for these knights fail to accomplish their wrongful task and gain not "worship" but Arthur's contempt, and one of them in fact incurs death; nor in the four valiant knights suborned by Pinabello in one of Spenser's sources (*Orlando Furioso* 22.47–98) who, though successful in their depredations, gain no visible "worship" by them and occasionally feel ashamed of them. Though Spenser admits some circumstances that justify joining wrongful quarrels, financial need is never one of them. Contrast these relatively sensitive glosses, however, with the paraphrase of line 9 by Hadfield, "Right must be backed up by force if it is to combat wrong," in his edition, *The Faerie Queene, Book VI* (Hackett, 2007), which distorts this surprising line into a more common opinion.

19. *Allegory and Epic in English Renaissance Literature: Heroic Form in Sidney, Spenser and Milton* (Cambridge, England: Cambridge University Press, 2000), 62

20. Prescott, "Foreign Policy in Fairyland: Henri IV and Spenser's Burbon" (titled more aptly for my purposes in the oral form, "Defending Knights Who Throw away Their Shields"), *Spenser Studies* 14 (2000):189–214, citation 206 n. 43, citing for example the biography of Henri by François Bayrou, *Henri IV: Le Roy Libre* (Paris: Flammarion, 1994), 261. Bayrou and Prescott claim "the jest proves nothing" because Henri often made jokes about serious matters; but it does allude to the suspicion of timeserving among his public. On this see also Ray Heffner in *Works of Edmund Spenser: A Variorum Edition, Book Five*), ed. by E. Greenlaw, C. G. Osgood, F. M. Padelford, and Ray Heffner (Baltimore, MD: Johns Hopkins University Press, 1936), Appendix II, 330.

21. Prescott, 205–6 and n. 42, 213; for up-to-date factual historical background, see Michael Wolfe, "Henri IV," *Encyclopedia of the Renaissance*, gen. ed. Paul Grendler (New York: Charles Scribner's Sons, 1999) hereafter cited in text. See also Heffner in *Works, Book Five*, 330–35; Wolfe mentions by implication the Edict of Nantes, as Heffner does not. See Wolfe 448–49; also Heffner, 330–35.

22. *Medusa's Gaze: Casuistry and Conscience in the Renaissance* (Stanford: Stanford University Press, 1991), 194 and 311n31 (citing William Perkins, *Epieikeia* 61. I cannot find this title among Perkins's works).

23. True, sins of violence like wrongful quarrels are not those toward which laxity is usually recommended, but they could easily have been so recommended once it is recognized that human frailty can manifest itself in aggression as well as self-indulgence—in Pyrochles as well as in Cymochles (II.vi. 40–51; see Hamilton's note on II.vi.40.4). *Commentarii in Ecclesiasten auctore R.. P. Cornelio Cornelii a Lapide . . .* (Antwerp, 1638); see 228 C, Verse 17, for his opening debate with himself. Although Cornelius à Lapide (van den Steen) lived after Spenser (he flourished in the early seventeenth century), the many commentators he cites on this verse often date from the Middle Ages or the sixteenth century and so would have been available to Spenser. Cornelius presents a full spectrum of interpretations from different times and cultures, some of which take the text literally and startlingly prohibit justice, whereas some (as do two of the English versions—the Geneva and the Douai-Rheims) claim that all that is prohibited is hypocrisy and vainglory. Versions and commentators often merge this prohibition of justice with the next prohibition, "be not overly wise" (7:17 or 18), which is less startling because familiar and easily limited to either the pretense or the hubristic ambition. The pragmatic threat, "Why should you invite desolation?" occurs in the Latin of Junius and Tremellius (London, 1585), which Spenser is likely to have read (translation mine); on this likelihood, see *Spenser and Biblical Poetics*, 11. See also the text and notes to the King James Version (1611). This pragmatic threat in one version or another represents a late importation from the Hebrew text; Cornelius presents it labeled as such in a separate paragraph.

24. Cornelius 231.1.D quoting Cajetan, presumably his commentary of 1534 on Ecclesiastes. The threat, as specified by *pernicies,* the word with which the Latin Bibles paraphrase "desolation," means earthly ruin, destruction, calamity, or disaster, not hell or the loss of the Holy Spirit. Just so, Artegall's justice is genuine, yet he sacrifices it for a worldly goal, to save Burbon not from sin or damnation but from a worldly calamity, loss of his beloved Flourdelis (V.xi.61–64).

25. See especially Prescott, "Foreign Policy in Fairyland," and Borris, *Allegory and Epic.*

JONATHAN E. LUX

"Th'eternal Brood of Glorie Excellent": Infants and the Battle for the Future in *The Faerie Queene*

Given the prominence of infants in *The Faerie Queene*—both literal children and questing "infant" scions of distinguished families— disappointingly little criticism has had anything to say about them. Even more disconcerting, most scholarship on the subject has focused almost exclusively on readings of separation anxiety and alienation; more extreme examples paint generation and reproduction themselves with broad brush strokes the color of disdain. Childhood becomes a tragicomic parallel to Hobbes's memorable specter of the chaotic condition of humanity before establishing a government: "solitary, poor, nasty, brutish, and [of course] short." It is now high time for a balanced reading of reproduction and children in *The Faerie Queene*. While Spenser's infants may suffer from alienation and what contemporary psychoanalysis calls separation anxiety, those developmental struggles are crucial steps in the transformative process of the quest. The next generation is born into grave conflict, but generation itself is a good and necessary thing that imbues progeny with the power of their ancestors and recalls the necessity of future (re)generation in the constant imperative of dynastic renaissance. Spenser's foundling children and infant knights are avatars of "th'eternal brood of glorie excellent" that will continue the allegorical struggle for the triumph of virtue when the current generation is dead and gone.

Spenser Studies: A Renaissance Poetry Annual, Volume XXVII, Copyright © 2012 AMS Press, Inc. All rights reserved.   DOI: 10.7756/spst.027.002.23-45

I. Generation, Regeneration, and Reproduction in *FQ*

G ENERATION, REGENERATION, AND REPRODUCTION appear in *The Faerie Queene* in a variety of metaphors; the poem is alive with tropes of generation. One worthy of attention occurs in Book I, when the monstrous Errour vomits her offspring onto the Red Cross knight. Her vomit of books and papers, frogs and toads, appears

> As when old father Nilus gins to swell
> With timely pride aboue the Aegyptian vale,
> His fattie waues doe fertile slime outwell,
> And ouerflow each plaine and lowly dale
> But when his later spring gins to auale,
> Huge heapes of mudd he leaues, wherein there breed
> Ten thousand kindes of creatures partly male
> And partly femall of his fruitful seed;
> Such ugly monstrous shapes elswher may no man reed.
>
> (I.i.21)

The sophisticated images of this simile house the potential for the kind of negatively charged reading of generation mentioned above. The alliterative images ("fattie" and "fertile" slime, "outwelling" and "ouerflowing" with muddy, monstrous shapes) leave a repulsive residue on the stanza. They conjure an impression of things rooting and wriggling in the dark. Even worse, Spenser follows the metaphor of "old father Nilus" with a description of the vomit of Errour's children, that "fruitfull cursed spawne of serpents small" (I.i.22). Reading this description—serpents wallowing in vomit or a vomit of snakes—one may indeed be inclined to think of reproduction in *The Faerie Queene* as a nasty, dubious process.

It might be well to pause here and link this description with the readings of separation anxiety, alienation, and a disdain for reproduction that have characterized scholarship on children in *The Faerie Queene*.[1] Joanne Craig has argued, citing the example of Errour's children, that "*The Faerie Queene* as a whole suggests a fastidious distaste for procreation."[2] According to Craig, Spenser develops separate principles for dealing with reproduction. He represents literal human procreation, associated with the "dangers and threats of all that is feminine," as a messy, undesirable practice producing problematic remainders. If one must reproduce, it is only the masculinized process of intellectual or artistic creation that the poet valorizes in strict opposition to the feminized act of physical reproduction. This process, associated with the "creativity of the male artists," produces "models and images belonging as monuments of unaging intellect to an enduring order."[3]

While one can certainly find evidence for this reading of procreation in *The Faerie Queene*, particularly in Book I, notice the problematic remainders that this reading leaves behind when applied to the earlier simile. Spenser chooses to describe the Nile as an "old father," whose spontaneously generative "fruitfull seed" creates both masculine and feminine offspring. The gender division in this simile does not seem to be as clear at a second glance. Furthermore, Spenser returns to "old father Nilus" later on in Book III, describing Belphoebe's spontaneous generation in terms far different from those of Book I. We may recall that the sun impregnates Belphoebe's mother, Chrysogone, while she lies "upon the grassy ground. . . . naked bare displayed." Spenser paints this moment of conception in glowing turns of phrase, as the sunbeams, "embayd / So sweet sence and secret power unspide, / That in her pregnant flesh they shortly fructifide" (III.vi.7). This description combines images neatly opposing the muddy, monstrous fruitfulness of the conception of Errour's children.[4] In fact, this moment of female conception receives some of the most elevated poetry in Book III, as the narrator reports that the heavens favored her so

> That all the gifts of grace and chastitee
> On her they poured forth of plenteous horne;
> Iove laught on Venus from his souerayne see,
> And Phoebus with faire beams did her adorne,
> And all the Graces rockt her cradle being borne.
> (III.vi.2)

These images of divine affirmation and boundless plenty in spontaneous or natural female conception stand in stark counterpoint to the model of generation discussed earlier.

Oddly enough, the analogy and the imagery to which Spenser returns in describing the generation of Belphoebe are *precisely* the same as those describing Errour's children. After acknowledging that this conception may seem strange to his readers, Spenser writes,

> But reason teacheth that the fruifull seades
> Of all things liuing, through impression

Of the sunbeams in moyst complexion,
Doe life conceiue and quickned are by kind:
So after Nilus inundation
Infinite shapes of creatures men doe fynd,
Informed in the mud, on which the Sunne hath shynd.

(III.vi.8)

This description corresponds almost exactly to the imagery of spontaneous generation in Book I—"fruitfull seades," the "infinite shapes of creatures" and the muddy banks of "Nilus." But Spenser differentiates this example of spontaneous generation by appealing to the universal. He argues that "reason" ought to teach his audience "of all things living," that they "conceiue and quickned are by kind."[5] The spontaneous offspring of Errour's generation follow their mother, and become a "fruitful cursed spawne of serpents small," wallowing in the "fertile slime." In contrast, the spontaneous reproduction of chaste Chrysogone, overseen by a pantheon of supporting gods and goddesses, produces Belphoebe, "Pure and unspotted from all loathly crime, / That is ingenerate in fleshly slime" (III.vi.2).

The number of parallels in these passages points to a conceptual dialogue Spenser presents to his readers on the consequences of reproduction. The results of this dialogue do not point toward a fastidious distaste for procreation, but rather toward a conception of procreation as the duplication of the parent. As fussy as Spenser may frequently be toward the subject of human *copulation*, and particularly copulation outside of marriage, he seems to present procreation according to different principles: the internal tendencies, the (sometimes disguised) core characteristics of Spenser's characters appear with unusual consistency in their children.

Gordon Braden's essay "Riverrun" sheds some helpful light on the depiction of the spontaneously generative Nile. Braden connects the Nile with

. . . the primordial, infinitely fertile and malleable substance that, in the Garden of Adonis derives from 'An huge eternall Chaos' . . . and outlasts all its forms . . . [generation in the form of] Mutability is not just an epiphenomenon of things, to be cleverly outwitted; it is an energized substance, an active reality that supplies us with all that we have—indeed, is what we are made out of.[6]

Nile mud itself, according to Braden, is a kind of raw material, not only the breeding ground of Errour's children, but the riverbed of the river flowing beside Alma's house.[7] The spontaneous generation of the Nile rearticulates a morally neutral theory of reproduction, with its roots in the Genesis account of reproduction "after kind." Spenser alludes to this theory in his description of the Garden of Adonis where all creatures "are borne to live and die / according to their kind" (III.vi.31).

This reproduction "according to their kind" is the crucial principle underlying Spenser's treatment of the singular type of procreation that forms the core of this essay. In another metaphor, one he deploys to describe the Red Cross Knight preparing for battle, Spenser writes,

> The noble hart, that harbours virtuous thought,
> And is with childe of glorious great intent,
> Can neuer rest, until it forth haue brought
> Th'eternall brood of glorie excellent:
> Such restlesse passion did all night torment
> The flaming courage of that Faery knight.
>
> (I.v.1)

Spenser's use of this metaphor to describe the Red Cross Knight's restless night before his battle with Sansfoy can obscure the fact that the independent referent of the metaphor is not the Red Cross Knight at all. Rather, Spenser's narrator steps outside of the poem's plot to craft an elaborate case study that can then be compared to the Red Cross Knight. The Red Cross Knight's restless night indicates desire for Duessa or for the dubious distinction that the House of Pride can bestow; but the subject described in this elaborate conceit is actually *the noble heart*.

The complexity of the metaphorical artifice involved disguises this reading. Spenser uses a metonymic symbol (the heart) personified as pregnant to establish a relationship between the symbol and its similarly metonymic offspring (the brood of glory). He then compares this relationship to the relationship between his character's interior state (courage, with a pun on the Latin root, *cor/cordis* "heart") and its outward manifestations (a restless night). But the noble heart, metonymic for the human core beneath its complicated exterior disguises, remains the subject that is "with childe of glorious great intent." Spenser's narrator here claims that pregnancy is the necessary state of the noble heart, which cannot rest until it (re)produces "Th'eternall brood of glorie excellent."

This metaphor contains some fascinating and adroit resonances. The adjective describing the parent's intentions (the "glorious great intent" of the progenitor) passes to the children "of glorie excellent." Also, the quietly contradictory implications of the term "eternal brood" deserve some consideration. Since both children and broods imply a finite or limited form of generation, one may anticipate that specifying that this brood is eternal implies a latent ability for such finite generation to stretch itself into the realm of the eternal. A virtuous heart laboring over a great (perhaps punning upon "pregnant") enterprise produces children who carry its "glorious intent" into the future. This principle is vital to understanding the role of reproduction in *The Faerie Queene*.

II. Readings of Renaissance Childhood and Childhood in *FQ*

It might be well here to point to the questionable historicity of one common theory underlying readings that treat children and generation in *The Faerie Queene* as negatively charged topics. As noted earlier, a simple majority of the few critical forays attacking these topics presents dark readings of childhood; children are born into danger and deal imperfectly with abandonment and separation anxiety. Indeed, this tendency is so prevalent that the field seems to be laboring under the shadow of Philippe Ariès's shop-worn thesis that a conception of childhood and infancy as a separate state did not develop in England until the seventeenth century.[8] This is a shade that must be conjured so that it can be exorcized.

As readers may recall, Ariès noticed a fascinating absence of children depicted *as children* in Medieval painting. Relying upon a number of sources, but with particular emphasis on these paintings, Ariès argued that the Medieval world did not theorize a fundamental difference between childhood and adulthood.[9] As soon as children left the care of their mother or nurse, they entered the harsh vicissitudes of the adult world.[10] In this mode of criticism, as expounded by a number of other capable scholars, a dark historical world of child neglect, abuse, and mistreatment emerged; children lacking clear theoretical space become the projected sites of contention among adults who neither recognize their special developmental needs nor engaged with them on a deep emotional level.[11] Invariably, high rates of child mortality and the dicta of prescriptive (rather than descriptive) writings about child-rearing became critical links in this chain of thought.

This "Ariès thesis" has come under devastating criticism from a group of scholars spearheaded by Linda Pollock. Pollock's book *Forgotten Children*, accompanied by other studies that rejected the Ariès thesis, questioned both the methodology that produced and the problematic definitions upon which Ariès built his claim.[12] Pollock argues that,

> Unfortunately, the very vagueness of Ariès' definition negates his whole argument: it would be impossible not to realize that a child was different from an adult, because children are all too obviously dependent on adult care and protection. If there is an appreciation of the *immaturity* of the child in either the physical . . . or mental sphere . . . then whoever has that appreciation possesses a concept of childhood, no matter how basic or limited this is.[13]

Children under the age of seven (the age Ariès himself uses to delineate transformation into the adult world), and particularly infants, die without extensive adult care that *cannot* be provided without some awareness of the need for that care. To describe a theoretical perspective that neatly erases a concept of childhood in the Renaissance seems to Pollock untenable, a misguided attempt at writing a history of child abuse rather than childhood. Rather than painting a fictitious transition between the dark childhood of the past and contemporary childhood, Pollock asks the field to consider why parental care, including deep emotional attachment, "is a variable so curiously resistant to change."[14]

A number of passages in *The Faerie Queene* display this deep repository of emotional connection between various figures and their offspring. A brief representative list would include Merlin's haunting description of Artegall stolen "while yet in infant cradle he did crall" (III.iii.26), the comparison of Britomart's joy to that of a "louing mother" seeing "her tender babe . . . safe appear" in childbirth (III.ii.11), or the language Claribell uses in celebrating the rediscovery of "her owne infant deare" (V.xii.20).[15] Indeed, Spenser hardly misses an opportunity to describe the cheerful (and critically pregnant) spectacle of parents and children reunited after a long absence.

But more than just reflecting the deep emotional involvement among parents and children, *The Faerie Queene* explicitly comments upon the process of child-rearing and upon the behavioral tendencies of children. In Book V, Spenser deploys another one of his elaborate metaphors in explaining how Clarinda, while attempting to seduce Artegall, beguiles Radigund. Spenser depicts her

> As a bad Nurse, which fayning to receiue
> In her owne mouth the food, ment for her child,
> Withholdes it to her selfe, and doeth deceiue
> The infant, so for want of nourture spoyld.
>
> (V.v.53)

This "feeding" metaphor plays a complicated game with the responsibilities of a Nurse in "nourturing" her ward, implying a level of social constraint on the part of a Nurse and recalling a Classical (as well as early modern) stock character, the malevolent guardian.[16] Spenser, after all, cannot describe a failure to perform appropriately the act of child-rearing without some conception of what child-rearing ought to entail.

Spenser performs a similar maneuver when addressing the behavioral tendencies of children. Notice that the same child metaphor Spenser applies to Radigund (who is the child in the "feeding" metaphor above) extends to Britomart a few stanzas later in Canto VI. In Britomart's furious "wrathful will" and "self torment" when she believes that Artegall has left her for Radigund, she behaves precisely like a child throwing a tempertantrum. Spenser describes her

> Like as a wayward childe, whose sounder sleepe
> Is broken with some fearefull dreames affright,
> With froward will doth set him self to weepe;
> Ne can be stild for all his nurses might
> But kicks, and squals, and shriekes for fell despight:
> Now scratching her, and her loose locks misusing,
> Now seeking darknesse, and now seeking light;
> Then crauing sucke, and then the sucke refusing.
>
> (V.vi.15)

It is difficult to imagine how an author living in an age that did not conceptualize childhood as a separate state, or the importance of child-rearing, could have written those lines. Spenser's metaphor infantilizes Britomart, as it had Radigund before her, fashioning her as a "wayward child" in her frustration and anger. The similarity between Britomart's "wrathful will" and the wayward child's "froward will" points to an uneasy series of parallels as Britomart's valorous martial demeanor is subsumed beneath a wave of solipsistic feelings of abandonment. Britomart puts on very literally the manner of a child in pining after the man she thinks has left her.[17]

A figure like Britomart cannot put on the manner of a child unless childhood itself has been conceptualized as a clear and distinct state—the metaphor would have no potency without a solid conceptual referent. Remembering that Spenser performed a similar maneuver in presenting the "bad Nurse" of Book V, one must conclude that *The Faerie Queene* showcases some fairly explicit ideas about childhood and child-rearing. It remains to unfold what implications these ideas hold for the infants of the poem.

III. Foundling Children of *The Faerie Queene*

Of the numerous children gracing the pages of *The Faerie Queene*, none have occasioned more comment than the foundlings that appear so prominently in Spenser's poem. Of these foundlings, few are actually "found" in the course of the poem itself—more are adults described as foundlings ex post facto, with the circumstances of their origin withheld from the reader until a later moment of revelation. In keeping with this spirit, I will withhold treatment of this second class of foundling for a later section of this essay, and focus here on some of the literal infants discovered during the course of the poem.

Barbara Estrin's *The Raven and The Lark* provides a nuanced and useful perspective on the narratives of foundlings and lost children recycled in Renaissance and Classical literature. According to Estrin, the foundling tale has a clear narrative formula that occurs with exceptional consistency in early modern England. The overall structure of the tale looks like this: "An exposed aristocrat . . . is saved by peasants, raised in primitive surroundings, discovered through a talisman or birthmark, and returned (usually at the moment he is about to marry) to his biological parents."[18] This structure (exposure, salvation, growth/development, and reunion) forms the core of the foundling tale. The last segment in particular, the reunion of the child with his or her biological parents, has a number of serious ideological implications. First, foundlings are meant to restore an aristocratic (and usually royal) dynasty thrown into disrepair by their absence.[19] They rectify the disorders of the state. Second, note the relevant assumption that the foundling's biological parents come from a higher lineage than their adopted ones; the rediscovery of one's lineage means the rediscovery of a higher, better social place in the world than the foundling had known. Finally, the concluding recognition and reunion affirm what Estrin terms "the affinities of kind," an ideal theory of natural and kinship relationships that endorses an underlying assumption of the natural good-ness of the world. As Estrin poetically notes, "the return of the real child surrounds the restoration of what was with the aura of rebirth. What was, even sinning man, seems all at once good enough."[20]

Spenser plays with and eventually subverts this set of generic expecta-tions in creating new paradigms for (re)generation. The two most promi-nent infants of *The Faerie Queene*, Ruddymane and the child Calepine rescues from a bear, both hearken back to the narratives of dying gener-ation and displaced generation that are so central to Spenser's work. Sir Guyon rides into a pitiful scene in Book II Canto i. Ruddymane's as yet unnamed mother reclines beside a fountain with a dagger thrust through her chest, "from which forth gusht a stream of goreblood thick" (II.i.39). In this stream of "goreblood," Spenser confronts his readers with a horrific spectacle:

> In her lap, a louely babe did play
> His cruell sport, in stead of sorrow dew;
> For in her streaming blood he did embay
> His little hands, and tender ioints embrew
> Pitiful spectacle, as euer eie did vew.
>
> > (II.i. 40)

The reader is probably inclined to agree with the analysis of Spenser's nar-rator: a child wallowing in his dying mother's blood does indeed provide a powerful spectacle, a shocking image to find in any poem. Within this traumatic setting, Sir Guyon encounters a tale of failure and despair. As the mother discloses to Sir Guyon the substance of her familial history, the story of her dead husband Sir Mortdant's seduction and the charmed cup of Acrasia, the clear narrative of a dying aristocratic family appears.

In the early description, Sir Mortdant had metaphorically borrowed the armor of a heroic, questing knight, just as Red Cross himself put on bor-rowed armor back in Book I. Mortdant's desire in stanza 50, moved by "high corage" to "seeke aduentures wilde" and "puissaunt force to prove," mirrors the longings of Red Cross when "with child of glorious great intent." But Mortdant's quest finds itself sabotaged by his human, "fleshly" nature, as he first becomes enthralled in the Bowre of Bliss and then drinks from the poisonous cup of Acrasia that causes his death. Amavia's description of her husband, one of the darker passages of *The Faerie Queene*, seemingly drives this point home. She tells Sir Guyon, "he was flesh: (*all flesh doth frayltie breed*)" (II.i.52; my emphasis). Flesh breeds flesh, and passes frailty from parents to children. Ruddymane is doomed to repeat Sir Mortdant's life cycle—glorious intentions negated by corruption, ending in death.

This episode has been read and reread by an earlier generation of critics as an allegory for original sin, following A. C. Hamilton's early work: "A Theological Reading of *The Faerie Queene*, Book II." According to Hamilton, (in a thesis expanded upon and considered by numerous other scholars[21]), this moment is significant because it contains, in the words of Spenser's *Letter to Ralegh*, "the beginning of the second book and *the whole subject thereof*" [Hamilton's emphasis].[22] Hamilton claims that ". . . the bloody-handed babe stands for mankind which, from its infancy, has been infected by original sin. (Blood upon the hands being the usual token of man's guilty state.) The name of the enchantress reveals that the cause of the babe's stained hands is Intemperance, seen as an enchanting woman."[23]

According to this reading of Book II, Ruddymane's bloody hands have cataclysmic implications; his inheritance reflects the guilt of fallen humanity, giving this foundling tale a dark, threnodic core.

But Spenser evenly balances this reading of transgenerational curse, repetitive failure, and death, with a very different narrative embodied in the figure of Ruddymane's mother. Her last words to her son do not point to recycled defeat concluding in death, but to a brighter future generation that can live to redeem their family legacy. She tells her son,

> Sith heuen thee deignes to hold in liuing state,
> Long maist thou liue, and better thriue withal,
> Then to thy lucklesse parents did befall:
> Liue thou, and to thy mother dead attest,
> That cleare she dide from blemish criminall;
> Thy little hands embrewd in bleeding brest
> Loe I for pledges leaue. So giue me leaue to rest.
> (II.i.37)

In these lines, the last that Ruddymane's mother speaks to him, she drapes him in her own mantle, covering the metaphysical "sins of the father" and claiming for him a lineage of valiant struggle against evil. Notice that Amavia is herself a heroic, questing figure, a fact disguised by her narration of the story. Putting on the "Palmers weed," she goes out to confront Acrasia and to reclaim her husband "through danger and great dreed" (II.i.52). She sallies out to contend with Acrasia over the fate of her family. It is true that Acrasia claims a clear victory over her familial past, emblazoned in Mortdant's smiling "dead corse," but Ruddymane's mother rescues a fragment that can continue the fight and carry her battle into the future—her infant son.

The assumption that Amavia commits suicide, which has been repeated numerous times without thorough examination, may be one of the reasons this lineage of valiant struggle against evil has been frequently overlooked. Returning to the moment in question, one may note that the poem is surprisingly ambiguous on the subject. Although Guyon does hear her disembodied voice welcoming "sweetest death," he does not see the dagger pierce her chest (II.i.36). While this does indicate that Amavia either wanted to die or was resigned to her fate, it does not necessarily indicate that she stabbed herself. In fact, Amavia's statement that she died "cleare" from "blemish criminall" points in the opposite direction (II.i.37). Suicide is a mortal sin, a serious breach of social and religious principle. If Ruddymane's mother has committed suicide her claim that she is "cleare" from "blemish criminall" must be insincere or, worse, delusional. Applying either of these readings to Amavia, however, leads an attentive scholar into an interpretive quagmire. For one thing, no one seems inclined to treat the rest of Amavia's tale as a simple delusion. For another, the words in question are delivered to an infant who it must be assumed cannot understand them. It is difficult to imagine a scene in the allegorical world of the poem in which Amavia stabs herself and then immediately turns to her infant son and claims to be innocent. The simplest conclusion given these considerations is that Amavia did not commit suicide.

Some readers may respond to this statement with a reflexive question: if Amavia did not commit suicide, how did she end up dying in the woods? This question should be answered in two ways. First, one must assert that the poem may not provide an answer. There is no reason to expect that *The Faerie Queene* finally reveals every sphere of its solar system—indeed some seem quite inaccessible. Readers who demand certainty in the mapping of the poem's universe inevitably find themselves adding endless cycles and epicycles without creating a successful model. Second, one must assert that an allegorical figure exists according to principles quite different from those familiar to contemporary forensic science. To insist that there must be a cause of Amavia's death is to attribute to an allegorical figure real world characteristics it does not necessarily contain. As Carol Kaske's catalogue of ways to translate "Amavia" makes clear, Amavia's name implies a direct connection between her continued existence and role as a lover. The catalogue includes "she loves in order to live," "[she] that loves to live," or "I have loved life."[24] Some of these translations imply a clear link between Amavia's death and Acrasia's curse, to give "losse of love to her that loves to live" (II.i.55). Maybe, by killing Sir Mortdant, Acrasia has killed his wife. Or maybe, for an allegorical figure like Amavia, loving and living are all the same thing.

In a fascinating moment of literary metacriticism, Sir Guyon and the Palmer offer different readings of Amavia's death and their own inability to clean the blood off of Ruddymane's hands. Sir Guyon's explanations of the infant's red hands all return to archetypal "sins of the father," but the Palmer corrects Sir Guyon, as he so often will throughout Book II. It is not the father's blood that stains Ruddymane's hands, but his mother's blood. The Palmer concludes by advising Sir Guyon not to attempt to wash Ruddymane's hands

> But let them still be bloody, as befell,
> That they his mothers innocence may tell,
> As she bequeathd in her last testament;
> That as a sacred symbole it may dwell
> In her sonnes flesh, to mind revengement,
> And be for all chaste dames an endlesse monument.
>   (II.ii.10)

The stone nymph refuses to wash the blood from Ruddymane's hands not because, as Sir Guyon mistakenly muses, the sins of the father cannot be cleansed, but because his red hands are a memento of his mother's struggle against the murderous, dehumanizing evil of Acrasia (II.ii.10).

From the beginning of this encounter, Spenser's readership must recognize that Ruddymane's foundling tale cannot end in cheerful restoration. The formula has been broken. Not only are Ruddymane's biological parents unavailable for eventual discovery, but his family history is not entirely a glorious affair. However, as Spenser reveals line by line the tale of Ruddymane's tragic family, it becomes clear that he inherits a tradition not only of recycled failure and death but also valiant deeds and faithful service. Amavia's last words to her son become a benediction: "Long maist thou live and better thrive withal/. . . Liue thou, and to thy mother dead attest" (II.i.37).

If Ruddymane's tale constitutes a creative reworking of the traditional foundling tale, Spenser's other newborn foundling reworks the genre yet again. The child Calepine rescues from the jaws of a bear enters the poem in much the same manner as Ruddymane: wandering through the woods, Calepine hears a "litle babe" that "did loudly scrike and squall, / And all the woods with piteous plaints did fill" (VI.iv.18). This call for help neatly parallels the woe-stricken exclamations that had drawn Sir Guyon toward Ruddymane's mother, as does the image of a child "betwixt his [the bear's] bloodie iawes, besprinckled with gore" (VI.iv.17). Recalling the description of Ruddymane covered in "goreblood," the preceding language ought to indicate to Spenser's readers that the poem is returning to an earlier theme and set of generic conventions.

But rather than rescuing this child from the dismal scene of a dismembered family, Calepine rescues this child from a bear. And rather than allowing this child to extend its biological parents' legacy into the future, Spenser grafts this child onto a different family tree. Calepine (one of the most comically nervous single parents in Renaissance literature) seems almost too eager to give the child to Matilde and Sir Bruin (Sir Bear), "Right glad . . . to be so rid / Of his young charge, whereof he skilled nought" (VI.iv.37). Matilde's reaction then underscores the weighty significance this gift contains. Matilde explains to Sir Calepine that the heavens have not given her, "The gladfull blessing of posteritie, / Which we might see after our selues remaine" (VI.iv.31). This lack of a child, of regenerate life, threatens the destruction of the family in question: a "Gyant" waits for Sir Bruin to grow weak enough to be overpowered. Matilde tells Calepine that "All is in time like to returne againe / To that foule feend . . . / Who now ginnes to despize / The good Sir Bruin, growing farre in yeares" (VI.iv.31). Calepine encounters here the specter of a disordered state that the foundling story banishes in its traditional telling. Sir Bruin's land may seem a "peaceable estate," but it is *an uneasy peace*, a peace that promises to be someday disturbed by a fiendish antagonist.

Into this uncertainty with the promise of coming violence Calepine "bears" an infant. The reader might expect Spenser's speaker to comment upon the trauma latent in this pathetic moment—an innocent babe separated from its parents by a bear must face the terrors of a strange land haunted by a monstrous enemy. Instead, Spenser makes this child the fulfillment of a prophecy that points to his future glory. Matilde tells Sir Calepine that

. . .this was prophesied,
That from his sides some noble chylde should rize,
The which through fame should farre be magnified
And this proude gyant should with braue emprise,
Quite ouerthrow . . .

(VI.iv.33)

The family, and by extension the familial estate, will be rescued by this protomessianic child, a child that will "be gotten, not begotten" (VI.iv.32). Indeed, in these two words Spenser has given the foundling tale a twist. Rather than restoring the fortunes of the state in reunification with his biological parents, the child Calepine rescues from the bear will restore the estate of his foster parents like a healthy shoot grafted onto a dying tree.

Calepine's address to Matilde calls attention to the position of this child, as a uniquely suited figure who can be nurtured into an ideal familial place-holder. He advises her that good fortune has sent her

This little babe, of sweet and louely face,
And spotless spirit, in which ye may enchace
What euer forms ye list thereto apply,
Being now soft and fit them to embrace;
Whether ye list him traine in cheualry,
Or noursel up in lore of learn'd Philosophy.

(VI.iv.35)

This argument hearkens back to the substantial body of Renaissance litera-ture that treated children essentially as blank slates that could be inscribed with whatever figures their parents chose.[25] Here Calepine believes that the child can be *trained* to represent the forms of the family into which he has been adopted. The transition is meant to be seamless. Matilde seems to ac-cept this explanation at face value, taking the child "as of her owne by liuery and seisin" (VI.iv.37). This last term, "seisin" has a special significance, as a legal term for the delivery of property into the possession of an individual. Calepine's infant has become a part of the household, a representative of their extended sway, of Matilde and Sir Bruin as a dynastic unit.

These diverging narratives of foundling children in *The Faerie Queene* display a sophisticated dialogue on the nature of children and child-rear-ing. It is tempting here to focus on either side of a dichotomy in Spenser's descriptions of children. On the one hand, he seems to imply that familial, biological lineage dictates the course of a child's life, as with Ruddymane. On the other, Calepine and Matilde seem to read children as blank slates upon which adults may compose as they see fit. Those favoring either of these conflicting perspectives can marshal significant evidence in favor of their disparate positions. But perhaps Spenser presents his readers with these diverging possibilities to call attention to just how complicated the figure of a child can be. The answer is not either/or but both/and—or rather, Spenser creates children in *The Faerie Queene* who can be explored like rooms with many doors containing ample beauty to engender moments of wonder. An appreciator of this art is not meant to bar a door any more than to remain outside, but to sit and enjoy the paintings.

IV. Infant Renaissance and the Battle for the Future

Calepine provides an intriguing moment in the midst of the foundling tale, described earlier, when he self-reflexively comments on the larger number of famous adult foundling "infants" making their way through the poem. Conversing with Matilde on the subject, he tells her,

> And certes it hath oftentimes bene seene,
> That of the like, whose linage was unknown,
> More braue and noble knights haue raysed beene,
> As their victorious deedes haue often showen,
> Being with fame through many Nations blowen.
>
> (VI.iv.36)

These "brave and noble knights" raised outside their patrilineal families cut quite a swath through Faerielond. Indeed, an attentive reader may be shocked by the number of figures in *The Faerie Queene* who were foundlings at some point in their fictive history. An incomplete list would include Arthur, Britomart, Red Cross, Artegall, Tristram, Satyrane, Pastorella, Belphoebe, and Amoret—an unusually large percentage of the starring figure in Spenser's poem who work out their quests in the traditional structure of the foundling story.

Criticism focusing on these foundlings has tended to follow the critical reading of childhood as the place of danger, separation anxiety, and neglect

described earlier in this article. Elizabeth Bellamy, writing about Britomart
and Arthur, describes the "paradigmatic (and traumatized) 'infants' of *The
Faerie Queene* . . . less as epic subjects than as sites of alienation."[26] Joanne
Craig suggests that the foundlings of *The Faerie Queene* have a tenuous
relationship to a generational maternal figure whom they desire and fear as
she alternately nurtures and menaces them.[27] And Barbara Estrin describes
a generational cycle enacted in the life of Red Cross and Una that points
to "separation anxiety" as infants born into battle cope with absentee par-
ents.[28] According to Estrin, these children lose themselves in a "mental dis-
placement" that leaves them "filled with powers not their own."[29]

Fortunately, Barbara Estrin's work has added to this scholarship the
reminder that these displaced children are, in some cases, fulfilling their
traditional roles *as foundlings*. The troubles and travails of their search for
identity fit neatly into the generic conventions preceding their restoration
to their dynastic family. One addition that can be made here is to identify
the particularly significant dynastic role assigned to that section of adult
foundlings Spenser also describes as "infants." If this emphasis on a term
best known for its Latin roots (from *infans/infantis*, "one who does not
speak") seems odd, it may help to recall that "infant" was a sixteenth-cen-
tury term for a prince or princess, particularly one of Spain or Portugal
(*infante* or *infanta*) who would not inherit the throne.[30] The term is thus
weighted with all the contemporary discourse concerning the politico-re-
ligious role of the royal family but oddly displaced, set aside from the cen-
tral axis of socio-political authority. Spenser uses the term "infant" nine-
teen times throughout the poem, eleven of which refer to adult figures. Of
these eleven, six refer to the royal infant knights (three to Arthur, two to
Britomart, and one to Tristram).[31] Two more refer to Artegall in the mo-
ments of his foundling discovery,[32] and three refer to Pastorella's role as a
foundling in Book VI.[33]

Pastorella's foundling tale, a seeming exception in the company of the
royal infant knights and Artegall, deserves special attention here because
it begins to explain the connotations of the term "infant" when applied
to these adult figures. Upon recognizing Pastorella, Melissa experiences a
moment of sudden dislocation as the adult Pastorella merges with the liter-
al infant she abandoned in the wild. During this moment "in her conceipt-
ful mynd" Melissa recognizes "that this fair Mayd / was that same infant"
(VI.vii.16). In these lines, Melissa implies that Pastorella's identity, even as
an adult, remains that of an infant. Her significance is determined by her
relationship to the structure of her larger family tree. Pastorella's mother

repeats this formula, realizing that "this young Mayd, whom chance to her present / Is her own daughter, her own infant deare" (VI.xii.20). Even as an adult, Pastorella remains an infant because that term indicates her position in an old dynastic familial structure, a position that does not change with age. Like the child Calepine rescued, Pastorella is part of a larger story in which, as a dynastic representative, she has an important part to play.

This unusual position extends to other adult foundling "infants" in *The Faerie Queene*. Other figures, such as Satyrane and Belphoebe, may share the foundling status of these adult infants, but it is the prerogative of the "infants" to play a significant role in the revivification of their dynastic families by rediscovering their biological roots. This is a critical point—the adult infants of *The Faerie Queene* may be involved in quests of self-discovery, but self-discovery is ancillary to dynastic renaissance, a particular type of dynastic renaissance that only the foundling can initiate. The connection here between dynastic renaissance and self-consciousness, one of the effects of self-discovery, cannot be emphasized firmly enough.

A. Bartlett Giamatti provides some insightful words on the personal development of these adult infants. He claims that the foundlings of Spenser's work must leave the dynastic "nest" as they "wex old" and become figures worthy to rediscover and inherit a legacy. He argues that, in *The Faerie Queene*, "old energy cannot be reshaped into new forms unless it is first recovered . . . without exploring origins, we have no originals from which to fashion ourselves."[34] Ultimately, Spenser's adult infants require exile to acquire self-consciousness—it is a precondition for their quest, rather than the object of the quest itself. The object of the quest is the rejuvenation of the dynasty.

The limitations of an essay make adequately exploring the significance of all of these individual figures (Arthur, Britomart, Artegall, etc.) as infants impractical. However, noticing their many similarities helps to reveal the significance of such adult infants in *The Faerie Queene*. First, these adult infants can be given that label only in reference to a larger dynastic lineage or tree. The word is absurd and meaningless without this context. Like Shakespeare's Henry V, each of Spenser's adult infants is "a stem of that victorious stock." The reader is meant to intuit not their anxiety, but their "native mightiness and fate" (II.iv.62–63). They carry the figure of the majesty and power of their ancestors like wax pressed with the family seal.

Second, these adult infants are *in media res,* acting out their destined roles as questing foundlings—but they have not achieved them yet. The object of the quest, a renaissance of their dynastic lineage remains a glorious destiny that is consistently deferred. Like the marriage of Red Cross with Una, Britomart with Artegall, and of course Arthur with Gloriana, the consummation of the present with a promised destiny remains tantalizingly located in the future, beyond the bounds of that part of the poem available to Spenser's readers. If Spenser's adult infants are meant to come of age and fulfill the quest, it has not happened yet.

Lastly, infants as representatives of the latest generation of a dynastic legacy are necessary to initiate the process of rebirth and restoration vital to the victory of the valorized institutions of *The Faerie Queene*. Without Red Cross, the dragon remains undefeated and the land of Una's dynastic family would continue to lie in ruins. Without the child Calepine rescues from the bear, Matilde and Sir Bruin will succumb to the "foule fiend." Arthur, Britomart and the others have similar roles to fulfill that demonstrate that renaissance in the form of a new generation is a moral, religious, and cultural imperative. Indeed, the poem itself seems to be straining to see Spenser's infants emerge and remake the world of Faerielond in their own image.

It is tempting to see in this straining the anxieties or insecurities Andrew Hadfield has described—an awareness that in contemporary England and its analogues in *The Faerie Queene* borders are not stable or undisputed, and dynasties must be defended.[35] The implications for England at the end of a childless queen's reign are obvious. But it should be remembered that, although the fulfillment of the quest remains unseen, it is no less secure. Red Cross's vision of his own sainthood and the prophecy spoken over the child Calepine rescues from a bear are assurances that will come to fruition; the fact that they have not yet appeared points to the dramatic tension that accompanies a heroic achievement. To become worthy of their own dynastic legacies, these infants must face the physical and spiritual testing required by the quest.

V. CONCLUSION

Far from the unwanted remainders of sinful fleshly reproduction, children have great allegorical significance in *The Faerie Queene*. The questing "infant" knights (Arthur, Britomart, et al.) are just a few examples, the offspring of dynastic lineages with a mandate to master and order the world. Ruddymane is another, covered or recovered by the legacy of his mother's innocence at the last moment, and sent out to "better thrive" in this struggle.

But perhaps the child Calepine rescues from the bear presents the most poignant example, grafted into a family longing for the prophesied figure that can beat back the "foule feend" of lurking, chaotic misrule. Spenser's narrator extends the narrative of this infant in the restoration of his adopted dynastic family beyond the purview of *The Faerie Queene*. He says that Matilde, bringing the child to Sir Bruin,

> Made him thinke it surely was his owne,
> And it in goodly thewes so well upbrought,
> That it became a famous knight well knowne,
> And did right noble deedes, the which elsewhere are showne.
>
> (VI.iv.38)

Spenser's language here implies that, although the great conflicts into which he is born must continue, this child will be equipped with the force and fate of a new generation to do noble deeds. Spenser's infants, questing knights and newly swaddled babes, are meant to carry on the battle for the future long after Spenser himself has run out of pages.

Saint Louis University

NOTES

1.   Prominent scholarly examples include Joanne Craig, "'All Flesh Doth Frailtie Breed': Mothers and Children in *The Faerie Queene*," *Texas Studies in Literature and Language* 42:1 (2000): 16–33, as well as Elizabeth Bellamy, *Translations of Power: Narcissism and the Unconscious in Epic History* (Ithaca: Cornell University Press, 1992), and Barbara Estrin, "Finding the Poet in the Narrator's Tale: The Lost Child in Book I of *The Faerie Queene*," *Cahiers Élisabéthains* 12 (1977): 21–43. Neither Bellamy nor Estrin represent generation itself as the messy, negatively charged process that Craig describes. They have been included here, however, because of the emphasis on alienation and separation anxiety in the infants of Spenser's poem. Bellamy in particular treats separation anxiety as *the foundational* characteristic of Arthur and Britomart.

2. Craig, "'All Flesh Doth Frailtie Breed,'" 16.

3. Ibid., 28.

4. This conception is a moment of spontaneous generation (despite Phoebus's role) because it does not involve copulation. It fits, therefore, with the interplay of natural forces rather than the consummation of sexual desire.

5. The language Spenser applies to this discussion picks up and elaborates upon the use of "kind" appearing in Genesis 1:12; "the earth brought foorth the bud of the herbe, that seedeth seede according to his kind, also the tree that beareth fruite, which hath his seede in it selfe according to his kinde: and God sawe that it was good." Both here and later in verse 25, God commands flora and then fauna to generate offspring like themselves.

6. See Gordon Braden, "Riverrun: An Epic Catalogue in *The Faerie Queene*," *English Literary Renaissance* 5 (1975): 25–48, 42.

7. Ibid., 44.

8. Ariès introduced this thesis in some earlier articles, but it is more thoroughly analyzed in his book *L'Enfant et la Vie Familiale sous l'Ancien Régime*, quoted here from the English translation by R. Baldick, *Centuries of Childhood* (London: Penguin, 1962).

9. Ibid., 411.

10. Ibid., 412.

11. The list of scholars influenced by the Ariès thesis is extensive, but some examples might include Lawrence Stone, *The Family, Sex, and Marriage in England 1500–1800* (London: Weidenfeld & Nicolson, 1977); Lloyd de Mause "The Evolution of Childhood," in *The History of Childhood*, ed. Lloyd de Mause (London: Souvenir, 1976), 1–74; Edward Shorter, *The Making of the Modern Family* (London: William Collins, 1976); Ivy Pinchbeck and Margaret Hewitt, *Children in English Society* (London: Routledge, 1969).

12. A number of scholars had already pointed tentatively to this conclusion before Pollock's work. See Mary McLaughlin, "Survivors and Surrogates: Children and Parents from the Ninth to the Thirteenth Centuries," in *The History of Childhood*, ed. Lloyd de Mause (London: Souvenir, 1976), 82–101. McLaughlin's research documents twelfth-century notions of children as formative bearers of "potential greatness." See also Richard Lyman, "Barbarism and Religion: Late Roman and Early Medieval Childhood," in *The History of Childhood*, ed. Lloyd de Mause (London: Souvenir Press, 1976), 75–100. Lyman points to twelfth-century interest in the stages of child development, and an awareness that children need affectionate contact with their parents to develop appropriately.

13. See Linda Pollock, *Forgotten Children: Parent-Child Relations from 1500–1900* (New York: Cambridge University Press, 1983), 96–97.

14. Ibid., 271.

15. This last passage ought to be cross-read with the parable of the prodigal son in Luke 15, as Claribell "stayd no lenger to enquire" but runs to catch up her daughter and embraces her "twixt her armes twaine" (VI.xii.19).

16. See Heather Dubrow, "'The Infant of Your Care': Guardianship in Shakespeare's *Richard III* and Early Modern England," in *Domestic Arrangement in Early Modern England* (Pittsburgh: Duquesne University Press, 2002), 147–68. Dubrow develops the figure of the improper guardian with impressive results.

17. Britomart emerges from this child-like state only upon learning that Artegall is not, in fact, wooing Radigund, putting on her armor, and leaping upon her horse (V.vi.17).

18. See Barbara Estrin, *The Raven and the Lark: Lost Children in Literature of the English Renaissance* (Lewisburg, PA: Bucknell University Press, 1985). I am indebted to Barbara Estrin for her work on this subject.

19. Ibid., 13.

20. Ibid., 17.

21. Scholars who followed and expanded the general course of this critical perspective include A. D. S. Fowler in his "The Image of Mortality in *The Faerie Queene*, II.i–ii," *The Huntington Library Quarterly* 24:2 (1961): 91–110. Fowler outlines and develops some of the implications that this idea has for Mortdant, Amavia, and other provocative passages in *The Faerie Queene*. Carol Kaske, "The Bacchus Who Wouldn't Wash: *Faerie Queene* II.i–ii," *Renaissance Quarterly* 24:2 (1976): 195–209, maintains the general thrust of this point while cross-reading it with Ezekiel 16, wherein the blood becomes afterbirth and the well becomes Mosaic law. A more recent critic to work with this thesis has been Harold Weatherby, who, both in "Dame Nature and the Nymph," *English Literary Renaissance* 26 (Spring 1996): 243–58, and "Two Images of Mortalitie: Spenser and Original Sin," *Studies in Philology* 85 (Summer 1988): 321–52, argues that Ruddymane functions as an allegory for disparate and nuanced readings of "original sin" both in the context of the old patristic tradition and in relation to Spenser's own reluctance to use the term itself.

22. See A. C. Hamilton, "A Theological Reading of *The Faerie Queene*, Book II," *ELH* 25 (1958): 155–62, 155. It seems that Spenser must have had in mind another episode that would introduce Rudymane, since his letter to Raleigh describes a scene in which the Palmer brings Rudymane into Gloriana's court to enlist Sir Guyon's aid in dismantling the Bowre of Bliss. This calls into question whether or not the scene Sir Guyon finds in the woods could also be called "the whole subject" of Book II, since Spenser clearly references a scene not in the 1596 edition of *The Faerie Queene*. He seems to have decided at some point between the writing of the letter and the final publication that the image of Rudymane wallowing in his mother's blood was simply too powerful a spectacle to pass up.

23. Ibid., 156.

24. See Carol Kaske, "Amavia," in *The Spenser Encyclopedia*, ed. A. C. Hamilton (Toronto: University of Toronto Press, 2006), 70.

25. See Michael Whitmore, *Pretty Creatures: Children and Fiction in The English Renaissance* (Ithaca: Cornell University Press, 2007), 69–70.

26. Bellamy, *Translations of Power*, 194–95.

27. Craig, 18.

28. Estrin, "Finding the Poet in the Narrator's Tale," 23.

29. Ibid., 27.

30. "infant, *n.2*" *OED Online*. December 2011. Oxford University Press. 19 February 2012. <http://dictionary.oed.com>.

31. They are: Arthur (II.viii.56; II.xi.25; VI.viii.25), Britomart (III.ii.50; III.iii.56), Tristram (VI.ii.28).

32. III.iii.26.

33. VI.xii.15; VI.xii.16; VI.xii.20.

34. See A. Bartlett Giamatti, "Primitivism and The Process of Civility in Spenser's *Faerie Queene*," in *First Images of America: The Impact of the New World on the Old*, ed. F. Chiappelli (Berkeley: University of California Press, 1976), 71–82, 76.

35. See Andrew Hadfield, "Spenser, Drayton, and the Question of Britain," *Review of English Studies* 51:204 (2000): 582–99, 585.

SEAN HENRY

Hot and Bothered: The Lions of
Amoretti 20 and *The Faerie Queene* I

This essay analyzes the lions of *Amoretti* 20 and the first book of
The Faerie Queene. The sonnet depends upon the comparison the
speaker makes between the behavior of his beloved and that of the
lion, according to the received natural history of Spenser's time.
The first simile of Spenser's epic compares Redcrosse to a lion and
thereby introduces a series of lions and leonine characters running
throughout Book I and embodying different attributes and associa-
tions of lions—and, by extension, different attributes of Redcrosse,
Una's proper companion, for whom the other characters stand in,
whether Una wants them to or not. Spenser expects his readers to
interpret the significance of the animals in a cumulative, multifac-
eted manner, rather than as a simple one-to-one correlation based
upon a single trait at a local moment in the poem.

> I will roar, that I will do any man's heart good to hear me; I will
> roar, that I will make the duke say "Let him roar again, let him
> roar again."[1]

*I*N SPENSER'S *AMORETTI* 20, the speaker complains about his be-
loved's lack of pity for his love by unfavorably comparing her behavior
to that of the lion:

> In vaine I seeke and sew to her for grace,
>   and doe myne humbled hart before her poure:

Spenser Studies: A Renaissance Poetry Annual, Volume XXVII, Copyright © 2012 AMS
Press, Inc. All rights reserved.   DOI: 10.7756/spst.027.003.47-76

the whiles her foot she in my necke doth place,
and tread my life downe in the lowly floure.
And yet the Lyon that is Lord of power,
and reigneth ouer euery beast in field:
in his most pride disdeigneth to deuoure
the silly lambe that to his might doth yield.
But she more cruell and more saluage wylde,
then either Lyon or the Lyonesse:
shames not to be with guiltlesse bloud defylde,
but taketh glory in her cruelnesse.
Fayrer then fayrest let none euer say,
that ye were blooded in a yeelded pray.[2]

Most obviously, the conceit contrasts the proverbial natural magnanimity of the lion with the cruelty of the beloved. To take a representative selection of comments by critics over the past twenty years, William C. Johnson, Donna Gibbs, James Fleming, Kenneth J. Larsen, Richard McCabe, and Joan Curbet all take the comparison at more or less face value—as the speaker asking his lady how even the most fierce of beasts can be merciful when she cannot.[3] However, the lion comparison has a number of other implications because of the complicated (and often contradictory) associations the lion held in early modern English culture. Some are more familiar than others, such as the idea of the lion as king of beasts; some are less so. I argue that Spenser expects his readers to interpret the significance of the sonnet's animal comparison in a cumulative, multifaceted manner, rather than as a simple one-to-one correlation based upon a single shared trait. This accumulation of meaning makes the comparison in *Amoretti* 20 much less trite and predictable, and much more problematic for readers. In the remainder of the essay, I apply this cumulative interpretation to the lions of Book I of *The Faerie Queene*—in part as a case study analysis of multivalent meaning of such animals to someone of Spenser's intellectual and cultural milieu, and in part to demonstrate the sudden force these leonine images gain through such a reading.

Of all the non-native animals known to early modern England, the lion was probably the most familiar. Because of its close associations with England, particularly through heraldry, the lion was a potent symbol for Spenser and his contemporaries. The arms of England, *Gules three Lions passant gardant Or* (three golden lions, each standing on three feet with one forefoot raised and looking at the viewer, on a red background), were quartered in Elizabeth's day with the fleurs de lys of France in the royal

arms, with another lion as a supporter. Across the Channel, the cartog-
rapher Michael Aitsinger represented the Netherlands (so important to
Elizabethan foreign policy) as *Leo Belgicus*, a lion-shaped map based on
the geographical outline of the Low Countries and the leonine heraldry of
nearly all the provinces, first published in 1583 and reprinted at least eight
times during Spenser's lifetime (see fig. 1).[4] Lions were familiar not only

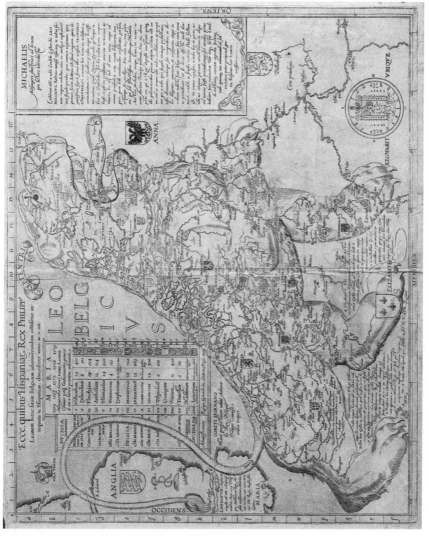

Fig. 1: Michael Aitsinger, *Leo Belgicus*, folding map from *De Leone belgico, ejusque topo-
graphica atque historica descriptione liber* (Cologne, 1583).

through heraldry, but also through representations in literature, the Bible, and the visual arts. Actual lions were not unknown. The poet Sir Thomas Wyatt as a child reputedly defended his father against a pet lion that had turned against the family (when the story came to Henry VIII's ear, he is said to have remarked of Wyatt that "He can tame lions").[5] Lions had been part of the collection of the Royal Menagerie at the Tower of London since at least the fourteenth century; archeological digs at the Tower over 1936–37 uncovered two lion skulls, the earliest of which has recently been radiocarbon dated to between 1280–1385.[6] During Spenser's lifetime, the lion quarters consisted of a yard with a hemicycle of dens for the lions, all of which were rebuilt in 1605. The Tower menagerie had by Elizabeth's reign become a public attraction. For example, Paul Hentzner, a German traveler to London in 1598, notes in his memoirs that among the animals he saw when visiting the Royal Menagerie were three lionesses and "one Lion of great size, called Edward VI, from his having been born in that reign."[7] Londoners must have joined foreign and country visitors in going to see the menagerie at the Tower. The Tower lions are among the wonders of England mentioned having been seen by a group of travelers met by "a certaine pretty quick witted fellow" in one of the jokes of *Pasquils iestes mixed with Mother Bunches merriments* (London, 1609).[8] A slightly later version of the same jest book describes how Mother Bunch, supposed author of some of the merriments, "spent most of her time in telling of tales, and when she laughed, she was heard from Algate, to the Monuments at Westminster, and all Southwarke stood in amazement, the Lyons in the Tower, and the Bulls, and Beares of Parish-Garden roar'd (with terrour of her laughter)."[9] Shakespeare's audiences would have been well-equipped to appreciate the mighty mildness of Snug the joiner's performance as a lion and the trusting pride Bottom has in his own ability to roar. To judge from such scattered references, enough people must have gone for the phrase "to see the lions" to become proverbial by the 1590s for seeing the London sights in general, at least according to Tilley.[10]

The Renaissance lion is a paradox. The beast is both clement and cruel by nature, and at the most extreme symbolic poles, representing both Christ (e.g., Genesis 49:9 and Revelation 5:5) and the devil (e.g., 1 Peter 5:8). Lions appear in saints' lives and serve as synonymous emblems for certain saints in art (such as St. Mark's lion, or the creature inevitably shown crouching like a house pet near St. Jerome at his desk). Lions were also an accepted generic part of romance, whether primary (e.g., *Yvain*) or secondary (e.g., *Don Quixote* or *The Faerie Queene*). Moreover, although "the king of beasts" seems an innocuous cliché, the monarchical associations of the animal in fact render it politically volatile and an interpretive challenge. The political overtones of the lion were central to the early modern definition of the creature. In the medieval tradition, Margaret Haist argues, the lion had particular importance precisely because "the bestiary lion entry addressed ideas of immediate concern to readers, who, if not themselves monarchs, were certainly living under monarchial rule."[11] The same could be said of Spenser's lions.

Contemporary natural history texts reveal the complex discourse around the lion, blurring the line between the "real" animal and its symbolic capital. For example, in discussing the paradoxical behavior of lions in his usefully derivative *Histore of Foure-Footed Beasts* (1607), Edward Topsell employs terms that could come from an exemplary civil history or a conduct manual for princes. Just as lions "excell in strength and courage," Topsell observes, "so also they doe in crueltie, deuouring both men and beastes, setting vpon troupes of horsemen, depopulating the flockes, and heards of cattell, carrying some aliue to their yoonge ones."[12] Elsewhere, echoing Pliny, Topsell comments on the paradox that

> Their clemencie in that fierce and angry nature is also worthy commendation, and to be wondered at in such beastes, for if one prostrate himselfe vnto them as it were in petition for his life, they often spare except in extremitie of famine; and likewise they seldome destroy women or children: and if they see women, children, and men together, they take the men which are strongest and refuse the other as weaklings and vnworthie their honor. (Rr6^r)[13]

Here, Topsell ascribes a kind of chivalry to the lion in its attitude toward women and children, as well as "weaklings" and those "vnworthie their honor." The behavior Topsell describes could just as easily be that of human monarchs as that of lions. Indeed, Erasmus derives didactic significance for rulers from this leonine chivalry in *Parabolae sive similia* (1514): "The lion attacks a man more readily than a woman . . . he spares simple folk and those who lie down before him. In the same way powerful men should have pity on those who are weaker than they are, and try their strength on others whose defeat would bring them credit."[14] Whether human or animal, monarchs are expected to be conversant with the arts of peace and war: zealous in the prosecution of violence when necessary, but also open to the claims of mercy and clemency.

Queen Elizabeth herself employed the connection between the behavior of lions and human monarchs for pointed purposes, drawing upon the totemic links between the animal and her person as "England." According to George Puttenham in *The Arte of English Poesie* (1589), "a noble Prince," like a lion, is

> not to be passionate for small detriments, nor to be a reuenger of them, but in cases of great iniurie and specially of dishonors: and therein to be the very sterne and vindicatiue, for that sauours of Princely magnanimitie: nor to seeke reuenge vpon base and obscure persons, ouer whom the conquest is not glorious, nor the victorie honourable.[15]

Puttenham goes on to recount an anecdote concerning Elizabeth I illustrating her own sense of "Princely magnanimitie" that equates the human sovereign with the king of beasts:

> Our soueraign Lady (keeping alwaies the decorum of a Princely person) at her first comming to the crowne, when a knight of this Realme, who had very insolently behaued himselfe toward her when she was Lady *Elizabeth*, fell vpon his knee to her, and besought her pardon: suspecting (as there was good cause) that he should haue bene sent to the Tower, she said vnto him most mildly: do you not know that we are descended of the Lion, whose nature is not to harme or pray vpon the mouse, or any other such small vermin? (Kk3ʳ)

Elizabeth's witty and characteristic response shows the queen's willingness to propound a correspondence between a human kingdom and that of the animals, even if only as a devastating retort to a "vermin" timeserver. Her choice of animal figure suggests the providential design of her accession; it must have seemed so to Elizabeth, given the tribulations of her life, though no doubt the queen also would have wished the suggestion embraced as fact by her subjects. Elizabeth Tudor is the proper ruler of England, just as the lion is the proper ruler of animals, both set in their places by divine order—and like the lion, the human monarch should have standards of conduct concerning the weak, the defenseless, or those merely beneath contempt.

Elizabeth's reign began and ended with lions as providential signs. She spent the night before her coronation procession in the Tower of London, where she had earlier been a prisoner during her sister Mary's reign. The next morning (according to an anonymous account published in 1559), Elizabeth stopped at the gate before leaving for Westminster, "lifted vp her eyes to heauen" and offered thanksgiving for the day's events:

> O Lord, almighty and euerlasting God, I geue thee most hearty tha[n]kes that thou hast been so mercifull vnto me as to spare me to beholde this ioyfull daye. And I acknowledge that thou hast dealt as wonderfully & as mercifully with me, as thou didst with thy true and faithfull seruant Daniel thy prophete whom thou deliueredst out of the denne from the crueltie of the gredy and rageing Lyons: euen so was I ouerwhelmed, and only by the deliuered. To thee therfore onely be thankes, honor, & prayse, foreuer. Amen.[16]

Some sources add that when Elizabeth mentioned Daniel and his lions, the lions of the Tower grew restive and roared; whether the outburst was stage-managed or not, the roar would have easily been heard at the gates of the Tower and must have impressed the crowd listening to Elizabeth pray as a propitious sign indicating the miraculous order that brought the queen to her throne.[17] That order was shown again at the end of Elizabeth's reign: during the Queen's final illness in March, 1603, a lion in the Tower named Elizabeth also grew sick and died, which was understandably considered an ill omen for the Queen's recovery. She died a few days after her animal namesake.[18]

Elizabeth seems to have been fond of the lion figure, for she compared herself to the king of beasts a number of times throughout her reign; others followed suit. I take but three further instances as illustration. The Calendar of State Papers for May 8, 1572 records the flattering overtures of some Scottish diplomats who called Elizabeth "a princess of honour and great courage, and in that point to resemble the noble nature of the lion, that the more they bow themselves and yield to her, the better speed they shall come."[19] Two years later, the French ambassador to Elizabeth's court reported in a dispatch of July 23, 1574 on a conversation he had had with the queen:

> Qu'encor qu'elle ne soit lyonne, elle ne layssoit d'estre yssue et tenir beaucoup de la complexion du lyon, et que, sellon que le Roy la traictera doulcement, il la trouvera doucle et traictable, aultant qu'il le scauroit desirer; et s'il luy est rude, elle mettra peyne de luy estre le plus rude et nuysible qu'elle pourra.

Although she is not a lioness, she is nonetheless descended from
the lion and displays much of its nature—in other words, if the king
treats her gently, he will find her as gentle and accommodating as he
would desire; similarly if he is ill mannered, she will go to great pains
to be as curt and malevolent as she can.[20]

Finally, almost at the end of Elizabeth's reign, the recusant loyalist Anthony
Copley, in an anti-Jesuit diatribe of 1602 seeking toleration for English
Roman Catholics, mused that "our Soueraigne is truly a Lionesse that
knowes her strength and how to vse it aswell as euer any her predecessor-
Kings of this Realme did."[21] From her accession until her death, Elizabeth
was linked to lions, though her own insistence when using the analogy that
she was descended from a lion rather than being a lion herself seems like
a concession to the uneasy comparisons made between the queen and her
father, Henry VIII, a man leonine in his passions and appetites.[22]

These connections between the human monarch and the lion are im-
portant because Spenser surely must have been aware of them; they could
not have been far from his mind in writing about another Elizabeth and
a lion. He shows his consciousness of the parallels between the different
Elizabeths framing his life in *Amoretti* 74. In *Amoretti* 20, the natural king-
ship of the lion suggests the corresponding reign of the beloved over the
speaker's world and implies that, at least from the speaker's point of view,
the beloved's reign is just as much according to natural, divinely sanctioned
order as that of the lion in the animal kingdom. To the speaker, she is "the
souerayne beauty which I doo admyre" (*Amoretti* 3.1), from whom he
seeks to "sew . . . for grace," as any courtier would from a monarch (20.1).
Moreover, one sonnet earlier, *Amoretti* 19 introduces monarchial order
to this point in the sequence, but also suggests that the beloved is a rebel
against such order. Cruelty beyond that of a lion does not alone set the
beloved beyond the pale of what is natural, however; the beloved's abroga-
tion of magnanimity as a ruler is as much a crime against natural order as
her being more bestial (and beastly) than an animal "blooded in a yeelded
pray" (*Amoretti* 20.9).

Then again, part of the irony Spenser plays with through the Petrarchan
pose adopted by the speaker is that whatever greatness there may be had
from ruling his heart has been thrust upon the beloved; she is an unwilling
queen of hearts. Spenser employs natural history on the one hand to set
the beloved on a throne corresponding to that of the king of beasts, and
on the other hand, to tear down that throne, making the beloved neither

human nor animal, but an unnatural, predatory monster, even as the abject speaker complains of his being ground into the "floure"—"floor" or "flower"—a deliberate touch of bathos either way, determined by rhyme scheme but emphasized by not being the "dust" or "ground" readers might expect. The tone and imagery playfully threaten to topple over into exaggeration. The speaker praises and chastises; the speaker has himself been torn apart, leaving the lady with "guiltlesse bloud defylde." Such exaggerated violence reappears in *Amoretti* 47, where the beloved "feeds at pleasure on the wretched pray" whom she has slain with her bloody hands (47.8). Even if the poem were limited to the single conceit of the beloved being more cruel than a lion, could any lover hope to woo and win, were such a comparison made in all seriousness?

Spenser introduces further elements of humor that depend on what pieces of information about lions the reader gives priority to when considering the simile. First, in a sense, the lady is too little a lion, inasmuch as she does not accept the position in the hierarchy of the speaker's world that corresponds with that of the lion in the animal world. However, she also exceeds the lion in cruelty and savagery, though presumably her violence is metaphorical and akin to the conventional cruelty of the sonnet beloved.

According to received natural history of Spenser's time, there is a far more overtly sexual association with the lion that is part of the cumulative significance of this leonine beloved. Topsell states that "There is no beast more desirous of copulation then a lionesse," and for this reason, "sometimes eight, ten, or twelue males follow one lionesse like so many dogges one sault bitch" (Rr5[r]). The social behavior of real lions is quite the opposite: prides conventionally consist of groups of females, with perhaps one or two males, rather than Topsell's image of a leonine *femme fatale* pursued by swooning troops of lions. Although he grudgingly adds that because of the heat of their constitution, "at all times of the yeare both sexes desire copulation," Topsell reflects in some detail on "the adultery of lionesses" (Rr5[r]), drawing upon Pliny the Elder for an explanation for the similarities among different species. Pliny, although he has no doubts about the beast's insatiable sexual appetite, refers only once to the lioness as "adultera";[23] the emphasis on adulterousness as a chief characteristic of the lioness is an innovation of the Reverend Mr. Topsell and post-classical natural history.[24] Topsell reasons that the passions of the female must be too much for the male of the species; he asserts that as a result of this imbalance of libido, the lioness "committeth adultery" with a grotesque variety of other creatures, including hyenas, dogs, and leopards—themselves, like panthers, animals also "begotten by the adultery of the lyonesse" (Rr1ᵛ). For these acts of "adultery," the lioness "is punished by her male if she wash not her selfe before she come at him" (Rr5ʳ); Topsell does not make it clear whether the lioness's offense is not washing herself or the adulterous act itself revealed by post-coital uncleanness ("Madam, you stink of leopards"). Although Topsell's remarks about the sexual proclivities of the lioness are immediately followed by praise for the lioness as a caring mother, his choice of the word "adultery" is a charged one, carrying with it overtones of moral judgment, as does the punishment meted out by the male to the unwashed female. The word suggests a system of morality and ethics among animals similar to that existing in the human world. Interbreeding between different species might occur to someone seeking to explain the resemblances between the great cats and the lion, but Topsell invokes a whole charged discourse of misogyny and cuckoldry in ascribing these resemblances solely to the breeding behavior of the lioness and not the lion.

Topsell's account of leonine sexuality of course mirrors the preoccupations and theories of his culture, which would include whatever titillated though scandalized fascination his readers would have in encountering the lascivious lioness. For Topsell, the creature's sexuality, rule, and tendency toward anger are according to contemporary notions of its natural order. In claiming that the lion's "naturall constitution is so hotte," Topsell makes the species subject to the traditions of astrology and elemental physiology and psychology, like any human being (Rr5ʳ). Elsewhere, Topsell uses the lion's temperament even to explain diet: young lions "cannot longe bee fed with Milke, because they are whot and dry," and therefore soon require flesh (Rr3ᵛ). Topsell uses the vocabulary of these systems without comment: in describing the antipathies of lions, Topsell observes that "They are . . . afraid of fire . . . For as they are inwardly filled with naturall fire (for which cause by the Egyptians they were dedicated to *Vulcan*) so are they the more afraide of all outward fire" (Rr5ʳ). Topsell slips between the internal fire of the lion's temperament and the external fire of the creature's fears, explaining the one through the other. Indeed, fire was so closely associated with lions and so essential to their nature in this tradition of natural history that Aristotle could assert that when a lion's bones are struck together, sparks fly out as from a flint and steel.[25]

Leo is a "fire" sign, associated with choler, as befits the lion's reputation. The association between lions and the choleric humor is a widespread commonplace. For example, the revised 1570 edition of *The kalender of shepardes* (a book that is something like a cross between a sacerdotal handbook, a home medicine guide, and *The Farmer's Almanac*) includes an illustration of the four temperaments matched by emblematic animals; a lion represents choler (fig. 2).[26] Astrology also associates Leo the lion with the Sun, as sixteenth-century practitioners confirm: John Maplet, in his 1581 astrological text, *The diall of destiny*, states that the Sun's "house or mansion is onely in Leo."[27] Leo governs the heart, the seat of passions like the courage and the valor ascribed to the lion, again blurring the distinctions between knowledge systems. As Topsell solemnly records, "As the Eagle is fained to feede vpon the heart of *Prometheus*, so also is the lion the ruler of the heart of man" (Rr3). For Maplet, both a natural historian and an astrologer, the distinction between knowledge systems is unthinkable. Among the creatures he lists in his astrology text that are under the influence of the Sun are "all such as be of bigge stature, and of hawty stomacke: likewyse such as are desierous of superiority, and haue naturally a pryde in themselues: Of which sorte is the Lyon" (E5ʳ). Like Topsell, Maplet conflates the zodiacal sign Leo (and the celestial body most closely linked to it)

Fig. 2: The Four Humours, woodcut from *The kalender of shepardes* (London, 1570; STC 22415), L6ʳ.

with the real animal used to represent the sign. Maplet's delineation of the attributes associated with those governed by the Sun reads very much like Topsell's description of the lion; where Topsell emphasizes the lordliness, the sense of dignity, and the danger in lions, Maplet describes the natural pride and desire for superiority over others in those ruled by the Sun.

Moreover, people governed by the Sun are also, according to Maplet, "hawty stomacked" and are "aduanced often to great honours and dignities . . . and are giuen much to procure the profit of their country" (E4ᵛ). Unlike animals, which astrological tradition assigns according to temperament or physiology to the rule of a certain heavenly patron, human beings are born under a specific set of influences that reputedly form their temperaments and physiological forms. But astrology is something of a chicken and egg system of interpreting natural history, as the situation of the lion suggests: is the lion ruled by the Sun because it is kingly and "hawty stomacked," or is the lion thought to be "hawty stomacked" and kingly because of the attributes associated with those born under the influence of Leo and the Sun (and is therefore itself subject to the same influences)? Topsell, however, does not engage with the questions behind his less scientific assumptions about the lion; his lion is just as "hawty stomacked" and regal as that of Maplet and as those men and women ruled by Leo. Rather, Topsell notes that lions are "ful of stomacke" (Rr3) and "can endure nothing which is vnsweete, stale, or stinking; but in my opinion they do it throgh the pride of their naturs, resembling in al things a Princely maiesty, and therefore scorne to haue one dish twice presented to their own table" (Rr4ʳ). Topsell's explanation rests entirely upon temperament: "the pride of their naturs" dictates the lion's diet. Just as the idea of cross-species interbreeding might occur to someone looking for a way to explain resemblances between those species, so a delicacy born of pride might explain why lions might eat some things and not others; both theories have a certain simple logic to them.

But again, as with the supposed adulterousness of lionesses, Topsell interprets his explanations according to the expectations of early modern human social systems rather than animal behavior. Topsell's logic is circular: if "the pride of their naturs" is the reason lions eat only certain things, then lions therefore resemble "in al things a Princely maiesty" (because of the delicacy of princely palates), which itself therefore "scorne[s] to haue one dish twice presented." Shakespeare makes a similar remark about the diet and nature of lions in *As You Like It*, when Oliver explains why the lioness that observed him sleeping did not attack:

For 'tis
The royal disposition of that beast
To prey on nothing that doth seem as dead.[28]

For Topsell, Maplet, and Shakespeare, diet is dictated by disposition. Upon analysis, at least in Topsell's natural history, the interpretation of disposition is dictated by diet, whether he acknowledges it or not: if it eats like a prince, then it must *be* like a prince.

The significance of these leonine associations to the lion analogy of *Amoretti* 20 should be apparent. Given the creature's reputation for rapacious and capacious desires, how serious is the speaker's complaint? In vain the speaker seeks for grace from the lady, but she is "more cruell and more saluage wylde" in her appetites than even a lioness, in that her graces are directed elsewhere (or at least not toward the speaker), like those of the wandering adulteress Topsell portrays. One wonders under which astrological sign Elizabeth Boyle was born. Yet the simile throughout the poem depends upon the beloved *not* being like a lion, and so what initially seems like libel becomes irony and nearly a compliment—if not a frank acknowledgement that the beloved has her own hot blooded passions. Moreover, just how is it that she is or is not "blooded"? "Let none euer say, / that ye were blooded in a yeelded pray," the speaker states, but will she instead be blooded by one that remains wholly prideful on that *Epithalamion* night? The speaker offers assurance that he is no dead prey, since such fare would not be to the liking of the lioness; perhaps a lion lurks beneath the speaker's own lambish clothing. In short, Spenser takes advantage of the inconsistencies of meaning. For the speaker, whether the beloved's refusal to be lion-like is something lamentable or laudable is contingent upon what piece of the lion's symbolic vocabulary governs the comparison. For the reader, her refusal can be both.

The speaker implicitly identifies himself with the lamb that the lion "disdeigneth to deuoure" when it "to his might doth yield" (*Amoretti* 20.7–8). The pairing of lion and lamb recalls Isaiah 11:6, where the prophet describes the return of idyllic harmony to the natural world that accompanies the arrival of the Messiah: "The wolfe also shal dwell with the lambe, and the leoparde shal lye with the kid, and the calfe, and the lyon, and the fat beast together, and a litle childe shal lead them."[29] By Spenser's lifetime, the pairing had also become a conventional symbol of the "antique age yet in the infancie / Of time . . . then like an innocent, / In simple truth and blamelesse chastitie," when "loyall loue had royall regiment" or rule (*FQ* IV.viii.30.1–7).[30] At that time,

The Lyon there did with the Lambe consort,
And eke the Doue sate by the Faulcons side,
Ne each of other feared fraud or tort,
But did in safe securitie abide,
Withouten perill of the stronger pride.

(IV.viii.31.1–5)

This description of the prelapsarian realm of love (whether ἀγάπη, Cupid, or both at once wrapped up in union with God) resembles that of the Garden of Adonis, Spenser's vision of generative love, where

Without fell rancor, or fond gealosie . . .
Franckly each paramour his leman knowes,
Each bird his mate, ne any does enuie
Their goodly meriment, and gay felicitie.

(III.vi.41.6–9)

The inhabitants of that garden "their true loues without suspition tell abrode" in perfect candor and trust (III.vi.42.9), quite in contrast with the conventional wrangling of the sonnet sequence, nor yet with any "perill of the stronger pride"—so assuring and important when considering a sonnet sequence that often addresses fears about desire in terms of bondage, violence, and suffering.

The lion and lamb pairing represents the unfallen "royall regiment" of love and the Messianic restoration of concord; the woeful speaker in *Amoretti* 20 and his beloved stand in marked contrast with both the prelapsarian beginning and the salvific conclusion to the narrative. The Geneva gloss on Isaiah proposes an interpretation of the prophecy that puts the symbolic significance of the animals first:

Men because of their wicked affections are named by the names of beasts, wherein the like affections reigne: but Christ by his Spirit shal reforme them, & worke in them suche mutual charitie that they shal be like lambes, fauoryng and louing one another, and cast of all their cruel affections.

The speaker identifies himself with the lamb and therefore one in conformity with Christ, but the beloved is "more cruell and more saluage wylde, / then either Lyon or the Lyonesse" (*Amoretti* 20.9–10). In her recalcitrance, the speaker therefore suggests, the lady stands in opposition to divine will. Birds do it, bees do it, even Millenarian lions and lambs do it: so why, the speaker asks his lady, can we not have "suche mutual charitie" as God would have of us? The logic seems worthy of John Donne; so also does the wry smile. The Second Coming *should* be something for which all Christians should make themselves as ready as possible; the lion *should* lie down with the lamb. Moreover, because the union the speaker seeks is a type for the perfected union of everlasting life, when lion, leopard, wolf, and all "shal be like lambes, fauoryng and louing one another," as the Geneva gloss puts it, the lion need not fear any unexpected cruelty from the lamb, but shall "in safe securitie abide, / Withouten perill of the stronger pride," as in the lost innocent antique age (*FQ* IV.viii.31.5). The couplet then turns about on itself to become an understanding reassurance of mutual charity and respect: blooded she may end up being on her wedding bed, but not as yielded prey.

Amoretti 20 shows Spenser employing the multivalent significance of the lion on a small, fairly self-contained scale. Even in a lyric, however, the meaning and implications of Spenser's lions are complex and allusive, if not elusive. Elsewhere, where they appear repeatedly in Spenser's longer poems, the lions accrue significance no less complex. The most familiar of Spenser's lions is that tamed by Una in the first book of *The Faerie Queene*, but this is not the only lion connected to Una in the book. As in Spenser's lion sonnet, the animal's moral register in the epic is often contradictory; its meaning is cumulative and derives not just from one attribute, anecdote, or discourse associated with lions in the poem or in Spenser's culture.[31]

The first simile of *The Faerie Queene* compares Redcrosse Knight to a lion. When her battle with the knight starts going wrong for her, the monster Error attempts to flee back into her den,

> Which when the valiant Elfe perceiu'd, he lept
> As Lyon fierce vpon the flying pray,
> And with his trenchand blade her boldly kept
> From turning backe, and forced her to stay.
> (I.i.17.1–4)

Spenser reiterates Redcrosse Knight's valor through the lion simile, invoking the positive parts of the lion's fierce nature, including its reputation for justice. Moreover, the lion simile foreshadows the revelation later in the book that Redcrosse is not an elf, but "Saint George of mery England, the signe of victoree" (I.x.61.9). Redcrosse's eponymous shield, marked with "a bloodie Crosse" (I.i.2.1), is bound to the leonine simile through the cross of St. George on the flag of England and the heraldic English lion. As patron of England, Redcrosse also should be likened to a lion under Maplet's astrological system, as one "giuen much to procure the profit of [his] country" (E4ᵛ). Later, of course, a real lion briefly replaces Redcrosse as Una's companion when the knight goes astray, confirming the equation the simile makes between Redcrosse and lions.

Throughout Book I, lions accompany Una. Spenser extends the initial leonine simile not just to make literal the comparison made with Redcrosse through the real lion that joins Una in Canto iii, but also to encompass some of Una's other companions while she is separated from the knight: Satyrane, the satyrs, and Sansloy. These other "lions" embody different attributes and associations of lions—and, by extension, different attributes of Redcrosse Knight, Una's proper companion, for whom the other characters stand in, whether Una wants them to or not.

To begin with Satyrane, the half-human, half-satyr, lion-taming knight who was "noursled vp in life and manners wilde, / Emongst wild beastes and woods, from lawes of men exilde" (*FQ* I.vi.23.8–9): like Alcyon in *Daphnaïda*, Satyrane enacts the Spenserian struggle for a disciplined identity; the leonine imagery associated with him reflects this struggle. He is a child of the wilds, born of a kidnapped human mother and a satyr father. Spenser intertwines two different conventional representations of satyrs in his epic, both of which contribute to his characterization of Satyrane. The first and more familiar image of the creatures is that formed by classical literature: carousing, ithyphallic rogues who are both comedic and perilous (the twinned sides of Bacchanalian frenzy). They represent the human potential for unchecked desires.

The second image is one that emerged at the turn of the sixteenth century as a result of the conflation of traditions concerning wild men with those of the satyr. This image is of a creature Lynn Frier Kaufmann calls the "noble satyr, a late intruder among ruffians," capable of improvement, just as nominally civilized human beings were capable of degeneration.[32] For all of their bestial qualities, these satyrs possess the potential in an instinctive way to recognize and admire supernatural virtue, as seen in their treatment of Una in I.vi.7ff—matched, however, by the potential to surrender completely and amorally to their (also instinctive) appetites, amply demonstrated in the spirited and extended welcome they give Hellenore at III.x.36ff.

This duality is not limited to the knight's background as satyr. In describing the origins of the satyr-knight, Spenser suggests little difference between the knight's human and satyr bloodlines. As H. M. Percival glosses the relevant passage in the *Variorum*, the name of Satyrane's mother, Thyamis, comes from Greek θυμός, meaning "passion." The name of the knight's human grandfather, Labryde, comes from λάβρος, "turbulent, greedy," and even the name of his mother's erstwhile human husband, Therion, θήριον, means "wild beast."[33] Whichever side of his family the knight takes after, Satyrane seems destined to struggle against a genetic inclination or predetermined tendency toward untempered passion and sinfulness: an emblem of the struggle universal to fallen humanity in Spenser's moral theology and an emblem of Redcrosse's own particular struggle in the first book of the poem.

In this struggle, Satyrane embodies the strengths and limitations of natural virtue. Although the satyrs, in John N. King's words, "live in a world without revelation,"[34] they and Satyrane are not without some virtue. Ronald A. Horton notes that "since childhood [the knight] has been at war with his bestial affinities," in a struggle to rise above the limitations of his heritage.[35] Spenser represents this inner conflict through Satyrane's battles with a variety of wild creatures of the forest, including bears, bulls, roebucks, leopards, panthers, pardals, boars, tigers, antelopes, and wolves—but especially lions. Satyrane's satyr father taught him "to banish cowardize and bastard feare" by seizing hold of lions (*FQ* I.vi.24.2), and in time, "he would learne / The Lyon stoup to him in lowly wise" (I.vi.25.6–7). Such an act, the narrator notes, was "a lesson hard," though whether it was hard for the lion or for Satyrane—or both—the context does not make clear; most likely, the lesson was hard for the lion, as king of beasts, being made to bow down in such a lowly manner. The narrator also reports that Satyrane made off with the whelps of a lioness before leaving the forest to become a knight. The theft is daring, considering that (as Topsell notes) "there is no creature that loueth her young ones better then the lionesse . . . death it selfe were nothing vnto her, so that her yonge ones might neuer be taken out of her den" (Rr5ᵛ). These acts of establishing mastery over beasts are at once a physical challenge for dominion over the natural world and also a psychomachian struggle, as Satyrane battles with his bestial or semi-bestial nature to tame the passions represented by the lions and other animals.

Such symbolic lion-taming has a long tradition. Dante acknowledges this function of the lion in the first canto of *Inferno*, when three beasts—a leopard (*lonza*), a lion (*leone*), and a she-wolf (*lupa*)—block his progress up the mountain, thereby precipitating his entire educative journey through the three realms.[36] Earlier in the sixteenth century, Lucas Cranach the Elder produced a number of paintings of club-wielding satyrs posed with their families beside dead lions, recalling Hercules's conquest of the Nemean lion, where the lion denotes ferocity subdued by the civilizing demigod, who with his club "subdew'd of old / So many monsters, which the world annoyed" (*FQ* V.24.5–6).[37] Another classical precedent for such educative fights is the training received by Achilles at the hand of Chiron the centaur in Statius's *Achilleid*, though battles with beasts also form a typical part of the training of the hero in medieval romance.[38]

Spenser employs this Tarzan-like trope elsewhere in *The Faerie Queene*, as in the pastoral struggles of Calepine with a bear (VI.iv.17ff), or in the story of Artegall, who "in iustice was vpbrought . . . by faire *Astræa*" (V.i.5.1–4), first learning how to establish equity by meting out justice to animals. The justice Artegall learns, R. S. White proposes, is all human law that is in accordance with natural law.[39] The animal struggles provide a training ground for Artegall in that justice. Moreover, Spenser shows that justice needs to recognize and incorporate the bestial (or, more properly, the seemingly inhuman) into the human. In A. Bartlett Giamatti's terms, "Justice, the power that shapes others for civil ends, must itself incorporate primitive energies in order to be effective."[40] Finally, even though the animals used in Artegall's training act as surrogate humans "for want there of mankind," the narrator's qualification that the animals are specifically those "with wrongfull power oppressing others of their kind" nevertheless suggests a need for Artegall's jurisprudence and implies a role for human beings even in the hierarchy of the animal kingdom, thereby fulfilling the divine and prelapsarian charge of dominion over the created world (*FQ* V.i.7.6–9). He is, in other words, Artegall, lord of the jungle.

Artegall's training differs from that of Satyrane. Both Satyrane and Artegall come to be feared by all beasts (*FQ* I.vi.24.9; V.i.8.4), but where the animals fear Artegall for his judgment, the lions and other creatures of the satyrs' forest fear Satyrane because of his violence. Does Satyrane go too far? Whatever else they are, Spenser's satyrs are comic figures, whether mistakenly worshipping Una's ass or busy having their Matins bells rung by Hellenore. In contrast, setting aside the symbolic implications of the young knight's actions, Satyrane's oppression of beasts comes perilously close to cruelty: the warped spitefulness of a maladjusted youth, unable to come to grips with his own identity. True, the animals he fights are, in the main, "wyld" (I.vi.24.6), "angry" (I.vi.25.5), "cruell" (I.vi.25.4), and "both fierce and fell" (I.vi.26.5). But Spenser takes pains to introduce elements of uncertainty concerning Satyrane's domination over the beasts of the forest. In bald, non-allegorical terms, the animals potentially threaten the satyr community; the poem, however, gives no indication that Satyrane's sport serves any purpose other than his own amusement, once he has mastered his fear. Casual violence against animals was a common entertainment in Spenser's England, and then—as now—such acts were often "merely a prologue to violence against man," as Thomas F. Arnold remarks.[41] But even the Renaissance had its limits on what was acceptable. Keith Thomas points out that although human beings were "fully entitled to domesticate animals and to kill them for food and clothing," men and women were "not to tyrannize or to cause unnecessary suffering."[42] Among the animals, Satyrane's will comes to be "tyrans law," with all the potential for arbitrariness and cruelty that term implies (*FQ* I.vi.26.9). The cruelty, anger, and wildness of the animals become ironic symbols of the violence Satyrane employs; in fighting against his own bestial passions, Satyrane gives rein to those passions.

The satyr-knight's parents note the trouble. Satyrane's human mother comments on how ambivalent—if not actually perilous—such "dreadfull play" is to the physical, emotional, and moral health of her son and of those around him (I.vi.28.7). His father the satyr "would him aduise, / The angry beastes not rashly to despise, / Nor too much to prouoke," only to find himself becoming fearful of his son's boldness and violence (I.vii.25.4–6). Donald Cheney sees the satyr-father's fear of his son as a mark of how Satyrane has "learned to overcome all that the forest can offer"; such a view denies the symbolic meaning of the animals, however.[43] Rather than just showing the limitations of the satyr, the warning about the beasts illustrates Spenser's awareness of the need to incorporate the passions the creatures represent into even the most civilized of identities. By reason of his being a satyr, the father cannot master "the angry beastes"—the forest predators themselves and the ungovernable passions they represent. In contrast, Satyrane can control both because of his human capacity for rationality. Passion and desire are not banished, nor yet destroyed (as in the usual misreading of Guyon's destruction of the Bower of Bliss), but brought under "vertuous and gentle discipline," as Spenser puts it in the *Letter to Ralegh* (*FQ* 714). Other authors similarly recognized the need for a bit of bestial grit in human nature: Machiavelli, for example, remarks that a prince must make use of both his humanity and the beast within himself, learning lessons in statecraft from the fox and the lion; Alciato echoes the sentiment in his emblem "Consiliarii Principum" (complete with an image of the half-human, half-animal centaur Chiron), advising that those who would counsel princes should teach them to be part human and part beast.[44] As Dorothy Yamamoto remarks, "Knights need an infusion of wild-man blood to launch them into battle"—to say nothing of the creative and procreative drives that depend upon the bestial edge in human nature, as implied in *Amoretti* 20.[45]

Satyrane goes too far in suppressing bestial passions because he has ironically not yet been able to act human enough. His asceticism becomes unruly passion itself; hence the necessity that the satyr-knight seek his fortune in the human world outside the forest. The bestial passions with which satyrs are most commonly associated are, of course, sexual, and so Satyrane's excesses in his battles with animals (and especially lions) can be taken as his attempts to reject or control those particular passions. Spenser introduces Satyrane in a section of the poem repeatedly concerned with threats or perceived threats to Una's chastity, linked together by the lion imagery that follows Una through the first book of the poem. Canto vi opens with Una held captive by Sansloy, who has killed her lion protector and seized her as booty. Sansloy "vildly entertaines" Una (I.iii.43.7);[46] she increasingly becomes the subject of the knight's desire until he attempts to rape her. Providence steps in, and the knight is interrupted by the arrival of a troop of satyrs who have heard Una's cries for help; Sansloy flees from the strange rabble and Una is left with the satyrs. The narrator reflects on the turn of events, marveling how providence "a wondrous way it for this Lady wrought, / From Lyons clawes to pluck the gryped pray" (I.vi.7.3–4).

Spenser jars his readers by calling Sansloy a lion, since the last one Una met was the protective lion killed by Sansloy. Any mention of lions must also recall Redcrosse, whom Una identifies as a lion when she pauses to consider the four-footed lion tamed by her truth and beauty:

> The Lyon Lord of euerie beast in field,
> Quoth she, his princely puissance doth abate,
> And mightie proud to humble weake does yield,
> Forgetfull of the hungry rage, which late
> Him prickt, in pittie of my sad estate
> But he my Lyon, and my noble Lord,
> How does he find in cruell hart to hate
> Her that him lou'd, and euer most adord,

As the God of my life? why hath he me abhord?
(I.iii.7)

The lion behaves as lions should when confronted with humble supplica-
tion. Spenser has Una neatly echo the first simile of the poem and makes
it the knight's identity, here transferred to the actual lion Una has met. But
whereas the literal lion finds "his bloody rage aswaged with remorse, / And
with the sight amazed, forgat his furious forse" in the face of Una's beauty
(I.iii.5.8–9), Sansloy as the "lyon" of I.vi.7.4 finds his wrath turned to lust.
Una's beauty does not tame him, but instead "burnt his beastly hart t'efforce
her chastitye" (I.vi.4.9). Sansloy is leonine not just in his wrath but also
in his fieriness and lustfulness. He has the same hot constitution associ-
ated with lions, whether expressed in his "wrathfull fyre" or "lustfull heat"
(I.vi.3.3), and his actions make it clear how "desirous of copulation" he is as
any of Topsell's lionesses or lions (Rr5ʳ).

At first, Una's rescue by the satyrs seems merely a new threat to her chas-
tity, given the classic reputation of satyrs. Spenser expresses her concern in
a figure that transfers the lion image to the next presumed foe:

> She more amaz'd, in double dread doth dwell;
> And euery tender part for feare does shake:
> As when a greedie Wolfe through hunger fell
> A seely Lambe farre from the flocke does take,
> Of whom he meanes his bloudie feast to make,
> A Lyon spyes fast running towards him,
> The innocent pray in hast he does forsake,
> Which quit from death yet quakes in euery lim
> With chaunge of feare, to see the Lyon looke so grim.
> (*FQ* I.vi.10)

Here, Spenser again changes the signification of the lion. Three stanzas ear-
lier, Sansloy was the lion; now, Sansloy is the wolf and the satyrs are the
lion. Redcrosse, the literal lion of Canto iii, Sansloy, and the satyrs are all in
turn "Una's lion" when serving as her protector, however much that role is
abused, as with Sansloy. The leonine image or title comes with the respon-
sibility of protecting Una. In one sense, Sansloy vitiates his claim to the title
of lion when he stops protecting Una and instead becomes her immediate
foe. His actions go against normal leonine behavior, according to Topsell,
who notes that lions "seldome destroy women," and "if one prostrate him-

selfe vnto [lions] as it were in petition for his life, they often spare" the suppliant (Rr6ʳ). With Sansloy, in contrast, Una's pleas seem a further incitement to the knight in his attempted rape. Sansloy completely lacks that clemency for which Topsell repeatedly commends lions, but displays other leonine characteristics similar to those against which Satyrane battles.

In another sense, Sansloy embraces his lion identity precisely when he attempts to violate Una. He is undeniably the lion from whose claws providential design rescues Una. Sanloy's sexuality is leonine (the point of Spenser's metaphor at I.vi.7.3–4) and aggressive to the point of wrathfulness; his wrath turns to lust, after all. Spenser notably includes another lion during the *entrelacement* between the appearances of Una's literal lion in I.iii and the lion in the metaphor describing her escape from Sansloy's attempted rape in I.vi: the lion upon which Wrath rides in the parade of deadly sins at the House of Pride (I.iv.33ff). Not that his lions are without pride,[47] but Spenser emblematically associates wrathfulness as well as pride with the creatures, and then suggests a development in passionate energy between wrath and lust. John M. Crossett and Donald V. Stump suggest that Spenser's ordering of the sins leading Lucifera's coach depends upon whether the sin is one of deficiency or excess. Spenser groups Wrath and Lechery, along with Gluttony, on one side of the wagon beam, linking them in his personified schema by their extroversion, lawlessness, and hot temperaments.[48] Sansloy rings the changes between wrath and lust in his dealings with Una. Later, he demonstrates his gluttony during the feasts at the Castle of Medina where he is quite literally a lover of excess, as "fitt mate" (*FQ* II.ii.37.2) to Perissa (from the Greek περισσός, "excessive, extravagant").

Wrath need not necessarily lead to lust or gluttony, as with the four-footed lion that first rushes at Una only to find his "bloody rage aswaged with remorse" (I.iii.5.8). But even this lion's initial wrathfulness has sexualized overtones. The lion seeks "to haue attonce deuourd [Una's] tender corse" (I.iii.5.6). As with that of the "salvage nation" of brigands (VI.viii.35.2), whose version of the sonneteer's blazon when examining Serena serves as a menu to whet both their erotic and cannibalistic appetites (VI.viii.42), the lion's hunger evokes the theme of consumption so common in Spenser's portrayal of sexual desire. Moreover, as the narrator states, the beast leaps "ramping" (if not actually erect) out of "the thickest wood . . . hunting fully greedy after saluage blood" (I.iii.5.1–3); such thick forest growth also covers the hill at the center of the Garden of Adonis. Although the word recalls the ramping and roaring lion of Psalm 22, in Spenser's vocabulary, "ramping" also evokes uncontrolled energy, if not specifically sexual passion: for example, Duessa's beast, "swolne with bloud," comes "ramping forth with proud presumpteous gate" to support Orgoglio in battle (I.viii.12.4–5).

In contrast, the "yielded pryde and proud submission" the lion offers Una (I.iii.6.6) suggest tempered passion, particularly given the common sixteenth-century meaning of "pride" as sexual drive or desire. Una unconsciously alludes to the sexual overtones of the lion's hunger when she pauses to consider how "mightie proud to humble weake does yield, / Forgetfull of the hungry rage, which late / Him prickt" (I.iii.7.3–5). Beside the "mightie proud," the prickly pun seems irresistible, recalling Una's "Lyon, and . . . noble Lord" (I.iii.7.6) and his "pricking on the plaine" at the beginning of the poem (I.i.1.1).

What is important in this reading is that the priapic lion is not made impotent, but rather is brought to "proud submission." Paul J. Alpers remarks that "a proud submission is a knowing one"; it acknowledges the dignity and strength of the lion, while at the same time suggesting the greater strength and dignity of the beast's willing service.[49] The scene stands as an emblem of the Pauline vision of matrimony, where at least in theory both parties have dignity in their distinct roles while at the same time submit themselves "one to another in the feare of God" (Eph. 5:21). Una matches the lion's "proud submission" with "great compassion" and "pure affection" (I.iii.6.8–9); if one role in the matrimonial emblem is the willing submission of desirous pride, then Spenser seems to say that the complementary role is one of compassion for that pride. Sexual desire becomes something, as the 1559 *Book of Common Prayer* puts it, "for the mutual society, help, and comfort, that the one ought to have of the other," utterly unlike the willful, self-serving desire of Sansloy.[50] Such "proud submission" by the lion to Una is a type for what should be the erring Redcrosse Knight's attitude toward his would-be bride; it is moreover a manifestation of what Anne Lake Prescott calls "the theme, apparently of great emotional significance to Spenser, of binding and loosing, of constraint that is liberating because freely choosen," that finds its ultimate meaning in the willing submission of Christ.[51] The association between the lion and Una as Christ and the Church also suggests this matrimonial reading.

Una is a lady with a lion and a lamb that travel in seeming harmony.[52] If the speaker of *Amoretti* 20 could tease his beloved over her unwillingness to make ready for the Second Coming, then here the roles are reversed: Truth waits upon her unready lover. Una bases her lament at *FQ* I.iii.7 on the disparity between the lion's behavior and that of Redcrosse. The knight obviously has troubles with desire. When he rejects the advances of the false Una conjured by Archimago in the enchanter's initial effort to tempt the knight, Redcrosse finds himself torn between priggish conceit and fantasy, first bewildered "to thinke that gentle Dame so light / For whose defence he was to shed his blood" (I.i.55.2–3), and then troubled with dreams of "bowres, and beds, and Ladies deare delight" (I.i.55.7). Redcrosse succumbs to the second of Archimago's conjured visions, however, and flees from the hermitage burning with "gealous fire" (I.ii.5.6) and full of "bitter anguish of his guilty sight" (I.ii.6.2): the guilty sight he has seen, but also the guiltiness of his own desires that go a long way in tainting his overly idealistic (and, I would suggest, bodiless) preconceptions about Una, both as an allegorical figure and as a woman. In Donald Cheney's estimation, Redcrosse is "too little the lion: he possesses the proud rage but lacks the intuitive capacity to recognize and pay homage to virginity."[53] Put another way, the knight has the lion's pride but not the creature's humility.

Redcrosse is compared to a lion one last time in Book I, when he undergoes a purgative treatment at the hands of Penaunce, Remorse, and Repentance in the House of Holinesse, during which "his torment often was so great, / That like a Lyon he would cry and rore, / And rend his flesh, and his owne synewes eat" (I.x.28.1–3). A. C. Hamilton in his gloss on the passage hears an echo of 1 Peter 5:8, where the apostle compares the devil to "roaring lyon," suggesting that Redcrosse's regimen is like casting out an evil spirit. But inasmuch as the lion could represent the devil, so it could also represent Christ: the suffering Redcrosse experiences for the sake of his own sinfulness is part of the knight's participation in the suffering of "his dying Lord," who is both Lion of Judah and suffering servant (I.i.2.2). Like the real lion Una encounters, Redcrosse must learn to set aside his hungry rage and yield himself to Una, leaving his erotic and theological adventures with Fidessa/Duessa and returning to the love of truth.

Spenser's lions in *Amoretti* 20 and Book I of *The Faerie Queene* are not just courageous, magnanimous, and royal. They are also dangerous; they excel in cruelty; they possess fierce and angry natures; they are capable of committing acts based upon pride, wrath, and lust—acts that would be sins were they committed by human beings. In comparing Redcrosse to a lion, Spenser alludes not merely to the knight's valor or courage, but also to the pride that pricks Redcrosse on to fight, with all the punning meaning that phrase encompasses, in spite of Una's careful and the dwarf's more frantic warnings about "the danger hid, the place vnknowne and wilde" (I.i.12.3). Like a lion, Redcrosse is "full of fire and greedy hardiment," and "could not for ought be staide" in his approach to Error's den (I.i.14.1–2). Spenser explores the implications of Redcrosse as a lion through the various other lions Una encounters in Book I and demonstrates the dilemma Redcrosse faces in finding some balance between the seemingly dichotomous leonine traits of magnanimous clemency and a sexuality that threatens to spill over into irrationality and wrath in its drive.

Amoretti 20 explores the complex ways in which the lady is and is not a lion—or is a lion in quite different ways—as well as the speaker's ambivalence over what animal he would have his love emulate. By *Amoretti* 21, she finds at least some balance in the speaker's eyes between "pride and meeknesse mixt by equall part" (21.3). Her transformation into a fellow lamb with the speaker comes only in the final consummation of *Epithalamion*, rich in echoes of the great marriage feast of the Lamb. We are never given the union of Redcrosse with Una in *The Faerie Queene*. Perhaps the absence of their wedding (and attendant nuptial night) is because of the incomplete state of the poem, but it may be a deliberate statement on Spenser's part that such an allegorical union must await their entrance into the New Jerusalem. Yet, inasmuch as the book concerns romantic human love, it is a poem working toward matrimony and teaches mutual submission. In *An Hymn in Honour of Love*, Spenser addresses Love as the power "That doest the Lions and fell Tigers tame, / Making their cruell rage thy scornefull game, / And in their roring taking great delight" (46–48). Spenser's position on human love emphasizes passion tempered with compassion. Only in willing submission of one to the other can the lovers of the *Amoretti* and Book I of *The Faerie Queene* jointly harness their passionate lions and drive Love's chariot, and thereby embrace the great delights derived from difference in concord.[54]

A final note: I have argued that the lion simile of *Amoretti* 20 in particular also brings to mind the analogies attached to the queen. The relationship between the Elizabeth Boyle of the sonnets and Elizabeth the queen comes across as fraught; as James Fleming says of the violence in the sonnet sequence, "When *Amoretti*'s discourse of slaughter and blame slanders the lady, it slanders the queen."[55] Spenser's interrogation of lion symbolism in *Amoretti* 20 might plausibly reflect back on the self-proclaimed descendant of the lion. How far does the lion's ample libido intrude upon the queen's analogy? Mercilla, for her part, keeps her lion securely chained: England, passions, and *Leo Belgicus* at heel, the vision of a poet who supports "the enterprise / for Belge for to fight" (*FQ* V.x.Arg.1–2). Although Elizabeth was united with lion England, Una, as a figure for Elizabeth, forever seeks union with her leonine Redcrosse. Yet again, the lady of the sonnet is not a lion; her fate is not (the speaker hopes) perpetual though magnanimous virginity, though the exigencies of this world sometimes dictate that others may never in life experience the mutual charity of lambs.

University of Victoria, BC

NOTES

I am grateful to Kaya Fraser, Clare Kinney, Roger Kuin, Lana Simpson, and the editors of *Spenser Studies* for their advice and comments on drafts of this paper.

1.   William Shakespeare, *A Midsummer Night's Dream, The Complete Works*, ed. Stanley Wells et al., 2nd ed. (Oxford: Oxford University Press, 2005), 1.2.66–69; all Shakespeare quotations are from this edition.

2.   Edmund Spenser, "Sonnet XX," *Amoretti and Epithalamion*, in *The Shorter Poems*, ed. Richard McCabe (London: Penguin Books, 1999), 397; all further citations from Spenser's shorter verse are given parenthetically from this edition.

3.   William C. Johnson, *Spenser's* Amoretti: *Analogies of Love* (Lewisburg, PA: Bucknell University Press, 1990), 105–6; Donna Gibbs *Spenser's* Amoretti: *A Critical Study* (Aldershot, Hants: Scolar Press, 1990), 72; James Fleming, "*A View from the Bridge: Ireland and Violence in Spenser's* Amoretti," *Spenser Studies* 15 (2001): 155; Kenneth J. Larsen, ed., *Edmund Spenser's* Amoretti and Epithalamion: *A Critical Edition* (Tempe, AZ: Medieval and Renaissance Texts and Studies, 1997), 150; McCabe, ed., *The Shorter Poems*, 676; Joan Curbet, "Edmund Spenser's Bestiary in the *Amoretti*," *Atlantis Revista* 24 (2002): 46–47.

4.   R. V. Tooley, *Leo Belgicus: An Illustrated List* (London: Map Collctors' Circle, 1963). Aitsinger's map first appeared in *De Leone belgico, ejusque topographica atque historica descriptione liber* (Cologne, 1583). I am grateful to Roger Kuin for reminding me of this cartographic lion.

5.   Colin Burrow, "Wyatt, Sir Thomas (c. 1503–1542)," *Oxford Dictionary of National Biography*, ed. Lawrence Goldman (Oxford: Oxford University Press, 2011), <http://www.oxforddnb.com/view/article/30111> (accessed 17 Jan. 2011).

6.   H. O'Regan, A. Turner, and R. Sabin, "Medieval Big Cat Remains from the Royal Menagerie at the Tower of London," *International Journal of Osteoarchaeology* 16 (2006): 386. The radiocarbon date range makes this lion notable as the earliest

recently known to have been in England since the European lion became extinct at about the end of the last Ice Age.

7.   Paul Hentzner, *A Journey into England in the Year MDXCVIII*, trans. Richard Bentley (Edinburgh: Aungervyle Society, 1881), 27, translation of *Iterarium Germaniae, Galliae, Angliae, Italiae* (Nuremberg, 1612). For the development of the physical plant of the Tudor and Jacobean Tower menagerie, see H. M. Colvin, D. R. Ransome, and John Summerson, eds., *The History of the King's Works: Volume III 1485–1660 (Part I)* (London: Her Majesty's Stationery Office, 1975), 272–73. For two popular accounts of the menagerie, see Daniel Hahn, *The Tower Menagerie: Being the Amazing True Story of the Royal Collection of Wild and Ferocious Beasts* (New York: Simon and Schuster, 2003) and Philip Drennon Thomas, "The Tower of London's Royal Menagerie," *History Today* 46 (1996): 29–35. Thomas mistakenly calls Hentzner's lion "Edward IV." Had Edward the lion been born during Edward IV's reign (which ended in 1483), the creature would have been well past his century and improbably ancient by any leonine standard, which is more in the range of 20 years. As it is, he must have been a pretty elderly lion even if he had been born in Elizabeth's brother's reign (1547–53), unless Hentzner misunderstood the explanation for the animal's name.

8.   *Pasquils iestes mixed with Mother Bunches merriments* (London, 1609; *STC* 19451.5), F3^r.

9.   *Pasquils iests with the merriments of Mother Bunch* (London, 1629; *STC* 19452), A2^r. Mother Bunch's laugh was apparently not the only loud thing about her, for "shee was once wrung with wind in her belly, and with one blast of her taile, she blew downe Charing-Crosse, with Pauls aspiring steeple" (certainly enough to frighten the horses, if not the lions). I am grateful to Anne Lake Prescott for sharing Mother Bunch with me.

10.   Morris Palmer Tilley, *A Dictionary of the Proverbs of England in the Sixteenth and Seventeenth Centuries* (Ann Arbor, MI: University of Michigan Press, 1950), L322.

11.   Magaret Haist, "The Lion, Bloodline, and Kingship," *The Mark of the Beast*, ed. Debra Hassig (New York: Routledge, 2000), 3.

12.   Edward Topsell, *The Historie of Foure-Footed Beastes* (London, 1607; *STC* 24123; facsimile rprt., Amsterdam: Theatrum Orbis Terrarum, 1973), Rr4^v; all further citations given parenthetically.

13.   See Pliny the Elder, *Naturalis historia*, ed. H. Rackham, vol. 3 (London: William Heinemann, 1967), 8.19.48.

14.   Desiderius Erasmus, *Parabolae sive similia*, trans. R. A. B. Mynors, in *Literary and Educational Writings 1*, ed. Craig R. Thompson, vol. 23 of *Collected Works of Erasmus*, ed. Peter G. Bietenholz et al. (Toronto: University of Toronto Press, 1978), 249. Erasmus also advises that the best way to defeat a lion is to throw a blanket over its head.

15.   George Puttenham, *The Arte of English Poesie* (London, 1589; *STC* 20519.5; facsimile rprt., Menston, Yorks: Scholars Press, 1968), Kk3^r; all further citations given parenthetically.

16. *The passage of our most drad Soueraigne Lady Quene Elyzabeth through the citie of London to westminster the daye before her coronacion* (London, 1559; *STC* 7590), E4^{r-v}. Raphael Holinshed includes this account of Elizabeth's prayer in *The firste volume of the chronicles of England, Scotlande, and Irelande*(London, 1577; *STC* 13568b), Ssss2^v; see also Thomas Heywood, *England's Elizabeth* (London, 1631; *STC* 13313; facsimile rprt., Amsterdam: Theatrum Orbis Terrarum, 1973), L5^{r-v}; and Elizabeth I, *Collected Works*, ed. Leah S. Marcus, Janel Mueller, and Mary Beth Rose (Chicago: University of Chicago Press, 2000), 53–55. Marcus et al. identify the author of *The passage of our most drad Soueraigne* as Spenser's future headmaster, Richard Mulcaster.

17. Hahn, 104–5.

18. Geoffrey Parnell, *The Royal Menagerie at the Tower of London* (Leeds, Yorkshire: Trustees of the Armouries, 1999), 8.

19. *The Calendar of State Papers, Foreign Series, of the Reign of Elizabeth*, ed. Allan James Crosby (London, 1876), 10:102.

20. Bertrand de Salignac Fénélon, Seigneur de la Mothe, "CCCXCV^e dépesche," *Correspondance diplomatique de Bertrand de Salignac de la Mothe Fénélon*, ed. Charles Purton Cooper (London, 1840), 6:191; my translation.

21. Anthony Copley, *Another letter of Mr. A. C. to his dis-Iesuited kinesman* (London, 1602; *STC* 5736), C1^r.

22. For the importance of lions as symbols of royal dynastic descent, see Haist.

23. Pliny the Elder, 8.17.43.

24. See similar comments by Topsell's great master, Conrad Gesner, *Historiae animalium* (Zurich, 1551–58), Ii1^r.

25. Aristotle, *Historia Animalium*, ed. A. L. Peck, vol.1 (London: William Heinemann, 1965), 516b9ff. Gesner dutifully repeats Aristotle's assertion (Hh5^r).

26. Cf. Henry Peacham's often-reproduced emblem "Cholera," in his *Minerua Britanna* (London, 1612; *STC* 19511), T2^r, which links the lion to the choleric temperament.

27. John Maplet, *The diall of destiny* (London, 1581; *STC* 17295), D1^v; all further citations are given parenthetically.

28. William Shakespeare, *As You Like It*, 4.3.118–20. Given the lion's association with choler, it is entirely appropriate that the beast, as an emblem of choleric rage, does not overcome Oliver, thereby matching the change in his temperament from the beginning of the play.

29. All biblical quotations derive from *The Geneva Bible: A Facsimile of the 1560 Edition* (Madison: University of Wisconsin Press, 1969) and are cited parenthetically. I have silently expanded tildes.

30. Quotations from *The Faerie Queene* come from A. C. Hamilton's 2nd edition (Harlow: Longman, 2001) and are cited parenthetically.

31. See, in contrast to my analysis of the lions, Kathryn Walls's more overtly theological interpretation, "Abessa and the Lion: *The Faerie Queene*, I.3, 1–12," *Spenser Studies* 5 (1985): 3–30.

32. Lynn Frier Kaufmann, *The Noble Savage: Satyrs and Satyr Families in Renaissance Art* (Ann Arbor, MI: UMI Research Press, 1984), xx. Spenser illustrates such degeneration elsewhere in his epic (notably in the fate of Malbecco).

33. *The Works of Edmund Spenser*, ed. Edwin Greenlaw et al. (Baltimore: Johns Hopkins University Press, 1932–58), 1:245.

34. John N. King, *Spenser's Poetry and the Reformation Tradition* (Princeton, NJ: Princeton University Press, 1990), 205.

35. Ronald A. Horton, "Satyrane," *The Spenser Encyclopedia*, ed. A. C. Hamilton et al. (Toronto: University of Toronto Press, 1990), 628.

36. Dante Alighieri, *La Divina Commedia: Inferno*, in *Le Opere di Dante Alighieri*, ed. E. Moore and Paget Toynbee (Oxford: Oxford University Press, 1924), Canto 1.31ff.

37. See, for example, the satyr family panel by Cranach (c.1526) in the collection of the J. Paul Getty Museum, Los Angeles (2003.100).

38. Although the text of *Sir Gawain and the Green Knight* was unknown to Spenser, that romance provides a useful example of a hero testing his mettle in fights with animals, almost as a place-holding formula. The narrator notes during the time before his assignation at the Green Chapel, Gawain

> Sumwhyle wyth wormez he werrez, and with wolues als,
> Sumwhyle wyth wodwos, þat woned in þe knarrez,
> Boþe wyth bullez and berez, and borez oþerquyle,
> And etaynez, þat hym anelede of þe he3e felle.
>
> (720–23)

The Gawain poet augments the animals (dragons, wolves, bulls, bears, and boars) with bestial semi-humans like *wodwos* (variously, "satyrs," "trolls of the forest," or "wild woodmen") and giants. For the Spenserian forest and its inhabitants as testing ground for virtue, see Corinne J. Saunders, *The Forest of Medieval Romance: Avernus, Broceliande, Arden* (Cambridge: D. S. Brewer, 1993), 187ff.

39. R. S. White, *Natural Law in English Renaissance Literature* (Cambridge: Cambridge University Press, 1996), 61.

40. A. Bartlett Giamatti, "Primitivism and the Process of Civility in Spenser's *Faerie Queene*," *First Images of America: The Impact of the New World on the Old*, ed. Fredi Chiappelli (Berkeley: University of California Press, 1976), 75.

41. Thomas F. Arnold, "Violence and Warfare in the Renaissance World," *A Companion to the Worlds of the Renaissance*, ed. Guido Ruggiero (Oxford: Blackwell, 2002), 466; cf. Bruce Boehrer, "Introduction," *A Cultural History of Animals in the Renaissance*, ed. Bruce Boehrer (Oxford: Berg, 2007), 23ff.

42. Keith Thomas, *Man and the Natural World: Changing Attitudes in England, 1500–1800* (London: Allen Lane, 1983), 153.

43. Donald Cheney, *Spenser's Image of Nature: Wild Man and Shepherd in "The Faerie Queene* (New Haven, CT: Yale University Press, 1966), 63.

44. Niccolò Machiavelli, *Il principe*, in *Opere*, ed. Mario Bonfantini (Milan: Riccardo Ricciardi, 1954), 3:56–57; Andrea Alciato, "Consiliarii Principum," *Emblemata* (Lyons, 1555; facsimile rprt. Aldershot, Hants: Scolar Press, 1996), 160.

45. Dorothy Yamamoto, *The Boundaries of the Human in Medieval English Literature* (Oxford: Oxford University Press, 2000), 187.

46. Spenser's word choice in this ominous phrase deserves notice. Although "vildly" is an acceptable, though dialectal, variation on "vile" in Spenser's English, the word also carries a punning connotation of both "vile" and "wild," suggesting much about the nature of Sansloy's treatment of Una. Attention needs to be paid to Spenser's fondness for portmanteau words.

47. According to the *OED*, the collective term for a group of lions, "pride," was one revived during the late nineteenth century from fifteenth-century use; see "Pride, *n.1*," def. 9a. However, William Gryndall includes "A pride of Lions" among "the proper tearmes and names of companies of Beasts and Foules, with others" listed in his *Havvking, Hunting, Fouling, and Fishing, with the true measures of blowing* (London, 1596; *STC* 12412; G2^{r-v}), so the term clearly had some currency during Spenser's lifetime.

48. John M. Crossett and Donald V. Stump, "Spenser's Inferno: the Order of the Seven Deadly Sins at the Palace of Pride," *Journal of Medieval and Renaissance Studies* 14 (1984): 214.

49. Paul J. Alpers, *The Poetry of "The Faerie Queene"* (Princeton, NJ: Princeton University Press, 1967), 309.

50. *The Book of Common Prayer* (London, 1559; *STC* 16292), ed. John E. Booty (Charlottesville: University Press of Virginia, 2005), 291.

51. Anne Lake Prescott, "The Thirsty Deer and the Lord of Life: Some Contexts for *Amoretti* 67–70," *Spenser Studies* 6 (1986): 61.

52. Some readers might protest that the lamb appears only in the first canto and then disappears—a loose lamb's tale that Spenser did not pursue. Yet why should one assume the creature vanishes or wanders off on its own, simply because Spenser does not mention it? In William Nelson's wise words, the reader need "not trouble to inquire how that poor lamb kept pace with the Red Cross Knight and Una; nor . . . feel inclined to suppose that, since it is never seen again, Una must have cooked it for supper." See Nelson, *Fact or Fiction: The Dilemma of the Renaissance Storyteller* (Cambridge: Harvard University Press, 1973), 91.

53. Cheney, 45.

54. *FQ* III.12.22; cf. Thomas P. Roche, Jr.'s analysis of Love's lion-drawn chariot in *The Kindly Flame: A Study of the Third and Fourth Books of Spenser's "Faerie Queene"* (Princeton, NJ: Princeton University Press, 1964), 23ff.

55. Fleming, 161.

MICHAEL ULLYOT

Spenser and the Matter of Poetry

Edmund Spenser resisted two forms of material constraints on poets: their reliance on historical circumstance for poetic subjects (or "matter"), and their reliance on patrons for material support. This article uses three poems that comment on these constraints to argue that Spenser used the mode of complaint to address the generic decorum of occasional texts, or poets' choices of genres to suit their social and historical circumstances: "The Tears of the Muses," "The Ruins of Time," and the October eclogue from *The Shepheardes Calender.*

WHEN SHAKESPEARE'S THESEUS hears a "brief" of the entertainments with which to pass the evening before the lovers' marriages in *A Midsummer Night's Dream*, one of the options he rejects may be familiar to Spenserians: "The thrice-three Muses mourning for the death / Of learning, late deceased in beggary." Theseus rejects it as unsuitable on generic grounds, calling it "some satire, keen and critical, / Not sorting with a nuptial ceremony."[1] Shakespeare likely refers to Edmund Spenser's "The Tears of the Muses," a poem from his *Complaints* (1591).[2] It is hard to imagine Spenser's complaint of the death of learning caused by beggary entertaining anyone, let alone these betrothed Athenians: it may not be a satire, but it is certainly keen and critical. Theseus has already banished melancholy from his own wedding, and will not risk its return with an indecorous genre.[3] Better an epithalamion, or a reenactment of famous lovers—Pyramus and Thisbe, say—even if they are impersonated by rude mechanicals.

Spenser Studies: A Renaissance Poetry Annual, Volume XXVII, Copyright © 2012 AMS Press, Inc. All rights reserved.   DOI: 10.7756/spst.027.004.77-96

Theseus bases his choice on generic decorum, or the suitability of a text's genre to its occasion and audience. Generic decorum combines elements of social, literary, and rhetorical decorum: social circumstances dictate the writer's choice of genre, whose tonal, narrative, and other conventions influence its effects on a receptive audience.[4] It determines the appropriateness (decorum) of a generic choice based both on its social conditions, and on the rhetorical ends that a writer (or audience like Theseus) deems most suitable or necessary to those conditions.

They have a public function, a burden of circumstance. Their decorum is not merely internal, or literary; but external, or social. An epithalamion suits a wedding because it celebrates marital unity; an elegy suits a funeral because it mourns human frailty. Their effects are variable and contingent, but they are limited (at least) by the determinate range of responses that each genre intentionally provokes: praise or blame, mirth or dole, complacency or change.

If these decorous limits make the writer's choice and execution of an occasional genre sound reductively automatic, they also account for Samuel Johnson's influential opinion that "occasional poetry must often content itself with occasional praise."[5] Occasional texts have both memorial and rhetorical aims: to describe occasions as they are; and to influence readers to undertake given courses of action, different from the way things presently are. They reflect their circumstances not only by representing things as they are, but also—and for my purposes, more importantly—by trying to change those circumstances. Their desire to rewrite history is evidence of their indelible historicity.

Only in admittedly rare instances does such a text surpass the limits of its occasion and earn the praise of readers in new circumstances. But if Johnson's view is based on occasional poetry's transparent concern with quotidian conditions, it is not nuanced enough to account for a poem such as Spenser's "Tears of the Muses" at the Athenian court. Prompted by entirely different circumstances, this poem suits them and others that deserve its "keen and critical" scrutiny. More broadly, Johnson's claim is unsuited to occasional texts such as complaint or satire, which criticize their conditions and demand better ones—just as it is unsuited to elegy, which I have called a reluctant genre because its writers resist its necessity.[6] All are provoked by failures, though they vary in the specificity and degree of blame they assign their subjects. The generic decorum of these anti-occasional texts, as we might call them, is more discomfiting to the comfortable, yet more necessary: these texts often posit alternate occasions (more noble, memorable actions) and the better memorials they would have provoked.

I have two purposes in this article: to consider (first) the generic decorum of Spenser's complaints as occasional poems, and thereby (second) to theorize his view of the "matter" of poetry. In Spenser's usage, the word "matter" acquires two meanings: the subjects that a poem describes or critiques, and the financial support of its patrons.

In Spenser's complaints, both are inadequate. In "The Tears of the Muses" and in the October eclogue of *The Shepheardes Calender* (1579), his rhetorical aim is more corrective than decorous. Facing a paucity of subjects to praise, from whom to receive "matter" in both senses of the word, Spenser counsels patrons to liberate poets from the whims of occasion so they can write more monumental verse, verse whose endurance is more important than its historical truth. In "The Ruins of Time," another poem in the *Complaints* collection (1591), Spenser looks past these earthly impediments. He turns away from his occasions and his subjects to demand better ones, to remind prospective subjects of their duty to do things worth remembering, and prospective patrons of their duty to cultivate their legacies. In his *Complaints* (1591), Spenser laments that his poetic ambition is impeded by failures of inspiration—at times underscored by the deaths or other failures of patrons, but always embroiled in the broader issue of worldly impediments to heroic verse.[7]

There are three sections to this argument. The first concerns Spenser's sense of the origins of poetry, and his claim (after Sidney) that it is distinct from oratory; I argue that occasional poems' overt concern with historical events makes this distinction problematic. The second takes its subject from a line in the October eclogue of *The Shepheardes Calender* that provoked this whole inquiry into the conditions of writing the kind of poetry that repudiates its conditionality. After Cuddy complains of the deaths of exemplary patrons, he adds that "all the worthies liggen wrapt in leade, / That *matter* made for Poets on to play."[8] In one sense his meaning of "matter" is straightforwardly the subject on which a poet writes. But as Cuddy has just cited Mæcenas and Augustus, the 'matter' of material support that patrons give to poets is not far from the reader's mind. My transition from "The Tears of the Muses" to "The Ruins of Time" in the third section is similarly a shift from worthy subjects to material support. I consider Spenser's assertions of the memorial duties of patrons—not only to conduct themselves memorably, but to be "friended" by the Muses.[9] Finally, I identify an echo of this word and an analogous argument (if not a source) in John

Harington's translation of Ariosto's *Orlando Furioso*, published the same year as Spenser's *Complaints* (1591). To assert the importance of funding poetry, Ariosto is more eager than Spenser to distinguish its longevity from its trustworthiness. Yet both poets counterbalance inherited, classical idealizations of poetry's divine origins with a more concrete, material sense of its subjects' and its writers' historical circumstances. That counterbalancing is where we begin with Spenser.

Where do poems come from? Stephen Guy-Bray raises this faux-naive question in the subtitle of his recent book *Against Reproduction: Where Renaissance Texts Come From.*[10] Early modern English responses focused on poetry's celestial origins, even if it manifested itself in earthly habitations. The "ancient-learned" opinion, according to Sir Philip Sidney in *The Defence of Poesy* (wr. 1583), is that poetry is "a divine gift, and no human skill."[11] In his unpublished and therefore lost discourse *"the English Poete,"* Spenser echoed this ancient opinion to describe poetry originating in *"celestiall inspiration."*[12]

But what happens next? What turns the ethereal into the concrete is the poet's wit and labor—often humbly inspired by the Muses or other intermediaries, but nonetheless concretized by the historical, material conditions of writing. Theorists of poetry appreciated the need to manifest and materialize their subject-matter, as their intellectual forebears had done: just as humanists saw the combination of wisdom and eloquence as essential to learning, and as orators saw the complementarity of *res* and *verba* (things and words) as essential to persuasion. These processes are essential but difficult.

I tend to think of Spenser's complaints both as a genre and a mode, on the basis of his usage.[13] His 1591 collection of poems by that name, *Containing Sundrie Small Poems of the Worlds Vanitie*, advertises in its subtitle that its poems lament the state of the world and the vicissitudes of Fortune.[14] More broadly, complaints are "plaintive poems, or plaintive passages within larger poems, expressing grief or lamentation for any variety of causes: unrequited love, the speaker's affairs, or the sorrows of the human condition."[15] As this definition suggests, a complaint either informs and shapes a whole text, such as "The Tears of the Muses," or it is subsumed by another text, such as Pastorella's "pitifull complaints" of her captivity in *The Faerie Queene* VI.x–xi.[16] We might even use Pastorella to provoke an analogy between complaint and pastoral. Both can preside over an entire text, and can even accommodate one another: the pastoral *Shepheardes Calender* is punctuated by Cuddy's complaints from January to December. And both can be inset within other genres; consider the pastoral modes that Shakespeare incorporates into a romance such as *The Winter's Tale*, or a comedy such as *As You Like It*.

Complaints are elastic in this way because they are prompted by the speaker's immediate subjects and experiences. Yet unlike satire, they concern abstract or conceptual problems over named, particular wrongdoers.[17] When the subject is historical, the speaker is "Spenser"—and the result is a genre lamenting his circumstances. When the subject is invented, like Pastorella's captivity, so too is the speaker—and the result is a mode inset in the poem, lamenting her own circumstances. Lamenting is not quite the right word, however: one laments in an elegy, but one criticizes in a complaint. Its speaker knows, and often says, that circumstances could be otherwise. One account of late medieval complaints describes them as a "rhetorical vehicle" to criticize social failings, even if (unlike satire) the particular "source of these failings was not analyzed by the [complaint's] limited moral critique."[18]

I began this argument with one faux-naive question, and will now pose another. How can we reconcile Spenser's recapitulation of the idealized, ethereal origins of poetry with his complaints about its earthly impediments? To put it another way, if poems come as divine gifts from heaven, just what is Spenser complaining about? The answer is not simply the material debasement of ethereal visions. Spenser's view of poetry survives in the paraphrase of his editor E.K., describing it as *"no arte, but a divine gift and heavenly instinct not to bee gotten by laboure and learning, but adorned with both: and poured into the witte by a certain* ἐνθονσιασμὸς. [enthusiasmos] *and celestial inspiration."*[19] The two denials in the first part of this definition distinguish poetry from rhetoric, that "arte" or skill which *can* "bee gotten by laboure and learning." Sidney argues that poetry cannot be led roughly, by industry without genius. His definition is also indebted to rhetorical theory: "For poesy must not be drawn by the ears; it must be gently led, or rather it must lead; which was partly the cause that made the ancient-learned affirm it was a divine gift, and no human skill. ... since all other knowledges lie ready for any that hath strength of wit; a poet no industry can make, if his own genius be not carried into it."[20]

Sidney's inquiry into the origins and effects of poetry in his *Defence* owes much to the labors of preceding writers on rhetoric such as Roger Ascham and Thomas Wilson, and their recapitulations of Cicero, Quintilian, and the *Rhetorica ad Herennium*. But even if poetry can teach, delight, and persuade as rhetoric does, the poet is no mere rhetorician, trained up by the "diligent practice and earnest exercise [that] are the only things that make men prove excellent."[21] Rather, Sidney cites the proverb *orator fit, poeta nascitur*: an orator is made, a poet born.

So is the ideal. Spenser's occasional poems temper his theory of poetry as a divine gift by emphasizing the circumstances of a poem's writing and reception. Occasional poems come closest to rhetoric because they bring words (*verba*) into close proximity with subject-matters (*res*), whose complementarity is one definition of rhetorical decorum. Spenser's complaints are especially preoccupied with this complementarity: they directly emerge from and explicitly respond to their material circumstances. Even if they are critical of those circumstances, the generic decorum of complaint prevails.

The elegy is an occasional text that similarly, if more surreptitiously, resists its occasion. In a typical example, Thomas Heywood begins his elegy for Henry, Prince of Wales (d.1612) "wishing with my soule, I might haue had a more pleasing subiect," but conceding that "since the Heauens haue giuen vs this cause it is a duty to entertaine the occasion, and an vnanswerable negligence to omit it."[22] Our "duty to entertaine the occasion" implies a duty to acknowledge and receive the occasion with a decorous genre, a death with an elegy. Heywood's claim that heaven gave this cause to poets attributes the prince's death to supernatural forces, as was conventional— and it echoes what (again) Sidney calls the "ancient-learned" opinion of poetry's divine origins. Heywood dutifully reconciles this divine matter with his earthly words, with scarcely a hint of resistance.

"The Tears of the Muses" focuses instead on poetry's earthly matter, with Spenser taking the more adversarial role of resisting and criticizing it, in order to change it. I will now show that Spenser counterbalances poetry's divine origins with a more material view of its circumstances, and argue that his ideals of what poetry ought to be are based on the generic hierarchies or (at least) preferences that he sets out in "The Tears of the Muses." The poem makes the absence of better genres rhetorically conspicuous. After a series of laments, the Muses "change the tenor of [their] joyous layes," "[their] praises into piteous cries, / And Eulogies turne into Elegies."[23] Thus Spenser explicitly names the kinds of genres he would prefer to write.

Each of the nine Muses has a sense of the ideal form of her respective art, the one that poets ought to be writing, and each complains accordingly. Their frustration lies with poetic subjects for their failure to cultivate and inspire better writing: error, folly, and spite prevail in place of virtue; infamy in place of fame. Among the lewd "dunghill thoughts" of men, Erato finds no reception for her lyric poetry, nor for the "high conceipt of that celestiall fire" whence love is "infused into mortall brests."[24] She finds no signs of Love, "the devicefull matter of my song."[25] Melpomene, the muse of Tragedy, uses the same word for poetic subjects when she complains that the petty tragedies of senseless men are poor "matter" compared to the "true Tragedies" she ought to relate: "I mourne . . . Because that mourning matter I have none."[26]

Both "The Tears of the Muses" and *The Shepheardes Calender* depict the failure of the world to provide poets with sufficient material, in both senses of the word "material." At the end of the former poem, Spenser's dissatisfied Muses renounce this world and its writers. They break their "learned instruments" in protest, a gesture that immediately silences the poet: "The rest untold no loving tongue can speake."[27] The finality of this gesture recalls Colin Clout hanging up his pipe at the end of *The Shepheardes Calender*, a gesture of resignation to age, cold, and the material failures that Spenser will elaborate in *The Complaints* some years later.[28]

The October eclogue conflates the two meanings of "matter" most directly. The shepherd Cuddy, "the perfecte paterne of a Poete," has found "no maintenaunce of his state and studies."[29] When his companion Piers urges him to "sing of bloody Mars, of wars, of giusts" and other heroic subjects, Cuddy complains that great patrons like Mæcenas and Augustus are dead, "And all the *worthies* liggen wrapt in leade, / *That matter made* for Poets on to play."[30] We take a muse like Clio more seriously when she makes a similar-sounding prediction in "The Tears of the Muses" that "all that in this world is *worthie*" will lie dead and forgotten unless patrons embrace their duty.[31] But Spenser repeats the same phrase in *The Faerie Queene* when he invokes the female knights "*That matter made* for famous Poets verse." This is immediately before he tells Britomart's story for the benefit of her descendent Queen Elizabeth, "O Queene, the matter of my song."[32]

The "matter" that these worthies, knights, and queens made is the poets' subjects, rather than the materials by which they live; this meaning is clear from their contexts in Spenser's repeated uses of the phrase (e.g., worthies are praiseworthy). It is also consistent with George Puttenham's use of "matter" interchangeably with "subject" in *The Arte of English Poesie* (1589), wherein "The Subject or Matter of Poesie" is one chapter-heading. Puttenham uses the term "the whole matter" to mean a complete thought or narrative, whether or not it is confined to a piece of writing; thus he describes a writer "fashion[ing] his tale to his matter."[33]

Spenser's repetitions of the word "matter" and its cognate "material," throughout his corpus, reveal the rhetorical quality of his poetics, its decorous combination of *res* with *verba*. Matter is the unformed source of all things, natural and artificial; it is always subject to the intervention of a divine or poetic artificer. It emerges from Chaos, in one definition from *The Faerie Queene*, as the material cause of Creation itself: "All things from thence doe their first being fetch, / And borrow matter, whereof they are made."[34] Matter is also the cause of everything from private moods to pitched battles, in a range of instances. In the oft-cited Proem to Book II of the poem, Spenser justifies his choice of poetic subject as a "matter of just memory" rather than as a painted forgery, a history of true events, not invented ones.[35]

Spenser offers this justification when addressing the historical quality of his subject, particularly as he prepares for the interleaving of British and Faery histories later in Book II, in the House of Alma. In this episode, when his knights Guyon and Arthur read their respective national chronicles in Eumnestes's chamber, Spenser links matter to historical memory in ways that evoke Cuddy's appeal for memorable poetic matters. Spenser abridges the book of Arthur's *Briton moniments*, glossing over "much materiall." It comprises "seuen hundred Princes" whose "sondry gouernments" are too tedious to recount, yet who stand as "famous moniments, / And braue ensample, both of martiall, / And ciuil rule to kinges and states imperiall."[36] Not all are worth recounting for his immediate purposes—admittedly, to the relief of this reader—but all remain firmly in the category of brave examples for princes, from Arthur to Elizabeth. Matter and material are the origins of all histories, then, real and invented—of stories with the power to persuade and guide their readers. As I will suggest in the next section of this argument, on Spenser use of the word's more venal sense, matter is also the source of future fame.

Cuddy's laments for a lack of matter are neither entirely poetic nor entirely venal. His matter in the October eclogue is his poetic subjects, the wars and "giusts [gests]" to which he would fashion his words, but he frequently uses financial terms: he lacks "good" and "gayne"; his rhymes give pleasure, but gain him "a sclender prise."[37] Augustus and particularly Mæcenas, whom he cites, are as famous for their patronage as for their achievements, for materially supporting poets rather than for being intrinsically worthy matters themselves.[38] In the accompanying woodblock, Cuddy looks past the offered pipes to the classical temples, the courtly milieu that should supply poets with both kinds of matter. The tenor of this eclogue is not thanks, but despair for that milieu. It supplies no worthy makers of matter for poets to sing about, and no patron willing to support the song.[39]

Spenser repeatedly conflates sources of stories with sources of funds—not because he is venal, but because he recognizes the material origins of all texts. His chief complaint in this eclogue is that patrons neglect their two duties, to create and to offer the matter that enables poets to write their words. These prospective subjects are neither doing memorable things, nor cultivating their legacies through patronage. Sidney uses a memorably fecund image for poets honing their innate abilities with art, imitation, and exercise: "the fertilest ground must be manured."[40] The same could be said for how patrons ought to cultivate the poet's divine gift, through reciprocal generosity.[41] This combination of material manure and imaginative fertility is where poetry comes from. Poetic praise is the due reward of virtuous actions, but praise is most forthcoming to those who pay for it; memorials do not emerge spontaneously from noble and memorable lives. Between things and words, subjects and poetry, stand the labor and imagination of poets.

The process of turning material into poetry has three stages. Patrons first recognize a poet's possession of this divine gift in a poet, then sense its potential, and finally facilitate its expression. In a more autobiographical text, Spenser's pastoral persona Colin Clout elucidates this process and draws a more explicit link between present patronage and future fame. *Colin Clout's Come Home Again* makes many references to the historians and poets writing accounts of Queen Elizabeth's life, and to the poet's own ambition to join them. For instance, Colin praises William Alabaster's "heroick" yet unfinished *Elisæis*, a Latin epic, in the hope that he can "end thy glorie which he hath begun."[42] Colin is ambitious for poetic immortality, specifically that "long while after I am dead and rotten: / Amongst the shepheards daughters dancing rownd, / My layes made of her [*Cynthia*, or Elizabeth] shall not be forgotten." But the unwelcome guest at this literate feast, as at any, is the bill that arrives at the end. Colin is explicit that his praise comes at a price. He says to the dancing shepherdesses, "When as ye heare her memory renewed, / Be witnesse of her bountie here alive, / Which she to *Colin* her poore shepheard shewed."[43] Indeed, Cynthia had already been generous to Colin before Spenser revised this poem in April 1594, awarding the poet an annual pension of £50 for his *Faerie Queene* I–III in 1591.[44]

The division between self-serving and magnanimous patronage may be fragile, but Spenser is determined to maintain it. His Calliope pointedly repeats Erato's lament for the proud, degenerate patrons careless both of "the aunceestrie / Of th'old Heroës" and "that late posteritie / Shoud know their [own] names, or speak their praises dew."[45] Clio and Calliope, the Muses of history and of epic, are both repositories and reporters of the past, but Calliope's function is more actively presentist: as both "the nurse of vertue, . . . And golden Trompet of eternitie," she ensures that men choose to be good because it is more praiseworthy.[46] Praise is the spur to virtue, so when praise is lost, what motive do men have to be virtuous?

In "The Tears of the Muses," Spenser's complaints about his subjects focus squarely on the failures of the nobility, who are neglecting their duty to provide poets with matter fit for eulogies rather than elegies. The Muses "Finde nothing worthie to be writ, or told" in the nobles' pride and ignorance; they "nothing noble haue to sing."[47] The implications of this failure extend beyond the present; it is a disservice both to their ancestry and to their descendants. Clio, the muse of history, protests that the Muses are mourning not because their poets are ill paid but (rather) because the nobility are neglecting their duty:

> It most behoves the honorable race
> Of mightie Peeres, true wisedome to sustaine,
> And with their noble countenaunce to grace
> The learned forheads, without gifts or gaine:
> Or rather learnd themselves behoves to bee;
> That is the girlond of Nobilitie.[48]

The peers are guilty of literally unbecoming behavior: their admiration for their ancestors amounts to their resting on their laurels, without becoming admirable in their own right. This paucity of matter leads to paltry verses, debasements of what ought to be written—or at least, what the poets and Muses would prefer to write.

One of the essential questions of "The Tears of the Muses" is whether or not the present will offer anything worth preserving in the future. If peers fail to sustain wisdom, the consequence for future ages will be a loss of memory, of "moniments of time":

> So shall succeeding ages have no light
> Of things forepast, nor moniments of time,
> And all that in this world is worthie hight
> Shall die in darknesse, and lie hid in slime. . . .[49]

The poet's bid for patronage invariably follows his implicit threats of slimy darkness and explicit promises of famous monuments. The preservation of worthy things in monuments for succeeding ages to appreciate and imitate is Spenser's ideal—both here, and in Arthur's appreciation of chronicles such as *Briton moniments* in *The Faerie Queene* II.x. But it receives the fullest articulation in another poem in his *Complaints* volume.

In "The Ruins of Time," Spenser is preoccupied with history's passage into memory, and the countervailing material media in which that memory is to be preserved. This is memory in both the civic, or national, and the personal sense. "[T]hings forepast" here refers to ruined cities like the British city Verulamium, conquered by the Romans and later overrun by Saxons. What remains are at most broken ruins, poor memorials that leave present-minded observers ignorant of their original grandeur.[50] But Spenser's complaints are also preoccupied with the deaths of great men, of Sidney (1554–1586) and his uncle Robert Dudley, earl of Leicester (1532/3–1588). He dedicates "The Ruins of Time" to Mary Sidney, offering it as a monument to her brother's memory. His narrator Verlame excoriates those who have neglected Leicester's memory, despite his good treatment of poets while he lived. She repeatedly testifies that she has witnessed his death, and that his virtues will live as long as her verses persevere: "For ever it shall live, and shall rehearse / His worthie praise," and vertues dying never."[51] She condemns men like William Cecil (without explicitly naming Lord Burghley) for their parsimonious "scorn" of the Muses. Spenser characterizes both Sidney's and Leicester's deaths as symptomatic of a broader degeneration, as an index for the decline of virtue itself. Vice has displaced heavenly discipline, as Richard McCabe notes, and ignorance prevails over enlightened patronage.[52]

The duty of historians and poets is to labor to preserve past and present, to offer corroborating and more enduring monuments. Verlame's testimony alone is hardly a sufficient legacy for Sidney and Leicester, just as a complaint is inadequate to express the memories of a ruined city. Verlame acknowledges that the evidence of her own past is unconvincing in isolation: "To tell the beawtie of my buildings fayre," my riches and my forces, "Were but lost labour, that few would beleeve, / And with rehearsing would me more agreeve." Without monuments to the past, "Wasted it is, as if it never were."[53]

Verlame's faith in the endurance of the written word is essential to Spenser's claims of the evidentiary purpose of poetic praise. Deserving poets offer not flattery or false monuments like the pyramids she disparages, but "wise wordes taught in numbers for to runne, / Recorded by the Muses" to outlast noble deeds and men's thoughts.[54] Verlame thus praises the historiography of the antiquary William Camden (1551–1623), whose *Britannia* preserves "the light of simple veritie, / Buried in ruines."[55] Verlame uses the familiar trope of written memorials outlasting physical monuments, claiming that Camden's "just labours ever shall endure," despite acknowledging that "Time all moniments obscure."[56] Spenser uses the word "monuments" forty-six times in ten works, to mean a textual or physical aid to memory, or a medium of its preservation. He most frequently modifies it with adjectives like "famous," "immortal," or "eternal"; and twice monuments are "endlesse," despite Verlame's claims to the contrary.

Patrons need to cultivate their reputations, both by doing things worth remembering in the present, and paying poets to write accounts evidencing their achievements in the future. So Colin Clout praised Elizabeth, and so Verlame urges patrons:

> Provide therefore (ye Princes) whilst ye live,
> That of the *Muses* ye may friended bee,
> Which unto men eternitie do give;
> ....
>
> And do those men in golden thrones repose,
> Whose merits they to glorifie do chose.[57]

There are echoes here of Calliope's "golden Trompet of eternitie" that urges consciousness of one's future reputation.[58] Being "friended" by the Muses is Verlame's elliptical appeal to foster the good intentions of poets, their earthly intermediaries, by offering them material forms of support to enable them to write these memorials. The language of patronage often borrows from the language of friendship, as McCabe has argued.[59]

But being "friended" by the Muses also evokes a parallel with John Harington's translation of Ariosto's *Orlando Furioso*, published the same year (1591) as Spenser's *Complaints*. Even if Spenser never read Harington's translation, he certainly knew the poem well enough to model parts of the *Faerie Queene* on it. For my purposes, he might have appreciated its privileging of poetic representations over historical and extra-poetic truths. Harington's translation offered Elizabethan poets one more example of both the power of poetry and the self-interested duty of its patrons.[60]

The parallel that I am pursuing follows the episode that has been called the "epitome" of *Orlando Furioso*, the English duke Astolfo's moon-voyage.[61] Harington writes that Dido, queen of Carthage "worthy was indeed to be commended," but that her reputation for histrionics is due only to her interference with Aeneas's progress from Troy to Italy: she is "subject now to slaunder and to shame / Because that she by *Virgill* is not frended."[62] Saint John the Evangelist, Astolfo's guide, tells him that the truth of history is the opposite of its representations: "*se tu vuoi che 'l ver non ti sia ascoso, / tutta al contrario l'istoria converti.*" ["If you wish that the truth be not hidden from you, turn all of history upside down."][63] Saint John, with his divine knowledge, probes beyond poetic representations into transcendent truths, indicting poets as he praises them.[64] Unfriendly poets, in this menacing view, exert more influence over your reputation than do the Muses.

Ariosto's is a more unflinchingly material view of poetic writing than Spenser's, which emphasizes the "merits" of those the Muses choose to "glorifie." Before I detail the Astolfo episode any further, consider another resonant connection between Harington's and Spenser's disdain for bad poetry. In "The Tears of the Muses," the failure of good patrons leaves the best poets without worthy subjects for enduring praise. Meanwhile, the worst poets are encouraged by bad patrons who pursue immediate pleasure, who mis-allocate "Their great revenues all in sumptuous pride": "And the rich fee which Poets wont divide, / Now *Parasites* and *Sycophants* doo share."[65] Good patrons do not brook such flattery; they cultivate their future fame by performing famous deeds and supporting the right poets with a "rich fee."

The word "parasite" is used frequently in this period to refer specifically to flatterers for hire, and always as a foil to more principled poets.[66] Samuel Daniel describes the parasite as a warning to all poets not to write for others' delight.[67] In 1596, Charles Fitzgeffrey laments that Sir Francis Drake cannot be eternized by classical poets in this corrupt age when "Onlie to flatter is to Poetize" and "[to] be a Poet is [to] be a Parasite."[68] In 1599 the anonymous author of a paean to Henry VII pledges to recount only the truth of his life: "Nor with a penne that is hyr'd . . . verse smoothly to compile, / Like glauering parasite."[69] William Herbert makes a smiliar pledge not to confuse praise with truth: "my pen . . . shunnes the hire / Of base reward."[70] Similarly Joseph Hall will not, like other poets, "[make] his pen an hyred Parasite."[71] The disdain these writers express is for a hired poet who misrepresents the truth of history for financial gain. This raises a difficult problem for Spenser, as he conflates the two meanings of matter: to what degree does one kind (the money) distort the other (the subject), or at least distort the poet's representations of that subject?

Spenser and Ariosto share this disdain for unprincipled poetry, as an encounter earlier in the moon-voyage episode reveals. Astolfo encounters an aged man throwing armloads of threads into a river. While ravens, vultures, magpies, and crows struggle in vain to recover these threads before they sink into the depths, a pair of swans retrieve a select few to install in a nearby shrine. Saint John explains that these threads spun by the Fates are mortal lives, which Time casts into the river Lethe. The birds are their only hope against obscurity, but their efforts have variable results. The swarming flocks are the "promooters, ruffins, [sic] bawds, and those / That can the parasites and jesters play," whose parodies and apish performances of their subjects are inevitably short-lived. The graceful swans are the "Historians learnd and Poets rare" who "Preserve them in cleare fame and good report," protecting their subjects from the threat of oblivion in the shrine of Immortality. "O happie Princes whose foresight and care / Can win the love of writers in such sort," Saint John concludes.[72]

Ariosto anatomizes the power of poetry in order to convince patrons that it is worth supporting. In the process, he divides poetry's longevity from its trustworthiness: poets' selective images and outright lies have the patina of truth, but only because of their resilience—because these misrepresentations outlast and override the historical truths that precede them. Saint John contrasts the poets' admiration for the emperors Caesar and Augustus with their vilification of Nero, who refused to patronize artists. As I have mentioned, he also cites their representations of subjects like Dido. Her unwitting impediment of the future designs of Virgil's patron, the emperor Augustus seeking praise for his ancestor Aeneas, leaves Dido subject to slanderous misrepresentation. Every prince chooses whether or not to respect the authority of poets, but if like Augustus they seek "cleare fame and good report," poets will represent them favorably. Ariosto's message is clear: with poets as the arbiters of reputations, those who patronize them will be favored and thus admired, while others are forgotten or (worse) vilified.

Inverting poetry to reveal the truth of history may well reveal—and Ariosto is coy even on this point—what the poets' and historians' whims have deliberately concealed: that (as he says) Aeneas was not pious; nor Hector nor Achilles brave; nor the Greeks victorious; nor Penelope chaste. Without corroborating or conflicting records, we cannot measure the truth-value of these reputations; we cannot know whether these heroes whose descendants have bought poets' praise of their ancestors truly deserve their veneration:

> But those fayre lands and castles out of doubt
> That their successours unto writers gave

Made them so famous over forren lands
Canonizd by the Poets sacred hands.[73]

We have only Homer's word to know that the Greeks prevailed over the Trojans, "Yet sure (for ought you know) he might have taught / The contrary to this if he had listed."[74] His representations have the patina of truth only because they are resilient: but longevity is not to be equated with trustworthiness. Ariosto assures readers that their own interpretations are equal arbiters of the truth.

There are elements in this episode of both deliberate and self-defeating hyperbole. Saint John overstates the case to make the poets' interference more stark, and their power more appealing to patrons. Even if an authentic, transcendent, and original (not originating) truth precedes every unreliable image, readers could hardly restore it by inverting poets' lies; to do so would presume that they themselves are consistent. Thus Ariosto indicts himself in this process of elevating his craft. But he also inducts himself into the company of Homer and Virgil, assuming their potential influence by portraying them as essentially familiar, or as subject to familiar exigencies of patrons and their interests, at least. The effect is not to dismantle their authority, but to assume it for every poet.

Ariosto's Homer is not Spenser's, who praises Homer in the *Letter to Ralegh* as his forebear, as the first of "*all the antique Poets historicall.*"[75] Spenser finds more to imitate in Ariosto's idealization of the "Historians learnd and Poets rare" than in his vision of an unreliable Homer.[76] The issue for Spenser, reading Ariosto's thought experiment, is that he is too motivated by the principles of decorum, of conjoining *res* with *verba*, to assert his poetic authority quite so far. He does not undertake to falsify his subjects, but to assert that a patron's neglect is as dangerous to her legacy as a poet's bad intentions.

All poets aim to create enduring fictions from the passing materials of history, whether those materials are their subjects or their circumstances. They aim not to strain credulity, but to narrow the divide so that the fictionality is more an elaboration, an augmentation, than an invention. A poet such as Ariosto reminds a poet such as Spenser that it must be an invention. The distinction between Ariosto rewriting history according to whim and Spenser augmenting his subjects and elaborating on his occasions is a matter of degree: both resist the limits of their subjects. When that subject is historical circumstance rather than a particular event, Spenser still aspires to rewrite history through complaints, which exert pressure on ideal readers to do better, to imitate better examples and cultivate better legacies.

Spenser and Ariosto engage in a mutual effort to counterbalance poetry's traditionally divine origins with a more modern, material view of its circumstances and exigencies. But Spenser is less eager than Ariosto to admit a clear implication of their efforts, that fictional endurance is more important than historical truth. His complaints show that Spenser holds fast to the rhetorical potential of generic decorum, to the belief that the right genre can prompt readers to deserve better genres.

University of Calgary

NOTES

For comments on previous versions of this article, I am grateful to the editors of *Spenser Studies*; to the manuscript's anonymous readers; and to my colleagues Stefania Forlini and Faye Halpern.

1.   William Shakespeare, *A Midsummer Night's Dream*, Norton Shakespeare (New York: W. W. Norton, 2008), 5.1.42, 39, 52–53, 54–55. On the question of this allusion, see James Bednarz, "Imitations of Spenser in a Midsummer Night's Dream," *Renaissance Drama* 14 (1983): 79–102.

2.   The first to make this identification was Thomas Warton, in *The Plays of William Shakespeare*, ed. Samuel Johnson and George Steevens, 10 vols. (London, 1773), 3:90n.

3.   "Turn melancholy forth to funerals— / The pale companion is not for our pomp" (Shakespeare, *Midsummer Night's Dream*, 1.1.14–15).

4.   My use of the term "generic decorum" refines its usual meaning, of the internal rules of particular genres. Freedman and Medway coin the term "generic rhetoric" for the choice of a genre to fulfill "attendant felicity conditions or conditions of success" (*Genre and the New Rhetoric* [London: Taylor and Francis, 1994], 99).

5.   Samuel Johnson, *The Lives of the English Poets* (Dublin, 1781), 159.

6.   Michael Ullyot, "The Fall of Troynovant: Exemplarity after the Death of Henry, Prince of Wales," in *Fantasies of Troy: Classical Tales and the Social Imaginary in Medieval and Early Modern Europe*, ed. Stephen Powell and Alan Shepard (Toronto: CRRS, 2004), 69–90. Elegists lament not only the deaths that have occasioned them, but that elegies are necessary at all (necessitated by their circumstances).

7.   The rhetorical intentions of Spenser's *Complaints* have been noted as long ago as Gerald Snare, "The Muses on Poetry: Spenser's the Teares of the Muses,"

Tulane University Studies in English 17 (1969): 31–52. For the place of this text in Spenser's career, see Katharine A. Craik, "Spenser's 'Complaints' and the New Poet," *Huntington Library Quarterly* 64:1/2 (2001): 63–79.

8. Edmund Spenser, *The Yale Edition of the Shorter Poems of Edmund Spenser* (New Haven: Yale University Press, 1989), 173, lines 63–64; my emphasis.

9. Spenser, *Yale Edition*, 248, line 366.

10. Stephen Guy-Bray, *Against Reproduction: Where Renaissance Texts Come From* (Toronto: Univesity of Toronto Press, 2009).

11. Sir Philip Sidney, "A Defence of Poetry (1595)," in *English Renaissance Literary Criticism*, ed. Brian Vickers (Oxford: Clarendon Press, 1999), 379. Sidney also refers to the poet endowed with "the force of a divine breath" creating works that surpass God's own nature (344).

12. Spenser, *Yale Edition*, 170. For a study of how poets' social positions affect their claims to poetic inspiration, see John Huntington, "Furious Insolence: The Social Meaning of Poetic Inspiration in the 1590s," *Modern Philology* 3 (1997): 305–26.

13. See R. H. Nicholson, "State of the Nation: Some Complaint Topics in Late Medieval English Literature," *Parergon* 23 (1979): 21; Richard Rambuss, *Spenser's Secret Career* (Cambridge: Cambridge University Press, 1993), 85; and John N. King, "Traditions of Complaint and Satire," in *A Companion to English Renaissance Literature and Culture*, ed. Michael Hattaway (Malden, MA: Blackwell, 2003), 367. Kietzman argues that complaint "extends to a wide range of narrative kinds including medieval tragedy, allegory, epic, prose history, and picaresque" ("'Means to Mourn Some Newer Way': The Role of the Complaint in Early-Modern Narrative" [Boston College, 1993], 1–2).

14. Richard Danson Brown, *"The New Poet": Novelty and Tradition in Spenser's Complaints*, vol. 32, Liverpool English Texts and Studies (Liverpool: Liverpool University Press, 1999), 7.

15. Hugh Maclean, "'Restlesse Anguish and Unquiet Paine': Spenser and the Complaint, 1579–1590," in *The Practical Vision: Essays in English Literature in Honour of Flora Roy*, ed. James Doyle et al. (Waterloo, ON: Wilfrid Laurier University Press, 1978), 30. Brown concludes from his analysis of the 1591 *Complaints* that "for Spenser it becomes a genre instinctively preoccupied with the status and value of poetry" (*Novelty and Tradition*, 24, n.72).

16. This is Spenser's description (6.10.44.2). To find this and other examples of Spenser's usage, I have used Wordhoard, an application for searching Spenser's texts, among others <http://wordhoard.northwestern.edu/>.

17. John Peter, *Complaint and Satire in Early English Literature* (Oxford: Clarendon Press, 1956), 59; Kirk Combe, "The New Voice of Political Dissent: The Transition From Complaint to Satire," in *Theorizing Satire: Essays in Literary Criticism*, ed. Brian A. Connery and Kirk Combe (New York: St. Martin's Press, 1995), 76–77.

18. Steven A. Owley, "The Voice of Complaint: A Study in Political and Moral Rhetoric" (Ohio State University, 1999), 16; see also Nicholson, "Complaint Topics."

19. Spenser, *Yale Edition*, 170. For the relation between E.K.'s glosses and Spenser's text, see Richard McCabe, "Annotating Anonymity, or Putting a Gloss on *The Shepheardes Calender*," in *Ma(r)king the Text: The Presentation of Meaning on the Literary Page*, ed. Joe Bray, Miriam Handley, and Anne C. Henry (Aldershot: Ashgate, 2000), 35–54.

20. Sidney, "Defence of Poetry," 379.

21. Thomas Wilson, "An English Rhetoric (1560)," in *English Renaissance Literary Criticism*, ed. Brian Vickers (Oxford: Clarendon Press, 1999), 78.

22. Thomas Heywood, *A Funerall Elegie Vpon the Death of the Late Most Hopefull and Illustrious Prince, Henry, Prince of Wales* (London, 1613), sig. A2r.

23. Spenser, *Yale Edition*, 283, lines 367, 371–72.

24. Spenser, *Yale Edition*, 283–84, lines 393, 391, 390.

25. Spenser, *Yale Edition*, 283, line 386.

26. Spenser, *Yale Edition*, 275, lines 155, 165, 167–68.

27. Spenser, *Yale Edition*, 291, lines 599, 600.

28. Hugh MacLean, "Complaints: The Tears of the Muses," in *The Spenser Encyclopedia*, ed. A. C. Hamilton (Toronto: University of Toronto Press, 1990), 182. See also Lin Kelsey and Richard Peterson, "Rereading Colin's Broken Pipe: Spenser and the Problem of Patronage," *Spenser Studies* 14 (2000): 233–72.

29. Spenser, *Yale Edition*, 170. Anne Lake Prescott has suggested (in private correspondence) that the placement of commas in this sentence suggests, rather, that Cuddy is the pattern of a neglected poet.

30. Spenser, *Yale Edition*, 173, lines 63–64; my emphasis.

31. Spenser, *Yale Edition*, 273, line 105; my emphasis.

32. Edmund Spenser, *The Faerie Queene* (London: Pearson Education, 2001), III.iv.1.6, III.iv.3.8; my emphasis.

33. George Puttenham, *The Arte of English Poesie. Contriued Into Three Bookes: The First of Poets and Poesie, the Second of Proportion, the Third of Ornament.* (London, 1589), book 3, chapters 2 and 5.

34. Spenser, *The Faerie Queene*, III.vi.37.1–2.

35. Spenser, *The Faerie Queene*, II.Proem.1.5. For a survey of sixteenth-century precedents to this privileging of truth in history see William Nelson's enduring *Fact or Fiction: The Dilemma of the Renaissance Storyteller* (Cambridge: Harvard University Press, 1973).

36. Spenser, *The Faerie Queene*, II.x.74.4, 3, 6, 7–9. On this episode see Chloe Wheatley, "Abridging the Antiquitee of Faery Lond: New Paths Through Old Matter in the Faerie Queene," *Renaissance Quarterly* 58:3 (2005): 857–80.

37. Spenser, *Yale Edition*, 171, lines 10, 16.

38. Thus in "Virgils Gnat" Spenser's praise of Augustus is conventional (Spenser, *Yale Edition*, 301, lines 57–64).

39. The woodcut also debates whether the poet's art ought to be solitary or social, mono- or dialogical (Rebeca Helfer, "The Death of the 'New Poete': Virgilian

Ruin and Ciceronian Recollection in Spenser's 'The Shepheardes Calender,'" *Renaissance Quarterly* 56:3 (2003), 728–30).

40. Sidney, "Defence of Poetry," 380.

41. Edmund Spenser, *The Shorter Poems* (London: Penguin, 1999), 559. McCabe notes that Mantuan and Theocritus are Spenser's classical sources for this reciprocity. See McCabe, "Annotating Anonymity."

42. Spenser, *Yale Edition*, 541, lines 404, 409.

43. Spenser, *Yale Edition*, 550, lines 640–42; 645–47.

44. Spenser, *Shorter Poems*, 560. On Spenser and patronage see also Judith Owens, *Enabling Engagements: Edmund Spenser and the Poetics of Patronage* (Montreal: McGill-Queen's University Press, 2002) and, more recently, William Oram, "Seventeen Ways of Looking At Nobility: Spenser's Shorter Sonnet Sequence," in *Renaissance Historicisms: Essays in Honor of Arthur F. Kinney*, ed. James M. Dutcher, and Anne Lake Prescott (Cranbury, NJ: Associated University Presses, 2008).

45. Spenser, *Yale Edition*, 285, lines 439–40, 441–42.

46. Spenser, *Yale Edition*, 286, lines 457–58.

47. Spenser, *Yale Edition*, 273, lines 100, 108.

48. Spenser, *Yale Edition*, 273, lines 79–84.

49. Spenser, *Yale Edition*, 273, lines 103–6.

50. See Rebeca Helfer, "Remembering Sidney, Remembering Spenser: The Art of Memory and the Ruines of Time," *Spenser Studies: A Renaissance Poetry Annual* 22 (2007): 127–51.

51. Spenser, *Yale Edition*, 243, lines 255–56.

52. Spenser, *Yale Edition*, 592.

53. Spenser, *Yale Edition*, 236–38, lines 85, 90–91, 12.

54. Spenser, *Yale Edition*, 249, lines 402–3.

55. Spenser, *Yale Edition*, 240, lines 171–72. Camden's Latin history had editions in 1586, 1587, 1590, 1594, 1600 and 1607 before its first English translation in 1610.

56. Spenser, *Yale Edition*, 240, 175, 174.

57. Spenser, *Yale Edition*, 248, 365–71.

58. Spenser, *Yale Edition*, 286, line 458.

59. Richard McCabe, "'Thine Owne Nations Frend / and Patrone': The Rhetoric of Petition in Harvey and Spenser," *Spenser Studies* 22 (2007): 47–72.

60. *Orlando Furioso* "provided a quasi-epic medium for the celebration of a patron but refused to exempt that celebration from irony," writes Scott-Warren (*Sir John Harington and the Book as Gift* [Oxford: Oxford University Press, 2001], 38). Elizabeth is supposed to have ordered Harington's full translation of *Orlando Furioso* after her godson circulated among her ladies-in-waiting his translation of a bawdy tale from Ariosto's poem (canto 28); see Scott-Warren, *Book as Gift*, 25–26; and Miranda Johnson-Haddad, "Englishing Ariosto: Orlando Furioso At the Court of Elizabeth I," *Comparative Literature Studies* 31 (1994): 323–50.

61. See Thomas Greene, *The Descent From Heaven: A Study in Epic Continuity* (New Haven, CT: Yale University Press, 1963); and David Quint, "Astolfo's Voyage to the Moon," *Yale Italian Studies* 1 (1977): 398–408

62. Lodovico Ariosto, *Orlando Furioso. Translated Into English Heroical Verse By Sir John Harington (1591)* (Oxford: Clarendon Press, 1972), 403, 35.27.2–5. Watkins argues that Virgil also repudiates the digressiveness of Homer's *Odyssey* in a Roman *renovatio* of Hellenic licentiousness; his "slander" of Dido is also motivated by this Augustan moral program (*The Specter of Dido: Spenser and Virgilian Epic* (New Haven: Yale University Press, 1995), 9–29).

63. Ariosto, *Orlando Furioso*, 403, 35.27.5–6; cit. and trans. Albert Russell Ascoli, *Ariosto's Bitter Harmony: Crisis and Evasion in the Italian Renaissance* (Princeton: Princeton University Press, 1987), 276.

64. Ascoli, *Ariosto's Bitter Harmony*, 278. Saint John turns "the humanist value of man shaping the historical world into an image of poets reshaping the world by lying about it" (276). Ariosto's irreverence extends to scripture itself, when even the Evangelist reveals that he relies on Christ's preferment for his eternal well-being. "Instead of dignifying poetry by raising it up to the Scriptures," adds Ascoli, "Scripture is lowered to the level of fiction" (290).

65. Spenser, *Yale Edition*, 286, lines 469, 471–72; my emphasis.

66. So Craig describes both as poisoning enemies indifferent to truth and prone to betraying those who patronize them. See Alexander Craig, *Against Sycophants and Parasits* (Edinburgh, 1609).

67. Samuel Daniel, *A Defence of Ryme: Against a Pamphlet: Observations in the Art of English Poesie* (London, 1603).

68. Charles Fitzgeffrey, *Sir Francis Drake: His Honorable Lifes Commendation, and His Tragicall Deathes Lamentation* (Oxford, 1596), lines 217, 224.

69. *The First Book of the Preservation of King Henry the Vij. When He Was But Earle of Richmond* (London, 1599), lines 61–62.

70. *Englands Sorrowe or, a Farewell to Essex With a Commemoration of the Famous Liues, and Vntimely Deaths of Many Woorthie Personages Which Haue Liued in England. By W. H. Gent.* (London, 1606), lines 757–59.

71. Joseph Hall, *Prologue From Virgidemiarvm* (London, 1598), line 10.

72. Ariosto, *Orlando Furioso*, 402, 35.20.5–6; 22.3–4; 22.5–6. Saint John thus "situates poetry in relation to power and economic value, as well as to historical and transcendental truth" (Ascoli, *Ariosto's Bitter Harmony*, 265).

73. Ariosto, *Orlando Furioso*, 403, 35.24.1–8.

74. Ariosto, *Orlando Furioso*, 403, 35.26.1–8. Harington's gloss of this passage asserts the authority of tradition to determine Penelope's reputation: "how so ever it is, for my part, seeing it hath been received so long for a truth that Penelope was a chast and vertuous wife, I will not take upon me (by S. John) to write the contrary though myne authour make S. John to cast a doubt of it" (409).

75. Spenser, *The Faerie Queene*, 715, line 13.

76. Ariosto, *Orlando Furioso*, 402, 35.20.5.

Judith H. Anderson

Milton's Compressed Memory in *Areopagitica* of Spenser's Cave of Mammon

Milton suffers, or at least seems to suffer, a lapse in memory regarding the plot of *The Faerie Queene*, Book II, when he refers to Spenser in *Areopagitica*. He seems to think that the Palmer accompanies Guyon, the Knight of Temperance, into the Cave of Mammon. Quite to the contrary, Guyon has been separated from the Palmer through the intervention of Phaedria in the preceding canto. Milton's apparent mis-remembrance is hardly inconsequential: it has encouraged erroneous suppositions about the distinctive character of Spenser's romance epic, about Milton's relation to his acknowledged Spenserian "Original," and about his reading of allegory. In brief, my argument will be that Milton's memory of Guyon's foray into the Cave is best understood as mnemonic compression or appropriation, and not as mnemonic weakness or error. Its major basis will be an interpretation of this foray itself.

MILTON'S BEST KNOWN REFERENCE to Spenser occurs in *Areopagitica*, the most familiar of his prose tracts, and it involves, or at least seems to involve, a mnemonic error. In a passage distinguished by rhetoric at its Miltonic best, the future epic poet rejects "a fugitive and cloistered virtue" in favor of the heroic trial by vice that purifies through the resistance of temptation.[1] This is the same famous

Spenser Studies: A Renaissance Poetry Annual, Volume XXVII, Copyright © 2012 AMS Press, Inc. All rights reserved.   DOI: 10.7756/spst.027.005.97-106

passage in which he describes "our sage and serious poet Spenser" as "a better teacher than Scotus or Aquinas" and thereby depicts the poet he elsewhere identified as his "Original" (or model) in what some modern readers have imagined as somber hues of puritanical grey.[2] Although others have tried to see Milton's valuing Spenserian teaching over the moral philosophy of the Scholastics as a preference for the imaginative and motivating powers of poetry over dry abstraction—a preference comparable to Sidney's in *The Defence of Poesy*—the puritanical paint job has persisted. Moreover, it has regularly been extended from Spenser to allegory per se, the most distinctive feature of Spenserian form. What better way to protect Milton's writing from contagion than to identify Spenser with allegorical moralism as opposed to Miltonic fullness and complexity, even if such identification clashes resoundingly with Milton's actual views and poetic practices?

The final deleterious effect of Milton's eloquent affirmation in *Areopagitica* of active engagement in a fallen world—again, an engagement resembling both Sidney's in *The Defence* and Spenser's in *The Faerie Queene*—has arisen from his apparently mis-remembering details of plot in the very episode of his poetic Original's epic that he cites as the culminating example of his ideal of active virtue in the life of "the true warfaring [or 'wayfaring'] Christian."[3] This mis-remembrance follows immediately on Milton's praise of Spenser's practical wisdom and focuses on the virtue that is everywhere central to the good life in Milton's writing, namely temperance, which is also the focal virtue of the knightly protagonist Guyon in the second book of Spenser's epic. Characterizing the purity of a cloistered virtue as "an excremental whiteness," one merely external and actually impure, Milton invokes his Original's description of "true temperance under the person of Guyon, [whom Spenser] brings . . . in with his palmer through the cave of Mammon and the bower of earthly bliss, that he might see and know, and yet abstain." Of course the problem with Milton's memory here is that Guyon separates from his Palmer in the sixth canto of Book II when Phaedria takes the knight aboard her boat but leaves the Palmer behind on the shore, refusing "To ferry that old man," Guyon's sober companion, "ouer the perlous foord."[4]

In Book II's seventh canto, which houses the Cave of Mammon, Guyon is conspicuously without the Palmer at his side as he first engages Mammon's arguments outside the Cave and then enters it, having accepted the need to "see and know" this place for himself. The Cave is in one sense the fallen world and in another the very heart of unrighteousness—

the Bible's wicked Mammon—with blood-guilty Tantalus and Pilate in its furthest depths. I have argued at length elsewhere that Guyon's actions in this canto, first outside and then inside the Cave, are reasonable, even though the whole experience is for him increasingly like a funhouse of mirrors—of distorting reflections, as when Mammon twists Guyon's arguments outside the Cave and then inside it, in a parody of the Palmer, openly assumes the role of Guyon's reason, or when Guyon washes his hands of Tantalus only next to see, with emblematic irony, the bloody hands of Pilate trying to wash themselves of their stain.[5] Reasonably, of course, Guyon is "with reason pacifyde" in the Cave by his mammonic guide, the parody Palmer, and he therefore does not futilely battle the indestructible Disdain when threatened by him (vii.43). Guyon, who has explicitly disdained both Phaedria and Mammon and been disdained in turn, meets in the figure of Disdain a self-mocking inversion who "did disdayne / To be so cald, and who so did him call" (vii.41). Mammon, as Guyon's reasonable pacifier in this last incident, explicitly impersonates the Palmer, who has virtually been labeled "reason" in the preceding episodes of Book II: for example, Guyon has earlier "hearkned to his reason" *immediately* on the conclusion of the Palmer's rationalization of the failure of the nymph's fountain to cleanse the blood-stained hands of baby Ruddymane; in other words, he has harkened to his Palmer, who both represents his reason and exercises reason to explain the character of the fountain (ii.11). Disdain is indestructible the way in Book I the figure Despair is, since he belongs simultaneously to the forever fallen past and forever fallen present. If earthly time is redeemable, it is never forever so until it ceases and never so without trace of blood stain. There is something undeniably reasonable about Guyon's heeding Mammon's advice, even if this advice suits the unavoidably fallen condition in which Guyon presently finds himself. Emerging from the Cave, Guyon will be both triumphant and errant, heroic and fallen, Christlike and, like the lifeless Mortdant, an image of mortality—of flesh and death. He will need divine intervention to rescue him.

Already at the outset of the seventh canto, Guyon is simultaneously an admirable model and an insufficient one. He is memorably compared to an expert pilot who firmly steers his vessel by compass and nautical chart when the Pole star has been occluded or, more exactly in Guyon's situation, when his Palmer has been separated from him by all that Phaedria represents, which critically includes circumstance and opportunity, or place and time, and not only or simply the affective, unruly side of human nature.[6] Alone, Guyon sustains and guides himself with his own habituated virtues and former experiences, what we nowadays (still) refer to as a moral compass. Such a compass is specifically temperate in Guyon's instance, but as described here it is also broadly prudential, an *"intellectual virtue . . . engendered and fostered by experience and time,"* and it looks ahead to the explicit allegory of prudence in the three sages of Alma's brain turret later in Book II.[7] Guyon, on his own, is incomplete at the outset of this canto and is also without "his trustie guyde," the Palmer, whose reason has become increasingly abstractive in Cantos ii to v and increasingly liable to the charge that it is becoming disconnected from human flesh, or in Milton's terms, increasingly Scholastic (vii.2). Feeding himself as Canto vii opens with the comfort of "his owne vertues, and praise-worthie deedes," Guyon, while equipped with a moral compass and admirable, also sounds self-centered and self-gratifying, much as Christian moral philosophy held that of Aristotle to be, even while basing itself firmly on Aristotle before adding supernatural virtues to the Greek philosopher's natural moral and ethical ones (vii.2). In Spenser's terms, Guyon might now be said to steer by reference to the basically Aristotelian ethic by which his Palmer has formerly guided him and which he has successfully internalized prior to his separation from this good old man. In this figurative sense, the Palmer is still with him when he enters the Cave.

Albeit without the Palmer in *propria persona* beside him, Guyon is hardly without reason when he argues at length with Mammon outside the Cave. Nor is Mammon without reason as he insidiously implies his own complicity with human nature, something Guyon tries his best to counter by invoking heroic values (shields, steeds, arms) or the experienced corruption wrought by riches or the ideal of an antique golden age or Aristotelian ethics in order to question the doubtful origin of Mammon's wealth. Indeed, when Guyon decides to enter the Cave, again in Milton's words, to "see and know" it for himself, the argument between the Knight and the mammonic "God of the world and worldlings" (vii.8) has reached such an impasse that it has begun to repeat itself, with Guyon again demanding to know how Mammon has managed to get and keep his horde (vii.7, cf. 20). Given this impasse, the next step for Guyon to take is obviously and reasonably to see and in this way to experience and understand, or to know, the Cave without embracing its corruption, very much as will pertain to the problem of knowing evil in *Paradise Lost*. The old view that Guyon is sinfully curious when he decides to enter the Cave is therefore suspect. Contrary to it, the *process* of dialogue outside the Cave and Guyon's embrace of experiential understanding as a result of this process—a choice the new science would (re)baptize in the name of curiosity—together become additional attractions that the Cave episode was to offer Milton.[8]

Once Guyon is within the Cave, while most readers probably find his answers to Mammon's temptations inadequate, puzzling, or simply dislocating, they are hard to label simply irrational; in fact they, too, are reasoned—explanations rather than simple denials and refusals. They maintain Guyon's moral standing and get him through the Cave without his falling and failing: evidence of heroic virtue in Milton's terms. But certainly the experience of the Cave also proves exhausting, debasing, and poisonous for Guyon, despite his victorious resistance. When he collapses outside the Cave, in retrospect his resistance looks as suicidal as surrender to Mammon would have been, and it would remain so, were it not swiftly followed and—to interpret sequence as causation—also justified by heavenly intervention.

When the angel descends to summon the Palmer to the unconscious Guyon's side, we learn that the Palmer "By further search had passage found elsewhere" after Phaedria denied him passage over her Idle lake (viii.3). I want to read the line just quoted as an indication that the Palmer, too, has changed or at least has got to the other side of Guyon's experience—*as if* he has really been with Guyon all the time, as indeed he has been, if we consider Guyon's internalization, or habituation, of the Palmer's earlier teaching.[9] The brightly colored wings and the more generally erotic character of the salvific angel contrast radically with the "blacke Palmer" who earlier banished love *tout court* in his exorcism of Phedon (II.i.34, iv.35).[10] The Palmer's values and demeanor have also changed by the time he reappears on the other side of Guyon's experiences with Phaedria's island and Mammon's Cave. It is again as if he had been with Guyon throughout the knight's trial in the Cave: *as if* is the sign of metaphor, and metaphorically and/or allegorically, the Palmer has indeed been there.[11] He has been so by virtue of his figurative presence, what Guyon, on reawakening, understands as faith: in Guyon's words, "Firme is thy faith, whom daunger neuer fro me drew" (II.viii.53).

Whereas in Canto v, the Palmer had earlier rejected the affective knightly values to which Pyrochles appealed and to which Guyon was prepared to respond just before being physically separated from his Palmer, now in Canto viii, with Guyon in mortal danger at the hands of

Pyrochles and Cymochles, "the Palmer suppliaunt" is the one who invokes precisely these values: "For knighthoods loue, doe not so fowle a deed, / Ne blame your honor with so shamefull vaunt / Of vile reuenge" (16).[12] As generally recognized, Book II moves into a more distinctly Christian context in Canto viii, one that arguably begins near the end of Canto vii, with the appearance of Pilate and references to "the Lord of life," or Christ, and to Mammon himself now as the traditionally satanic "Guyler" (62, 64). A palmer might by definition have been to Jerusalem, but the full significance of this Palmer's figure is not realized in the early cantos; like the major protagonists of Books I and II, earlier he does not fully embody the virtue he nominally represents.[13] Insofar as he is Guyon's reason and not *simply* reason in general, he is, after all, in some degree a developing aspect of Guyon. In Miltonically relevant terms, he, too, is sorely tested by Guyon's experience in the Cave, and he, too, is changed by faith. He even participates actively in rescuing Guyon, handing the sword of temperance to Arthur when it is most needed.

I imagine it evident by now that I want to suggest that Milton's misremembering a feature of the plot of Spenser's Mammon episode is not the result of superficial acquaintance or even of hazy memory. Milton was an acute, close, and recurrent reader of Spenser if we judge on the basis of the explicit references to Spenser in his writings and biography, on the basis of the many, clear verbal echoes of Spenser in his writings, and on the basis of his complex, allusive use of allegory first in Satan's hell and then in various allegorical extensions of Satan's character throughout *Paradise Lost*.[14] Milton was a sophisticated, not a naive, literal, or reductively abstractive reader of Spenser's allegorical romance epic.

Yet I would be a little more careful: Milton undeniably makes a factual mistake or mistakenly expresses himself when he indicates that Guyon's Palmer is literally, in terms of the physical plot, beside him in the Cave of Mammon. The Palmer is not present, and yet Milton asserts that he is there with Guyon. Either we assume that Milton is writing figuratively here and supposing his readers will understand him this way, a possibility with profound implications for the history of reception, or else we assume that his memory has imposed a figurative reading on the literal one to the extent that the two have simply coalesced. Although my argument has moved from text into speculation, I cautiously take this latter possibility to be the case. Compressed memories are common enough in human experience. A central temptation to temperance that is realized in the powerfully imaginative art of Mammon's Cave, to which the poets Shakespeare, Milton, and Keats all responded,[15] clearly affected Milton's memory of it, which might best be understood as an instance of mnemonic compression, or even mnemonic appropriation, rather than merely as an instance of mnemonic weakness or error.

Having reached my conclusion, with the phrases "mnemonic compression" and "even mnemonic appropriation" I have also reintroduced into it what I shall ingloriously label the proverbial can of worms, in this case an invitation to more complicated, systemic theorizings of Milton's mistake. With this invitation, I have also come full circle, returning to the critical suspicion of Spenserian allegory to which Milton's mistake has lain open. On the one hand, the phrase "mnemonic compression" is susceptible to psychoanalytical extension, as, for example, in Harold Bloom's *Map of Misreading*.[16] On the other hand, the phrase "even mnemonic appropriation" is itself susceptible to systemically theorized capture, of which a strong example can be found in John Guillory's *Poetic Authority*. Building on a mid-twentieth-century reading by Ernest Sirluck, Guillory sees Milton's mistake as an apparently deliberate rejection of Spenserian allegory.[17] This is surely a leap, although it is rationalized within a larger argument as Milton's appropriative internalizing of Spenser and as part of the march of literary history toward the Romantic imagination. This is a march that many, myself included, have observed with a variety of historical emphases, cultural, formalist, philosophical, Marxist.[18] The assumption of appropriation, however, has still left us with the persistent literalness and simple brevity—the blatant compression in view of the Spenserian text—of Milton's self-evident error. So open an error, stated so plainly by Milton, asks for reflection but also resists—even clashes with—elaborate theorizing. Milton's statement itself, in all its expressive substance, and I mean full verbal substantiality, stubbornly remains. While I have argued both that this statement is more than simply error and that, when seen in its Spenserian context, it is not a rejection by Milton of his Spenserian Original, I have also tried to respect its obvious inaccuracy instead of appropriating it in a move that effactually substitutes for what Milton wrote. Habituation only makes sense as a Miltonic shorthand for the relation of Guyon to his Palmer if it is understood not as an abstraction but instead as the evolving relation between virtue and embodiment, or abstract, rationalized Temperance and Guyon. Thus understood, it simultaneously encapsulates and represents the allegorical narrative of Mammon's Cave, which begins with Guyon's necessary and humanly inevitable departure from his too exclusively rational Palmer and ends with their reunion in transformative faith.

Indiana University

NOTES

1. Unless otherwise specified, reference to Milton's prose is to *John Milton: Complete Poems and Major Prose*, ed. Merritt Y. Hughes (New York: Odyssey, 1957); in this paragraph and the next, 728–29. *Areopagitica* was published late in 1644 when Milton still had his eyesight.

2. Barbara K. Lewalski, *The Life of John Milton: A Critical Biography* (Oxford: Blackwell, 2000), 508: Milton's fellow poet John Dryden is the source for this acknowledgment by Milton of his debt to Spenser.

3. Hughes, ed., 728n102, notes that "wayfaring" is the reading of the first edition but argues for "warfaring" on the basis of immediate context, sources, and the written, possibly authorial corrections of three extant copies of the first edition. Ernest Sirluck, ed., *Areopagitica*, in *Complete Prose Works of John Milton* (New Haven: Yale University Press, 1959), 2:515n102, agrees with Hughes, noting that all known presentation copies, and some others, correct "wayfaring" to "warfaring." On the active engagement argued in *The Defence*, see Robert E. Stillman's illuminating *Philip Sidney and the Poetics of Renaissance Cosmopolitanism* (Aldershot: Ashgate, 2008).

4. *The Faerie Queene*, ed. A. C. Hamilton, with text by Hiroshi Yamashita and Toshiyuki Suzuki, 2nd ed. (Harlow, UK: Pearson, 2001), II.vi.19. Subsequent reference is to this edition.

5. For discussion see my *Growth of a Personal Voice: "Piers Plowman" and "The Faerie Queene"* (New Haven: Yale University Press, 1976), 50–65; and especially on Pilate's bloody hands, "Mutability and Mortality: Reading Spenser's Poetry," in *Celebrating Mutabilitie: Essays on Edmund Spenser's Mutabilitie Cantos*, ed. Jane Grogan (Manchester, UK: Manchester University Press, 2010), 246–74, here 255–56.

6. For further discussion of Phaedria, see my *Reading the Allegorical Intertext: Chaucer, Spenser, Shakespeare, Milton* (New York: Fordham University Press, 2008), 194, 228–33.

7. Quotation from Aquinas, *Summa theologica*, trans. Fathers of the Dominican Province, 2nd rev. ed., 22 vols. (London: Burns, Oates and Washbourne, 1916–29),

10:27 (2–2.47.16, 49.1); see also *Summa theologiae*, Blackfriars Edition, 60 vols. (London: Eyre and Spottiswoode, 1964–76), 36:50–51: "Sed ad generationem prudentiae necessarium est experimentum, quod fit ex multis memoriis, ut dicitur in princ. *Meta*. [Now to produce prudence experience is necessary, and this is formed of many memories, as remarked at the beginning of the *Metaphysics*]" (2–2.47.16); "Quid autem in pluribus sit verum oportet per experimentum considerare. Unde et Philosophus dicit quod *virtus intellectualis habet generationem et augmentum ex experimento et tempore*. Experimentum autem est ex pluribus memoriis, ut patet in 1 *Meta*., unde consequens est quod ad prudentiam requiritur plurium memoriam habere [Now to know what is true in the majority of cases we must be empirical; Aristotle says that intellectual virtue is produced and developed by time and experience. Experience is stocked with memories, as noted in the *Metaphysics*; consequently recalling many facts is required for prudence]" (2–2.49.1). On Spenser's allegory of prudence, see *Books I and II of "The Faerie Queene,"* ed. Robert Kellogg and Oliver Steele (New York: Odyssey, 1965), 343n47.8–9; also Hamilton, ed., 243nn47–48.

8.　On scientific curiosity, see Joanna Picciotto, *Labors of Innocence in Early Modern England* (Cambridge: Harvard University Press, 2010), 35–36, 255–319: my reading would not appeal to Picciotto, who is committed to the opposition of Milton to Spenser and to a radical break between the new science and the intellectual culture of the sixteenth century. On Guyon's supposed sinful curiosity, see Patrick Cullen, *Infernal Triad: The Flesh, the World, and the Devil in Spenser and Milton* (Princeton: Princeton University Press, 1974), 71–74.

9.　See, for example, Sirluck, ed., *Complete Prose Works of John Milton*, 2:516n108: Sirluck interprets Milton's error as an avoidance of Aristotelian-Spenserian habituation and cites his earlier article "Milton Revises *The Faerie Queene*," *Modern Philology* 48 (1950): 90–96. In this article, Sirluck sees Guyon as "Aristotle's temperate man . . . immune to temptation and having no need to call upon reason to assist him with its active intervention" (96). Such a view privileges abstraction over embodied experience to the extent that it questionably represents allegory, as distinct from Aristotelian dogma. Guyon exercises reason throughout the Cave episode.

10.　For recent discussion of the angel as embodied sympathy, see Jonathan Goldberg, *The Seeds of Things: Theorizing Sexuality and Materiality in Renaissance Representations* (New York: Fordham University Press, 2009), 101–2. Goldberg draws this concept from Joseph Campana, "On Not Defending Poetry: Spenser, Suffering, and the Energy of Affect," *PMLA* 120 (2005): 33–48, here 45.

11.　On *as if* as the sign of metaphor, see, for example, Paul Ricoeur, *Time and Narrative*, trans. Kathleen McLaughlin and David Pellauer (Chicago: University of Chicago Press, 1984), 1:45; also Ricoeur's "The Metaphorical Process as Cognition, Imagination, and Feeling," in *On Metaphor*, ed. Sheldon Sacks (Chicago: University of Chicago Press, 1979), 141–57.

12.　A perverse or cynical reading might see the Palmer's embrace of knightly values, along with the progressive Christianizing of the context, as mere expediency:

chacun à son goût. Yet it might be remembered that the reader I posit in this essay is Milton and might also be noted that the quality of the Palmer's words, like belief itself, is at this stage of Book II affective in tone.

13. The obvious and significant fact that a Palmer is "one who has been to Jerusalem" goes all the way back for me to William Nelson, *The Poetry of Edmund Spenser* (New York: Columbia University Press, 1963), 179.

14. See my *Reading the Allegorical Intertext*, 280–320.

15. Harold F. Brooks refers to the Cave of Mammon in "'Richard III': Antecedents of Clarence's Dream," *Shakespeare Survey* 32 (1979): 145–50. Keats finds in the Cave what Paul Alpers has described as "a metaphor for the poet's activity": *The Poetry of The Faerie Queene* (Princeton: Princeton University Press, 1967), 264; and *The Letters of John Keats, 1814–21*, ed. Hyder Edward Rollins, 2 vols. (Cambridge: Harvard University Press, 1958), 2:322–23.

16. *A Map of Misreading* (New York: Oxford, 1975), 127–29.

17. For Sirluck, see note 9 above; for Guillory's argument, see *Poetic Authority: Spenser, Milton, and Literary History* (New York: Columbia University Press, 1983), 133–39.

18. For persuasively historicized resistance to and revision of Guillory's argument, see Janet Leslie Knedlick, "Fancy, Faith, and Generative Mimesis in *Paradise Lost*," *Modern Language Quarterly* 47 (1986): 19–47, here 19–29. Knedlick especially invokes the theories of Mazzoni and Tasso, with both of which Milton was familiar, as evidenced in his *Of Education: Complete Prose Works of John Milton*, 2:404.

GILLIAN HUBBARD

"Send your angel":
Augustinian Nests and Guyon's Faint

When the Palmer covers the pulse of Guyon in *Faerie Queene* II.viii, the action evokes the covering wings of the mother hen of Matthew 18:10 and God's protective wings in the Psalms. These images come together in the writings of Augustine, in particular his *Confessions* and his commentary on Psalm 91. In the *Confessions* Augustine conveys carnal understanding and rejection of the redemptive simplicity of the Scriptures by the metaphor of a fall out of the nest of faith. An angel's prayer for the rescue of an unfledged chicken in Book XII of the *Confessions* is strongly echoed in the passage of Guyon's faint. This metaphorical fall appears in the Palmer and Guyon's combination of presumptuous overconfidence in ethical precepts and despair over mortality in the opening of *Faerie Queene* II, which betrays a regressive carnality opposed to Pauline spiritual renewal. In Augustinian terms, the Word of God and sufficient ecclesiastical support for the "little one" in the faith provide the proper path to self-control through hope in the promise of eternity. In both Augustine's early theology, and Book II of *The Faerie Queene*, conversion and temperance are equated in a neo-Platonic return to God.

Spenser Studies: A Renaissance Poetry Annual, Volume XXVII, Copyright © 2012 AMS Press, Inc. All rights reserved.   DOI: 10.7756/spst.027.006.107-132

I. As a Hen Gathereth Her Chickens

AT THE END of Canto vii of Spenser's *Faerie Queene* Guyon suffers a death-like faint after emerging from the Cave of Mammon. Guyon's life "did flit away out of her nest" (II.vii.66.8),[1] and in the opening stanzas of the following canto, the Palmer finds a beautiful winged angel sitting protectively by the fallen knight, who assures him that "life ere long shall to her home retire" (II.viii.7.8). Guyon's life, then, leaves a "nest" in Canto vii but will return to a "home" in Canto viii. This promise is made by a winged "faire young man" (II.viii.5.1), whose beauty is compared to that of the divine Cupid. After handing on "the charge of [Guyon's] deare safety" (II.viii.8.1–2) to the Palmer, this angel displays "[h]is painted nimble wings, and vanisht quite away" (II.viii.8.9). The Palmer tremblingly tests Guyon's pulse, "Where finding life not yet dislodged quight, / He much reioyst, and courd it tenderly, / As chicken newly hatcht, from dreaded destiny" (II.viii.9.7–9).

Spenser's imagery of nests and chickens draws on a set of biblical sources and associations in Christian writing that would resonate with a readership used to hearing the Bible read and to the exegesis of biblical passages in preaching. This is the familiar imagery of God's care and spiritual protection for both the individual and the church. Less familiar is Spenser's association of a descending angel, through the Palmer, with the tendering of the maternal care by a biblical mother hen. But for this association a precedent does exist: that of a prayer in Augustine's *Confessions*. The effect of reading this episode in the light of this Augustinian prayer is to make its concerns both strongly ecclesiastical, and focussed, as Augustine so often was, on how to read the Scriptures. An Augustinian Guyon is, I will argue, at this point in his journey, a *parvulus*, a "little one" in the faith. Augustine accords such little ones a particular dispensation if they stray away from the faith through misreading and misinterpreting scriptural messages. Indeed, Augustine saw himself as such a *parvulus*, one who went astray by reading the nature of the world in terms of classical philosophy and the Manichean heresy.

In the *Confessions* Augustine recounts his discovery that to read the world with (essentially) Pauline faith and hope is to see it spiritually, and not carnally. This spiritual orientation runs counter to the underlying premise of classical philosophy (based as it is, according to Augustine, in the temporal world) that virtue is the highest good. In an Augustinian light the precepts and premises of classical philosophy introduced in the early parts of Book II of *The Faerie Queene* are out of tune with the Christian principles established in Book I. Like the church when it has gone astray, Guyon must be called back to faith and admonished as well as protected. Spenser's reminder is also directed to the reader of his allegory who, as Guyon is regaining his proper spiritual orientation, receives the poet's homiletic address on the nature of divine grace.

While my discussion here draws primarily on Augustine, he is merely one conduit for a set of ideas and images important in Reformation exegesis and preaching deriving particularly from the Psalms, the Gospels and the Pauline Epistles. These include the imagery of divine supporting wings, chickens and nests. A. C. Hamilton's edition of *The Faerie Queene* cites Christ's words in Matthew 23:37[2] (both comforting and admonishing) as the source of the tender action by which the Palmer, replacing the angel, "courd" Guyon's life: "I have gathered thy children together as a hen gathereth her chickens under her wings." The New Testament metaphor of the protective mother hen in turn draws on the image of God's powerful wings in the Psalms[3] and Exodus, wings whose shelter brings hope or trust in God and defence against foes. Such imagery is also directed toward the church. The German theologian Strigelius, in his commentary on the covering wings in Psalm 17—"Keepe me as the aple of thine eie, hyde me vnder the shadowe of thy winges,"—sees the divine protection as naturally belonging not to the individual but to the community of God's chosen: "Here David doth most pleasantly painte out the defence of the churche setting before his eyes the similitudes of the eye, and of a henne."[4] The association of the nest and the church in turn derives from Psalm 84, where "the sparow hath found her an house, and the swallow a nest where she may lay her younge, euen they aulters O Lord of hostes."

In Calvin's exposition of Psalm 91:4 we see how naturally exegesis of the Old Testament—"Hee will couer thee under his winges, and thou shalt be sure vnder his feathers: his trueth shall be thy shield and buckler"[5]—is conflated with the New Testament metaphor of the maternal hen of Matthew 23:37. Calvin argues (in Arthur Golding's 1571 translation) that the incongruous homeliness of the sheltering mother bird is the very point of the image.

The similitude (the which the Scripture useth in other places also) dooeth beawtifully peint out God's wonderful charinesse in preferring our welfare. Surely if the maieste of God be considered in itself, it can have no allyance with hennes or other birds that he shold spred

out his wings to cherish his chickens. Howbeit to the intent to suc-
cor our infirmitie, he disdeyneth not to descent after a sort from his
heauenly glory, to allure us more gently under the image of a henne.
Therefore there is nothing that should stoppe us from familiar access
unto him, seeing he humbleth him selfe so lovingly unto us.[6]

Calvin's point is that the tenderness and humility of biblical metaphor is
a path to participation in the grace that comes from divine humility, the
humility that lies as the central paradox of Christian faith. The progression
he traces from "the maieste of God . . . considered in itself," to the more
alluring because more humble "image of a henne" is mirrored in Spenser's
progression in the opening of Canto vii from "th'exceeding grace / Of high-
est God, that loues his creatures so" (II.viii.1.5–6), to a mediating descent
in the form of angels, first those who "watch and dewly ward" (II.viii.2.6),
then in the particular angel discovered sitting protectively at Guyon's head,
and finally in Spenser's echo of Matthew 23:37 when the Palmer covers
Guyon's pulse. Christ's grace in the passage as the source of Guyon's spiri-
tual "deare safety" (II.viii.8.2) is suggested both by this action of "couring"
and by the echoes of angelic annunciation in the Palmer's response to the
angel, of "feare and wonder, that he nought could say" (II.viii.7.2).

II. Protect the Chick without Wings. Send Your Angel.

In his early and still heavily Neoplatonic *De Ordine*, Augustine identifies
purification, temperance and conversion with each other: "After all, from
what things do you think we pray to be turned [*convertamur*] towards God
so that we can see his face if not from the mud and filth of the body, and
similarly from the shadows in which error wraps us? And what is it to
be turned [*converti*] if not to turn away from the excesses of vice and to
be raised into ourselves by virtue and temperance?"[7] As Augustine tells
the story of his own wandering away from God and return to Him in the
first nine books of the *Confessions* he combines this essentially Neoplatonic
view of conversion with imagery of epic voyaging, the wayward Prodigal
Son and Old Testament idolatry as fornication. The *Confessions* also mixes
biblical imagery of admonition and with that of comfort. God rebukes me-
dicinally, and his hand turns the human head back to face the truth, but

more gently and maternally the infant is suckled by its nurse and carried in its mother's arms, protected as a fledgling in the nest until ready to be thrust forth into independent flight.[8]

In the last four books of the *Confessions* Augustine moves from his personal story of redemption to a quest for a deeper understanding of spiritual truth. This quest includes the bishop's pastoral concerns with how the spiritual flock understands scripture. In Book XII Augustine considers a range of exegetical readings of the formless matter in the Genesis story (modeling the generous view of spiritual interpretation through love also found in *On Christian Doctrine*) before arguing that all these readings can be accepted. He compares believers spiritually ready for exegesis to newly fledged birds searching for fruit in dark thickets, chirping with delight when they find it (*Confessions* XII.xxvii.37). The one reading Augustine will not endorse, because it contradicts the spiritual exegesis he has been exploring, is the literal one, which sees God as uttering the words of creation as if standing in time and space. But ruling out this literal reading presents Augustine with a problem. He has already argued in Book III of the *Confessions* that one cause of his own fall away from orthodox Christian faith was his inability to see the superficially absurd imagery of the Bible as a path to faith accessible only to the humble. Yet at this point in Book XII he is rejecting just such a child-like literal reading of the Scriptures as wrong. In seeking to resolve this problem he returns to the very sort of simple biblical imagery at issue, the sort used more commonly in the earlier parts of the *Confessions*.

Those Christians who visualize God standing and speaking physically in time and space do so, Augustine says, "because of their familiarity with the fleshly order of things [*ex familiaritate carnis*]."[9] This literal level of understanding is still healthy, he concedes, as long as believers are receiving support of the church's love: "In such people who are still infants [without higher insight], faith is built up in a healthy way, while in their state of weakness they are carried as if at their mother's breast by an utterly simple kind of language" (XII.xxvii.37). Such infant believers, however, face a unique risk, a form of "proud weakness" that results in "scorning the humble style of biblical language." The risk is that they will reject the absurdity of the surface before seeing beyond the surface to the beauty of its spiritual truth.

It is this risk that could potentially require the rescue of an angel, and it leads us to a crucial prayer:

If any among them comes to scorn the humble style of biblical language and in proud weakness pushes himself outside the nest in which he was raised he will fall, poor wretch. Lord God, have mercy, protect the chick without wings from being trodden on the path by passersby. Send your angel to replace it in the nest, so that it can live until it can fly. (XII.xxvii.37)

Quorum si quispiam vilitatem dictorum aspernatus extra nutritorias cunas superba inbecillitate se extenderit, heu! cadet miser et, domine deus, miserere, ne implumem pullum conculcent qui transeunt viam, et mitte angelum tuum, qui eum reponat in nido, ut vivat donec volet.

There are several ways of seeing the angel in this Augustinian prayer. A literal angel evokes Matthew 18:10 (as Chadwick suggests in his annotated translation): "Take heed that ye despise not one of these little ones; for I say unto you, That in heaven their angels do always behold the face of my Father which is in heaven." But reference to angels is sparse in the *Confessions* (and of course it is neither prominent nor unproblematic in Reformed theology). The Augustinian context of Scriptural exegesis suggests another possibility, one associated with the figure of Ambrose, whose scriptural exegesis was critical to Augustine's conversion. It was only as Ambrose enabled Augustine to read scriptural imagery spiritually and not literally that the latter gained access to its deeper truth. Reading and preaching the Word in its spiritual sense becomes central to the act of conversion in the *Confessions*, as it is also for Protestant thought. In the *Confessions* Augustine describes his mother as having loved Ambrose "as an angel of God" (VI.i.1). The biblical source for this epithet is the Paul who came to the Galatians "as an angel of God, even as Christ Jesus" (Gal. 4:14).

Augustine's hypothetically fallen ecclesiastical chicken, needing the support of Scriptural interpretation, requires primarily the intervention of an ecclesiastical angel, one whose purpose, like that of the evangelists themselves, is to deliver understanding of the Old Testament in terms of the comforting promise of the New, and to open minds to a truth beyond the limitations of the material. Or (in tune with Spenser's description of the angel as divine), the ecclesiastical messenger may be The Word in the form of the "angel of great counsel of God" of Isaiah 9:6.5 (the *megales boules angelos* of the Septuagint), Christ in his role as messenger and Incarnate Revealer. John Michael Owens has shown that the Augustinian among other exegeses lies behind this usage in the Scottish Confession of 1560 to describe the birth of Christ: "and sa was borne of the iust seid of Dauid / the Angell of greit counsel of God the uerray Messias promesit."[10]

What is striking about the prayer in Augustine's *Confessions* is that it, uniquely as far as I have been able to ascertain, calls for the rescue of an unfledged chicken by an angel and so gives us in direct form the combination of rescuing angel and unfledged chicken more subtly offered by Spenser. Augustine, we should note, evinces no Calvin-like concern with the apparent incongruity of his request for the rescue of a tiny wingless chicken and its restoration to a nest by a much larger winged angel. Spenser however quite carefully avoids this incongruity, conveying like Calvin the nature of "similitude," which to some extent disguises the association. So Guyon's life is "cou'rd, as chicken newly hatcht" and the agency of the angel is transferred to the Palmer before the covering begins. The relationship of rescuing angel and defenceless, newly hatched chicken nevertheless remains central to Spenser's passage as it is in Augustine's prayer. The chicken is rescued by the angel.

Augustine's prayer to "send your angel" is thus in effect enacted in the passage describing Guyon's faint. Guyon's life has left "her nest" and he has fallen like Augustine's fallen chicken. But Spenser's highest God embraces all his works with mercy, and an angel, discovered next to Guyon, promises the return of his life to its home. Guyon, the "chicken newly hatcht," discovered on the path leading into and out of the Cave of Mammon, is returned to a nest, the Palmer's protective presence and covering hands, just before the onslaught of Pyrochles and Cymochles (Spenser's equivalent of Augustine's careless passersby), who seek to despoil Guyon's apparently lifeless form.

To see Spenser's Guyon in this Augustinian way, as a chicken temporarily fallen from an ecclesiastical nest of love and so needing New Testament rescue, draws strength from the imagery of *Faerie Queene* I. The sudden intervention of Spenser's narrator at the opening of *Faerie Queene* II.viii, with a praise of God and his descending angels, invites a return to the earlier preoccupations of the Legend of Holinesse. In the House of Holinesse Redcrosse, at his own moment of spiritual rebirth, meets a Charissa who has just "left her fruitfull nest" (I.x.29.8). Charissa is a figure of abundant maternal nurture familiar in a range of Christian iconography: "Her necke and brests were euer open bare, / That ay thereof her babes might sucke their fill" (I.x.30.7–8); and she continues to feed these babes "whiles they were weak and young" (I.x.31.3). But in the spirit of the imagery we have been discussing, like a mother bird with her fledglings, she "thrust[s] them forth still, as they wexed old" (I.x.31.4). Redcrosse, who is about to gain a vision of eternity, is in the process of being successfully "thrust forth."

By contrast, in *Faerie Queene* II, Guyon's collapse figures his frailty. He is anagrammatically "young" and exemplifies the state of being "weak and young" in the sense of needing the continued spiritual nurturing and sustenance of Charissa. And so he is returned to the embrace of "highest God, that loues his creatures so" (II.viii.1.6).

If we place the two quests for knowledge, that in the House of Holinesse and that in the Cave of Mammon, next to each other, the Augustinian dichotomy between the spirit and matter—for Augustine the difference between things as they are and things as they seem[11]—becomes very pointed. Redcrosse, with the allegorical assistance of Mercy, Fidessa, and Contemplation, ascends to see "The Citty of the greate king" (I.x.55.8) and "The blessed Angels to and fro descend, / From highest heuen" (I.x.56.2–3). By contrast, Guyon collapses after descending into the gloom and feasting his eyes on the sources of material wealth in the Cave of Mammon, accompanied by Mammon, unable even to see the angel who comes to minister to him.

Harry Berger has cogently argued, partly in Augustinian terms, for the sin of curiosity in Guyon's passage through the Cave.[12] In *De Moribus Ecclesiae* Augustine opposes curiosity about the things of the world to the important definition of temperance as "love keeping itself entire and incorrupt for God."[13] In other words, the problem with curiosity about things of this world lies in not questing for the things of the spirit. In entering the Cave of Mammon, Guyon is wandering away, in Augustinian terms, into the realm of the material, the realm of all that merely seems, and away from the path to what is true and real because spiritual—the vision that Redcrosse can see from the Hill of Contemplation. Guyon is looking in the wrong place, and instead of spiritual truth, he finds at the heart of his search the presumption of Tantalus and the spiritual blindness of Pilate.

In Book XII of the *Confessions* the significance to Augustine's thought of the apparently incidental prayer for the rescue of a chicken fallen from the nest appears in the increased imagery of nests and covering wings. In his *First Sermon on the New Testament* he characterizes himself as a fledgling that once fell out of the nest of faith. This imagery of fall from and return to a nest thus stands in little for the process of fall away from and return to God in the *Confessions* as a whole, and this deepens its application to Spenser's passage. Intellectual arrogance and intemperance in the form of an "irregular life" (together representing the tripartite sin of pride, curiosity, and carnal concupiscence) have

joined forces to separate Augustine from God, he tells his congrega-
tion. Searching in pride for that which only the humble can discover,
he closed the gate that would open (as Redcrosse finds in *Faerie Queene*
I.x, entering the House of Holinesse) to simple knocking. His naïve
congregation was more secure than he:

> How much more blessed now are you [the congregation], in what
> sure confidence do you learn, and in what safety, who are still
> young ones in the nest of faith and receive the spiritual food;
> whereas I, wretch that I was, as thinking myself fit to fly, left the
> nest and fell down before I flew; but the Lord of mercy raised me
> up, that I might not be trodden down to death by passersby, and
> put me in the nest again; for those same things then troubled me,
> which now in quiet security I am proposing and explaining to you
> in the name of the Lord.[14]

In the *Confessions* Augustine provides examples of this intellectual ar-
rogance and of the classical texts that seemed to him more elegant and
more valid than the Scriptures. In his early questing Cicero had seemed
more worthy than the Bible, and Augustine recalls his own spiritual
pride. "It [the Bible] seemed unworthy in comparison with the dignity
of Cicero. My inflated conceit shunned the Bible's restraint, and my gaze
never penetrated to its inwardness. Yet the Bible was composed in such a
way that as beginners mature, its meaning grows with them. I disdained
to be a little beginner (*parvulus*). Puffed up with pride I considered my-
self a mature adult" (III.v.9).

In Book IV he returns to the now familiar imagery of the nest to de-
scribe his intellectual pride further (this time his self-satisfaction at the
facility with which he conquered Aristotle's difficult *Ten Categories*):

> What profit, then, was it for me at that time that my agile mind found
> no difficulty in these subjects, and that without assistance from a hu-
> man teacher I could elucidate extremely complicated books, when
> my comprehension of religion was erroneous, distorted, and shame-
> fully sacrilegious? Or what serious harm did it cause your little ones
> that their intelligence was much slower? They did not wander away
> from you. In the nest of the Church they could grow like fledglings in
> safety and nourish the wings of charity with the food of sound faith.
> (IV.xvi.31)[15]

In the important and metaphorically complex prayer that follows this exclamation of regret and that closes Book IV of the *Confessions,* Augustine makes explicit a critical point (also claimed for *Faerie Queene* II by Hugh MacLachlan)[16]—that being turned out of the nest of faith and the Church results from the dangerous sin of self-sufficiency. Spenser's apparently inconsequential statement that Guyon's life flits out of a *nest* (a flitting which echoes Augustine's thinking himself fit to fly and immediately falling) and an angel's promise of a return to a *home* is explained by this prayer (and by other similar occasions of its use in Augustine, as for example in the *Commentary on Psalm 84*). The nest from which one may be turned out is the Church, for the home (*domus*) is eternity.

> O Lord our God, under the covering of your wings we set our hope. Protect us and bear us up. It is you who will carry us; you will bear us up from our infancy until old age. When you are our firm support, then it is firm indeed. But when our support rests on our own strength it is infirmity. Our good is life with you for ever, and because we turned away from that we became twisted. Let us now return that we may not be overturned. Our good is life with you and suffers no deficiency for you yourself are that good. We have no fear that there is no home to which we may return because we fell from it. During our absence our home suffers no ruin; it is your eternity. (IV.xvi.31)[17]

In this prayer we have the two halves of a fall out of a spiritual nest and a return to an eternity, the two halves, I am arguing, that we can see on the one hand in Guyon's fall and rescue by an angel in *Faerie Queene* II.viii and on the other hand in Redcrosse's vision in I.x. There Contemplation tells Redcrosse that Fidelia has the keys to his vision of "that most glorious house, that glistereth bright with burning starres, and euerliuing fire" (I.x.50.5–6). Redcrosse understands the importance of his vision of eternity to the spiritual stability Augustine describes, later begging Contemplation that he might remain, "That nothing may my present hope empare" (I.x.63.5), rather than returning to the world "whose ioyes so fruitlesse are" (I.x.63.2). But Redcrosse's return to Una involves an important aspect of faith and hope: that the member of the temporal church also and always participates in some way in the eternal city (the underlying premise of Augustine's *City of God*).

III. The Fowles in Aire Doe Flocke

Augustine's commentary on Psalm 91 links the eternal city with the path of the Christian in the temporal world. The eternal city is also the church of all believers from Abel onward, of which Christ is both the body and head. While angels and saints (which Protestant Spenser recasts in *Faerie Queene* I.x as the community of the faithful) await the toiling pilgrim in the city, the city also reaches out.

> Letters have reached us too from that city, apart from which we are wandering: those letters are the Scriptures, *which exhort us to live well*. Why do I speak of letters only? The King himself descended, and became a path to us in our wanderings: that walking in Him, we may neither stray, nor faint nor fall among robbers, nor be caught in the snares that are set near our path.[18]

"Walking in Christ," enables one of the chosen, such as Redcrosse, to return from the contemplation of the divine world to the fallen world while still participating safely in the eternal city that is Christ's body and also the church. The Scriptures in this Augustinian passage play an intermediary role, reminding the wanderer of the need for moral behavior, also the topic of Spenser's legend *Of Temperaunce*.

In the prayer with which my essay concerns itself, Augustine portrays a risk to a fledgling posed by trampling passersby. The commentary on Psalm 91 extends this risk to Scriptural straying, including fainting, falling among robbers, or being caught in snares. Augustine portrays these and similar risks interchangeably, as we will see later. That Guyon is at risk during his faint further points the contrast with the Redcrosse of *Faerie Queene* I.x, who has had his face set toward eternity. Having strayed from his quest in entering the Cave of Mammon, Guyon faints and lies at the mercy of robbers of the worst sort, those who despoil the dead. This straying, fainting, and falling among robbers indicates, in Augustinian terms, a failure to remain spiritually safe by "walking in Christ," and this risk of attack indicates a separation from the eternal city, anticipated in the form of the temporal church.

Images of snares and birdlime to catch birds recur in Augustine (for example, in *On Christine Doctrine*) and include that of a circling devil and his angels hovering in the air like hawks. Augustine describes this risk in his

Exposition on Psalm 91:4: "He will couer thee under his winges, and thou shalt be sure vnder his feathers: his trueth shall be thy shield and buckler." The protective nest of God's powerful wings is (in a way now familiar to us) the best protection against this foe.

It is clear that the protection of the wings of God expanded places thee between His shoulders, so that God's wings on this side and that have thee in the midst, where thou shalt have no fear lest any one hurt thee: only be thou careful never to leave that spot, where no foe dares approach. If the hen defends her chickens under her wings; how much more shalt thou be safe beneath the wings of God, even against the devil and his angels, the powers who fly about in the mid-air like hawks to carry off the weak young one?[19]

The sense of potential threat is here strongly emphasized. Augustine's hen is not only sheltering but actively defending her chickens, and from a foe who waits to approach and against whom warning is needed (just as the angel gives warning to the Palmer).

The onslaught of Pyrochles and Cymochles, and Arthur's battle with them on Guyon's behalf in *Faerie Queene* II, enacts what happens when threat becomes struggle. Spenser evokes an aerial battle of birds of prey warring over the recumbent fallen "chicken newly hatcht." Cymochles has already threatened Guyon (when finding him in Canto vi with Phaedria) telling him that "the fowles in aire / Doe flocke, awaiting shortly to obtayn / Thy carcas for their pray" (II.vi.28.7–9). Pyrochles wants Guyon to be "entombed in the rauen or the kight" (II.viii.16.9) and is in turn captured by Arthur "as a Bittur in the Eagles clawe" (II.viii.50.2). Pyrochles and Cymochles are already associated with Archimago (II.vi.41–51), whose demonic status, already clearly established in *Faerie Queene* I, is reinforced in Book II when "The Northerne winde his wings did broad display" (II.iii.19.3). The dichotomy between such a devil and God's sheltering wings is established in the *Confessions*: "The enemy is he who 'decided to place his throne in the north' . . . but look Lord, we are your little flock, take possession of us. Stretch out your wings and let us find refuge under them."[20] And so, to make this Augustinian echo explicit, Spenser's Arthur does battle, on Guyon's behalf, if not with the devil, at least with the devil's angels, "who fly about in the mid-air like hawks to carry off the weak young one."

Arthur's battle with Cymochles and Pyrochles is thus an aerial struggle for Guyon's soul against both demonic agency and the inner concupiscence and irascibility represented by the allegorical brothers. This in turn echoes Augustine's early and very Neoplatonic definition of temperance in his dialogue *De Musica*. There the "powers of the air" are combated while temperance allows the soul's ascent with divine support. "But this action by which the soul, with the help of its Lord God, frees itself from the love of lower beauty, overcomes and destroys the habit that wars against it, and by its victory in itself *triumphs over the powers of this air* that envy and try to hinder it, and then flies up to God, its strength and support: — doesn't it seem to you that this is the virtue known as temperance?"[21]

It should be noted that, in his aerial battle for Guyon's soul, Spenser very carefully avoids an early Augustinian emphasis on human agency: Guyon is completely recumbent while Arthur, who "offers hope of help and timely grace," fights on his behalf. We can be less sure that Spenser knew this early dialogue than that he read the well known *Confessions* and commentaries on the Psalms. Even so, applying this Augustinian definition of temperance to the battle of Arthur with a Cymochles already identified with concupiscence and a Pyrochles already identified with irascibility helps us see this battle as not just about ethical self-control but, much more significantly, about such self-control as both a path to God and a path supported by God. Temperance in other words has a teleological purpose in Augustinian theology. Its purpose is union with God. That purpose can be achieved only through divine agency (a view that strengthens as Augustine's theology develops, as I have noted). It is from Temperance's teleological function, I suggest, that Spenser's Guyon, and to some degree his Palmer, have become separated in the early cantos of *Faerie Queene* II and to which they are restored by the interventions of an angel and Arthur.

Ultimately, in Christian theology, divine support comes to fallen man through Christ's incarnation. Augustine's commentary on Psalm 91 uses the image of divine supporting wings to make this point. While Calvin, as I have noted, argues that the humble imagery of the mother hen makes the divine more approachable, for Augustine, who had taken the same point further, it reveals the nature of the Incarnation itself. He makes a contrived but charming analogy as he explicates Psalm 91:4: "You will be safe under his feathers." While all birds hatch their eggs and keep their young warm, none weakens itself in sympathy as the hen does, Augustine explains: "[W]e know the hen to be a mother by the weakness of her voice, and the loosening of her feathers: she changes altogether from love for her chickens: she weakens herself because they are weak." Augustine then reaches a central conclusion. "Thus since we were weak, the wisdom of God made Itself weak, when the Word was made flesh, and dwelt among us, that we might hope under its wings."[22]

Augustine repeats the idea of weakness answered by weakness in the *Confessions*. Here the Word builds a humble house in the inferior material of human clay. This image is close to Spenser's imagery of the nativity in the Histories of Briton: "What time th'eternall Lord in fleshly slime / Enwombed was, from wretched Adams line / To purge away the guilt of sinfull crime: / O ioyous memorie of happie time" (II.x.50.2–5). Through the Incarnation, Augustine tells us, Christ heals the proud swelling of those willing to be made his subjects, detaches and carries them over to himself, and nourishes their love. Humility and the abandonment of self-sufficiency enable this spiritual transformation: "They are no longer to place confidence in themselves, but rather to become weak. They see at their feet divinity become weak by sharing in our 'coat of skin.' In their weariness they fall prostrate before this divine weakness which rises and lifts them up" (VII.xviii.24).

This humble acceptance of weakness does not apply only to the moment of conversion itself but is at all times (and this is the importance for Spenser's Legend of Temperance) the source of both spiritual understanding *and* moral behaviour. As Augustine considers his ecclesiastical duties in Book X of the *Confessions* he sees humility together with the example of Christ as the source of his spiritual *and* moral strength. "It would be a far too perilous responsibility unless under your wings my soul were submissive to you. My weakness is known to you. I am a child [*parvulus*]. But my Father ever lives and my protector is sufficient to guard me . . . . You yourself are all my good qualities" (X.iv (6)).

Spenser emphasizes weariness and weakness in the passage on Guyon's faint. The Knight's weary and "enfeebled spright" (II.vii.66.5) is overcome as he leaves the Cave of Mammon, his "vitall powres gan wexe both weake and wan" (II.vii.65.2), and he falls and remains recumbent. The Palmer's feet, following the calling voice, are also "feeble" (II.viii.4.5). As an expression of Christian humility (and as MacLachlan demonstrates particularly in terms of the Protestant doctrine of justification by faith alone), a recumbence demonstrating a complete dependence on God's grace is also the path to his redemption. The Christian paradox lying at the heart of this episode is informed by a view of Guyon as a carnally-minded "little one."

IV. I Gaue You Milke to Drink & Not Meat

I have explained that the chicken, which falls from the nest of faith through "proud weakness" in Augustine's prayer for rescue by an angel, is put at risk by a limited carnal and thus literal understanding of the Scriptures. It is helpful at this point to address the theological distinction between two sorts of carnality. Augustine gives his definition of these two varieties in *De Diversis Quaestionibus*. One is much more reprehensible than the other, and it is the second, less reprehensible variety that applies to Guyon. The first type of carnality involves those still under the Law. One still under the Law, according to Augustine, is "carnal in this sense, that he is not yet reborn from sin but is 'sold under sin,' since the price of mortal pleasure that he embraces is that sweetness by which he is deceived; and he loves to break the law, and the more illicit the act the more he likes to do it."[23] The second type of carnality involves those who have been reborn through faith as "little ones" (*parvuli*) in Christ, and who may still be carnal, according to Augustine, in the sense that they still need to be fed with milk. It is Christians exhibiting this kind of carnality who require ecclesiastical protection. The sermon on the New Testament cited earlier is directed at this second type, the still carnal believer for whom Augustine as a bishop is directly responsible as a shepherd and preacher.

This distinction is a helpful one for the action of *Faerie Queene* II. Death comes to Mordant, and also to Amavia, precisely because they remain under the Law. Mordant strays with Acrasia, loving the illicit in the way described by Augustine. This straying is inevitably lethal to both Mordant and Amavia when its true nature is revealed as if under the Law.[24] The punitive action of avenging Mordant and Amavia, finally enacted in the Bower of Bliss, is in turn directed against this first kind of carnality, the carnality of sinning under the Law. Guyon and the Palmer however (as the initial encounter with Redcrosse Knight makes clear) are already reborn from sin. They are placed at risk after Guyon visits the Cave of Mammon by something different, the second sort of carnality: an as yet restricted spiritual understanding.

The Elizabethan homily *On the Reading of the Scripture*, in the spirit of Augustine, is compassionate toward still carnally-minded readers of the Scriptures: "And concerning the hardness of the Scripture, he that is so weak that he is not able to brooke strong meat, yet he may still sucke the sweet and tender milk and deferre the rest, until he wax stronger, and come to more knowledge." The biblical image of feeding with milk is more severe, coming as it does when Paul admonishes the Corinthians (1 Corinthians 3:1) for their squabbling and moral backsliding: "And I could not speake vnto you, brethren, as vnto spirituall men, but as vnto carnal, euen as vnto babes in Christ, I gaue you milke to drinke, & not meat: for yee were not yet able to beare it [the *Bishops' Bible* gives "ye then were not stronge"] neither yet nowe are yee able." (Guyon, we must note, like the backsliding Corinthians has become entangled with several variants of the occasion to wrath along his way.) Calvin's commentary on Corinthians paints an even sterner picture of regression: "Hence, with beating down so much the better their insolence, he [Paul] declares, that they belong to the company of those who, stupefied by too much carnal sense, are not prepared to receive the spiritual wisdom of God. . . . He does not mean, however, that they were altogether *carnal*, so as to have not one spark of the Spirit of God—but that they had still greatly too much of carnal sense, so that the flesh prevailed over the Spirit, and did as it were drown out his light."[25] It is in this way that Guyon is carnal and needs rescue.

As Guyon emerges from the Cave, he seems to be *microchristus*, cheating Mammon by resisting temptations such as those laid before Christ in the wilderness. But there is a strong sense that, much as the "want of food, and sleepe" (II.vii.65.3) has made him "wexe both weake and wan" (II.vii.65.2), he has also been overwhelmed by his exposure to a "liuing light" (II.vii.66.4) with which his recent journey in the gloom has made him unable to cope. As soon as he sucks its vital air into his breast he collapses. This overwhelming spiritual "liuing light" is analogous to the strong meat of Corinthians that is too rich to stomach, and it reveals Guyon as, to use the more negative Calvinist language, "stupefied with too much carnal sense." It is important to note that, as with Paul's admonitions to the Corinthians, there is rebuke as well as comfort in the opening message of Canto viii. If there were not care in heaven "much more wretched were the cace / Of men then beasts" (II.viii.1.4–5). God sends his blessed Angels to and fro "to serue to wicked man, to serue his wicked foe" (II.viii.1.9). "O why," Spenser's narrator asks in a voice that may be full of wonder and yet also contain the despairingly admonitory tones of Paul, "should heuenly God to men haue such regard" (II.viii.2.9)?

V. ARE YE NOT CARNAL, AND WALKE AS MEN?

In the light of the preceding discussion I would like to offer a reading of two key speeches in the initial cantos of *Faerie Queene* II in terms of a wandering away from God. This wandering is not unlike that in the early parts of the *Confessions* but in an incipient form. Augustine is led astray by pride, curiosity and carnal concupiscence. If, as I have suggested, we should see Guyon as a still carnally-minded "little one" we can also see his faults as just developing, so that his mode of going astray is a "proud weakness" rather than the full-scale carnal concupiscence in the Bower of Bliss (which in the *Confessions* might also be seen as idolatrous fornication) of Mordant with Acrasia, or Acrasia with Verdant. By contrast, Guyon is only carried to Phaedria's concupiscent island, from which he immediately struggles to be returned, and his latent concupiscence waits until the Bower of Bliss to be more seriously aroused. But his pride and curiosity show a more worrying initial tendency. Like the Augustine of the *Confessions*, Guyon is overcome in the opening cantos of *Faerie Queene* II by a despair that is the natural partner of presumption (two extremes opposed to Christian hope) and that together with it signals the distance from God.

Regression from faith was a strong religious concern in Spenser's period. The Elizabethan homily entitled *How dangerous a thing it is to fall from God* uses the language of turning away from God familiar to us in Augustine: "All they that may not abide the word of God, but, following the persuasions and stubbornness of their own hearts, *go backwards and not forward* (as it is seen in Jeremy), they go and turn away from God."[26] The homily also describes the spiritual disinheritance that follows. God will "no longer dig and delve" around his vines: instead one is left in a frighteningly oblivious state of self-sufficiency. It is this state of oblivion that characterizes Guyon. "But when he [God] withdraweth from us his word, the right doctrine of Christ, his gracious assistance and aid, which is ever joined to his word, and leaveth us to our own wit, our own will and strength, he declareth then that he beginneth to forsake us." Luther's widely read *Commentary on Galatians* gives us another view of this regression as a struggle in the soul: "In the midst of the conflict when we should be consoling ourselves with the Gospel, the Law rears up and begins to rage all over our conscience. I say the Gospel is frail because we are frail . . . nothing is more perilous than to be weary of the Word of God. Thinking he knows enough, a person begins little by little to despise the Word until he has lost Christ and the Gospel altogether."[27]

Being left, as the Elizabethan homily has it, to "our own wit, our own will and strength" as a sign that God has abandoned us, is also a sign of carnality. This is made clear in a side note in the Geneva Bible for Corinthians 3:3. The text (following the spiritual feeding on the carnal discussed earlier) reads: "for yee are yet carnal: for whereas there is among you enuying, and strife, and diuisions, are ye not carnall and walke as men?" The Geneva Bible side note for "walke as men" reads: "by the square and compas of mans wit and iudgement."

When Guyon cannot wash the hands of the Bloodie-handed Babe he is filled with wonder and doubt. His words over the Babe show that he sees the Babe's condition, then generalized to the whole of humanity, in terms of the disinheritance and abandonment read in the Elizabethan homily as the sign of God's withdrawal of his gracious aid.

> Poore Orphane in the wide world scattered,
> As budding braunch rent from the natiue tree,
> And throwen forth, till it be withered:
> Such is the state of men: Thus enter we
> Into this life with woe, and end with miseree.
>
> (II.ii.2.5–9)

The babe is an orphan because he has lost his parents to the poison of Acrasia. Just as Mordant has been associated with the Old Adam (as "him that death doth giue" [II.1.55]) so Ruddymane is born into the misery of original sin under the Law. In Matthew 3:10 John the Baptist proclaims that every tree that does not bear fruit will be cut down (it is in this sense that the "budding braunch" is torn from a "natiue tree"). What Guyon fails to see, but would see through a more unified reading of John 15 is that Christ's promise redeems John the Baptist's essentially pre-Christian judgment.

> Nowe ye are cleane through the worde which I haue spoken vnto you. Byde in me, and I in you. As the braunche can not bear fruite of it selfe, except it byde in the vine: no more can ye, except ye abyde in me. I am the vine, ye are the braunches. He that abydeth in me, and I in hym, the same bryngeth foorth much fruite: For without me ye can do nothyng. (John 15:3–5 Bishops' Bible)

Guyon uses John 15 to support his view that the happiness of the Babe (who "gan smyle on them") is mistaken: he "rather ought to weepe" (II.i.1.6). This amounts to a misreading of the wider Scriptural passage. We are wrong to overlook this misreading. It is as if Guyon has regressed to the state of mind of one under the Law, as described by Luther, who has forgotten the promise of hope. In seeing things entirely in terms of human mortality and misery, the "dreade of death and dolour" that the angel will tell the Palmer to "doe away" (II.viii.7.7), Guyon shows himself unable to find the consolation of the Gospel. It is in this way that he is again like Augustine's chicken falling out of the nest of faith. A deep anxiety about mortality and innate sinfulness appears when Guyon picks up Mordant's armour with its ambiguous pronoun: "his sad fathers armes with blood defilde" (II.ii.11.3), which very quickly "did him sore disease" (II.ii.12.4). Guyon's deep anxiety sounds an unresolved counter-note to the confident delivery of ethical precepts throughout the early cantos of *Faerie Queene* II.

Calvin's *Commentary on John* 15:4 emphasizes the New Testament injunction to abide in the vine and gives the negative consequences of not doing so, a flitting away out of the nest that is an abandonment of grace.

> *Abide in me.* Hee exhorteth them againe to be desirous & carefull to retaine that grace wherewith they are endowed. For the carelessnesse of our flesh can neuer be sufficiently awaked, And this is Christs only drift to keepe vs under his wings as an hen keepeth her chickins: lest being carried away with our lightnesse, we fly hence to our owne destruction.[28]

Guyon's despair over Ruddymane stands in an odd disjunction to the cheerful advocacy, over the bodies of Mordant and Amavia, by the Palmer and Guyon of the essentially Aristotelian ethical solution of the mean. Here we see the carnality of the Geneva Bible's "walking as men" "by the square and compas of mans wit and iudgement."

> But temperaunce (said he) with golden squire
> Betwixt them both can measure out a meane,
> Neither to melt in pleasures whott desyre,
> Nor frye in hartlesse griefe and dolefull tene.
> *Thrise happy man,* who fares them both atweene.
> (II.i.58.1–5; my emphasis)

The promise of happiness in this confident delivery of precepts also rings theological warning bells and Spenser's tone may be gently mocking in this early, rhythmically jaunty presentation of an apparently straightforward solution to the dilemmas of his book.

In *The City of God* Book XIX Augustine launches a full-frontal attack on systems of classical philosophy as laid out by Varro and by others such as the Stoics, the Old and New Academies, the Peripatetics and all the varied and possible combinations of their thought that place virtue as the highest good in this life. These philosophers, according to Augustine, "attempt to fabricate for themselves *a happiness in this life* based on a virtue which is as deceitful as it is proud" (XIX.4; my emphasis).[29] The deceit lies in their exaltation of virtue. While Augustine has in this later work lost the imagery of covering wings, nests and Neoplatonic return, what remains is the Pauline stress on hope in eternity: "As . . . we are saved, so we are made happy by hope." Temperance is as always a central virtue to Augustine: "that virtue which the Greeks call *sophrosyne*, and we temperance, and which bridles carnal lusts, and prevents them from winning the consent of the spirit to wicked deeds." But this virtue has efficacy only when human behaviour is approached in terms of the City of God, in other words when it has the teleological purpose described earlier.

> The actual possession of the happiness of this life, *without the hope of what is beyond*, is but a false happiness and profound misery. For the true blessings of the soul are not now enjoyed; for that is no true wisdom which does not direct all its prudent observations, manly actions, virtuous self-restraint and just arrangement, to that end in which God shall be all in all in a secure eternity and perfect peace. (XIX.20; my emphasis)

Augustine's surprising conclusion, and one that counters both Guyon's despair over Ruddymane and his overconfident certainty in the ethical promise of the golden mean, is that happiness in the present life is eminently possible for those with "true piety."

> For if these are true virtues—and such cannot exist save in those who have true piety—they do not profess to deliver the men who possess them from all miseries; for true virtues tell no such lies, but they profess that *by the hope of the future world* this life, which is miserably involved in the many and great evils of this world, is happy as it is safe. (XIX.4; my emphasis)

When the soul is properly orientated to God (and here we see a conso-
nance with the definition of temperance cited previously from *De Moribus
Ecclesiae*, "love giving itself entire and incorrupt for God"), then there will
be a just order of nature in the individual "so that the soul is subjected to
God, and the flesh to the soul, and consequently both soul and flesh to
God" (XIX.4).

The ability to see things in terms of the hope of the future life, with spiri-
tual insight (rather than carnally and in material terms), is precisely what
is missing as Guyon approaches the Cave of Mammon and finds himself
travelling "through wide wastfull ground, / That nought but desert wil-
dernesse shewed all around" (II.vii.2.8–9). The spiritual aridity is reminis-
cent of the Augustine who found himself early in the *Confessions* "far from
your unmoved stability. I had become to myself a region of destitution"
(II.x.18). Guyon comforts and feeds himself with his "card and compass"
(II.vii.1.6) and "his owne vertues, and praise-worthie deedes" (II.vii.2.5).
But this cannot be a substitute for the biblical comfort and spiritual safety
directly delivered by Spenser's angel in Canto viii. Guyon, whose very en-
trance into the Cave of Mammon shows he is choosing to see the world
carnally and not spiritually, puts himself at perilous risk of the "dreaded
destiny" (II.viii.9.9) that comes from wandering away from God.

VI. Dread of Death and Dolour Doe Away

I have suggested Spenser's sequence in the first nine stanzas of Canto viii
moves (like Calvin's commentary on Psalm 91:4) from highest God to the
tender action with which the Palmer "courd" the pulse of Guyon. Both
Calvin and Spenser are concerned with human dependency on divine
grace. Spenser's narrator at the opening of Canto viii, himself like an angel
descending to rescue a chicken, intervenes into the allegory with a small
homily of two stanzas that, like a Protestant preacher, gathers up the read-
ers after their journey with Guyon through the Cave of Mammon and re-
turns them to a nest, one where bright squadrons of angels protect wicked
man, watch, ward and fight fowle feends (with an inclusive use of "vs") on
our behalf. This care comes from "th'exceeding grace / Of highest God,
that loues his creatures so, / And all his workes with mercy *doth embrace*"
(II.viii.1.5–7; my emphasis). Here Spenser emphasizes the power of renew-

ing love (as in the picture of Charissa's nest) because angels are sent "all for loue, and nothing for reward" (II.viii.2.8).

This embrace of divine love and compassion, ministered first to the reader, is then extended to the Palmer and Guyon as a message delivered by one "like flying Pursuiuant" (II.viii.2.4), an angelic messenger in the Greek sense of *angelos*. Although the angel promises the return of Guyon's life, he also delivers the central meaning of the Nativity (that according to Luther in his *Preface to the New Testament* lies like the richest treasure at the heart of the Scriptures[30] and in this sense counters the false treasure of the Cave of Mammon), the message of the divine incarnation. This message will be delivered to Arthur in the House of Alma following the battle over Guyon's recumbent form. It is not irrelevant to the connection between Book II and Augustine's interpretation of the Scriptures that the message of the incarnation will then come through an act of reading.

The hope that results from the incarnation does away with "dread of death and dolour" (II.viii.7.7), overcoming despair at the nature of human mortality and its innate miserable sinfulness. The Palmer is "abasht . . . / Through fear and wonder, that he nought could say" (II.viii.7.1–2), like Mary or the shepherds at the angelic annunciation of the New Testament (or as Luther again tells us *Evangelion*, "good tidings"). His hand trembles as he seeks for Guyon's pulse, as one now charged with Guyon's "deare safety" (II.viii.8.2), for this charge of care was laid on the angel by God.

In Book XIII of the *Confessions* Augustine exhorts his flock, citing Paul, not to remain carnally-minded: "[Y]our minister, who generates sons by the gospel and does not wish to have permanently immature believers fed on milk and cherished as if by a nurse says, 'Be renewed in the newness of your mind to prove what is God's will, which is a thing good and well-pleasing and perfect'" (XIII.xxii.[32]). It is the Scriptures that provide the Christian model of continence and temperance, according to Augustine: "[B]y your word through your evangelists the soul achieves self-control by modelling itself on the imitators of your Christ"(XIII.xxi.[31]). As a chicken *"newly* hatcht" (my emphasis) in this Pauline sense of spiritual renewal and always with the proviso that self-sufficiency is never possible (because "under Him the greater, always we be chickens," Augustine tells us in the *Commentary on Psalm 63*), Guyon can now little by little be fledged for the oncoming battles of temperance. These are intrinsically, in Augustinian terms, also a return to God.

In the early *Confessions,* as Augustine describes his quests for alternative sources of truth and rejects the simple language of the Bible for the more elegant language of Cicero he knows something is missing: "[T]he name of Christ was not contained in the book. This name, by your mercy Lord, this name of my Saviour, your Son, my infant heart had piously drunk in with my mother's milk, and at a deep level I had retained the memory" (III. iv.[8]). In the Chronicles of Briton the incarnation of Christ is also rediscovered in Spenser's Legend of Temperance as a "ioyous memorie of happy time" (II.x.50.5)

But instead of being a memory, the winged angel who ministers to Guyon and passes this care to the Palmer brings Christ's protective wings directly into the fallen world of the present, as Spenser indicates with the echo of Matthew 23:37. In the prayer of the covering wings in Book XII of the *Confessions* Augustine describes his fall away from God and his return. "I slipped down into the dark and was plunged into obscurity. Yet from there, even from there I loved you. I erred and I remembered you. I heard your voice behind me calling me to return" (XII.x.10). This is also the voice of "the beauty so old and so new" of Book X: "You called and cried out and shattered my deafness. You were radiant and resplendent, you put to flight my blindness" (X.xxvii.(38)). Augustine's message, which also counters Guyon's despair and Scriptural misreading over Ruddymane, is one of hope.

Guyon faints in a moment of extreme weariness after emerging from the Cave of Mammon. But his Palmer hears "a voyce, that called lowd and cleare, / Come hether, come hether, O come hastily; / That all the fields resounded with the ruefull cry" (II.viii.3.7–9), and then again a "more efforced voyce, / That bad him come in haste" (II.viii.4.3–4). Augustine prays to a merciful God at the opening of Book XIII of the *Confessions*: "[W]hen I forgot you, you did not forget me." Spenser's merciful God who sends angels "all for loue and nothing for reward" (II.viii.2.8) will also "[neither] forgoe, ne yet forgett" (II.viii.8.3) the care of Guyon's life and soul. Through a dangerous combination of despair at the human condition and a presumptuous over-reliance on carnal human ethical formulae the knight has been wandering further and further from the spiritual solutions of Scriptural truth. But "th'exceeding grace / Of Highest God" (II.viii.1.5–6) sends a beautiful winged angel to return the life of a both fallen and "newly hatcht" chicken to a nest and a home that is, in the Pauline terms adopted by Augustine, human and temporal and yet at the same time stable and eternal.

Victoria University of Wellington

NOTES

I would like to thank Anne Lake Prescott for her generous respondent com-
mentary at Kalamazoo 2006, William Oram for his persistence and helpful revi-
sion, and Kathryn Walls for first agreeing that Augustine's Book XII rescuing angel
sounded very like Spenser's.

1.   Edmund Spenser, *The Faerie Queene*, ed. A. C. Hamilton (London: Pearson
Educational, 2001), 224. All subsequent quotations are from this edition.

2.   Hamilton, 226n.

3.   The relevant psalms in the 1587 Psalter are: Psalm 17:8: "Keep me as the apple
of an eie; hide me under the shadow of thy wings; Psalm 36:7: "How excellent is thy
mercie, O God: and the children of men, shall put their trust under the shadow of
thy wings"; Psalm 57:1: "Be mercifull unto me, O God, be mercifull unto me, for
my soule trusteth in thee: and under the shadow of thy wings shall bee my refuge
untill this tyrannie bee ouerpast." Psalm 61:4: "I will dwell in thy tabernacle for euer:
and my trust shall be under the couering of thy wings." Psalm 63:8: "Because thou
hast beene my helper: therefore under the shadow of thy wings will I reioise." Psalm
91:4: "For he shall defend thee under his wings, and thou shalt be safe under his
feathers: his faithfulness and truth shall be thy sheeld and buckler." See *The Psalter
or Psalmes of David after the translation of the great Bible: pointed as it shall be said
or soong in churches. Imprinted at London: by the assigne of William Seres, 1587*. It is
hard to overestimate the familiarity for an Elizabethan readership of phrases heard
regularly as part of the liturgical cycle and permeating much other Christian writing.
Augustine includes biblical quotation in the fabric of his writing by policy, believing
nothing could adequately replace the revealed word of Scripture. There are some dif-
ferences between the Latin translations Augustine worked from and the Bibles of the
Tudor period (see below), and smaller differences between the translations of these
Bibles. I will cite this Psalter unless specifying otherwise.

4.   *Part of the harmony of King Dauids harp. Conteining the first XXI. Psalms of
King Dauid. Briefly & learnedly expounded by the Reverend D. Victorinus Strigelius
Professor of Diuinitie in the Vniuersity of Lypsia in Germanie. Newly translated into
English by Richard Robinson* (London: Iohn Wolfe, 1582). In eebo.chadwyck.com.

5.   I have cited the Geneva Bible translation here as most appropriate for
Calvin's commentary that follows it, but the difference is insignificant.

6.   *The Psalmes of Dauid and others* (London: Thomas East and Henry
Middleton,1571) in eebo.chadwyck.com.

7.   *De Ordine* 1.8.23. The Latin text is: "A quibus enim rebus putas nos orare ut
convertamur ad Deum eiusque faciem videamus, nisi a quodam coeno corporis
atque sordibus et item a tenebris quibus nos error involvit? Aut quid est aliud
converti, nisi ab immoderatione vitiorum, virtute ac temperantia in sese attolli?"
(I was assisted in this and subsequent translations by A. Hubbard.)

8. For further discussion of this imagery see R. J. O'Connell, *St. Augustine's Confessions: The Odyssey of the Soul* (Cambridge: Harvard University Press, 1969), 31–36.

9. H. Chadwick, trans., *Saint Augustine's Confessions* (Oxford: Oxford University Press, 1991). All subsequent references to the *Confessions* in English are to this edition.

10. John Michael Owen, "The Angel of the Great Counsel of God and the Christology of the *Scots Confession* of 1560," *Scottish Journal of Theology* 55:3 (2002): 303–24.

11. "Book 12 is . . . the book of God's words; that is, of scripture; that is of knowledge—for all authentic knowledge comes from divine revelation. The formal pretext for the discussion of Book 12 is the distinction between heaven and earth, which Augustine takes allegorically to represent the differences between spirit and matter—between things as they are and things as they seem. God's knowledge, manifested to us, reveals this distinction. Otherwise we would be caught forever in the world of appearances . . . Revelation is ambivalent and multileveled. The enhancement of human knowledge is thus a constant transition from surface reality to inner knowledge, from letter to spirit, from material appearances to spiritual, inner reality" (J. O'Donnell, *Augustine* [Boston: Twayne, 1985], 117).

12. Harry Berger, *The Allegorical Temper: Vision and Reality in Book II of Spenser's "Faerie Queene"* (New Haven: Yale University Press, 1957), 26. Berger cites E. B. Pusey's translation of the *Confessions*.

13. *De Moribus Ecclesiae*, trans. Richard Stothert. New Advent website, 15.25.

14. Translation from <www.newadvent.org/fathers>.

15. The Latin reads: "quid ergo tunc mihi proderat ingenium per illas doctrinas agile et nullo adminiculo humani magisterii tot nodosissimi libri enodati, cum deformiter et sacrilega turpitudine in doctrina pietatis errarem? aut quid tantum oberat parvulis tuis longe tardius ingenium, cum a te longe non recederent, ut in nido ecclesiae tuae tuti plumescerent et alas caritatis alimento sanae fidei nutrirent?"

16. Hugh MacLachlan. "The Death of Guyon and the *Elizabethan Book of Homilies*," *Spenser Studies* 4 (1983): 91–110.

17. Chadwick, 71. The Latin reads: "o domine deus noster, in velamento alarum tuarum speremus, et protege nos et porta nos. tu portabis et parvulos et usque ad canos tu portabis, quoniam firmitas nostra quando tu es, tunc est firmitas, cum autem nostra est, infirmitas est. vivit apud te semper bonum nostrum, et quia inde aversi sumus, perversi sumus. revertamur iam, domine, ut non evertamur, quia vivit apud te sine ullo defectu bonum nostrum, quod tu ipse es, et non timemus ne non sit quo redeamus, quia nos inde ruimus. Nobis autem absentibus non ruit domus nostra, aeternitas tua."

18. *Exposition on Psalm 91*, 13; my emphasis. Translation from <www.newadvent.org/fathers>.

19. *Exposition on Psalm 91*, 5. It is here that a difference between the Latin and Tudor texts is apparent—Augustine is working with a Latin translation, "He shall

defend thee between His shoulders, and thou shalt hope under his wings," and may have in mind the reference in Exodus when God bore the Israelites away to safety like an eagle. He seems therefore to feel the need to establish whether the weak young Christian is above or below God's shoulders. James O' Donnell cites Knauer's citation of *Epistle*.148.4.13. God's wings are metaphorical to distinguish the divine from merely human limbs and so convey how divine protection is possible. O'Donnell, 2:279.

20. *Confessions*, Chadwick, trans., 214.

21. *De Musica* 6.15.50; my emphasis. The Latin text is: "Sed haec actio qua sese anima, opitulante Deo et Domino suo, ab amore inferioris pulchritudinis extrahit, debellans atque interficiens adversus se militantem consuetudinem suam, ea victoria triumphatura in semetipsa de potestatibus aeris huius, quibus invidentibus et praepedire cupientibus, evolat ad suam stabilitatem et firmamentum Deum; nonne tibi videtur ea esse virtus quae temperantia dicitur?"

22. *Exposition on Psalm 91*, op cit, 5.

23. *De Diversis Quaestionibus* 1.1.7. The Latin text is: "Qui autem nondum est sub gratia sed sub lege ita carnalis est, ut nondum sit renatus a peccato sed venundatus sub peccato, quoniam pretium mortiferae voluptatis amplectitur dulcedinem illam qua fallitur, et delectatur etiam contra legem facere, cum tanto magis libet, quanto minus licet."

24. Carol Kaske's seminal article "Augustinian Psychology in *The Faerie Queene* Book II" (*University of Hartford Studies in Literature* 15:3 (1984): 93–98) shows both the effect of Augustinian negative suggestibility for one under the Law and demonstrates that the Patristic Fathers are a direct source for Spenser. James Schiavone has recently demonstrated Spenser's access to Erasmus's complete and correctly ordered edition of Augustine's works at Pembroke College in Cambridge (*Spenser Studies* 20 [2005]: 271–81).

25. Calvin, *Commentary on 1 Corinthians*, 1. Taken from website <www.ccel. org/c/calvin/comment>.

26. *Tudor Book of Homilies*, op. cit., p 82.

27. Martin Luther, *Commentary on the Epistle to the Galatians* (1535), trans. Theodore Graebner (Grand Rapids: Zondervan, 1949), 200. (Text available on Project Wittenberg website.)

28. Calvin, *A harmonie vpon the three Euangelists, Matthew, Mark and Luke with the commentarie of M Iohn Calvine: faithfully translated out of Latine into English, by E.P. Whereunto is also added a commentarie vpon the Euangelist S. Iohn, by the same authour: London: Thomas Dawson, 1584*. On eebo.chadwyck.

29. W. Benton, ed., *The Confessions, The City of God, On Christian Doctrine.* (Chicago: Encyclopaedia Britannica, 1952), 416. All further references to *The City of God* are to this edition.

30. Martin Luther, *Preface to the Old Testament* (1545), in *A Reformation Reader*, ed. Denis R. Janz (Minneapolis: Fortress Press), 110.

RACHEL EISENDRATH

Art and Objectivity in the House of Busirane

This essay analyzes a sequence of descriptions of art objects
near the end of the 1590 edition of *The Faerie Queene*. In the
first room of the House of Busirane, Britomart encounters a
tapestry that, as the romance's longest ekphrasis, provides an
immersive experience of art. The second room, however, treats
art differently: No longer animated by the viewer's imaginative
involvement, these objects appear to be mere objects, antiquar-
ian refuse from a dead past. I argue that this progression from
immersion to detachment parallels a larger historical develop-
ment in the period toward epistemological objectivity. By em-
bodying imaginative forms in antiquarian objects, Spenser dis-
tances his readers from what he perceives as the imagination's
dangers. But he is ambivalent about the resulting detachment,
as an analysis of his final metaphor of the Roman hermaphro-
dite statue shows. In the end, his highly imaginative poetry de-
pends on the very same interfusion of subject and object that
his poetry also seeks to reject.[1]

FOR FRANCIS BACON, the imagination is a wayward tendency,
like original sin, that must be controlled—not by grace, but by the
application of technique and method. The problem with the imagi-
nation is that it creates grotesque mental amalgams by "mingling" a per-
son's internal nature with the external things he observes in the world.[2] In

Spenser Studies: A Renaissance Poetry Annual, Volume XXVII, Copyright © 2012 AMS
Press, Inc. All rights reserved.   DOI: 10.7756/spst.027.007.133-161

his 1605 *Advancement of Learning*, Bacon compares credulous and super-
stitious man to the mythic Ixion, who brought forth the race of centaurs
and other chimeras by accidentally copulating with a cloud: "So whosoever
shall entertain high and vaporous imaginations, instead of a laborious and
sober inquiry of truth, shall beget hopes and beliefs of strange and impos-
sible shapes."[3] Bacon's language may be saturated with the same imagina-
tive waters from which he claims to be leading his readers;[4] however, de-
spite such implicit complexity, much of today's scholarship presents itself
as continuing to employ the subject-object separation that his work most
overtly promotes. In regard to literary-historical scholarship, for example,
Margreta de Grazia probes in a recent article the shared working under-
standing of anachronism, defining it as "a violation of the basic principle
of epistemology: the viewing subject must remain distinct from the viewed
object. When one collapses into the other, knowledge cannot take place."[5]
Learning is no longer supposed to entail entering into the experience of the
object, but rather holding oneself apart from it. The reign of *pathei mathos*
(Aeschylus's "suffering is knowledge") is over.[6]

The broadscale shift toward modern European epistemological detach-
ment had already been manifesting in the formal tensions of sixteenth-cen-
tury literature before Bacon overtly expressed objectivity as a systemized
procedure and ideal. It may only be in retrospect that the world seems to
go where a "new" idea like Bacon's points; more often, according to Ernst
Kantorowicz, people have accepted only those doctrines that "confirmed and
justified what one thought or did anyhow. . . ."[7] Intellectual history is, truly,
no smoothly turning machine, but a squeaking, lurching, wonky concatena-
tion. In this essay, I explore how the unsteady movement toward objectiv-
ity appears in one set of images near the end of Spenser's 1590 *The Faerie
Queene*. It is my argument that Spenser's poetry in these aesthetically height-
ened episodes participates in the complex and contradictory historical pro-
cesses ultimately associated with the early modern rise of objectivity.

The current moment of literary-historical Renaissance scholarship, with
its predominant focus on the synchronic richness of the period, has tended
to downplay diachronic intellectual history. I argue that the formal ten-
sions in Spenser's poetry can be more fully understood by studying not
only their relations with aspects of the period's culture, but also with long-
term developments, especially in regard to understandings about the dan-
gers of imaginative immersion and the need for detachment. More specifi-
cally, I examine the emergence of objectivity in Spenser's treatment of art
in the House of Busirane. In the first room of this occult house, Britomart

encounters a tapestry depicting the Ovidian metamorphoses of the gods. This tapestry, the longest ekphrasis in *The Faerie Queene*, draws the viewer into Spenser's immersive poetics. The second room, though, is different: the artworks on this room's walls are minimally described so that they no longer elicit the involvement of the viewer's imagination. The art objects seem more like mere objects, antiquarian artifacts from a dead past. I will argue that this shift from the first room to the second corresponds to a historical process of subject-object differentiation, even as Spenser's highly imaginative poetics in these passages also resists this process.

To immerse oneself in Spenser's elaborate tapestry in the first room of the House of Busirane is to enter a world where everything is shifting around in a single, continuous, protean medium. The tapestry depicts the highly varied, often bestial forms the pagan gods adopted in order to gratify their lusts for mortals:

> Therein was writt, how often thondring *Ioue*
> Had felt the point of his hart percing dart,
> And leauing heauens kingdome, here did roue
> In straunge disguize, to slake his scalding smart;
> Now like a Ram, faire *Helle* to peruart,
> Now like a Bull, *Europa* to withdraw:
> Ah, how the fearefull Ladies tender hart
> Did liuely seeme to tremble, when she saw
> The huge seas vnder her t'obay her seruaunts law.
> (III.xi.30)[8]

In this ekphrasis, which draws on Ovid's ekphrasis of Arachne's tapestry in the *Metamorphoses* Book VI, nothing preserves its own autonomy: people, things, and gods morph into and out of one another. This is a world of mutual interpenetration on many levels. The sea moves by the pulse of Jove, whom we also see metamorphosing into a ram and a bull. Fear makes Europa's heart move in a kind of correspondence with the movement of the sea, and the sea's heaving seems both like a subjective account of the disorienting experience of her terror and an objective account of what causes her terror. Spenser melds subjects with objects by creating reciprocal formal relationships between inner states of feeling and external actions of things.[9]

Spenser calls into question the amorphous subject-object interplay of this tapestry's poetics most obviously by setting it within the House of Busirane, a place of dark magic and destructive sexuality. But the poetry of the tapestry itself is insidious, especially in the way that it blurs the boundaries between things:

> Wouen with gold and silke so close and nere,
> That the rich metall lurked priuily,
> As faining to be hidd from enuious eye;
> Yet here, and there, and euery where vnwares
> It shewd it selfe, and shone vnwillingly;
> Like to a discolourd Snake, whose hidden snares
> Through the greene gras his long bright burnisht back declares.
>
>   (III.xi.28)

Subjective and objective meanings fold very tightly around one another. The adverbs expressing privation, "vnwares" and "vnwillingly," link the viewer's subjective experience with an imaginative version of the *material*'s subjective experience: "euery where vnwares[10] / It shewd it selfe, and shone vnwillingly." It is as if the viewer's surprise at what she sees is projected into the work, so that it seems that the work is what lacks awareness—it shines "vnwillingly"—which is also a realization of the objective fact: the work does, of course, shine unwillingly. But then this negation immediately implies the reverse, for to say that the material shines unwillingly is also, paradoxically, to suggest that this object has a will or subjectivity. Spenser's language presupposes animistic magic at the very moment he denies it. And he implicitly questions—even demonizes—this magic's seductive effect by, in his long sinuous last line, likening the way the gold moves in and out of the tapestry's weave to the way a snake moves in and out of the grass.

   Just as the metamorphosing gods seduce mortals, so, too, can art seduce its viewers. Through the verisimilitude of its representations, the poetry ensnares the subject in the object and obviates their distance. In describing Jove's transformation into an eagle and his abduction of Ganymede from Mount Ida, for example, Spenser considers the shepherds looking at the rape, who inevitably reflect the audience looking at the tapestry:

> Wondrous delight it was, there to behould,
> How the rude Shepheards after him did stare,
> Trembling through feare, least down he fallen should
> And often to him calling, to take surer hould.
>
>   (III.xi.34)

Through this doubling of onlookers, the text sets up a mirror by which the spectator of the tapestry finds her activity of looking represented within the tapestry. We stare, just as the shepherds stare, and the idea is that we become so drawn into the picture that we seem to hear the shepherds' voices as they call to Ganymede from down below. As an artwork within an artwork, this elaborate ekphrasis is a *mise en abyme* that reflects back on the imaginative or subjectively immersive experience of Spenser's own poetics. However, Spenser makes problematic such effects of illusionist art at the same time as he uses them.

In Spenser's lines, the similarity between the gazes of the audience and the shepherds reveals a difference: our ecstatic pleasure as spectators of the tapestry contrasts with the shepherds' genuine concern for the boy. They want Ganymede to hold on more tightly so that he does not fall. Implicit in this contrast between our "wondrous delight" in the artistic image and their concern for what will happen is Augustine's moral criticism of mimetic art in the *Confessions*, where he complains that it encourages us hedonistically to enjoy the spectacle of other people's suffering rather than do anything about it.[11] In Spenser's critical rendering of this tapestry, boys and girls are raped, yet we are enraptured.[12]

As spectators of this aesthetically-animated ("liuely") tapestry, we are drawn into its moral corruption—and, in being so drawn, our faculties of judgment are suspended. The ekphrasis concludes: "So liuely and so like, that liuing sence it fayld" (III.xi.46).[13] The object's apparent liveliness has been mistaken for the viewer's real liveliness, and her powers are thereby deposed.

Britomart herself seems not to exist for this part of the poem; the experience of looking is expressed in an impersonal form that denies the looker any specific identity—"Wondrous delight *it was*, there to behould. . ."—as if Britomart has forgotten herself and disappeared into the world of the tapestry's images.[14] Spenser refers to Britomart again only later in the scene, in the description of Cupid's statue, in front of which she appears in an altered condition without self-possession:

> That wondrous sight faire *Britomart* amazd,
> Ne seeing could her wonder satisfie,
> But euermore and more vpon it gazd,
> The whiles the passing brightnes her fraile sences dazd.
> (III.xi.49)

In the first line quoted above, the grammatical subject is the "wondrous sight," which acts on Britomart. In the second line, the agent of action becomes "seeing," and, oddly enough, it is this seeing that is doing the gazing in the third line. Britomart's own agency has been peculiarly circumvented.[15]

Spenser's critical exploration of fused subjects and objects evokes what Ernst Cassirer once called, in paradigmatic terms, "the subject-object problem" of Renaissance thought. Students of the Renaissance will recall that Cassirer described how, for European thinkers of the fifteenth and sixteenth centuries, the world began to take on a "strong, strictly 'objective' character" evident in a newly emergent methodology of empirical investigation.[16] This methodology developed among European intellectuals working in a wide variety of fields that included, perhaps surprisingly, the study of magic.[17] While important work has been done on Spenser's treatment of art in the House of Busirane in terms of mostly Protestant anxieties about idolatry,[18] my focus will be on the aesthetic impact of this broader European epistemological development.

Part of the tapestry's deceptiveness specifically concerns its relation to its own expensive materiality. Although the costly "gold and silke" wish or pretend to want not to be seen—"As faining to be hidd from enuious eye" (III.xi.28)—Spenser exposes this apparent lack of concern as one of the tapestry's almost coquettish techniques of seduction. Indeed, tapestries made with gold-wrapped silk were, in this period, specifically associated with the display of wealth—so expensive that hardly anyone but royalty could own them in any number.[19] Edward Hall, who witnessed Henry VIII's displays, writes of the "riche and marveilous clothes of Arras wroughte of golde and silke, compassed of many auncient stories, with which . . . every wall and chamber were hanged, and all wyndowes so richely covered, that it passed all other sightes before seen."[20] The moral message of some tapestries' images, such as of the one depicting the sin of avarice in the series known as the *Triumphs of the Virtues over the Vices*, does not appear to have been as compelling as the expense of the object. Hall relates in copious detail the extravagant decorations accompanying one masque in which was debated whether love or riches is better; afterwards, the "hanginges and all other thinges" were left standing for three or four days so that "al honest persones might see and beholde the houses and riches, and thether came a great nombre of people, to see and behold the riches and costely devices."[21] If such tapestries were praised for their verisimilitude,[22] Spenser suggests that the illusion of lifelikeness does not really make anyone forget the expense of the material object.

In contrast to Poliziano, who, in a closely-related Ovidian ekphrasis, celebrates the power of illusionist art to seem alive or real,[23] Spenser is a more anxious guest in the house of the imagination, and can be heard pacing back and forth as he employs its image-making capacities at the same time as he criticizes them.

The development of objectivity is already perceptible arising from within Spenser's critical representation of this enchanting tapestry. For Spenser, illusion entails a loss of critical distance from the object; the subject loses herself in what simply seems real. In contrast to this experience of immersion, a more logical or scientific mode of thought posits "a mental space," as Aby Warburg puts it, between internal and external worlds.[24] This "mental space" fully structures the treatment of art only in the second room, where subjects no longer cavort with objects in a dangerous and unlawful realm of imaginative interplay, but stand apart from them and observe them from a position of detachment.

TRODDEN IN DUST: GROTESQUES AND THINGS IN THE SECOND ROOM

Whereas the tapestry in the first room conveys the sexual escapades of the gods in the fullness of nearly twenty ekphrastic stanzas, the art in the second room has suddenly become less vivid. The "passing brightnes" (III.xi.49) that dazzles Britomart's frail senses in the first room has, for the most part, passed. The second room is as bright as the first—objectively, it is even brighter (all overlaid with gold, the second room is "much fayrer" [III.xi.51])—but the objects seem to have receded into the status of artifacts. Instead of a long description of the sexual metamorphoses depicted in the tapestry, the reader gets only brief allusions to the subject matter of the paintings and to the types of old weapons on the walls.

The second room's artworks and things do not seem animated, the way the first room's tapestry did. Spenser has shifted into a mode of objectifying detachment:

> Much fayrer, then the former, was that roome,
> And richlier by many partes arayd:
> For not with arras made in painefull loome,
> But with pure gold it all was ouerlayd,

Wrought with wilde Antickes, which their follies playd,
In the rich metall, as they liuing were:
A thousand monstrous formes therein were made,
Such as false loue doth oft vpon him weare,
For loue in thousand monstrous formes doth oft appeare.

And all about, the glistring walles were hong
With warlike spoiles, and with victorious prayes,
Of mightie Conquerours and Captaines strong,
Which were whilome captiued in their dayes,
To cruell loue, and wrought their owne decayes:
Their swerds and speres were broke, and hauberques rent
And their proud girlonds of tryumphant bayes,
Troden in dust with fury insolent,
To shew the victors might and mercilesse intent.

The warlike Mayd beholding earnestly
The goodly ordinaunce of this rich Place,
Did greatly wonder, ne could satisfy
Her greedy eyes with gazing a long space,
But more she meruaild that no footings trace,
Nor wight appear'd, but wastefull emptinesse,
And solemne silence ouer all that place:
Straunge thing it seem'd, that none was to possesse
So rich purueyaunce, ne them keepe with carefulnesse.
                                                (III.xi.51–53)

The actual description of the artwork and objects is immediately subordinated to the overall richness of the room—the word "rich" is used four times in the space of two stanzas (stanzas 51 and 53). And the space for whatever Ovidian amorphous mingling there may be is shut down by being quickly and neatly allegorized: "A thousand monstrous formes therein were made, / Such as false loue doth oft vpon him weare, / For loue in thousand monstrous formes doth oft appeare." None of these thousand forms is named; in fact, they are kept sealed in Spenser's self-enclosed, chiastic lines (thousand monstrous forms : love :: love : thousand monstrous forms). These lines might remind the reader both of the "thousand shapes" in which Cupid disguises himself (III.vi.11), or the "thousand thoughts" that Britomart has of her future lover (III.iv.5). Yet Spenser leaves entirely undeveloped these connections, which could provide the ground for the subject's involvement in the object; in doing so, the lines seem to close down the possibility of that entwinement, rather than actualize it in any way.

I noted earlier that Britomart's agency in looking at the things in the first room was peculiarly eclipsed: Spenser constructed the lines so that the wondrous sight acted on her. However, here in the second room, objects no longer seem like subjects, and subjects no longer like objects. No less fascinated by what she sees, Britomart is the active grammatical subject who is "beholding earnestly" (III.xi.53).

The paintings seem like objects partly because Spenser has made them continuous, in the second stanza quoted above, with the "warlike spoiles" displayed on the same wall—a possible reference to the Roman practice of hanging the arms of defeated men in the Temple of Jupiter.[25] In Leonard Barkan's language, spoils are "alienated" from their cultural context,[26] quite literally stripped (*spolium* originally meant skin stripped from an animal). Barkan shows that Roman collections of spoils, both as displayed at the time in triumphal processions and as then found in the Renaissance represented on monuments, often appeared randomly heaped and torn from context.[27] The point is that these objects, in being plundered, are deprived of their interiority or culturally accrued meaning: they are now understood in terms of their material value as gold. Conquering involves desecrating a culture's things—which means, in a sense, making things of its things, as well as of its people. In this context, Barkan's note is especially helpful that the term *spolia* was used not only in the ancient Roman context, but also commonly in the Middle Ages and Renaissance to describe pagan art used as material for Christian buildings when marble was in high demand.[28]

In Spenser's sixteenth-century English context, the dissolution of the monasteries produced a new experience of spoliation, comparable to that described in the pages of Livy and Josephus, and this experience gave rise to a corresponding interest in historical reconstruction. Keith Thomas writes with characteristic vividness of the Reformation's impact on the lives of ordinary people: "Altar-stones were turned into paving stones, bridges, fireplaces, or even kitchen sinks. Dean Whittingham of Durham used two ex-holy-water stoups for salting beef and fish in his kitchen, and his wife burned St Cuthbert's banner."[29] This disturbing experience of sudden cultural desacralization evoked nostalgia and galvanized a desire on a new scale for antiquarian conservation.[30] Having witnessed buildings and living traditions become ruins seemingly overnight, England had established by the late 1580s the

Elizabethan Society of Antiquaries, which counted William Camden, Sir
Robert Cotton, and John Stow among its members, and with which Spenser
was well familiar.[31] At the same time, the experience of this loss, as Margaret
Aston puts it, "reached out beyond the work of antiquarians and historical
researchers into more indefinable areas of literary consciousness."[32]

For Britomart, what's especially mysterious is the fact that the room
seems to have been abandoned: the poem emphasizes the place's "solemne
silence," "wastefull emptinesse," and the absence of any "footings trace."
The room seems like an archeological site requiring decipherment: the
weapons are from the past; their original users are nameless; the material's
value is impressive; no one is around; things are dusty; it is not clear who
owns the place.

If this second room seems like an archeological site, that is because it is
based, at least partly, on an archeological site—on the rediscovered Domus
Aurea, Nero's Golden House.[33] Barkan notes this connection—and remarks
on the pun: the "wilde Antickes" referred to in stanza 51 ("Wrought with
wilde Antickes, which their follies playd, / In the rich metall, as they liuing
were") are antic figures with a specifically antique origin: "a quite particular
set of antique antics," Barkan writes.[34] Before Nero's palace was completely
unearthed, a generation of painters had descended on ropes to study by
candlelight these painted grotesques[35] (the word grotesque derives from
the erroneous belief that these buried rooms were grottos), which were the
best-preserved ancient paintings yet found.[36]

In order to understand Spenser's reference to the grotesques in this sec-
ond room, and their significance for the process of objectification repre-
sented in *The Faerie Queene*, we need to try to recover their culturally-
accrued meaning—and, in this way, to reverse their spoliation. To do so
is to try to develop knowledge about these figures, but not to obviate our
distance from them or re-animate them magically. Historicist scholarship
cannot but preserve, it seems, epistemological detachment.

Following the discovery of the Domus Aurea at the end of the fifteenth
century, grotesques started to generate a great deal of excitement. Raphael
and his circle decorated the Vatican's loggia with colorful, flowing, fanciful
grotesques. The influence of the grotesques increased outside Italy after the
sack of Rome in 1527, an event which dispersed Raphael's pupils into the "di-
aspora" of Europe.[37] In England, some walls of Henry VIII's Nonsuch Palace
seem to have been decorated with grotesques by Italian artists,[38] and, most
importantly, grotesques were integral to many designs of Henry VIII's mas-
sive tapestry collection. In 1542, the king acquired a duplicate set of the series

Grotesques of Leo X, inspired by the Domus Aurea and based on Raphael-school cartoons probably by Giovanni da Udine.[39] And Italy was not the only source: The pseudo-Rabelaisian *Songes drolatiques de Pantagruel* (Paris, 1565), with its pages filled with woodcuts of wonderfully bizarre grotesque figures, was also in circulation. Before Inigo Jones used these figures as the basis for costumes in the 1640 masque *Salmacida Spolia,*[40] they had appeared in 1581 ceiling decorations in Prestongrange in East Lothian.[41] Also important was Netherlandish work: Jacob Floris's grotesque cartouches directly influenced Christopher Saxton's English maps beginning in 1576;[42] and Jan Vredeman de Vries's architectural treatises of the 1560s and 1570s, with prints showing grotesque architectural details, were well-known in England.[43]

A critical conversation about the grotesques became especially intense during the forty years immediately preceding the first edition of *The Faerie Queene.*[44] It is hard, if not impossible, to know exactly how closely Spenser followed this debate, but his usage of the grotesques, as we'll see, draws on this intellectual history.

Grotesques were intimately linked with the imagination. David Summers has called them fantasy's "symbol,"[45] and Dacos says that grotesques and the imagination were in some contexts "almost synonymous."[46] Even outside artistic circles, it is not unusual to find Renaissance depictions of the imagination that sound like descriptions of grotesques. For example, in his *De anima et vita* of 1538, Juan Luis Vives describes the imagination as "prodigiously unrestrained and free; it can form, reform, combine, link together and separate; it can blend together the most distant objects or keep apart the most intimately connected objects."[47] In England, Timothy Bright writes in his 1586 *A Treatise of Melancholy* that the imagination, swayed by melancholy, "compoundeth, and forgeth disguised shapes."[48] Especially important is the composite nature of the imagination's means of production; that is, it makes new forms by putting together parts of things and animals found in the world.

These associations were equally strong among those who revived the use of the grotesques as among those who were adamantly *against* their use: Gregorio Comanini defines the grotesque as an "image of an imaginary thing, something that existed only in the mind," which, following I Corinthians 8:4, he equates with an idol [*idolo*], "nothing that exists in this world."[49] But the rejection of the grotesques on such a basis also predates Christianity. Comanini is drawing on the ancient authority of Vitruvius, who questions and explicitly condemns grotesques in Book VII of *De architectura* for their lack of fidelity to the real:

How is it possible for a reed to support a roof, or a candelabrum to
bear a house with the ornaments on its roof, or a small and pliant
stalk to carry a sitting figure; or, that half-figures and flowers at the
same time should spring out of roots and stalks? And yet the public,
so far from discouraging these falsehoods, are delighted with them,
not for a moment considering whether such things could exist.[50]

As the only surviving ancient critical manual on architecture and sculp-
ture, such a condemnation holds enormous authority in the Renaissance.
Further, Vitruvius's position seems to be supported by the negative refer-
ence to a grotesque in the opening of Horace's so-called *Ars poetica*, which
proves no less programmatic for Renaissance readers.[51]

In this way, grotesques become an arena for a longstanding argument
about the imaginative basis of art. Renaissance writers stress the gro-
tesques' unsettlingly ambiguous relationship with external reality. Anton
Francesco Doni determines in a 1549 dialogue on art that they exist only
"in the chaos of my mind."[52] And Daniele Barbaro first compares them to a
person's dreams—and then, as though to position them even farther from
reality, to the painting's dreams:

They are like animals which carry Time, columns of straws, claws
of monsters, deformities of natures, mixtures of varied species:
Certainly, as the Fantasy in the dream represents to us confusedly the
images of things and often puts together diverse natures, things that,
we could say, would make the Grotesques, which without doubt we
could name "the dreams of the painting."[53]

While expressing disapproval of grotesques, Barbaro's language seems,
almost despite itself, to toy with their fecundity and strangeness; his line
mimetically does for a moment what the grotesques do: through the
paratactic string of its first five clauses, the sentence engenders a line of
fantasy-beings that follow each other according to no order, or according
only to the anarchic creative order of more.

Grotesques represent what logic pushes to the margins. Like the gi-
gantomachia that decorates the outer wall of the temple of wisdom at
Pergamon, the grotesques serve as the counter-principle to the rational-
ity celebrated in the center. For certain Renaissance artists, they are a fe-
cund middle ground, "an intermediate world," as Leo Spitzer describes
Rabelais's poetic, "between reality and irreality, between the nowhere that

frightens and the 'here' that reassures."[54] So unstable are these figures that Renaissance thinkers seem to hesitate even to determine a name for them: some call them *chimere, grottesche,* or *mostri.*[55] Spenser, perhaps emphasizing their historicity, calls them *Antickes*—from *antico grottesco.*[56]

Historicizing the Imagination

If, for sixteenth-century Renaissance artists and writers, grotesque figures represent the imagination's ambiguous relation with the world, so, too, do they for Spenser—but with, for him, a distinctly negative valence. In the House of Alma, there is a room where sits, among the buzzing flies, *Phantastes,* an unappealing character who is described as beetle-browed, beady-eyed, melancholy, mad, and foolish. As David Evett has pointed out, *Phantastes's* room is decorated with grotesques,[57] or, at the very least, is heavily associated with grotesques:

> His chamber was dispainted all with in,
> With sondry colours, in the which were writ
> Infinite shapes of thinges dispersed thin;
> Some such as in the world were neuer yit,
> Ne can deuized be of mortall wit;
> Some daily seene, and knowen by their names,
> Such as in idle fantasies doe flit:
> Infernall Hags, *Centaurs,* feendes, *Hippodames,*
> Apes, Lyons, Aegles, Owles, fooles, louers, children, Dames.
> (II.ix.50)

In fantasy's chamber, Spenser distinguishes between two categories of images. Some images are of things which have never existed and cannot by a mortal mind be described or possibly contrived (in *The Faerie Queene,* the word "deuized" carries both meanings). And there are some that are regularly seen since they flit as "idle fantasies" and have names. The list that follows is a confusing amalgam that mixes the unreal with the real, and, as Hamilton suggests, the use of asyndeton creates the impression, at least upon first reading, that all the figures are connected with one another: the lyons almost combine with the aegles, he says, to make a griffin. With *Hippodames*, Spenser even offers his own version of the mixed objects he describes. Hamilton suggests that it is a variant spelling of hippopotamus, sometimes spelled *hippotame*; however, I suspect that, while punning on *hippotame*, Spenser is actually creating a female version of the centaur mentioned just before (from the Greek *hippos* = horse + *dames*). Like Barbaro, Spenser seems to be creating in this passage his own paratactic line of strange beings, some that seem monstrous in and of themselves, and others that become monstrous when linked together without reason in his long list.

Spenser's portrait of *Phantastes* may offer an oblique glimpse of himself as the poet. In *The Defense of Poesy*, Sir Philip Sidney had portrayed poets in similar terms, depicting them "making things either better than Nature bringeth forth, or, quite anew, forms such as never were in Nature, as the Heroes, Demigods, Cyclops, Chimeras, Furies, and such like. . . ."[58] However, the inventiveness that Sidney celebrated Spenser endows with an ambiguous if not out-and-out negative quality. In this respect, Spenser's use of grotesques seems closer to Michel de Montaigne's description of his own tortured mental fecundity. Retiring to his family estate in the early 1570s, Montaigne finds that his mind "gives birth to so many chimeras and fantastic monsters, one on top of another, without order and without aim [. . . m'enfante tant de chimeres et monstres fantasques les uns sur les autres, sans ordre et sans propos. . . .]" that he decides to record in writing this clambering riotous nothingness, "hoping in time to make my mind ashamed of itself [esperant avec le temps luy en faire honte à luy mesmes]."[59]

Like Montaigne,[60] Spenser associates the literary imagination with grotesque paintings. But, in Spenser's case, the paintings on the walls of *Phantastes*'s chamber are of a particular kind: Spenser explicitly mentions the "sondry colours" and the "Infinite shapes of thinges dispersed thin." These qualities may refer specifically to the vibrant, flowing paintings found in the Domus Aurea. Previous to this discovery, Renaissance artists had to rely largely on recovered sculptures for their understanding of ancient art. Painterly qualities of color and brush handling were matters for speculation, tantalizingly alluded to in incomplete and sometimes contradictory ancient verbal descriptions of the work of such "immortal" painters as Apelles, of whom nothing survives.[61] In this situation, it is hard to overestimate the importance of the Domus Aurea, as Hetty Joyce explains: "The discovery of ancient relics was of course no novelty. But in place of the stained, abraded, monochrome surfaces of old marbles, artists could see here [in the Domus Aurea] the fresh, vivid, and abundant revelation of the ancient artistic consciousness. Here, at last, was ancient Rome *in color.*"[62] This color was soon registered in the more polychromatic, looser grotesques of certain Renaissance painters, such as Pinturicchio.[63]

The possible association of the colorful paintings in the Domus Aurea with the multicolored paintings on the walls of *Phantastes*'s chamber is important because one of the ways that Spenser detaches his reader from the imagination is by historicizing its symbol, as we'll see below. He thereby pushes this symbol into the past as an antiquarian object from which the spectator can, by the end of Book III, claim an objective distance.

Antiquarianism was linked in this period with the rise of objectivity. H. J. Erasmus explains that as attention shifted from the literary form of history to the events and institutions that such histories describe, history started to become, in the language of Mark Pattison, "the object of science."[64] Like scientists, sixteenth-century antiquarians needed to remain detached from what they studied in order to aspire to, in Lorraine Daston and Peter Galison's words, "the viewpoint of angels,"[65] or, as the title of Thomas Nagel's book trenchantly describes the objective perspective, *The View from Nowhere.*[66] The strength of this shift is evident in the monumental works of antiquarian study that were appearing at this time by such humanists as Onofrio Panvinio and Carolus Sigonius.

It is known that Spenser is deeply familiar with antiquarian methods of inquiry and even committed to them. In "The Ruines of Time," Spenser praises the antiquarian William Camden, "the nourice of antiquitie" (169), for rescuing from oblivion the old Roman settlement of Verulam, and Spenser uses Camden's *Britannia* as a direct source for this poem.[67] But Spenser was also aware that antiquarianism could conflict with poetry. In his *A Vewe of the Present State of Ireland*, Eudoxus and Irenaeus discuss the problem of extracting historical truth from the accounts of Irish bards:

Eudox. You doe very boldly Iren. adventure upon the histories of auncient times, and leane too confidently on those Irish Chronicles which are most fabulous and forged, in that out of them you dare take in hand to lay open the originall of such a nation so antique, as that no monument remaines of her beginning and first inhabiting; especially having been in those times without letters, but only bare traditions of times and remembrances of Bardes, which use to forge and falsifie every thing as they list, to please or displease any man.

Iren. Truly, I must confess I doe so, but yet not so absolutely as you sup-
pose. I do herein rely upon those Bardes or Irish Chroniclers, though
the Irish themselves through their ignorance in matters of learning and
deepe judgement, doe most constantly beleeve and avouch them, but
unto them besides I adde mine own reading; and out of them both
together, with comparison of times, likewise of manners and customes,
affinity of words and names, properties of natures, and uses, resem-
blances of rites and ceremonies, monuments of churches and tombes,
and many other like circumstances, I doe gather a likelihood of truth,
not certainly affirming anything, but by conferring of times, language,
monuments, and such like, I doe hunt out a probability of things, which
I leave to your judgment to believe or refuse.[68]

Bart van Es describes the historiographical interest of this passage as
Spenser's "defense of antiquarian practice": It is through Irenius, van Es
says, that "Spenser channels his knowledge of, and enthusiasm for, anti-
quarian research."[69] What's important for my purposes to note is the way in
which this expression of Spenser's antiquarian commitments also articu-
lates a tension with imaginative poetry. Spenser sounds like a conventional
detractor of poetry, like Stephen Gosson for example,[70] when he says of the
bards that they "use to forge and falsifie every thing as they list, to please
or displease any man."[71]

In the second room of the House of Busirane, Spenser makes historical
objects of the grotesque figures, which represent the imagination. In so do-
ing, he objectifies the imagination and detaches the viewer from its spell.
The viewer, disengaged, detached, no longer participates in the mimetic
fantasy that is represented. The artwork has lost any dialectical relation-
ship with its own condition as an object, and has become instead *simply* an
object—one more thing in a world of things. Britomart, adopting a stance
that Jeff Dolven calls one of "exemplary detachment,"[72] is made to see the
artworks for the things that they are, but in being so perceived, they be-
come less like artworks, and more like artifacts.

What's most striking in the second room of the House of Busirane is
the sense of hiatus, of caesura, of aporia. Here is the poetry of the *un*-
filled: "ne could satisfy," "a long space," "no footings trace," "Nor wight
appear'd," "wastefull emptinesse," "solemne silence," "none was to pos-
sesse." Rather than describing the grotesques, or listing their forms, or in
some manner engaging us in their varied play of images (for example, by
recreating a version of the grotesque in language, as in Book II's House

of Alma, as well as in Barbaro's condemnation), Spenser objectifies them
as historical artifacts in a room that has all the stillness, desolation, and
uncertainty of an archeological site heaped with spoliated fragments.
Artworks no longer represent intersubjective imaginative worlds, but,
instead, decayed artifacts.

HALFE ENUYING THEIR BLESSE: ON HERMAPHRODITES

Near the end of the 1590 edition, *The Faerie Queene* provides an image
that, I will argue, uniquely crystallizes the poem's dynamic relation to the
process of epistemological detachment that I have been considering.
Immediately after the scene I have focused on, Britomart endures the
ultimate display of enargeic art, Busirane's sadistic masque of love, and
survives the test unfazed: "Nether of ydle showes, nor of false charmes
aghast" (III.xii.29). She progresses into the next room, unchains Amoret,
and forces Busirane to undo his spell. Finally, she emerges from the now
disenchanted house, where the rich display has vanished (III.xii.42), and
she observes the joyful reunion of Amoret and Scudamour:

> Lightly he clipt her twixt his armes twaine,
> And streightly did embrace her body bright,
> Her body, late the prison of sad paine,
> Now the sweet lodge of loue and deare delight:
> But she faire Lady ouercommen quight
> Of huge affection, did in pleasure melt,
> And in sweete rauishment pour out her spright:
> No word they spake, nor earthly thing they felt,
> But like two senceles stocks in long embracement dwelt.
> (III.xii.45)

In the lovers' happiness, mutual physicality, escape from linguistic media-
tion ("No word they spake"), Amoret and Scudamour seem to have re-
turned to a golden state intimate with nature. Spenser in fact compares the
loving couple to entwined branches of a tree, "two senceles stocks."[73] Yet,
the addition of "senceles" implies that a distanced perspective—if not an
outright criticism—is already imposed on the pair.

And just as in the first and second rooms of the House of Busirane, where Spenser juxtaposed subjective modes of perception with historically objectified things, the poet immediately answers this image of amorphous emotional melding with a very different kind of image in the stanza that follows:

> Had ye them seene, ye would haue surely thought,
> That they had beene that faire *Hermaphrodite*,
> Which that rich *Romane* of white marble wrought,
> And in his costly Bath causd to bee site:
> So seemd those two, as growne together quite,
> That *Britomart* halfe enuying their blesse,
> Was much empassiond in her gentle sprite,
> And to her selfe oft wisht like happinesse,
> In vaine she wisht, that fate n'ould let her yet possesse.
> (III.xii.46)

The lovers are now compared to a hermaphrodite, but not simply a hermaphrodite. They are compared, strangely, to a Roman statue of a hermaphrodite[74]—and, I would like to emphasize, one that has a pseudo-antiquarian quality. Spenser describes this statue (as he did Arthur's sword[75]), as if it were a real object that could be found somewhere, out there, in the world—that is, an object with an objective status: "*that* faire Hermaphrodite / Which *that* rich Romane of white marble wrought / And in his costly Bath causd to bee site" [my italics]. Like those grotesques found in the Baths of Titus (or what was believed to be the Baths of Titus, but was really Nero's Domus Aurea[76]), this statue of the hermaphrodite is an archeological object depicted in situ near a Roman bath. And, as in the second room, this antiquarian or historically objectified quality of the object distances Britomart from what she sees. The ecstasy of the lovers' embrace, which is associated first with happy primitivism through the reference to nature, is registered but then immediately pushed off to a distance with the metaphor of the Roman statue of the grotesque-like hermaphrodite.

The hermaphrodite metaphor suggests an erotic union of self with other, in opposition to a stance of detachment, and the metaphor does so by associating this union with an object that is explicitly from the deep past. In fusing a man and a woman, the hermaphrodite becomes a composite figure not unlike a grotesque. Spenser's hermaphrodite is, in fact, more grotesque-like than real Roman statues of hermaphrodites, which, as Donald Cheney has pointed out, were not of two people melding into one another but of one bisexual individual.[77] The threat Spenser's hermaphrodite image poses is of the self's loss of differentiation from the world. It is certainly true that the hermaphrodite serves as an emblem of Christian marriage,[78] but Spenser brings out also the figure's association with older forms of thought by emphasizing the hermaphrodite's ancient origins. The image's ambiguous power belongs to the dual way it is both a rejected thing (the archaic) and an object of longing (the erotic).[79]

The unreconciled dual quality of the hermaphrodite metaphor is brought to the surface through Britomart's "*halfe* enuying their blesse." While retaining a sense of her distance, Britomart also imagines herself participating in the couple's happiness. By employing an image of forms that lack separation (the embracing couple) to describe a position of separation (Britomart standing apart), the poem articulates for the reader an emergent historicized distance against a kind of prehistorical memory of undifferentiated union with the other in nature. Britomart desires the lovers' condition, at the same time that she expresses her sense of difference from this condition. This scene of Britomart looking at these embracing figures is, ultimately, an image of the tension of intellectual separation: it concretizes the conflictual process by which early modern consciousness defines itself in relation to that which it is in the process of renouncing.

Spenser has specifically marked this scene as important for our understanding of the poem as a whole by using an ekphrastic convention to refer to the audience: "Had ye them seene, ye would haue surely thought. . . ."[80]—thus framing the scene with a meta-textual resonance (as he did in the earlier ekphrasis of the tapestry, referring to what "ye mote haue liuely seene" [III.xi.37]). In her role as spectator, Britomart becomes, to use Lauren Silberman's words, "the reader's surrogate as an onlooker."[81] Britomart's ambivalent longing for that from which she is distanced speaks to the poem's conflicted relation to the historical process of detachment it has absorbed.

Whatever the sadness involved, poetry may ultimately entail such betrayal of its own imaginative worlds: For James Nohrnberg, "it is precisely some capacity to betray, or qualify, or call into question its own mode of existence, that characterizes fictionality in literature."[82] This betrayal of the imagination is not the end of poetry, but integral to its motivating process. Focusing on the unit of the poetic word, Thomas M. Greene writes that poetic language "seems to maintain a permanent conflict with archaic intuitions which persist despite all the well-intentioned logic of a society that considers itself modern." For Greene, words originally had a cultic power to affect the external world: by naming, we could create something, make it obey us, belong to us, or unite with us. If words have lost their originally magic vocation in the current more rational situation, this situation is also what has given birth to poetry. A poem "remains for us a text which carries itself *as if* [comme si] it were endowed with magical efficacy, the power of invoking, connecting and enchanting, but which at the same time implicitly renounces this power." It is by means of this *as-if* quality that a poem inscribes itself with the defeat of its longing for imaginative concretization. But this as-if quality is also that which we call "poetic."[83] In the end, an imaginative world is imaginative precisely because we have the distance to step back and see it as such.

The scene with the hermaphrodite crystallizes in a single image the ambivalent relationship with pseudo-magical illusionism that is, in fact, scattered throughout the poem as a whole. As much as Spenser demonizes illusionistic art in *The Faerie Queene*, readers of the poem are constantly made to feel that they are wandering through a long "picture gallery," as one reader reported to Alexander Pope in the eighteenth century.[84] I have tried to show the ways that Spenser's nineteen-stanza development of the illusionist tapestry in the first room of the House of Busirane reflects on his own illusionism, despite the way he condemns this same illusionism. The historical development from subjective imaginative immersion to objective detachment is both a historical transition and also a dialectic preserved within the artwork.

I might speculate that Spenser had to eliminate, as he did, the metaphor of the Roman statue of the hermaphrodite when he continued the poem for the 1596 edition not because, as various critics have long believed, Elizabeth's chief advisor William Cecil, Lord Burghley, found it too erotic.[85] Rather, the image concretizes a dynamic that energizes the self-problematizing push-and-pull of Spenser's poetic world. In forming this image, the poem overcomes the tension that had, in no small way, generated the poem; that is to say, the poem goes beyond the poem. The effect is that of closure, and, for this reason, Spenser had to change the image in order to be able to continue the poem for the 1596 edition.

Donald R. Kelley is certainly right that no person can rise so far above his own cultural ocean as to become an oceanographer instead of a fish.[86] But the startling effect of the 1590 edition's final image is that, in it, the reader seems to witness Spenser for a moment leaping out of the mental waters of his own *Faerie Queene*, and looking around with his bulbous eyes.

Barnard College

NOTES

1.   I am grateful to Bradin Cormack, Allyson Celeste González, Victoria Kahn, Anna Kalish, Michael Murrin, William A. Oram, Joshua Scodel, and the anonymous readers at *Spenser Studies* for their comments on drafts of this essay.

2.   Francis Bacon, *Great Instauration* in *Selected Philosophical Works*, ed. Rose-Mary Sargent (Indianapolis: Hackett Publishing, 1999), 96.

3.   Francis Bacon, *The Advancement of Learning*, ed. William Aldis Wright (Oxford: Clarendon Press, 1869), 123.

4.   Ronald Levao cites this passage in exploring central paradoxes of Bacon's approach to science, such as his "polymorphous curiosity about the world and ways of knowing it that turns repeatedly into the fields it has declared off limits." See "Francis Bacon and the Mobility of Science," *Representations* 40 (Fall 1992): 1–32.

5.   Margreta de Grazia, "Anachronism," in *Cultural Reformations: Medieval and Renaissance in Literary History*, ed. Brian Cummings and James Simpson (Oxford: Oxford University Press, 2010), 13.

6.   See Aeschylus, *Agamemnon*, ll. 177, 250ff. To take the long view: the process of epistemological detachment is already implicit in the *Oresteia's* story of the emergence of the Athenian legal process of trial by jury through the delimitation of the Furies' archaic reign.

7.   Ernst H. Kantorowicz, *The King's Two Bodies: A Study in Mediaeval Political Theology* (Princeton: Princeton University Press, 1957), 273.

8.   All citations of Edmund Spenser, *The Faerie Queene* refer to the revised edition edited by A. C. Hamilton, Hiroshi Yamashita, Toshiyuki Suzuki, and Shohachi Fukuda (Harlow, U.K.: Longman, Pearson Education Limited, 2007).

9.   Michael Murrin writes that Spenser's fairyland is "the literary expression of a complex mental experience": instead of just expressing external characteristics, "it includes both perceiver and the thing perceived." See "Spenser's Fairyland," in Murrin, *The Allegorical Epic: Essays in Its Rise and Decline* (Chicago: University of Chicago Press, 1980), 143.

10.   Hamilton glosses "vnwares" as "unexpectedly," 393.

11.   In Book III of the *Confessions*, trans. R. S. Pine-Coffin (London: Penguin, 1961), 56, Augustine describes the solipsism entailed in an Aristotelian cathartic response to the theater: "But what sort of pity can we really feel for an imaginary scene on the stage? The audience is not called upon to offer help but only to feel sorrow, and the more they are pained the more they applaud the author." Augustine's criticism does not by any means suggest his rejection of all pagan art: In *On Christian Teaching*, he offers strategies for the moral reading of pagan literature, the "spoil of the Egyptians."

12.   Page DuBois comments: "The images on Busyrane's tapestries show false, repetitious, potentially monstrous Ovidian love, which poet, hero, and reader

might find delightful, but whose consequences are finally the torture to which Amoret is subjected. The chaste lover, like Britomart, must learn to suspect the vehicle of these images, the classical *ekphrasis* and other such inherited literary forms." *History, Rhetorical Description and the Epic: From Homer to Spenser* (Cambridge: D. S. Brewer, 1982), 85.

13. As Hamilton notes, "fayld" means "deceived; caused to fail," 396.

14. The reader knows from earlier parts of the book that these images represent a version (a very dark version) of Britomart's own erotic desires. For example, likening the sea's violent tempests with her own, she says: "At length allay, and stint thy stormy stryfe, / Which in thy troubled bowels raignes, and rageth ryfe" (III.iv.8).

15. Paul J. Alpers associates Britomart's apparent disappearance with the reader's intensified involvement in this scene in *The Poetry of* The Faerie Queene (Princeton: Princeton University Press, 1967), 15–16.

16. Ernst Cassirer, *The Individual and the Cosmos in Renaissance Philosophy*, trans. Mario Domandi (Chicago: University of Chicago Press, 1963), 123–91.

17. Tommaso Campanella's major work on natural philosophy, for example, announces its association with magic in its title: *De sensu rerum et magia*. Ibid., 54.

18. See Ernest B. Gilman, *Iconoclasm and Poetry in the English Reformation: Down Went Dagon* (Chicago: University of Chicago Press, 1986), 61–83; Kenneth Gross, *Spenserian Poetics: Idolatry, Iconoclasm, and Magic* (Ithaca: Cornell University Press, 1985); and John N. King, *Spenser's Poetry and the Reformation Tradition* (Princeton: Princeton University Press, 1990).

19. Tapestries made with gold and silk threads were approximately fifty times more expensive than those made with coarse wool. Thomas P. Campbell, *Henry VIII and the Art of Majesty: Tapestries at the Tudor Court* (New Haven: Yale University Press, 2007), 94.

20. Edward Hall, *The Triumphant Reigne of Henry the VIII* (London: T. C. & E. C. Jack, 1904), 1:191. Campbell, *Henry VIII and the Art of Majesty*, 145.

21. Hall, *Henry VIII*, 2:88.

22. Campbell, *Henry VIII and the Art of Majesty*, 145.

23. In the *Stanze*, Poliziano describes without ambivalence the illusionistic images of metamorphosis that decorate the golden palace of Venus: "You would call the foam real, the sea real, real the conch shell and real the blowing wind. . ." (C.1–2). Poliziano explains that this effect of lifelikeness results from the viewers' imaginative involvement in what they see: "whatever the art in itself does not contain, the mind, imagining, clearly understands" (CXIX.7–8). *The Stanze of Angelo Poliziano*, trans. David Quint (University Park: The Pennsylvania State University Press, 1993), 51, 61.

24. Aby Warburg, *The Renewal of Pagan Antiquity: Contributions to the Cultural History of the European Renaissance*, trans. David Britt (Los Angeles: Getty Research Institute for the History of Art and the Humanities, 1999), 599.

25. See Lawrence A. Springer, "The Cult and Temple of Jupiter Feretrius," *Classical Journal* 50:1 (1954): 27–32. In medieval literature, broken bows can be

found on the wall of the temple of Venus in Chaucer's *Parlement of Foules*, ll. 281–84. These bows belonged to women who, Chaucer's narrator reports, had once wasted their time in Diana's service.

26. Leonard Barkan, *Unearthing the Past: Archeology and Aesthetics in the Making of Renaissance Culture* (New Haven: Yale University Press, 1999), 129.

27. Ibid., 130. Barkan illustrates his point by quoting Josephus, who describes the Romans' spoliation of Jerusalem after the destruction of the Second Temple (an event well-known in the Renaissance both from Josephus's text and from the often-reproduced image carved into the Arch of Titus in the Roman Forum): "The rest of the spoils were borne along in random heaps. The most interesting of all were the spoils seized from the Temple of Jerusalem: a gold table weighing many talents, and a lampstand also made of gold" (VII.5.148). But in this example, the decontextualization goes even further than Barkan suggests, for this "lampstand" [λυχνια] is actually the Temple's menorah. The complete quotation continues: ". . . though its [the lampstand's] construction were now changed from that which we made use of: for its middle shaft was fixed upon a basis, and the small branches were produced out of it to a great length, having the likeness of a trident in their position, and had every one a socket made of brass for a lamp at the tops of them. These lamps were in number seven, and represented the dignity of the number seven among the Jews. . . ." Josephus specifically records that this gold "lampstand" used to have a different meaning for the conquered people: in explaining what this meaning used to be, he cannot but translate it into terms comprehensible to his own conquerors. Thus, Josephus emphasizes the menorah's value in gold, and describes its shape as a trident [τριαινης], the same word typically used for Poseidon's pronged weapon. I am quoting from *The Works of Flavius Josephus*, trans. William Whiston (Belfast: Simms and M'Intyre, 1841), 769. A reproduction of this famous image from the Arch of Titus, which Barkan provides, can be found online: <http://commons.wikimedia.org/wiki/File:Arch_of_Titus_Menorah_22.jpg>.

28. Barkan, *Unearthing the Past*, 132.

29. Keith Thomas, *Religion and the Decline of Magic* (New York: Charles Scribner's Sons, 1971), 75.

30. Margaret Aston, "English Ruins and English History: The Dissolution and the Sense of the Past," *Journal of the Warburg and Courtauld Institutes* 36 (1973): 231–55; Arthur B. Ferguson, *Clio Unbound: Perception of the Social and Cultural Past in Renaissance England* (Durham: Duke University Press, 1979), 84.

31. For recent work on Spenser's involvement with antiquarianism, see Tom Muir, "Specters of Spenser: Translating the *Antiquitez*," *Spenser Studies* 25 (2010): 327–61 and Bart van Es, *Spenser's Forms of History* (Oxford: Oxford University Press, 2002). For the history of English antiquarianism, see Joan Evans, *A History of the Society of Antiquaries* (Oxford: Printed at the University press by Charles Batey for The Society of Antiquaries, 1956), 1–32; Ferguson, *Clio Unbound*, 78–125; F. J. Levy, *Tudor Historical Thought* (San Marino: Huntington Library, 1967), 124–66; Kevin Sharpe, *Sir Robert Cotton, 1586–1631: History and Politics in Early Modern*

England (Oxford: Oxford University Press, 1979); Angus Vine, *In Defiance of Time: Antiquarian Writing in Early Modern England* (Oxford: Oxford University Press, 2010); C. E. Wright, "The Elizabethan Society of Antiquaries and the Formation of the Cottonian Library," in *The English Library before 1700: Studies in Its History*, ed. Francis Wormald and C. E. Wright (London: Athlone Press, 1958), 176–212.

32. Aston, "English Ruins and English History," 254.

33. It is now known that these grottos were part of Nero's palace, but there was significant confusion about this point in the sixteenth century. Many people, including Vasari (see especially his life of Giovanni da Udine), incorrectly believed that the buried rooms containing the grotesques were part of the Baths of Titus. As Nicole Dacos explains, the rooms presented an archeological puzzle partly because the Domus Aurea, which became almost immediately a symbol of imperial decadence (as is obvious in Suetonius's and Tacitus's accounts of the villa), was abandoned so soon after Nero's death and used as the foundation for the Baths of Trajan. The erroneous identification of the grotesques as part of the Baths of Titus was widespread and not generally corrected until the end of the seventeenth century. Yet evidence shows that at least some people in the sixteenth century did have the correct information. Most convincingly, a 1538 watercolor by the Portuguese artist Francisco de Holanda depicts the Domus Aurea's so-called "Volta Dorata" with the following inscription in the margin: "Domus aureae Neronis." The image with the full inscription can be found in Elías Tormo y Monzó, *Os Desenhos das Antigualhas que vio Francisco d'Ollanda, Pintor Portugués, 1539–1540* (Madrid, 1940), 37–38. I am grateful to Nicole Dacos for clarifying this matter. As is the case with most scholars' accounts of Renaissance grotesques, my discussion of these images depends heavily on her seminal *La découverte de la Domus Aurea et la formation des grotesques à la Renaissance* (London: Warburg Institute; Leiden: E. J. Brill, 1969).

34. Leonard Barkan, *The Gods Made Flesh: Metamorphosis and the Pursuit of Paganism* (New Haven: Yale University Press, 1986), 234.

35. Francis Ames-Lewis, *The Intellectual Life of the Early Renaissance Artist* (New Haven: Yale University Press, 2000), 128–29.

36. David Evett reviews the Renaissance history of the grotesque and discusses the grotesque's possible importance for the "esthetic of *The Faerie Queene* as a whole" (181). In this regard, he mentions "the poem's unresolved concern with the proper relationship between nature and art, its fascination with the ambiguities of visual experience, and its deep and incessant dualism" (204); his ultimate focus is on the structure of the poem, which, he says, could have evolved from the grotesques as a mnemonic system that disposes vivid images around an edifice (205ff). See his "Mammon's Grotto: Sixteenth-Century Visual Grotesquerie and Some Features of Spenser's *Faerie Queene*," *English Literary Renaissance* 12 (1982): 180–209.

37. Dacos, *The Loggia of Raphael: A Vatican Art Treasure*, trans. Josephine Bacon (New York: Abbeville Press, 2008), 10.

38. Ibid., 308. Nonsuch was destroyed in the late seventeenth century, but some panels with grotesques that are believed to be from the palace are preserved in Loseley Park, Surrey. These are reproduced in Edward Croft-Murray, *Decorative Painting in England, 1537–1837*, vol. 1 (London: Country Life, 1962), figs. 17–20. It is not known who painted these panels, but scholars believe that one likely candidate is Toto del Nunziata, who was working in the English court and who was, according to Vasari, responsible for Henry VIII's "principale palazzo"—a likely reference to Nonsuch, Henry's last major building project, as Edward Croft-Murray notes (18). Dacos concurs with Croft-Murray, but adds that the panels are also related to popular engravings by Agostino Veneziano, which were based on the Raphael-school grotesques in the Loggia (See Dacos, *The Loggia of Raphael*, 313).

39. These tapestries, which are also referred to as the *Triumphs of the Gods*, each depict a god in a fanciful architectural setting, "obviously inspired by those in the Domus Aurea," writes Thomas P. Campbell, *Tapestry in the Renaissance: Art and Magnificence* (New Haven: Yale University Press, 2002), 228. Leo X's original series is now lost, but from Henry's seven-piece set two pieces survive at Hampton Court Palace, as well as three pieces from a later weaving in the Mobilier National in Paris. See Campbell, *Tapestry in the Renaissance*, 225–29.

40. See Percy Simpson and C. F. Bell, *Designs by Inigo Jones for Masques & Plays at Court* (Oxford: Printed for the Walpole and Malone Societies at the University Press, 1924), pl. xlv, 337 (verso).

41. M. R. Apted and W. N. Robertson, "Four 'Drollities' from the Painted Ceiling Formerly at Prestongrange, East Lothian," *Proceedings of the Society of Antiquaries of Scotland* 106 (1974–75): 158–60.

42. Anthony Wells-Cole, *Art and Decoration in Elizabethan and Jacobean England: The Influence of Continental Prints, 1558–1625* (New Haven and London: Published for the Paul Mellon Centre for Studies in British Art by Yale University Press, 1997), 53.

43. L. E. Semler, "Breaking the Ice to Invention: Henry Peacham's 'The Art of Drawing' (1606)," *Sixteenth Century Journal* 35:3 (Fall 2004): 744–45.

44. André Chastel, "Sens et non-sens à la Renaissance. La question des chimères," *Archivio di filosofia* (1980): 188.

45. David Summers, *Michelangelo and the Language of Art* (Princeton: Princeton University Press, 1981), 139.

46. Dacos, *La découverte de la Domus Aurea*, vii.

47. Quoted in Summers, *Michelangelo and the Language of Art*, 113. Juan Luis Vives, *De anima et vita*, ed. Mario Sancipriano (Torino: Bottega d'Erasmo, 1959), 32–33.

48. Quoted in William Rossky, "Imagination in the English Renaissance: Psychology and Poetic," *Studies in the Renaissance* 5 (1958): 57.

49. See *The Figino, or, On the Purpose of Painting: Art Theory in the Late Renaissance*, trans. and ed. Ann Doyle-Anderson and Giancarlo Maiorino (Toronto: University of Toronto Press, 2001), 16. Summers, *Michelangelo and the Language of Art*, 140.

50. Vitruvius, VII.5.4. I am quoting the text provided in William Audsley and George Ashdown Audsley, *Popular Dictionary of Architecture and the Allied Arts* (New York: G. P. Putnam's Sons, 1881), 2:6.

51. *De arte poetica*, 1–5. Horace, *Satires, Epistles and Ars Poetica*, trans. H. Rushton Fairclough (Cambridge: Harvard University Press, 1929), 450–89.

52. Anton Francesco Doni, *Disegno* (Venice, 1549), 3:20; cited by Paola Barocchi, *Scritti d'Arte del Cinquecento* (Milan and Naples: R. Ricciardi, 1971), 1:584–85. Chastel, "Sens et non-sens à la Renaissance. La question des chimères," 185.

53. "Come sono animali, che portano Tempi, colonne di cannuccie, artigli di mostri, difformita di nature, misti di varie specie: Certo si come la Fantasia nel sogno ci rappresenta confusamente le imagini delle cose, e spesso pone insieme nature diverse, cosi potremo dire, che facciano le Grottesche, le quali senza dubbio potemo nominare sogni della pittura." Cited in Dacos, *La découverte de la Domus Aurea*, 123–24. My translation from the Italian. I am grateful to Susan Raye for her correction.

54. Leo Spitzer, *Linguistics and Literary History: Essays in Stylistics* (Princeton: Princeton University Press, 1948), 16–17.

55. Chastel, "Sens et non-sens à la Renaissance. La question des chimères," 183–89.

56. In *Henry VIII*, Edward Hall regularly uses the same word when describing grotesques in Henry VIII's tapestries and other palace decorations. Henry Peacham's *The Art of Drawing* (London, 1606) also employs this word to mean "an vnnaturall or vnorderly composition for delight sake, of men, beasts, birds, fishes, flowers, &c without (as wee say) Rime or reason, for the greater variety you shew in your inuention, the more you please. . . . you cannot bee too fantastical" (36).

57. See Evett, "Mammon's Grotto," 200.

58. Sir Philip Sidney, *An Apology for Poetry, or, The Defense of Poesy*, ed. Geoffrey Shepherd; revised and expanded for third edition by R. W. Maslen (New York: Palgrave, 2002), 85.

59. Michel de Montaigne, *Essais*, book 1 (Paris: Garnier-Flammarion, 1969), 70.

60. Ibid., 231.

61. For example, Pliny wrote in regard to color that Apelles used only four pigments (*Naturalis historia*, XXXV.32), but Cicero said that Apelles advanced the art of painting by using a full palette (*Brutus*, 70). In regard to paint handling, Pliny derived the ineffable charm of Apelles's work from the fact that he "knew when to take his hand away from a picture" (*Naturalis historia*, XXXV.80).

62. Hetty Joyce, "Grasping at Shadows: Ancient Paintings in Renaissance and Baroque Rome," *Art Bulletin* 74:2 (1992): 219.

63. Dacos, *La découverte de la Domus Aurea*, 64.

64. Mark Pattison, *Isaac Casaubon, 1559–1614* (London: Clarendon Press, 1892), 509; cited by H. J. Erasmus, *The Origins of Rome in Historiography from Petrarch to Perizonius* (Assen: Van Gorcum, 1962), 32. See also Evans, *A History of the Society of Antiquaries*, 11.

65. Lorraine Daston and Peter Galison, "The Image of Objectivity," *Representations* 40 (Autumn 1992): 82.

66. The roots of the New Science were deeply intertwined with antiquarianism; many doctors were also antiquarians. See Arnaldo Momigliano, "History between Medicine and Rhetoric," in his *Ottavo contributo alla storia degli studi classici e del mondo antico* (Rome: Edizioni di Storia e Letteratura, 1987), 13–25; Nancy G. Siraisi, "*Historiae*, Natural History, Roman Antiquity, and Some Roman Physicians," in *Historia: Empiricism and Erudition in Early Modern Europe*, ed. Gianna Pomata and Nancy G. Siraisi (Cambridge: MIT Press, 2005), 325–54.

67. *The Yale Edition of the Shorter Poems of Edmund Spenser*, ed. William A. Oram, Einar Bjorvand, Ronald Bond, Thomas H. Cain, Alexander Dunlop, and Richard Schell (New Haven: Yale University Press, 1989), 236, notes the close relationship between Spenser, "The Ruines of Time," lines 85–98, and Camden, *Britannia*, 411.

68. *A View of the State of Ireland: From the First Printed Edition (1633)*, ed. Andrew Hadfield and Willy Maley (Oxford: Blackwell Publishers, 1997), 46.

69. See Bart van Es, *Spenser's Forms of History*, 89; Ferguson, *Clio Unbound*, 83. Aspects of antiquarian methodology evident in this passage include antiquarianism's emphasis on non-literary remains, its cautious suspension of judgment, and its typically multi-tiered process of collection, observation, and comparison. I am drawing from Peter N. Miller's account of antiquarian methodology in *Peiresc's Europe: Learning and Virtue in the Seventeenth Century* (New Haven: Yale University Press, 2000).

70. Peter C. Herman, *Squitter-wits and Muse-haters: Sidney, Spenser, Milton and Renaissance Antipoetic Sentiment* (Detroit: Wayne State University Press, 1996), 145–72.

71. Van Es, *Spenser's Forms of History*, 78–84, relates the publication history of this text: the antiquarian Sir James Ware included it in a 1633 volume of Irish history, *The Historie of Ireland, Collected by Three Learned Authors*, presenting Spenser's text as though it were itself an antiquarian treatise.

72. Jeff Dolven, *Scenes of Instruction in Renaissance Romance* (Chicago: University of Chicago Press, 2007), 171.

73. As Hamilton notes, this metaphor connects Spenser's lines with Ovid's version of the story of Hermaphroditus; Arthur Golding translates Ovid's description of the union of Hermaphroditus and Salmacis: "Two twigges both growing into one and still togither holde" (IV.465).

74. Donald Cheney draws attention to this point in "Spenser's Hermaphrodite and the 1590 *Faerie Queene*," *PMLA* 87:2 (1972): 192–200, although he ultimately rejects any real Roman statue as the metaphor's source. His point, which informs mine, is that an important function of the metaphor is to rebuff our attempts fully to understand it, and thereby position us as distanced spectators, trying "to make what we can of the spectacle" (196).

75. Of this sword, Spenser writes: "But when he dyde, the Faery Queene it brought / To Faerie lond, where yet it may be seene, if sought" (I.vii.36). Arthur's sword, which, as Hamilton points out, is likened through a parallel passage to Caesar's sword (II.x.49), is precisely the kind of treasure that would hold a prized spot in an antiquarian cabinet. And, in fact, the question of whether Arthur was a real historical figure was of debate among English antiquarians such as John Leland in this period. See Ferguson, *Clio Unbound*, 104–9. Murrin, "Spenser's Fairyland," makes a related argument about the objective existence of Fairyland.

76. See note 33.

77. Cheney, "Spenser's Hermaphrodite and the 1590 *Faerie Queene*," 194.

78. Thomas P. Roche has rightly drawn attention to the emblem tradition that lies behind this image: In Sambucus's and Reusner's collections of emblems of 1564 and 1591 respectively, one finds the ideal of male-female Christian union depicted in images of lovers who have physically grown into one another. The biblical source is probably Matthew 19:5 or Mark 10:8, both of which refer to a man cleaving to his wife and becoming one flesh with her. Or, as many commentators have suggested, the source might be Genesis 1:27: "Male and female He created them," a version of creation which has implied to some an original hermaphroditic oneness of the sexes, not unlike the fantasy attributed to Aristophanes in the *Symposium*. See *The Kindly Flame: A Study of the Third and Fourth Books of Spenser's* Faerie Queene (Princeton: Princeton University Press, 1964), 133–36.

79. Theodor Adorno writes of the aesthetic that "what is menacing in the domination of nature is wed with a longing for the vanquished, a longing stirred by domination." See his *Aesthetic Theory*, trans. Robert Hullot-Kentor (Minneapolis: University of Minnesota Press, 1997), 52.

80. This reference to what the audience would have seen has Virgilian origins and recurs throughout the ekphrastic tradition. In his ekphrasis of Aeneas's shield, Virgil marks the difference between the audience's ability to comprehend the depicted images of Roman history and Aeneas's inability by three times addressing the audience with verbs in the second-person subjunctive: *aspiceres* (VIII.650), you would look at; *videres* (VIII.676), you would see; *credas* (VIII.691), you would believe. These verbs are in the subjunctive because they occur outside the context offered by the narrative.

81. Lauren Silberman, *Transforming Desire: Erotic Knowledge in Books III and IV of* The Faerie Queene (Berkeley: University of California Press, 1995), 67.

82. James Nohrnberg, *The Analogy of* The Faerie Queene (Princeton: Princeton University Press, 1976), 776. Nohrnberg argues that Spenser's decision to represent Nature in the Mutabilitie cantos is, on one level, an act of disenchantment: "To represent a noumenon is in some sense to annul it" (775). By representing Nature, Nature becomes a discrete being, no longer magically interfused with the contemplating mind of the poem. But, on another level, the poem's unveiling of its own animating force is also what makes the artwork art: "if the gods be not gods, they may still be allegories" (776).

83. Thomas M. Greene, *Poésie et magie* (Paris: Julliard, 1991), 42, 52, 57. Translation from the French mine.

84. Jean H. Hagstrum, *The Sister Arts: The Tradition of Literary Pictorialism and English Poetry from Dryden to Gray* (Chicago: University of Chicago Press, 1958), 76.

85. See Hamilton, 409n; Anne K. Tuell, "The Original End of *Faerie Queene*, Book III," *Modern Language Notes* 36:5 (1921): 309–11.

86. Donald R. Kelley, *Faces of History: Historical Inquiry from Herodotus to Herder* (New Haven: Yale University Press, 1998), xi.

PATRICIA WAREH

Competitions in Nobility and Courtesy: *Nennio* and the Reader's Judgment in Book VI of *The Faerie Queene*

This paper brings into conversation two texts that have not yet been explored in detail together: *The Faerie Queene*, Book VI, and *Nennio, or a Treatise on Nobility*, originally written in Italian in 1542 and published in English translation in 1595, with a commendatory sonnet by Spenser.[1] *Nennio's* debate between nobility of blood and nobility of mind concludes with a relatively straightforward victory for nobility of mind, cemented by the generosity of the lower-born Fabricio; Calidore's competitions with Meliboe and Coridon in Canto ix of Book VI have differing outcomes and have encouraged a variety of critical responses to his character. I argue that in contrast both to *Nennio* and to his own commendatory sonnet, Spenser's concern throughout Book VI is not to direct his readers toward a particular view of nobility, but to train their judgments in understanding the complexity of courtesy in action. By navigating interrelated examples, Spenser's readers revisit and revise their interpretations and come to understand the shifting relations between nobility and courtesy, and between inner character and outward show.

Spenser Studies: A Renaissance Poetry Annual, Volume XXVII, Copyright © 2012 AMS Press, Inc. All rights reserved.   DOI: 10.7756/spst.027.008.163-191

Spenser and *Nennio*

R EADERS OF BOOK VI of Spenser's *Faerie Queene* are familiar with
Calidore's competition with Coridon in Canto ix. A pastoral setting
provides the leisure for conversation and recreation. Two men of
different social stations compete for the favor of a lovely woman. Finally,
one of them gains victory over the other in part through his insistent gen-
erosity. Less familiar is another passage perfectly described in these same
terms, the parallel conclusion to the dialogue *Nennio, or a Treatise on
Nobility*. *Nennio*, originally written in Italian by Giovanni Battista Nenna,
was published in Venice in 1542; in 1595 William Jones brought out an
English translation that included commendatory sonnets by Spenser and
others.[2] While there is no critical consensus about Spenser's familiarity
with the dialogue, there is at least a reasonable possibility that he made a
study of *Nennio* before completing the 1596 *Faerie Queene*. Spenser's praise
of the translation's accuracy in his commendatory sonnet even implies that
he has read the text in both English and Italian.[3]

   Nennio and Book VI of *The Faerie Queene* share a common vocabulary
as well as a sense that competitions in generosity can serve as a means of
defining nobility. In *Nennio*, when a group sets out to avoid plague and war,
their idyllic place of recreation is visited by the noble Lady Virginia. Before
she departs, she leaves a ring with the company, saying: "I doe bestow this
ring upon him that is the most noble of you two, whom I incharge to weare
it in remembrance of me" (B3ʳ).[4] Possidonio, a wealthy man of noble blood,
and Fabricio, a man of noble learning, both immediately claim the ring.
In the remainder of the dialogue they make their cases until Nennio, their
judge, passes sentence in favor of Fabricio, who then unexpectedly gives
the ring to Possidonio.

   Spenser's commendatory sonnet to *Nennio* emphasizes the need for
readers to have accurate insight in choosing between the dialogue's two
opposed forms of nobility. In *Nennio*, inherited nobility of blood (closely
connected to nobility based on wealth) is revealed to be inferior to nobility
of mind, and though Spenser does not declare his own preference directly,
he strongly hints at it when he contrasts "painted shewes & titles vaine" to
"true Nobility":

     Who so wil seeke by right deserts t'attaine
     unto the type of true Nobility,

And not by painted shewes & titles vaine,
Derived farre from famous Auncestrie,
Behold them both in their right visnomy
Here truly pourtray'd, as they ought to be,
And striving both for termes of dignitie,
To be advanced highest in degree.
And when thou doost with equall insight see
the ods twixt both, of both them deem aright
And chuse the better of them both to thee,
But thanks to him that it deserves, behight:
To *Nenna* first, that first this worke created,
And next to *Jones*, that truely it translated.[5]

Spenser here asks the reader to regard the two kinds of nobility and "behold them both in their right visnomy,"[6] to look at them "with equall insight," and to "chuse the better of them both"—yet he also offers clues so heavy-handed as to foreordain the proper decision. Further, his emphasis is on making a *correct* decision, rather than on a higher level of thinking. Spenser similarly praises the justness of the dialogue's portraits of nobility ("truly pourtray'd, as they ought to be") even as he praises the accuracy of Jones's translation rather than any more creative aspect of his writing. Spenser here offers readers a simple choice, and even steers them in the proper direction. Indeed, in criticizing inherited nobility explicitly at the outset of the dialogue, he seems to take for granted the victory of nobility of mind. While the dialogue's moderator will give at least some credit to the value of titles, Spenser here brushes them aside.

Possidonio and Fabricio's conflict contributes to a debate over the definition of nobility that has a long history and was particularly active in Spenser's day.[7] Spenser's assertion in his commendatory sonnet that defining nobility is about making a simple choice is belied by his own extended treatment of noble virtue in Book VI of *The Faerie Queene*, which at times supports the view of Possidonio, that nobility is physically inherited, and at other times supports the view of Fabricio, that "true and perfect nobilitie, doth consist in the vertues of the minde" (H4^v).[8] Readers have, understandably, been divided over what this sonnet reveals about Spenser's own attitude. A. C. Judson acknowledges that Spenser shows here a "democratic" sympathy, but suggests that he may be merely indulging Jones and the "conclusions" reached in *Nennio*.[9] Millar Maclure goes even further in claiming that Spenser is "at one" with Possidonio's view that aristocratic grace is a gift from God.[10] More recently, however, critics such as Louis Montrose and John Huntington have seen a greater willingness on Spenser's part to agree with *Nennio*'s critique of nobility of blood, though even Huntington, who provides the most thorough recent attention to this sonnet, sees Spenser's endorsement of *Nennio*'s ideas as rather lukewarm. For Huntington, Spenser's agreement with the dialogue is primarily on "moral" grounds rather than representing any real recognition of its "social implications."[11]

   Nennio has not yet to my knowledge been systematically studied in relation to Book VI of *The Faerie Queene*, especially Canto ix,[12] and I propose that bringing these two texts into conversation with one another affords additional insight into Spenser's method of open-ended literary argument, whether or not he read *Nennio* early enough to influence his treatment of courtesy.[13] *Nennio* provides a portrait of generous nobility that has much in common, on its face, with that of Calidore's liberality, but the dialogue also offers a lens through which Spenser's reader may consider Calidore's techniques critically, in an exercise requiring something other than outright acceptance or dismissal. Moving from a wide-ranging consideration of *Nennio*'s debate and its resolution, I will next consider Canto ix in the context of other moments from Book VI in which Spenser's multifaceted examinations of nobility, rhetorical deception, greed, and generosity require readers to be alert to connections and willing to refine their judgments. I will argue that in contrast to *Nennio*'s relatively straightforward presentation of the victory of nobility of mind, the intertwined narratives of *The Faerie Queene*'s Book of Courtesy require readers to exercise their own discernment.

NENNIO'S DEBATE

Though *Nennio* is structured as a debate, both Nenna and his translator foreshadow the outcome in their front matter.[14] The dialogue's pastoral setting offers the possibility of a new social order toward which Nenna gestures in his dedicatory letter to the Duchess of Bari. This letter expresses a longing for a golden age unspoiled by the strife that accompanies riches, honor, and nobility, even as it contradicts this sentiment in addressing the Duchess herself as someone who encompasses "le vere qualità della perfetta nobiltade."[15] Jones does not include a translation of the dedication, though he may well have been informed by the spirit of this letter. His own front matter—a dedication to the Earl of Essex and a Letter to the Courteous Reader—is also full of contradiction on the topic of nobility, even as he ultimately makes his preference clear. In his dedicatory letter to the Earl of Essex, Jones insists on the modesty of his achievement as well as on the perfections of the earl; referring to the dialogue's debate between "Nobilitie by descent" and "Nobilitie, purchased by vertue," he asserts that Essex exemplifies both of these. Further, he insists that Essex's noble blood "is well knowne to all men" and that his "perfections can well witnesse" his nobility of virtue (A2^r). If Essex wishes to learn about perfect nobility, he merely has to look in a mirror instead of reading the book (A2^v). While Jones's address to the earl sidesteps any complicated view of nobility, the Letter to the Courteous Reader undermines the notion of nobility of blood by referring to the descent of all people from "one Stocke" and claiming that uncertain family fortunes mean that nobles "have smal reason to bragge so much of their Nobility" (A3^r). One wonders what the flattered Essex would have made of this. Jones proceeds to anticipate the outcome of the dialogue with further criticism of mere inherited titles, suggesting that "without vertue, it [nobility] is as a ring of gold, wanting the ornament of some pretious stone" (A3^v–A4^r). Even as Nenna and Jones effusively praise their dedicatees, they indicate that the dialogue itself will favor nobility of mind.

As the debate begins, Possidonio is unwilling to recognize any real question to be decided, which also foreshadows a resolution against his view. He insists that his case is self-evident, saying that the company might as well debate "whether the day be more cleerer than the night, or the sunne more hote then the Moone" (B4^v). It makes sense that Possidonio would be "desirous to be the first that should enter into the listes" (B4^r); his view that his case is obvious is closely connected to his lack of deference to his competitor. For Possidonio, nobility is akin to an inherited physical trait such as skin color: "if a man be white, the child shal likewise be participant of his whitenes: if he be blacke, he shall be partaker of his blacknes" (D2^v). He argues further that it is "a general and common custome" to see nobility as inherited by birth in this way, and that taking a different view would be the same as using "sophisticall arguments, to make men deeme, that white is black" (D4^v). Possidonio sees the superiority of his own inherited nobility as a manifest truth, and he therefore disdains Fabricio's acquired nobility of learning as coming from art, rather than nature (F3^v), just as he mocks Fabricio's case as derived from the colors of rhetoric rather than the legitimacy of a natural, physical truth.

Possidonio's argument betrays logical flaws that Fabricio will later exploit. He oddly supports his case with examples of historical figures who sought to obscure their base lineage as they rose in status (E4^v–F^r). He also comes close to conflating nobility of blood and nobility of riches with his striking image of a garden hidden by darkness: this figures how nobility is vulnerable to being obscured without the light of riches to make it apparent (G2^v). These arguments are intended to show the desirability of noble blood paired with riches, yet they also acknowledge that nobility of blood may be falsified or hidden, refuting Possidonio's repeated claims of its *obvious* superiority. Even as Possidonio insists that it would be "an easie matter for a man of a slender capacitie, to decide this controversie" (G4^v), he reveals that nobility of blood depends on both riches and the maintenance (or creation) of an illustrious reputation.

Proving something that is self-evident ends up being more of a challenge than Possidonio anticipates. As the dialogue progresses, Fabricio points out the problems with a mode of thinking which asserts that thought is not necessary. Though he also considers his case to be the clear truth, Fabricio looks forward to the *argument*, asserting that he will "plainly" reveal Possidonio's "manifest error" (I^r) and claiming, "let everie one of them alleadge the most pregnant and strong reasons they can, for I shall not want courage sufficient to confute them all" (E3^v). Fabricio makes his case at greater length than Possidonio, asking a number of pointed questions: Who now knows about the descendants of such ancient nobles as the Scipios (I2^v)? What about the fact that ignoble children can come from noble blood (I3^{r-v})? Don't we all descend from Adam anyway (I2^r)? He provides new interpretations of Possidonio's examples as well as his own counterexamples, such as Moses' disavowal of Pharaoh's "royall blood" and Jesus' preference for disciples "of base estate" (L2^v, L^v). In contrast to Possidonio's insistence on the physical manifestation of nobility, Fabricio anticipates Spenser's claim that "vertues seat is deepe within the mynd" (VI.Proem.5) when he asserts that true nobility "consisteth in the vertues of the mind, whither the sight of our outward eies cannot pierce" (I3^r).[16] In a similar vein, Fabricio takes on Possidonio's assertion that nobility is inherited like skin color:

I saie that his similitude is not worth a rushe: In asmuch as blacknesse, or whitenesse, are demonstrative dispositions of the body; but Nobilitie is a hidden propertie of the minde, in regard that it proceedeth of vertue: So that a painter may by arte easily alter either the

whitenesse or blacknesse of man: but he can never paint forth with
his pensill, the nobilitie of the mind, as being a thing not subiect unto
the sight of bodily eyes. (I4^v)

Fabricio makes a case for a more nuanced understanding of worth than
Possidonio's view that art is simply inferior to nature, masterfully rework-
ing the terms of Possidonio's mocking suggestion that he will attempt to
reverse white and black through the distortions of his argument. Here
Fabricio readily concedes that apparently firm physical categories may be
more readily changed through art than the interior worth of the truly noble
person may be depicted or conceived. Nobility of mind, Fabricio asserts,
cannot be reached with physical eyes, and it does not lend itself to the rhe-
torical coloring that Possidonio claims.

Most crucially, Fabricio denigrates riches in order to assert the superior
value of learning, insisting on the unreliability of wealth as something ex-
ternal to the self, the cause of more harm than good. Comparing the rich
man to Tantalus, Fabricio asks, "Who is then so unadvised to terme such a
one rich[?]" (L4^v). Insisting on the deceptive quality of inherited nobility,
Fabricio goes on to assert that the sight of riches paralyzes the judgment
and makes discernment of true nobility impossible:

riches . . . is a thing most deformed, wearing on the naturall visage
thereof, a masque of most fine gold, denoting thereby, that it is faire
in apparence, but foule within: wherefore they who travell so many
Countries, and take such paines to seeke it, are enamoured with the
outward shewe, which blindeth the eyes of the understanding: so that
they can hardly discerne how hurtfull the inward deformitie thereof
is. (M^v)

In its condemnation of the deceptive pleasures of glittering surfaces,
Fabricio's image resonates with Spenser's assertion that the contemporary
practices of courtesy lead others to "thinke gold that is bras" (VI.Proem.5) as
well as with his related claim that "learnings threasures . . . doe all worldly
riches farre excell" (VI.Proem.2). As he continues to insist on the superi-
ority of learning over riches, Fabricio adduces such examples as Philip of
Macedon and his son Alexander the Great. Philip's hiring of Aristotle as
tutor for Alexander shows that he saw "learning and science, as treasures of
far more inestimable value, then his nobilitie" (M3^v). He further recounts
how Alexander, presumably having learned well from Aristotle, also valued

learning over riches. When he had conquered Darius of Persia, Alexander found a beautiful golden casket decorated with precious stones. He used this casket not for ointments, as Darius had done, but for Homer's poetry. Fabricio describes Alexander as "imagining he had not in al his treasure, a jewell of greater value" than these "poeticall workes" (O4ᵛ). Fabricio's many examples in this vein work together to suggest the greater importance of essence over appearance as well as the fundamental role of scholars and poets. Needless to say, Spenser too holds these values dear. Also, needless to say, the arguments of the smug and entitled Possidonio cannot stand up to Fabricio's intellectual assault.

The resolution of the dispute between Possidonio and Fabricio depends on the judgment of Nennio, who is daunted by the task. He initially avoids a decision altogether, declaring that both sides have made arguments that appear "probable," and that therefore it "scarsely . . . may be discerned, which of them draweth nearer the troth" (S3ᵛ). Still, Nennio reveals his fundamental sympathy for Fabricio's position when he compares a noble man without virtue to a marble and gold sepulcher, an image that is worth quoting at length:

For a noble man by bloud, who is deprived of vertue, is made no oth-
erwise, then as a sepulchre of white marble, inriched with fine gold,
which at the first shewe is pleasant to the sight of those, that behold
it: but considering afterwards the rotten body, and filthy stinch, that
is within it, it seemeth unto them hideous and horrible. Such a one is
hee who is descended of noble bloud, for at the first sight he seemeth
gratious, & pleasing, but looking afterwards to the foule corruption
of his maners, and to the default of the gifts of his mind, by which he
shuld become worthie, neither this grace, nor the pleasure which was
found therein, is anie more seene, but in steede thereof basenesse,
and deepe contempt. Whereof hee may be called noble in apparance
by the which the common people (whose eyes are blinded, that they
cannot see the trueth) doe lightly judge, and holde him as a noble-
man, which is farre different from him, whose minde is fraught with
vertues, because that hee holdeth not an apparance of true Nobilitie,
but the verie essence thereof. (Xʳ⁻ᵛ)

The image of the golden sepulcher recalls Fabricio's argument about the hollowness of "outward shewe" as well as providing an analogue to the casket challenge in Shakespeare's *Merchant of Venice*; there, too, the need to disregard "outward shows" is emphasized, with some irony.[17] Though the slapdash judgment of the multitude is criticized here, Nennio also suggests the possibility of correcting one's initial evaluation of what seems obvious, moving beyond the surface to consider the true nature of things. Perhaps, too, the legacy of nobility based on an inheritance from the dead is questioned through the gruesome imagery of the decaying body. In any case, Nennio underscores the need to reflect before coming to a proper decision about the worth of noble blood when it lacks virtue. His view, like Spenser's commendatory sonnet, emphasizes accurate judgment; it may not be easy to decide at first, but there is indeed a right way to see things. Nennio does not completely discount the value of nobility of blood, however, precisely because of its practical value in influencing the opinions of the crowd, who are taken in by surface appearances. He therefore invents another possibility, "compounded nobility," which combines material riches and learning (S3^v). This "compounded" form is clearly his preference; he asserts, "The nobility of bloode then, and noblenesse of the minde, when they concur togither in one subject, surely both the vulgar sort, and men of wisedome, will hold such a one to be most noble" (Bb^v).[18] Only one person can wear a ring, however, and when Nennio must ultimately decide between the two competitors, he awards the ring to Fabricio.

Fabricio's superiority is underscored by his greater skill in the courtier's art of *sprezzatura*.[19] He too can sometimes seem unappealingly certain of himself, but unlike Possidonio he at least hesitates before launching into the praise of his own learning necessary for his argument (O3^r). And in the resolution of the dialogue, he demonstrates further his mastery of generous savoir-faire when he passes on the contested ring to Possidonio. In performing this noble act, Fabricio shows an ability to make use of modesty for self-aggrandizing purposes, carrying out an action that Possidonio himself had only sarcastically expressed a willingness to do, if the terms of the debate were changed so that the prize would go to the "most unworthy" (H^r). Yet Fabricio too changes the terms of the debate by his apparently magnanimous transfer of the ring.

Fabricio has already paved the way for his renunciation of material goods through his insistence that the truly noble reject riches just as Pompey the Great refused to touch the treasure of the temple of Jerusalem (M^v–M2^r). His gesture of generosity to Possidonio therefore cements his status as truly noble even as it adds support to his own definition of nobility, causing their competition to shift from a debate to a kind of potlatch. Marcel Mauss's now-classic account of the potlatch, which he describes as "above all a struggle among nobles to determine their position in the hierarchy," shows how the giving or even the scorning of goods may be one way of indicating superiority.[20] In recent years critics have paid much fruitful attention to the instrumentality of generosity in early modern literature, and in particular to the ways in which different kinds of gifts, both literary and otherwise, worked to augment the status of the giver as much as, or more than, the receiver.[21] Versions of Mauss's model of the potlatch were theorized *avant la lettre* in the early modern period by authors such as Stefano Guazzo and Lodowick Bryskett. Pettie translates Guazzo as asserting that "the more loftie we are placed, the more lowly wee ought to humble our selves: which is in deed, the way to ryse higher,"[22] and, even more pointedly, Bryskett in *A Discourse of Civill Life* describes the magnanimous man in this way:

> knowing right well that whoso offereth iniury to another, cannot be rightly called Magnanimous, he abstaineth from doing any: and if any man haue offered him iniurie, he holdeth it for the greatest and honorablest reuenge to forgiue, though he haue the partie in his power, & maye satisfie himselfe; and thinketh that the greatest displeasure he can worke to his enemy, is to shew himselfe euermore garnished with vertue.[23]

Bryskett's account highlights the disguised competition—even hostility—that might be expressed through apparent generosity. While Possidonio credits the importance of liberality in contributing to "a glorie farre exceeding al other" (G3ᵛ), making it part of his argument for the importance of riches,[24] Fabricio, in contrast, exhibits a metaphorical understanding of generosity. Just as Fabricio insists that scripture must be read with attention to its figurative rather than to its literal meaning (T4ᵛ–Vʳ), his gift of the ring to Possidonio reveals the true meaning of his assertion that "Nobilitie is nothing else, but an excellencie, by the which things that are most worthy, do take place before those that are lesse worthy" (P3ᵛ). Passing on the physical prize becomes the means by which Fabricio asserts his superiority on a higher level, encouraging readers to recall the recent assertion of one of the interlocutors that "gifts of the mind" are "not easie to be transported from one body to another" (Bb3ʳ). His gift thus changes the meaning of the contested token; as Fabricio ever-so-graciously rubs it in, asking Possidonio to be a "partaker" of the "sentence" that has just judged him unworthy, he also instructs Possidonio to wear the ring in remembrance of *him*, rather than the lady Virginia. Fabricio's supremacy is now undoubted, and Possidonio is finally prevailed upon by the whole group to take the ring as a "signe of brotherlie friendship" (Dd^r). Possidonio, who has spent the whole of the dialogue loudly trumpeting his superiority is, at the end, compelled to accept the condescension of the one he proclaimed his inferior. Fabricio, for his part, is given a crown of olive leaves, a plant associated with peace as well as with Minerva's learning, that he is to wear as a "signe of victorie" (Dd^v). The narrator does offer faint praise of Possidonio's contributions to the argument as "no weake reasons" (Dd^v), but there is no real advocacy in the remainder of the text for nobility of blood and wealth. While one reader of *Nennio* has suggested that its end reveals an "Elizabethan love of compromise,"[25] that view discounts the extent to which the competing views of nobility are not so much reconciled as left to stand in tension. As Huntington has noted, "this is a text that seems intent on voicing a critique but at the same time achieving deniability."[26] Still, though Nennio's positive gestures toward inherited nobility may serve to make the dialogue's scathing critique of its vices more palatable, the mere fact that nobility of blood is being offered a consolation prize demonstrates just how much it has suffered over the course of the dialogue. Though it is true that readers of Nenna's dialogue are asked to weigh the merits of differing views, these readers, like those of Spenser's commendatory sonnet, have not been given a very challenging task.

NOBILITY AND COURTESY IN *THE FAERIE QUEENE*

The Faerie Queene follows in many ways the humanist emphasis on virtue in action over inherited nobility, while at the same time making it impossible to regard that virtue as straightforwardly as *Nennio* does. The Spenserian narrator asserts in Book VI *both* that "gentle bloud will gentle manners breed" (iii.2) *and* that "vertues seat is deepe within the mynd,/ And not in outward shows, but inward thoughts defynd" (Proem.5).[27] In offering such apparently simple—and contradictory—statements about the nature of noble virtue, the narrator encourages the reader to *test* his varying assertions rather than to adopt any one of his claims as definitive. Even as the proem to Book VI suggests a close link between nobility and courtesy, then, it points to the work that will be required of the reader in interpreting this connection:

Amongst them all growes not a fayrer flowre,
    Then is the bloosme of comely courtesie,
    Which though it on a lowly stalke doe bowre,
    Yet brancheth forth in braue nobilitie,
    And spreds it selfe through all ciuilitie:
    Of which though present age doe plenteous seeme,
    Yet being matcht with plaine Antiquitie,
    Ye will them all but fayned shows esteeme,
    Which carry colours faire, that feeble eies misdeeme.
                                                    (4)

In his attack on contemporary expressions of courtesy and nobility (here
tightly connected), the narrator insists that his readers perform the mental
exercise of contrasting the world around them with the world portrayed
in his book. Here the narrator addresses the readers directly, speaking of
their own thought processes: "*Ye* will them all but fayned showes esteeme"
(emphasis mine). Having been counseled to be suspicious of assumptions
based on visual evidence, however, these readers are also in a good position
to evaluate the narrator's own claims, including his association of courtesy
with "nobilitie," a term that he declines to define specifically. While the
description "noble" is frequently used in the first few cantos of Book VI, it
is used quite sparingly in the later cantos. Book VI as a whole emphasizes
more and more the movement from nobility as an inherent attribute of a
person, to nobility as the characterization of an *action* that may admit of
more than one interpretation.

In *Nennio* the judgment of the reader is likely to be in accord with the
judgment of the dialogue's characters. In Book VI of *The Faerie Queene*
there are multiple possibilities for the reader's sympathy, as the differing
assessments of Calidore in the past decades of scholarship can well attest.[28]
Calidore, identified as a knight on Book VI's 1596 title page, could be seen
as *Nennio*'s ideal of compounded nobility, linking him to the Earl of Essex,
but it is not at all clear that his character blends in equal measure inherited
nobility as represented by Possidonio and acquired nobility as represented
by Fabricio. The narrator's early description of Calidore in Canto i sug-
gests that he has a "naturall" "gentlenesse of spright" but also that he can
"add" to that the learned art of "gracious speach" which is able to "steale
mens hearts away" (2). Though the narrator goes on to assert that Calidore
"loued simple truth" (3), this description points toward the nuanced rela-
tionship between "speach" and "truth" in the poem rather than clarifying

Calidore's character. Readers know much more about what Calidore does than what he thinks, rendering decisive judgment of him impossible. In the end, the poem emphasizes his courteous techniques rather than his ability to epitomize one form of nobility over another. The poem's valuing of "inward thoughts" over "outward shows" thus makes it necessary for the reader to consider how outward shows—at their best, benevolent actions rather than subterfuge, though the distinction will prove difficult to maintain—may serve as an imperfect guide to a character's motivations and virtue.

The opening cantos of Book VI demonstrate the troublesome nature of the connection between courtesy and nobility on which the narrator insists in the proem. In Canto i, Calidore himself connects the two concepts in his criticism of those who "defame/ Both noble armes and gentle curtesie" (26), but readers of the poem may share Briana's disgust with his indiscriminate violence and her sense that these ideals do not combine as neatly as he claims. Canto ii's depiction of Tristram seems to illustrate the process by which courtesy moves from occupying a modest place to bursting onto the scene in the full-blown expression of nobility, yet in so doing it invites an interrogation of its own terms.[29] This canto contains an explosion of instances of the word "noble," insisting on the way in which Tristram's inherited gentle blood shines through despite his appearance; he is referred to as or associated closely with the term "noble" no fewer than eleven times in this canto, many more times than any other character in Book VI. Tristram's claim to true nobility is complicated, however, by his grasping relationship to material goods, revealed by his intense interest in the spoils of the knight he has vanquished. Jeff Dolven has argued convincingly that the greed Tristram shows here is part of Book VI's "creeping anxiety about proof."[30] I would add that his display of greed also encourages readers to evaluate Calidore's thought process in determining Tristram's nobility. Having been told *twice* in parallel lines that Calidore views Tristram's nobility with certainty ("That sure he deem'd him borne of noble race" [VI.ii.5] and "That sure he weend him borne of noble blood" [VI.ii.24]), Spenser's readers are now in a good position to judge just what is meant by this confident label. As they watch how Tristram "Long fed his greedie eyes with the faire sight/ Of the bright mettall" (39), they may connect his ostensibly certain nobility of birth to the problems with counterfeit courtesy, especially its ability to "please the eies of them, that pas," and make one "thinke gold that is bras" (VI.Proem.5). Tristram is here subjected to a "triall of true curtesie" (VI.Proem.5)—a trial requiring the reader's discrimination and work to bring together different parts of Book VI—and, with his disordered values, it is not at all clear that he passes. As readers begin to wonder if Tristram's golden character may actually be brass, the connection between apparent nobility and true courtesy becomes more and more suspect.

Spenser's readers are also required to be attentive in the opening lines of Canto iii, in which conflicting claims about the true nature of gentility are presented as if they form a seamless whole.[31] The canto opens with the simplistic assertion "True is, that whilome that good Poet sayd, / The gentle minde by gentle deeds is knowne," which Spenser credits to Chaucer and invites readers to question precisely by insisting on its obvious truth. This formulation emphasizes action as a reflection of a noble mental state, and it echoes the Wife of Bath's claim (in the persona of the old woman to the knight) that "gentil dedes" are what characterize the "gentil man" (1115-16), and emphatically *not* anything that is inherited ("For, God it woot, men may wel often fynde/ A lordes son do shame and vilenye" [1150-51]) or possessed ("genterye/ Is nat annexed to possessioun" [1146-47]).[32] And yet, immediately after citing Chaucer's criticism of blood and wealth, the narrator offers Possidonio's view of the obvious worth of inherited gentle blood, claiming "For a man by nothing is so well bewrayd,/ As by his manners, in which plaine is showne/ Of what degree and what race he is growne," and even bringing in the example of horse breeding (1).[33] The logical evidence that the narrator seems to offer with the conjunction "for" actually stands in contrast to the claim that precedes it; one statement points toward the mind's reflection in noble deeds, and the other points toward the physicality of noble inheritance. In giving equal weight to two contradictory statements, the narrator provokes his readers to notice a discrepancy and to consider the relation between these conflicting assertions and the tale that follows.[34] As Canto iii's episode unfolds, characters demonstrate their mastery of the narrator's claim that gentility is closely linked to outward manners. This means, however, that they actively seek to preserve the appearance of a quality that the narrator has insisted is natural. Priscilla, who has been absent from home against her father's wishes, seeks to preserve her reputation with "coloured disguize," and Calidore thinks in similar terms: "He can deuize this counter-cast of slight,/ To giue faire colour to that Ladies cause in sight" (VI.iii.8, 16). In "coloring" the tale that he tells to Priscilla's father, Calidore demonstrates his skill in precisely those contemporary practices of rhetoric that the narrator criticizes as "fayned showes . . . which carry colours faire, that feeble eies misdeeme" (VI.Proem.4).[35] This rhetorical coloring of nobility is not as easily rejected

as it is in *Nennio*, however. Calidore's use of the head of the corpse slain by
the "noble Tristram" (VI.iii.17) does provide an ironic commentary on the
nature of the nobility that he works to preserve, but readers may well con-
tinue to sympathize with Priscilla's situation and feel that Calidore's aims
are worthy despite his suspect means of accomplishing them. Though the
episode is introduced with the claim that "gentle bloud will gentle manners
breed" (VI.iii.2), readers may come to regard this as a hypothesis to be
tested and refined rather than as an obvious and simple truth.

Similarly, when readers encounter the narrator's assertion, "O what
an easie thing is to descry/ The gentle bloud, how euer it be it be wrapt"
at the outset to Canto v (1), they will recall the tale that has immediately
preceded it: Calepine's satisfaction of Matilde's desire for a "noble *chyld*"
with a foundling who will go on to accomplish "right noble *deedes*"
(VI.iv.33, 38; emphasis mine). The characterization of nobility here has
shifted toward outward action, and, furthermore, it has been supple-
mented by Calepine's speech suggesting that proper *training* forms "more
braue and noble knights" than being "dandled in the lap" (VI.iv.35–36).
Here too, the very confidence with which both Calepine and the narrator
speak invites readers' attention.

While the narrator asserts that the Salvage Man is a source of obvious
proof for the ease with which "gentle bloud" manifests itself ("That plainely
may in this wyld man be red . . . For certes he was borne of noble blood"
[VI.v.2]), readers have already been abundantly cautioned to be skeptical
of such evidence. As the account of the Salvage Man proceeds, the nar-
rator's claim for his *obvious* nobility is complicated, though not under-
mined completely. He is misunderstood by Arthur and Timias when they
first approach him (VI.v.25), and his displays of violence, though aimed
in the proper direction, are unsettlingly animalistic, such as when, lion-
like, he attacks Turpine's groom and "him rudely rent, and all to peeces
tore" (VI.vi.22), when he is "found enuironed about/ With slaughtred bod-
ies" (VI.vi.38), and when, in his attack on Enias, "He flew vpon him, like
a greedy kight/ Vnto some carrion offered to his sight" (VI.viii.28). The
Salvage Man may indeed contribute to the poem's portrait of gentility—the
lion is a noble beast—but his verbal associations with rudeness, slaugh-
ter, and greed undermine the correspondence between "gentle bloud" and
"sparkes of gentle mynd" (VI.v.1) as well as the link between "noble armes
and gentle curtesie" (VI.i.26). When readers of Book VI reflect on these
early examples of nobility in action, they may be inclined to feel that its
definition is not so obvious.

CALIDORE'S GENEROUS COURTESY

In the latter cantos of Book VI, the term "noble" falls away almost completely, and, beginning with Calidore's pastoral sojourn in Canto ix, readers are asked to consider instead how Calidore's courtesy may be both troubling and efficacious. Both *Nennio* and Canto VI.ix depict contests between noble and lower-born characters, and both texts place the reader in the position of judge in these contests, yet they also differ in important ways. While *Nennio's* Possidonio and Fabricio are in open competition with one another, and readers of that competition are steered toward a decided preference for one over the other, Calidore deals with others in ways that admit of less definitive judgments. By re-staging Calidore and Coridon's rivalry in Cantos x and xi, Spenser requires his readers to revise their conclusions and resist simple distinctions.

Calidore reveals himself in Canto ix to be susceptible to genuine overwhelming emotion but also adept at self-mastery and ready to use conversation as a tool of manipulation. After being caught by Cupid and "surprisd in subtile bands," Calidore is unable to do much more than gaze (11, 12). When he masters himself again, however, he has the presence of mind to orchestrate the conversation with the shepherds in his favor, drawing it out "to worke delay," and speaking to the shepherds but aiming his words at Pastorella's "fantazy" (12). Having gained a dinner invitation to Pastorella's house, Calidore chooses a post-prandial topic of conversation designed to appeal to his hosts. The narrator describes him in this moment as "the gentle knight, *as* he that did excell/ In courtesie, and well could doe and say" (18; emphasis mine). While "gentle" describes Calidore directly, his courteous actions are distanced from him by the term "as," which suggests that he is *like* a courteous person in his pose, rather than simply *being* courteous. Despite his courteous skill, Calidore is at cross-purposes with Meliboe, Pastorella's foster father, for much of their discussion. It may be that they are speaking in different genres: what Calidore seems to mean as pleasing after-dinner *talk* becomes, in Meliboe's responses, a debate about the way to live one's life, with Meliboe insisting on the value of withdrawal from the world of commerce. Calidore's expression of envy for Meliboe's low station in life, which may be no more than making conversation, is greeted with serious rebuke by Meliboe and a lesson about the true nature of contentment. When Meliboe talks without interruption for six stanzas, Calidore is yet again left to gaze, and yet again left with divided attention, affected by both the sound of Meliboe's speech and the sight of Pastorella. His "greedy eare" suggests a link to Tristram, though the "double rauishment" he feels is not due to gold, but to the myriad attractions of a pastoral world in which he does not really belong (26).

Even as he experiences a real desire to become part of Pastorella's world, Calidore reveals his outsider status by making use of techniques that link him to rich show-offs such as Possidonio or even Mammon.[36] In an echo of Guyon's words to Mammon ("To them, that list, these base regardes I lend" [II.vii.33]), Meliboe asserts to Calidore the importance of rejecting ambition and its attendant spectacles, saying "To them, that list, the worlds gay showes I leaue,/ And to great ones such follies doe forgiue" (22).[37] Calidore appears to share this condemnation, declaring, "Now surely syre, I find,/ That all this worlds gay showes, which we admire,/ Be but vaine shadowes to this safe retyre/ Of life, which here in lowlinesse ye lead" (27), but his audience here includes Pastorella. The narrator explains that Calidore condemns the court in order "to occasion meanes, to worke his mind,/ And to insinuate his harts desire" (27), lines that echo the narrator's previous description of how Calidore makes conversation with the shepherds in order to create delay.[38] Calidore's carefully chosen words suggest the "painted shewes" of Spenser's commendatory sonnet to Nennio despite his attempt to distance himself from court life. Calidore's show is not completely insincere, nor is it completely convincing to either Meliboe or the reader. When Calidore goes too far in wishing for the shepherd's life, Meliboe offers him a sententious rebuke, calling into question the judgment of the many and telling him "It is the mynd, that maketh good or ill,/ That maketh wretch or happie, rich or poore" (29, 30).[39] Meliboe's emphasis on retirement is misinterpreted by Calidore, however, who immediately sees in his assertion that "each vnto himselfe his life may fortunize" the possibility of an active self-fashioning (30, 31).

With his emphasis on the mind and on the need for proper judgment, Meliboe resembles Fabricio,[40] while Calidore in turn resembles Possidonio when he offers to repay Meliboe for his hospitality. He continues to look to outward expressions of generosity, even flashy generosity, regardless of what he has just heard Meliboe say about internal contentment. Here Spenser rewrites Tasso's Gerusalemme liberata, his source for this exchange, in an important way. In Tasso, Erminia, the outsider guest who is Calidore's counterpart, shows that she has understood the words of her host by not offering the money adored by the vulgar crowd; she only acknowledges that she would have been willing to do so.[41] In contrast, Calidore actually produces the gold and thrusts it toward Meliboe: "forth he drew much gold, and toward him it driue" (32). In offering a "recompense" (32) to Meliboe, one of a series of humble hosts in Book VI, Calidore potentially deprives him of his means of enacting courtesy, and also shows that he was not paying attention to Meliboe's scorn for the time when he sold his services (24). Further, Calidore shows an uncomfortable resemblance to Turpine, who himself uses a disguise of courtesy "[t]o cloke the mischiefe" when he offers a "goodly meed" to Enias and his companion (VI.vii.4).[42] Meliboe, for his part, practically recoils: "Sir knight, your bounteous proffer/ Be farre fro me, to whom ye ill display/ That mucky masse, the cause of mens decay" (33). Meliboe's alliteration turns Calidore's attempt to "golden guerdon giue" (32) into an emphatic rejection of the "mucky masse," which he wants to be "farre . . . farre" away from him. Not only is Meliboe's scorn another echo of Guyon to Mammon, as Judith Anderson has noted,[43] it is also a condemnation of Calidore's sensibilities; Meliboe is criticizing both Calidore's decision to offer him money and his doing so through show and "display." As Fabricio asserts in his own critique of Possidonio's view of liberality, "true liberalitie springeth not from riches, but from the love of the minde" (M2ᵛ). Spenser's characterization of courtesy as "forgerie" in the proem to Book VI is well illustrated by Calidore's practice of it here; Meliboe rejects his offers just as Guyon rejects Philotime's "art and counterfetted shew" (II.vii.45).[44] Readers are left to decide whether Calidore and Meliboe engage in a competition of values or merely of courteous one-upmanship in this conversation, but in any case it is Meliboe who emerges victorious, a victory of the mind's treasures over the power of golden speech and golden gold.

Spenser's readers must continue to exercise discernment in evaluating Calidore's decision to present himself as a shepherd the better to woo Pastorella, who has also rejected his "courteous guize" in another alliterative series ("His layes, his loues, his lookes she did them all despize" [35]). Spenser writes of Calidore that "who had seene him then, would haue bethought/ On *Phrygian Paris*" (36), a suggestion that Calidore's garb could provoke a critical response. The association of the Judgment of Paris with a bad choice of life paths was conventional;[45] Book II of *Nennio* begins with an allegorical reading of the myth as showing the greater value of the contemplative life over the active life or the life of pleasure, indicating the narrator's own sympathy for the case that Fabricio will make about the nobility of Pallas Athena's domain of learning, and foreshadowing the end of the debate. This reading of the Judgment of Paris in *Nennio* also provides a useful lens for viewing Calidore, who, with his shepherd's garb and lovesickness, may be likened to the Paris of poor choices.[46] Indeed, readers may well remember, yet again, Spenser's description of the Cave of Mammon, which includes the golden apple of discord among the fruits of Proserpina's garden and a reference to "partiall *Paris*" in the same position in the stanza as the reference to "*Phrygian Paris*" in Book VI (II.vii.55); while the term "Phrygian" may have connotations of effeminacy, the word "partiall" is clearly disparaging and evokes the relevant issue of faulty judgment. What is crucial is that Spenser does not just compare Calidore to Paris, he represents the *thought process* of those who might see him in this condition ("who had seene him then, would haue bethought"). Spenser's readers are thus implicitly included among those who would have been *reminded* by Calidore's dubious disguise of a Paris whom they know to be prejudiced and foolhardy. Nonetheless, by pointing to a connection that Calidore's costume might cause others to make, rather than simply declaring Calidore to be *like* Paris, the narrator also hints that the similarity need not be the whole story. The reader's mind also forms part of the tale.

As the disguised Calidore goes on to compete with Coridon for Pastorella's love, his insistent deference involves him in another competition in generosity from which Coridon emerges as the loser even as readers are left to decide what to make of Calidore's courtesy. The narrator clearly describes Coridon's disposition and actions as both base and ineffective; he scowls, pouts, lowers, frowns, and repeatedly bites his lip (38, 39, 41), and he sets up a wrestling contest for the express purpose of embarrassing Calidore ("t'auenge his grudge, and worke his foe great shame" [43]). Coridon is unpleasant company. Yet even as readers are told explicitly of Coridon's motives, they are left to conjecture about Calidore's thoughts, being told merely that his actions arise from "courteous inclination" (42). Calidore's generosity could be ingrained disposition, calculated technique, or a combination of the two. The narrator simply reveals how Calidore's actions *appear* to others, that he "did *seeme* so farre/ From malicing, or grudging his good houre,/ That all he could, he graced him with her,/ Ne euer *shewed* signe of rancour or of iarre" (39; emphasis mine). Calidore's gifts to Coridon further call into question his motives. In an action similar to Fabricio's gesture to Possidonio, Calidore places a "flowry garlond" (42) that Pastorella has given him on Coridon's own head. Soon after, he duplicates this action in a wrestling contest.[47] Calidore has to lighten his fall to prevent breaking Coridon's neck, but he downplays his success:

Then was the oaken crowne by *Pastorell*
Giuen to *Calidore*, as his due right;
But he, that did in courtesie excell,
Gaue it to *Coridon*, and said he wonne it well.
(44)

Calidore emphasizes the inappropriateness of the gift by saying that
Coridon is the rightful recipient of this token of victory; as Stanley
Stewart has noted, this only serves to turn the crown into a "token of
defeat."[48] Precisely by shifting the crown from his own head to Coridon's,
Calidore underscores that what makes him noble, his generous courtesy,
cannot be shifted from one person to another. The more Calidore down-
plays his own efforts in a classic display of *sprezzatura*,[49] the more he is
able to win over his rivals; the narrator's very suggestion that Calidore *ex-
cels* in courtesy emphasizes the efficacy of courtesy as a means of achiev-
ing success in public competition rather than Calidore's inward dispo-
sition. The narrator goes on to comment that "courtesie amongst the
rudest breeds/ Good will and fauour" (45), a hereditary metaphor that
could mean that courtesy is recognized *even* "amongst the rudest," but
which also suggests that the rustic crowds who witness Calidore's courte-
ous performance lack the critical judgment whereby Meliboe knows to
reject a display of generosity motivated, at least in part, by self-interest.
If the pastoral audience for Calidore's generosity is taken in, however,
the reader who has witnessed his previous encounter with Meliboe may
well have a more complicated reaction. While *Nennio's* Fabricio shows
a certain savvy in passing on the ring to Possidonio, he does so as the
winner of a contest with explicit terms, and he also makes the meaning
of the gift explicit. Calidore, in contrast, doesn't reveal the motivation of
his generosity, and Spenser similarly declines to tell readers directly what
to think of it. When Coridon is jealous because Calidore is leading the
dance, the narrator recounts that Calidore kindly "set him in his place"
(42); the double meaning of the line perfectly captures the ambiguity of
Calidore's action.

   At the same time that Calidore appears suspiciously adept at manipu-
lating his gifts to secure public favor, he also has a real instinct for gener-
ous courage, as subsequent cantos reveal; these two aspects of his char-
acter work together to such a degree that it becomes impossible to reject
one without rejecting the other. In Canto x, his *teleological* desire for the
"guerdon" of Pastorella's love (2) stands in tension with the vision of the

Graces on Mount Acidale, who represent the ideal *circulation* of gener-osity.[50] Calidore is overcome by Colin Clout's explication of the vision in the same manner that he is by Meliboe's talk and Pastorella's beauty in Canto ix; he feeds "his greedy fancy," and "his sences" are "rauished" (30). It is tempting to imagine Calidore as learning from this vision, and the narrator does describe him as "voide of thoughts impure" when he resumes his pursuit of Pastorella (32). Soon after he gives her the gift that really wins her over: the head of the tiger from which he has just saved her (36–37). In this moment of unhesitating bravery and self-sacrifice, which Maurice Evans likens to "put[ting] on the mantle of the good shep-herd,"[51] Calidore is clearly distinguished from Coridon and his "cowherd feare" (35). And yet Calidore immediately follows this deed with actions that underscore his showiness and questionable sincerity, taking the odd step of "hewing off" the tiger's head, presumably with his "shepheards hooke," rather than attending to the immediate needs of the "scarcely" recovered Pastorella (36).[52] While killing the tiger should speak for it-self, Calidore adds a superfluous proof of his bravery for which Pastorella is bound to repay him with "a thousand" thanks (36). In this, Calidore seems more courtier-like than Christ-like, supplementing actual sacri-fice with performative flourishes. The reader who pauses to imagine this messy scene is forced to appreciate the messiness of courtesy itself; as in Canto iii, when Calidore makes use of another head, the real-world relationships that courtesy forges resist the narrator's idealizing formula-tions. Calidore's display of a head here is strange, rather than deceptive, but it does suggest that readers should connect two moments from Book VI, and all the more so when the narrator refers to Calidore's use of rhe-torical coloring in the very next stanza. In what are perhaps the narrator's most critical words so far, readers are told "Yet *Calidore* did not despise him [Coridon] quight,/ But vsde him friendly for further intent,/ That by his fellowship, he colour might/ Both his estate, and loue from skill of any wight" (37). Calidore's ability to respond to the changing demands of his situation, a fundamental attribute of the courtier,[53] means that he can take on the tiger *and* that he continues to make use of others.

Canto xi also insists on the practical value of Calidore's courtesy, and even, perhaps especially, his craftiness in deploying it. Though Calidore may be associated with a vocabulary of use and greed, he also saves Pastorella from the worst examples of such forces by rescuing her from the brigands to whom, as Douglas Northrop and Heather Dubrow have noted, he bears some resemblance.[54] If Spenser's narrator suggests that readers pass judgment against Calidore's efficacious manipulation in Canto ix, he also requires them to revisit that judgment in Canto xi, when the idealistic Meliboe is summarily "slaine" (18),[55] when Calidore's ability to influence Coridon with both "meed" and "words" is the only means by which he can locate Pastorella (35), and when Calidore's disguise as a shepherd and his willingness to let the brigands "hyre" him become the means by which he saves Pastorella (36, 40). When Calidore acquires the "victors meed" after his battle with the brigands,[56] he passes on the best of the treasure to Pastorella, his primary concern, and also gives all the recovered flocks to Coridon (51). Readers who have seen how both Calidore's courage and his grief at Pastorella's apparent death (41) exceed Coridon's may well be inclined to feel that he is the proper victor in spite of their lingering reservations, reservations not provoked by the conclusion of *Nennio*. By presenting more than one version of the competition between Calidore and Coridon, Spenser requires his readers to see the issues at stake from several angles, and to recognize that the meaning of nobility in action cannot be decisively pinned down.

When Calidore captures the Blattant Beast at the end of Book VI, the narrator calls him "noble" for the first time, a word that he has not used since Arthur's defeat of Disdaine in Canto viii (xii.36). While the appellation underscores Calidore's achievement, it also hints at the precariousness of this achievement; Book VI's series of agons has taught readers to be suspicious of the term "noble" as definitive or final. In rendering Calidore's victory over Coridon in Canto ix hollow while going on to show how Calidore's real-world generosity is comprised of craftiness, display, *and* courage, Spenser shows a reluctance to direct the argument of his poetry toward a clear-cut definition of nobility or a simplistic evaluation of courtesy. Still, with his nuanced consideration of Calidore's goal-directed actions, Spenser suggests a different possibility for his own poetry: that he will require readers to take their time in assessing competing values, so that they may recognize what is at stake in a question rather than answering it in only one way. Though Spenser praises accurate decision-making in the commendatory sonnet to *Nennio*, in his own poem he shows that Calidore's generous virtue derives from a combination of inward thoughts and outward shows that is impossible to untangle, provoking his readers to adopt a view of courtesy that moves beyond simple choices.

Union College

NOTES

1.   For their generous responses to this article at different stages of its develop-
ment, I would like to thank Victoria Kahn, Lorna Hutson, Albert Ascoli, Timothy
Hampton, the audience at the October 2010 Sixteenth Century Society conference,
the editors of *Spenser Studies*, and the journal's anonymous reviewers. I would also
like to thank the English Department and the Humanities Research Fund at Union
College for supporting this work.

2.   Raffaele Girardi includes a brief biography and discussion of the dialogue in
the introduction to his edition of the text. See Giovan Battista Nenna, *Il Nennio*,
ed. Raffaele Girardi (Rome: Laterza, 2003), v–xxxii. Girardi's modern edition of
Nennio is rare in the United States; I have appreciated consulting Middlebury
College's copy. Jones published translations of Lipsius and Guicciardini in 1594
and 1595 with Spenser's publisher Ponsonby. For the scant bibliographical infor-
mation available on Jones, see Leslie Shepard's biographical note in Alice Shalvi's
facsimile edition of the 1595 *Nennio* (Jerusalem and London: Israel Universities
Press and H. A. Humphrey, 1967), xiv, as well as the *Spenser Encyclopedia* article
on the commendatory sonnets by Franklin B. Williams, Jr. (Toronto: University
of Toronto Press, 1990). The other commendatory sonnets to Jones's *Nennio* were
written by Samuel Daniel, George Chapman, and Angel Day.

3.   Willy Maley notes that Sonnet 80 of the *Amoretti*, which claims that *The
Faerie Queene* is complete, was entered in the Stationers' Register in November
1594 (*A Spenser Chronology* [London: Macmillan, 1994], 62). But the editors of
the Norton edition allow for the possibility that it was revised before itself being
entered in the Stationers Register in January 1596 (Hugh Maclean and Anne Lake
Prescott, ed., *Edmund Spenser's Poetry*, 3rd ed. [New York: W. W. Norton, 1993],
619). A French translation of the dialogue was published in 1583. Shalvi also notes
the accuracy of Jones's translation, an assessment with which I concur (xii).

4.   *Nennio, or A treatise of nobility: VVherein is discoursed what true Nobilitie
is, with such qualities as are required in a perfect Gentleman. Written in Italian
by that famous Doctor and worthy knight Sir Iohn Baptista Nenna of Bari. Done
into English by William Iones Gent.* London, 1595. Early English Books Online. I
have also appreciated the opportunity to consult this edition and the original 1542
Italian edition in the Folger Library. In citing *Nennio*, I have modernized u/v, i/j,
tilde, and long s.

5.   The poem is printed after A4; John Huntington notes that the commenda-
tory sonnets were "clearly a late edition" (*Ambition, Rank, and Poetry in 1590s
England* [Urbana: University of Illinois Press, 2001], 168n14).

6.   The use of "visnomy," or physiognomy, is interesting in this context, as it
points to a relation between the exterior and the interior that is especially compli-
cated in *The Faerie Queene*.

7.   For the Italian tradition of this debate, both primary texts and introductions, see Albert Rabil, Jr., *Knowledge, Goodness, and Power: The Debate over Nobility among Quattrocento Humanists* (Binghamton, NY: Medieval & Renaissance Texts & Studies, 1991). Rabil locates the beginning of the Italian debate in Dante's *Convivio*, which emphasizes virtue over wealth (3, 12). On the contested meaning of the categories of nobility and gentility in the English Renaissance, Ruth Kelso's work remains particularly useful. See Kelso, *The Doctrine of the English Gentleman in the Sixteenth Century* (Urbana: University of Illinois Press, 1929). Quentin Skinner in *Foundations of Modern Political Thought: The Renaissance* (Cambridge: Cambridge University Press, 1978) notes that the "the equation between virtue and nobility became a humanist commonplace" (82), though he also emphasizes the conservative attitude toward the aristocracy held by many northern humanists (238). On the topic of nobility in Spenser, see Lila Geller, "Spenser's Theory of Nobility in Book VI of *The Faerie Queene*," *English Literary Renaissance* 5:1 (1975): 49–57, an article that places more emphasis on the importance of aristocratic blood than I believe the text warrants. William A. Oram also makes brief reference to *Nennio* as well as to the different definitions of nobility of which Spenser's Dedicatory Sonnets make use: see "Seventeen Ways of Looking at Nobility: Spenser's Shorter Sonnet Sequence," in *Renaissance Historicisms: Essays in Honor of Arthur F. Kinney, ed.* James M. Dutcher and Anne Lake Prescott (Newark: University of Delaware Press, 2008), 106–7 and 110.

8.   Nenna here uses the term *animo*. Jones makes use of the term "mind" to translate both *anima* and *animo*, though he will also at times translate *anima* as "soul," as on N3[v] when he translates both *anima* and *animo* in the same passage.

9.   A. C. Judson, "Spenser's Theory of Courtesy," *PMLA* 47:1 (1932): 123.

10.   "Nature and Art in *The Faerie Queene*," *ELH* 28:1 (1961): 16.

11.   Huntington, 75. On Spenser's agreement with Fabricio in this sonnet, see also Montrose, "Spenser and the Elizabethan Political Imaginary," *ELH* 69:4 (2002): 922–23. For the view that Spenser is sympathetic to the possibility of social mobility in this sonnet, see also Arthur F. Marotti, "'Love Is Not Love': Elizabethan Sonnet Sequences and the Social Order," *ELH* 49:2 (1982): 418.

12.   Lila Geller does briefly connect the two texts, but for purposes very different from mine.

13.   My sense of Spenser as an author who insists on examining the nuances of his subject matter despite the risk of contradiction has been influenced by critics such as Paul Alpers, who characterizes Spenser as an author who "makes us see a moral question from all sides" ("How to Read *The Faerie Queene*," in *Essential Articles for the Study of Edmund Spenser*, ed. A. C. Hamilton [Hamden: Archon Books, 1972], 334). On Spenser's lack of interest in producing a "coherent fiction," see also Alpers's *Poetry of "The Faerie Queene"* (Princeton: Princeton University Press, 1967), 19. Other critics who emphasize Spenser's tolerance for tension and open-endedness in his poem include A. Bartlett Giamatti (*Play of Double Senses: Spenser's "Faerie Queene"* [Englewood Cliffs, NJ: Prentice-Hall, 1975]); Bill Nestrick ("The Virtuous

and Gentle Discipline of Gentlemen and Poets," *ELH* 29:4 [1962]: 357–71); James Nohrnberg (*The Analogy of "The Faerie Queene"* [Princeton: Princeton University Press, 1976]); and Jonathan Goldberg (*Endlesse Worke: Spenser and the Structures of Discourse* [Baltimore: Johns Hopkins University Press, 1981]). See also Jeff Dolven, *Scenes of Instruction in Renaissance Romance* (Chicago: University of Chicago Press), 229–30.

14. On Jones's front matter, including the other commendatory sonnets, see Huntington, 69–76.

15. Girardi edition, 6. At the end of his dialogue, Nenna also includes a letter to his readers that addresses criticism of his text's language and topic (though not its actual argument). See Shalvi for a translation, xvii–xix.

16. I cite throughout the edition of A. C. Hamilton, Hiroshi Yamashita, and Toshiyuki Suzuki (Harlow, UK: Longman, 2001).

17. The image also recalls the House of Pride, whose "golden foile" obscures its adjacent "Donghill of dead carcases" (I.iv.4, I.v.53).

18. Compounded nobility is also proclaimed the ideal in Castiglione, though not of course without the dissension characteristic of that work. See Baldassare Castiglione, *The Book of the Courtier*, I.xvi (Venice, 1528).

19. See *The Book of the Courtier*, I.xxvi.

20. *The Gift: Forms and Functions of Exchange in Archaic Societies*, trans. Ian Cunnison (New York: W. W. Norton, 1967), 1–4.

21. For theories on the paradoxical nature of the gift, see Pierre Bourdieu, *Practical Reason: On the Theory of Action*, trans. Randall Johnson (Stanford: Stanford University Press, 1998), 75–91. I find Bourdieu's formulation of how groups such as the nobility may have an "interest in disinterestedness" (85) especially compelling. See also Jacques Derrida, *Given Time: I. Counterfeit Money*, trans. Peggy Kamuf (Chicago: University of Chicago Press, 1992). On the contradictions in early modern gift-giving, see Natalie Zemon Davis, *The Gift in Sixteenth-Century France* (Madison: University of Wisconsin Press, 2000); Alison V. Scott, *Selfish Gifts* (Madison: Fairleigh Dickinson University Press, 2006); and Louis Montrose, "Gifts and Reasons: the Contexts of Peele's *Araygnement of Paris*," *ELH* 47:3 (1980): 433–61. For gift-giving in Spenser, see Patricia Fumerton, *Cultural Aesthetics: Renaissance Literature and the Practice of Social Ornament* (Chicago: University of Chicago Press, 1991), 29–66. See also Patricia Wareh, "Humble Presents: Gift-Giving in Spenser's Dedicatory Sonnets," *Studies in the Literary Imagination* 38:2 (2005): 119–32.

22. M. Steeven Guazzo, *The Civile Conversation*, trans. George Pettie and ed. Edward Sullivan (London and New York: Constable and Alfred A. Knopf, 1925), 192.

23. *Literary Works*, ed. J. H. P. Pafford (England: Gregg International, 1972), 232. I have modernized his spelling very slightly throughout (changing "ſ" to "s," but leaving "u" and "i.")

24. Cf. Mammon's argument to Guyon about the usefulness of money for

chivalry (II.vii.11). Ruth Kelso notes that "Liberality, one of the chief distinguishing virtues of the gentleman and Christian, was not possible without wealth" (28).
25. Shalvi, xi.
26. Huntington, 74.
27. On courtesy as a virtue that "must eventually manifest itself in society and public life," see Anthony Low, *The Georgic Revolution* (Princeton: Princeton University Press, 1985), 45. Low takes a positive view of the character of Calidore but also sees a "criticism" of court culture in Book VI through its emphasis on the value of work over aristocratic leisure (67). John D. Staines has recently argued for Spenser's "dissatisfaction with a pastoral fantasy where poetry and virtue are isolated from action" ("Pity and the Authority of the Feminine Passions," *Spenser Studies* 25 [2011]: 150).
28. For a reading of Book VI that emphasizes the cynicism in its depiction of Calidore, see especially Richard Neuse, "Book VI as Conclusion to *The Faerie Queene*," *ELH* 35:3 (1968): 329–53. Other accounts that emphasize the negative portrayal of courtesy in Book VI include Montrose, "Gifts"; Dolven, 207–37; Bruce Danner, "Courteous *Virtù* in Book 6 of *The Faerie Queene*," *Studies in English Literature* 38:1 (Winter 1998): 1–18; Jacqueline T. Miller, "The Courtly Figure: Spenser's Anatomy of Allegory," *Studies in English Literature* 31:1 (1991): 51–68; and Michael Schoenfeldt, "The Poetry of Conduct: Accommodation and Transgression in *The Faerie Queene*, Book 6," in *Enclosure Acts: Sexuality, Property, and Culture in Early Modern England*, ed. Richard Burt and John Michael Archer (Ithaca: Cornell University Press, 1994).

For more positive readings of Calidore and courtesy in Book VI, see Lila Geller, "Spenser's Theory of Nobility"; Donald Cheney, *Spenser's Image of Nature* (New Haven: Yale University Press, 1966), 176–238; Kathleen Williams, *Spenser's World of Glass: A Reading of* The Faerie Queene (Berkeley: University of California Press, 1966), 189–223; Mark Archer, "The Meaning of 'Grace' and 'Courtesy': Book VI of *The Faerie Queene*," *Studies in English Literature* 27:1 (1987): 17–34; Debra Belt, "Hostile Audiences and the Courteous Reader in *The Faerie Queene*, Book VI," *Spenser Studies* 9 (1988): 107–35; and P. C. Bayley, who calls Calidore "a paragon, almost the apotheosis, of the virtues Spenser has displayed in earlier books" ("Order, Grace, and Courtesy in Spenser's World" in *Patterns of Love and Courtesy: Essays in Memory of C. S. Lewis*, ed. John Lawlor [Evanston: Northwestern University Press, 1966], 195).

Critics who deal with the tensions at work in Book VI include Maurice Evans, who takes issue with some of Calidore's decisions but underscores the "redemption" at work in Book VI as a whole (*Spenser's Anatomy of Heroism: A Commentary on "The Faerie Queene"* [Cambridge: Cambridge University Press, 1970], 209–28); Humphrey Tonkin (*Spenser's Courteous Pastoral* [Oxford: Clarendon Press, 1972]); James Nohrnberg, who emphasizes Book VI's treatment of "questions of essential and feigned sincerity" (668); Derek Alwes, ("'Who knowes not Colin Clout?': Spenser's Self-Advertisement in *The Faerie Queene*, Book 6," *Modern*

Philology 88:1 [1990]: 31 and passim); and Douglas Northrop ("The Uncertainty of Courtesy in Book VI of *The Faerie Queene*," *Spenser Studies* 14 [2000]: 215–32). See also Jane Grogan, *Exemplary Spenser* (Farnham, UK: Ashgate, 2009), 137–75. Grogan observes that, with his emphasis on "interior virtue, Spenser gives courtesy a rigorous and well-nigh impossible brief: to be a virtue that defies expression" (149).

On Book VI as a place for reflection, see Gordon Teskey, "'And therefore as a stranger give it welcome': Courtesy and Thinking," *Spenser Studies* 18 (2003): 343–59. On the contradictions in the definition of courtesy in Book VI, see also Catherine Bates, *The Rhetoric of Courtship in Elizabethan Language and Literature* (Cambridge: Cambridge University Press, 2006), 151–72, and on courtesy more generally, see Jennifer Richards, *Rhetoric and Courtliness* (Cambridge: Cambridge University Press, 2003).

29. See also Hamilton's note on the link between VI.ii.35 and Book VI's proem.

30. Dolven, 219–23.

31. On the complicated relations between the narrator's precepts and his text, see especially Berger, "Narrative as Rhetoric in *The Faerie Queene*," *English Literary Renaissance* 21:1 (1991): 3–48. For the narrator's ability to provoke with an "overly neat syllogism," see also Neuse, 341.

32. The speech goes on at some length, and places a strong emphasis on "gentillesse" as a gift from God (1162–63). It also specifically credits Dante for this emphasis on Christian virtue (1125–30). As the *Riverside Chaucer* notes explain, the speech is also indebted to Boethius's *Consolation of Philosophy*, which Chaucer translated. Note, for example, Chaucer's translation of Philosophy's words: "Certes dignytees . . . aperteignen properly to vertu, and vertu transporteth dignyte anoon to thilke man to whiche sche hirself is conjoigned" (III.Prosa 4.37–40, *The Riverside Chaucer*, 3rd ed., ed. Larry D. Benson [Boston: Houghton Mifflin, 1987]).

33. Note that Fabricio mocks Possidonio for implying a similar connection between human and animal breeding (I3ᵛ).

34. See also Judson, 123–24, for Spenser's distortions of Chaucer.

35. Tonkin also remarks on this echo in his discussion of Priscilla and Aladine, though for somewhat different purposes (45–48). Critics who have commented on Calidore's deception in this canto include Neuse, Danner, and Grogan, who sees Calidore as an "accomplished storyteller" (156–57).

36. On Calidore's problematic relationships with Meliboe and Coridon, see also Cheney, 218–27, and Tonkin, 115–23.

37. Judith Anderson also notes how Meliboe echoes Guyon, though she does not treat this particular instance (*Reading the Allegorical Intertext: Chaucer, Spenser, Shakespeare, Milton* [New York: Fordham University Press, 2008], 91–105).

38. Schoenfeldt also notes the connection, and draws a similar conclusion (157).

39. On Meliboe's *sententiae*, see Judith Anderson as well as the notes by A. C. Hamilton.

40. Cf. Fabricio: "And that his felicity is greater . . . whose mind resteth contented with povertie, then his happines, who hath attained to the height of worldly welth, and lordly authoritie" (Q3ᵛ).

41. "Ché se di gemme e d'or, che 'l vulgo adora/ sí come idoli suoi, tu fossi vago,/ potresti ben, tante n'ho meco ancora,/ renderne il tuo desio contento e pago" (VII.16, Torquato Tasso, *Gerusalemme liberata*, ed. Lanfranco Caretti [Turin: Einaudi, 1971]). On the relation between this scene and Tasso, see Jason Lawrence, "Calidore *fra i pastori*: Spenser's Return to Tasso in *The Faerie Queene*, Book VI," *Spenser Studies* 20 (2005): 265–76, and Cheney, 219–22. Lawrence does not explore Spenser's alteration of Tasso in Calidore's offer, though Cheney does (221).

42. Schoenfeldt also connects the economic vocabulary of Canto vii with this discussion in Canto xi (162–63).

43. Anderson, 101–2. Anderson's comparison of Meliboe to Guyon is for a different purpose; she is particularly interested in pointing out the problems with Meliboe's idealism rather than in comparing Calidore to Mammon.

44. Cf. as well Guyon's rejection of Mammon's "ydle offers" and "vaine shewes" (II.vii.39).

45. On Spenser's poetic choices and the Judgment of Paris tradition, see especially Stanley Stewart, "Spenser and the Judgment of Paris," *Spenser Studies* 9 (1988): 161–209. Montrose also sees this passage as describing a "choice among life patterns" ("Gifts," 434).

46. On the troubling implications of Calidore's costume, see Stanley Stewart, "Sir Calidore and 'Closure,'" *Studies in English Literature* 24:1 (1984): 78–79. On Calidore's connection to the Trojan Paris, see also Cheney, 223–25, and Tonkin, 274–80.

47. In her brief connection of these two moments, Lila Geller sees Fabricio's action as "a gesture that anticipates Calidore's gentle removal of the sting of Coridon's defeat by passing the victor's garland to him" (55). An important part of my own argument is that Spenser's account of the episode as a whole makes descriptions of it as simply "gentle" impossible.

48. For Calidore's self-interested courtesy in Canto ix, see, for example, Neuse, 347–49, Nohrnberg, 709–10, and Stewart, "Calidore," 79–80. Stewart makes use of Spenser's commendatory sonnet to *Nennio* to hint, very briefly, at Calidore's bad behavior. Schoenfeldt comes closest to my own argument in asserting that Spenser in Book VI "exposes the brutal economy of exchange buried within courtesy's terminology of disinterested gift giving" (152); he also notes that Book VI "oscillates between a definition of courtesy as an internal moral virtue and as a repertoire of shrewd social practices" (151).

49. On the fundamental link between *sprezzatura* and the courtier's need "to disguise his efforts at outperforming others," see Daniel Javitch, *Poetry and Courtliness* (Princeton: Princeton University Press, 1978), 33. See also Frank Whigham's discussion of "self-deprecation" as a "trope of personal promotion" (*Ambition and Privilege: The Social Tropes of Elizabethan Courtesy Theory* [Berkeley: University

of California Press, 1984], 102–12) and Richard Helgerson on the poet's self-promoting self-deprecation (*Self-Crowned Laureates: Spenser, Jonson, Milton, and the Literary System* [Berkeley: University of California Press, 1983], 30 and passim).

50. The maidens of the vision dance in a "ring" that is also compared to a "girlond" (VI.x.11, 12), recalling the circular shape of the contested tokens in both *Nennio* and *The Faerie Queene*, VI.ix. On the "circulation" of courtesy, see also VI.Proem.7 as well as Fumerton, 31–36.

51. Evans, 223.

52. A. C. Hamilton also notes the strangeness of this detail.

53. On the courtier's ability to draw on strategies suited to the occasion, see Wayne Rebhorn, *Courtly Performances: Masking and Festivity in Castiglione's "Book of the Courtier"* (Detroit: Wayne State University Press, 1978).

54. See Northrop, 226–27, and Dubrow, "'A Doubtfull Sense of Things': Thievery in *The Faerie Queene* 6.10 and 6.11," in *Worldmaking Spenser: Explorations in the Early Modern Age*, ed. Patrick Cheney and Lauren Silberman (Lexington: University Press of Kentucky, 2000), 204–16. Dubrow rightly cautions readers to see Calidore and the brigands as being "compared," not "equated" (207).

55. For Meliboe's lack of efficacy, see also Low, 43.

56. The similes with which this battle is described also complicate Calidore's character; his comparison to a beast swatting flies recalls an image used in Canto i.24, as Hamilton notes, and his comparison to a lion further recalls the Salvage Man at VI.vi.22. In both cantos indiscriminate killing and generosity are combined.

EVAN GURNEY

Spenser's "May" Eclogue and Charitable Admonition

This essay places Spenser's "May" eclogue in the context of the Admonition controversy, which dominated much of the religious conversation in England during the 1570s. Rather than aligning Spenser with a particular ecclesial camp, however, this article suggests that he used the pastoral dialogue of "May" to dramatize the challenges of conducting religious discourse in a contentious atmosphere. Piers and Palinode articulate differing contemporary attitudes to the role of charitable admonition in building and sustaining a reformed community, and, in voicing the principles underlying their respective positions (including their limitations), Spenser purposefully replicates many of the rhetorical failures of the Admonition controversy. Ultimately the eclogue offers few answers to the dilemma—indeed, it participates in the failure—but by subjecting both perspectives to close ironic scrutiny "May" achieves its own kind of charitable success.

ROM ITS VERY INCEPTION, Spenser's "May" eclogue in *The Shepheardes Calender* has been understood as a representation of contemporary ecclesial disputes in Elizabethan England. According to E.K.'s confident gloss, the "moral" eclogue is framed as a debate between two pastors, a Protestant with a satirical pedigree named Piers (Plowman) and a "Catholique" named Palinode, "whose chiefe talke standeth in reasoning, whether the life of the one must be like the other."[1] E.K.'s easy di-

Spenser Studies: A Renaissance Poetry Annual, Volume XXVII, Copyright © 2012 AMS Press, Inc. All rights reserved.   DOI: 10.7756/spst.027.009.193-219

chotomy, accompanied by the implicit supposition that Piers represents an authoritative Spenserian voice, has propped up most scholarly examinations of the piece.[2] Summing up the conventional approach to reading the "May" eclogue, Harry Berger notes, with the slightest hint of irony, "For most commentators the ecclesiastical allegory makes the debate coherent."[3] Berger's remark subtly calls attention to the fact that a separate camp of readers exists, who, setting E.K.'s tidy allegory to the side, find the eclogue unstable and its pastoral dialogue often illegible, as Piers and Palinode resolutely defy the simple roles E.K. assigns to them. Why does Piers, for example, who "list none accordaunce make / With shepheard, that does the right way forsake" (164–65), almost immediately disregard his own austere principles, leave his flock, and sit down with a troublesome interlocutor to tell a fable? Moreover, as Berger himself observes, the two shepherds employ radically different allegorical registers, essentially talking past each other for the entire eclogue, and several scholars have identified other complicated aesthetic and dialectical dynamics present in the poem.[4] Readings of this kind, in which both Palinode and Piers are joint recipients of Spenser's critique, generally ignore the ecclesial context entirely and focus instead on the failure of dialogue when perspectives "confront each other as two separate, incommensurate poetic discourses."[5] So, much like the pastoral dialogue of "May," members of these two opposing scholarly positions continue to talk past each other.

This essay attempts to combine both approaches to the "May" eclogue, engaging the problematic aspects of Spenser's dialogue but placing this dynamic within the context of contemporary religious debate. Rather than using the ecclesiastical allegory to make Spenser's pastoral debate coherent, I intend to make sense of its incoherence by way of the ecclesiastical allegory. I suggest that Piers and Palinode replicate certain rhetorical failures of the Admonition controversy, which dominated religious conversation during the 1570s, and reflect cultural concerns about the status and exchange of charitable interpretation more generally. As best I know, nobody has provided a sustained analysis that links the "May" eclogue to the Admonition controversy, despite the close proximity between the publication of *The Shepheardes Calender* in 1579 and Thomas Cartwright's *Rest of Second Replie* in 1577, when the polemical artillery of Cartwright and John Whitgift finally fell silent.[6] Spenser was a student at Cambridge when Whitgift relieved Cartwright from the Lady Margaret chair because of his inflammatory lectures on the primitive church and episcopacy. Perhaps the controversy has not merited further comment among Spenser scholars because its influence is too obvious, but I intend to examine the controversy closely before moving to the "May" eclogue. I will demonstrate how the polemical exchange arose not merely from specific ecclesiological disputes but also from a fundamental disagreement over the aim and function of charitable admonition within the Church of England.

There are striking similarities between the eclogue's conversation and larger contemporary discussions of ecclesial polity, as many others have noted, and Piers articulates persuasive arguments for church reform that Palinode's rejoinders only partially blunt. But rather than aligning Spenser with one camp or another, I hope to show how he dramatizes the challenges of conducting religious discourse in a contentious atmosphere. Even if it is unclear whether Spenser intends the allegory E.K. suggests, he has obviously constructed a problematic dialogue between two different ethics of concord: one, Palinode's, which refuses to acknowledge that which "may not be mended" and thus avoids "conteck," and another that envisions a community in which careful governance and sober conduct is clearly visible and safe from "such faitors, when their false harts bene hidde" (170). Neither Piers nor Palinode, however, is able to sustain his ideology under the pressures of debate. Palinode, the friendly voice of fellowship, almost immediately assumes a defensive posture and curtly dismisses Piers's efforts at reform, while Piers, who desires stable guarantors marking his reformed community, ultimately shrouds his own ethics in the murky world of poetic fable-making. E.K., meanwhile, by polarizing the dispute in his commentary, contributes to the larger cultural and conversational dilemma the eclogue stages. Treating both sides with ironic understanding, Spenser simultaneously participates in and comments on the problematic tension that threatened to derail contemporary church-building and communal reform. In probing the religious controversy, Spenser demonstrates a concerned interest in the contestatory processes of writing and reform, as well as an appreciation for the comparable responsibilities and challenges shared by poets and priests.[7]

Admonition Controversy: "Whereby charity, the knot of all Christian society, is loosed"

During the early 1570s, the Church of England still struggled to define itself as a political and ecclesiastical institution. Attempting to accommodate a number of disparate religious groups as it clumsily framed a supposed *via media* between religious extremes, the Church faced vexatious unrest, not merely from Anabaptists and a resilient Roman Catholic population composed of recusants and church papists, but from so-called Puritan detractors as well.[8] Nor was the political and religious establishment that governed the church comprised of a single or coherent identity, but instead consisted of "an uneasy partnership of court bishops, prominent politicians, civil lawyers, divines and the more important heads of house at the universities working, directly or indirectly, with the monarch."[9] Given this insecure ecclesial structure and amalgam of ideologies and interests, it is no surprise that charity, which was supposed to foster concord, figured so prominently in debates over church government. In fact most disputes drew matter and energy from a fundamental disagreement about how charity ought to shape the Church of England. Puritans exhorting the political and ecclesial authorities to reform the carnal practices of a religious state still mired in Roman Catholicism might invoke Paul's first epistle to the Corinthians, which underscores the role of charity in establishing a godly community of Christian believers. Conformists would cite the same scriptural passages to plead on behalf of the establishment and levy an implicit critique of reformers unwilling to compromise for the sake of unity. Various factions attempted to appropriate the concept of charity in order to construct their own vision of church and commonwealth. They used essentially the same means (charity) but to slightly different ends.

The paradoxes of charitable conduct were not merely scriptural and religious but also implicated in cultural norms that can often seem contradictory. Elizabethan conceptions of charity were flexible enough to allow for severe discipline, and sixteenth-century developments in schemes of poor relief, for example, simultaneously distributed alms to deserving poor and whippings to able-bodied beggars. Whipping and almsgiving, if they were appropriately administered, were both understood as expressions of charity. A similarly rigorous imperative governed charitable social relations, which compelled neighbors to provide fraternal correction as a means of rectifying immoral behavior. But this created its own peculiar dilemma. Because of its pride of place among cultural values, charity was often invoked by contemporary laws and social norms as a guarantor of one's good name, functioning as one of the core legal and moral principles intended to protect individuals from defamation. Debora Shuger's recent study of censorship underscores this role of charity in contemporary regulation of language, or what Shuger (following John Weever's Whipper pamphlet) calls the "law of all civility."[10] Members of a community were obligated to observe decorum in their language to preserve a neighbor's reputation and honor from scandal or malice. The truth or falsity of public assertions was often irrelevant, as Shuger clearly demonstrates, since the priority of charity outweighed claims to verity. This posed a vexing challenge to members of the Elizabethan Church of England, especially those who felt compelled to discharge their charitable obligations by articulating the need for reform. Nor did it help that polemic, which encouraged or even depended on ad hominem attacks, was the characteristic (or at least most prominent) mode of debating important aspects of the religious body. In the ideal scenario a charitable reader would recognize the admonisher's charitable intent, but a different kind of reciprocity was more likely to emerge in the ecclesial discourse of the 1570s: a supposition of malice generally provoked a malicious reading—"Most mischievous foul sin, in chiding sin," as Duke Senior would say—and perpetuated the divisions separating both sides. Public discourse was dynamic and unstable, and the line distinguishing charitable admonition from uncharitable slander was a fine one. Those who offered moral correction were often accused of violating the social ethic, charity, which motivated their utterance in the first place.

These tensions received full expression in the Admonition controversy of the 1570s. After a decade and a half of Elizabeth's reign, a number of reformers had grown increasingly dismayed by the lack of reformation made by the Church of England, frustrated by vestiges of "papism" that remained entrenched in the episcopal infrastructure and ritualistic formalism of ecclesial devotion. Much of the dissent was concentrated among adherents of Presbyterian discipline who wished to model the Church of England explicitly after Geneva's polity. Their demands for further church reform eventually reached the public forum in 1572 with an anonymous manifesto penned by John Field and Thomas Wilcox, the *Admonition to the Parliament*, that outlined the various problems plaguing the church and posited Presbyterianism as an obvious and easy solution. In the Admonition controversy that followed, church authorities and religious reformers debated whether or not the genre of admonition might be used as an instrument of charity. As numerous recent works of scholarship have convincingly demonstrated, Puritans differed from conformists in degree rather than kind, a phenomenon that applies to the concept of charity as well. They agreed that charity lay at the heart of any effort to build and shape a Christian church, but they placed a stricter emphasis on the ethical responsibilities of charitable conduct, which reinforced their stringent cri-

teria for church membership. This led to inevitable conflict. Should char-
ity serve as the "the knot of all Christian society" in an inclusive vision of
the visible church, as conformists believed, encouraging reconciliation and
mutual recognition of sinfulness? Or should it be clearly evident in the
refining of the church body by the good and right conduct of the godly,
an instrument with which the church actively opposes any vestige of papal
carnality? More to the point in the contemporary debate, does charity jus-
tify the continued use of *adiaphora*—the ceremonies, traditions, and "fur-
niture" inherited from the Roman church, maintained by Elizabeth, and
generally agreed to be irrelevant to personal salvation? Or should charity
be extended to those whose consciences are somewhat more precise, whose
notion of "Christian liberty" would not countenance worldly state-build-
ing that does not conform to their vision of a godly church? Finally, should
charitable brethren avoid engaging in controversy altogether, or does the
scriptural injunction to edify others require such controversy in the ongo-
ing process of reforming the church? In the polemical exchanges between
Puritans and conformists, notions of charity remain unstable, adapted to
suit context and circumstance, as both sides appropriate the concept in
order to defend a more inclusive vision of church discipline (suggesting
that the opposition lacks fraternal affection) or use it to sanction an exclu-
sive vision of the church and excommunication (suggesting that the other's
charity is too carnal or too malicious for a reformed church).

Puritan adherents of Presbyterian discipline would quickly assert that
their vision of charity was motivated not by exclusivity, however, but
by edification, a work commanded to the Ephesians in particular and
Christians in general:

> But let vs followe the trueth in loue, and in all things growe vp into
> him, which is the head, that is Christ, / By whome all the bodie being
> coupled and knit together by euerie ioynt, for the furniture therof (ac-
> cording to the effectual power, which is in the measure of euerie parte)
> receiueth increase of the bodie, vnto the edifying of itselfe in loue.[11]

John Coolidge notes how Elizabethan Puritans traced this Pauline metaphor
back through a rich scriptural legacy that conceived of the communal order
in living, organic terms, a direct contrast to the lifeless edifices privileged by
the world.[12] Charity was the transformative principle by which such com-
munal glory could be achieved ("knowledge puffeth up, but love edifieth").
Coolidge observes that this subtler, more dynamic understanding of the

term "edification" encouraged Puritans to demand an active opposition to the temporal priorities of Elizabethan politics, which placed civic harmony before spiritual perfection. Conformists flattened the definition of "edify" to mean transmitting information or preaching doctrine, which, in the context of this particular debate, one could not do without wearing the vestments ordered by Elizabeth. But Puritans conceived of God's living temple in more emphatic terms—anything that was not done precisely for the health of the community contributed to its destruction. Any priest who in order to edify wore vestments, "the garments of Balamites, of popish priestes, enemies to God and all Christians," well, he had already missed the point entirely.[13] Or, to employ a phrase used by Piers in the "May" eclogue, "Who touches Pitch mought needes be defiled" (74).

The original *Admonition*, in broaching the topic of vestments and other faulty aspects of church discipline, lays bare this fundamental difference in emphasis among contemporary interpretations of Pauline charity. By incorporating ceremonies and vestments into worship, the pamphlet claims, the church was operating under a false notion of charity and building a hollow spiritual edifice: "These were the meanes and instrumentes to foster and cherishe riotousnesse, to neglecte true charitie, and to be shorte, to bring in folish and stagelike furniture."[14] The conformists might invoke the spirit of charity to justify ecclesial compromise, but Puritans claimed such an approach neglected *true* charity, which ought to assume a more active role in shaping and reforming the congregational body. Indeed, in Thomas Cartwright's *Replye to an answere made of M. Doctor Whitgifte*, he vociferously (and repetitiously) defends the ecclesial function of elders by declaring their role integral to the administration of charity. Such administration did not, however, consist of relieving the poor—a task left in Presbyterian discipline to deacons—but rather involved the supervision and private exhortation of congregational members to conduct themselves in godly behavior under the ultimate threat of excommunication: "That the principal offices of charity cannot be exercised without this order of ancients it may appear for that he which hath faulted and amended not after he be admonished once privately and then before one witness or two cannot further be proceeded against according to the commandment of our Saviour Christ."[15] A decade later John Udall would articulate demands for Presbyterian discipline with even more force: "Without admonition by the Eldershipp, all duties of charitie cannot be exercised towards sinners."[16] Both Cartwright and Udall used Matthew 18 as a scriptural blueprint for ecclesial administration, envisioning a community of Christian believers who demonstrate continued spiritual reformation in a process of discipline carefully governed by elders, while the reprobate would be progressively lopped off the congregational body. This was the "principal office" of charity, its most important function. And just as elders reproached sinners at the congregational level, spiritual leaders sometimes needed to rebuke political authorities. Thus Cartwright and others, most notably Walter Travers, implicitly justified the polemical action initiated by John Field and Thomas Wilcox, who were fulfilling their charitable obligations by admonishing Church, Parliament, and Queen for a wrongheaded approach to religious governance.

This attitude is evident in the preface to an anonymous pamphlet, *An exhortation to the byshops to deale brotherly with theyr brethren*, which was published immediately following the imprisonment of the *Admonition* authors. Puritans considered their inflammatory rhetoric as harsh discipline or tough love motivated by a concern for the spiritual community:

> We have in charity framed ourselves to be come all things unto all men, that at the least we mighte winne some to Christ; and have therfore thought meete to publishe this small woorke, wherein the bishops and prelates of this realm (much like to galled horsses, that cannot abide to be rubbed) are frendly admonished of their duetie towards God, and of love towardes their brethren.[17]

The writer conveniently ignores the possibility that Elizabethan authorities imprisoned Field and Wilcox because of similar communal imperatives. Instead the pamphlet boldly claims to be administering a curative discipline to a group of overly sensitive patients, meting out the sort of "charitable hatred" Alexandra Walsham discusses in her work on toleration.[18] Despite his initial gesture of apostolic charm, the writer quickly trades in his Pauline rhetoric for a less conciliatory allusion to Matthew 18, suggesting that the bishops have failed to honor the "laste and newest commaundement that Christe lefte unto us, that we should love one another, even as he loved us," and ought to be put out of their misery (and England's no doubt) as a consequence: "And therefore better it were for them, that a milstone were hanged about their neckes, & they drouned in the middest of the sea."[19] The scriptural analogy would have been clear to Elizabethan readers: church authorities were playing the role of Pharisees and obstructing the kingdom of God. According to the paradoxical logic of charity, such chastisement could be conceived as a good and loving act, a "frendly" admonishment to reform church government. It was important to frame the polemic as fraternal correction rather than malicious abuse for legal and ethical reasons, but in this case the function of charity was not merely rhetorical—it was driving the spirit of the whole enterprise.

It was the radical conception of "offices of charity" as a spiritual force edifying the godly community that buttressed the Puritans' furious appraisal of what they deemed to be ecclesial neglect, but their role as spiritual gadflies was already sanctioned, albeit in a modified manner, by the Elizabethan 1559 *Injunctions* that galled so many reformers. The injunction against slander, although concerned with public controversy, appears to license a process of charitable rebuke:

> Item, because in all alterations, and specially in rites and ceremonies, there happen discords amongst the people, and thereupon slanderous words and railings, whereby charity, the knot of all Christian society, is loosed; the queen's majesty being most desirous of all other earthly things, that her people should live in charity both towards God and man, and therein abound in good works, wills and straitly commands all manner her subjects to forbear all vain and contentious disputations in matters of religion, and not to use in despite or rebuke of any person these convicious words, papist or papistical heretic, schis-matic or sacramentary, or any suchlike words of reproach. But if any manner of person shall deserve the accusation of any such, that first he be charitably admonished thereof; and if that shall not amend him, then to denounce the offender to the ordinary, or to some higher power having authority to correct the same.[20]

Although the injunction recognizes the discord produced by "alterations" and implicitly discourages reform, Elizabethan officials clearly identify "rites and ceremonies" as a particular source of contention, since opinions about the form and function of these events will differ according to a "papistical heretic" or a "schis-matic." The rituals intended to foster social concord inevitably provoke "convicious words," it seems, just as the festivals at the beginning of Spenser's "May" eclogue occasion a heated debate between Piers and Palinode. In order to facilitate moderate reform, the injunction endorses a process of admonition similar to the role afforded to elders in Presbyterian discipline. Intended to uphold charity and maintain the bonds of civil society, the injunction demonstrates how mainstream was the Puritan approach to charitable admonition. Puritans and conformists might have differed in specific aspects of application—many Puritan communities exceeded the rubric provided by the Prayer Book in proceeding with excommunication[21]—but both sides in this dispute agreed on the important and contentious role of charity in shaping a community. Essentially the political orientation between Elizabeth (and the conformists who tacitly supported her) and reformers was reversed, which illustrates the loggerheads at which both sides had arrived: Elizabethan government invoked charity as a means of protecting the established order by forbearing "all vain and contentious disputations in matters of religion"; Puritans believed that charitable edification involves just such active participation in the life of a church community, and that order will follow by virtue of that edification.[22]

The injunction also shows how the polemical exchange initiated by Puritans, however charitable in its intention, nevertheless ignored the officially prescribed method of admonition. Instead Presbyterians preferred to enact their own censure outside the established channels of justice, a tactic born of expedience since the injunction ordered that Cartwright and others bring their objections to the very people—the ecclesial ordinaries—about whom they were complaining. Whitgift's response to the *Admonition* does not ignore the causes of Puritan dissent, but he reminds Presbyterians to adhere to contemporary standards of charitable privacy. It is as much a matter of process as principle: "Charitie doth not so couer open and manifest sinnes, that it suffereth them to be vnreprehended, but it remitteth priuate offences, it doth not publish secret sinnes at the first: neither doth it disclose all things that it knoweth to the defamation of a brother, when he may be otherwise reformed."[23] Although he intends to mitigate its effects, Whitgift allows for potential censure of established authorities, but other conformists were less cautious in their defense of ecclesial superiors. Conceiving of charity as a hermeneutic that willfully ignored errors, they employed the biblical trope of charity as a cloak or veil—from 1 Peter 4 (which was citing Proverbs 10:12)—either to encourage polemicists to cease their rhetorical violence or to persuade readers to disregard potential calumnies or slanders. Henry Howard uses the trope, in addition to the analogy of the mote and beam in Matthew 7, to emphasize Puritan hypocrisy: "A mote cannot escape their censure in their neighbours eye, & yet great beames & rafters lie couered vnder their owne. I maruayle what is become lately of charitie, *Quae operit multitudinem peccatoru: which couereth the multitude of sinnes.*"[24] Later, in his *Admonition to the people of England*, Thomas Cooper underscores the divisive nature of Presbyterian discipline, with its fault-finding and formal admonishment, reminding his audience that "christian charitie will hide the blemishes and faultes of their brethren, and specially of the preachers of the gospell sincerely teaching Gods trueth."[25] One can hear in these statements Palinode's reproach to Piers: "And sooth to sayne, nought seemeth sike strife, / That shepheardes so witen ech others life, / And layen her faults the world before" (158–60).

Conformists generally marshaled charity in behalf of an irenic plea for decorum and moderation. Many bishops were genuinely sympathetic to the arguments of some nonconformists, who were still recognized as valued, albeit troublesome members of the Church, but this was also a deliberate strategy to characterize their opponents as irrational extremists. There is obvious rhetorical value in deploying charity in polemic, investing the writer with scriptural authority and conditioning the audience to favorably interpret the writer's supposedly benevolent argument, but Elizabethan conformists were hardly interested in toleration.[26] Instead, by characterizing charity as the spiritual and material bond unifying the Church, conformists implicated Puritans as inhospitable promoters of disorder, or even as potential separatists. They would employ logical arguments to oppose the content of Puritan polemic and then invoke charity to censure the mode or manner of Puritan disputation. Regarding *adiaphora*, conformists like John Bridges flipped on their head the arguments of Puritans, claiming that Puritans were neglecting true charity by nurturing dissent and condemning rituals in corporate worship: "Without concord, they are vtterly no Churches at all: for which cause, if we will haue good regard to the safety of the Church, we must wholy with diligence looke to that which Paule commaundeth, that all things be decently done, and according to order."[27]

Puritans, of course, were voicing dissent expressly in behalf of church order. The conformists' deliberate refusal to see anything amiss—to cover their multitude of sins for the sake of charity—struck reformers as irresponsible. It is a relatively safe generalization to remark that Puritans desired to use charity as an instrument whereby the godliness of both individuals and communities might become more visible, establishing clearly demarcated boundaries between the devout and the impious. Rather than ignoring the errors of church officials, Puritans believed clerics should be held to even more stringent ethical standards. Cartwright seemed to be responding directly to the Whitgift's use of charity as a cloak in his *Replye*, in which he attacks a false notion of Christian love: "Abuse not his graces in devising cloakes to cover their disorders / but that they would set before them the love of Christ."[28] Henry Barrow, in *A brief discouerie of the false church*, partially justifies his separatist movement by observing that the charity of conformists contributes to a false sense of concord. Because it obscures the spiritual condition of the church and its individual members, Barrow claims, "Charitie had need haue a good ground in these high matters, & not walke by rote, least yt destroy both them & yt self."[29] A similar anxiety about the church's vulnerability, exacerbated by political insecurities and the threat of Rome, motivates the dire vision of Piers in "May": "Tho vnder colour of shepeheards, somewhile / There crept in Wolues, ful of fraude and guile" (126–27).[30] Puritans worried that charity, as understood by conformist clergy, would destroy the Church of England.

I have attempted to trace general trends among the Puritans and conformists in the Admonition controversy, but both approaches to charity, while consonant with contemporary values, were too inflexible to survive the exigencies of polemical exchange. Conformists occasionally mirrored the combative rhetoric of Puritans, for example, invoking charity to articulate a powerful and even painful defense of the church body. Rather than use the transformative power of charity to create and edify a godly church as Puritans wished, conformists considered charity an instrument to protect and defend an orderly church that had already been established. They were not upset with the disciplinary underpinnings of Puritan charity, just opposed to its specific application to their own church governance. Conformists could employ this approach with even more efficacy than Puritans because the metaphorical discipline present in their polemic was reinforced by the threat of real violence by the magistrate. Consider John Whitgift's initial reply to Cartwright in the *Admonition* controversy, when he apologizes for the severe discipline of charity:

> I whet the sworde no otherwise agaynst you, than Christian charitie and the state of the Church requireth. It is neither the sworde that taketh away life, nor fire that consumeth the body, which I moue vnto, but it is the sworde of correction and discipline, which may by sundrie other meanes be drawne out, than by shedding of bloud.[31]

Emphasizing the figurative nature of his violence—a violence he claims is at once justified and rendered obligatory by charity—Whitgift likewise reminds readers of the "sundrie other meanes" by which a Christian magistrate might enforce conformity, an implicit reference to the current church establishment's continued, albeit restrained policy of combating heresy with "fire that consumeth the body."[32] Like the earlier generation of English religious conservatives who defended the Roman church against Protestant reformers, Whitgift aligns Christian charity with the "state of the Church." That is, by situating the precedence of ecclesial unity and claiming that the Church defines charity rather than the other way around, he suggests that adherents of extreme ecclesial reform are motivated by a perverse kind of anti-charity. Thus Whitgift was embodying the very office Cartwright wished to invest in elders, admonishing the Puritans and tacitly threatening excommunication. Meanwhile, neither conformists nor Puritans acknowledged the close kinship their conceptions of charity bore to the argument made by "Bloody" Edmund Bonner in his *Homily on Charity*, which articulated the two offices of charity as a twin task of encouraging the godly and chastising sinners:

And such evil persons, that be so great offenders of God and the commonweal, charity requireth to be cut off from the body of the commonweal, lest they corrupt other good and honest persons; like as a good surgeon cutteth away a rotten and festered member for love he hath to the whole body, lest it infect other members adjoining to it.[33]

Quite simply the virtue of charity could be coopted by any religious faction. Whitgift and other figures in the religious establishment were perfectly content to justify coercion based on a communal imperative, even as they exhorted Puritans to soften their censure in behalf of Christian love.

Puritans noticed this discrepancy. Unwilling and no doubt frustrated to receive their own "charitable" chastisement, Puritans suggested that conformists intentionally misinterpreted their efforts at fostering concord. Cartwright—who elsewhere emphasizes the crucial role of excommunication in safeguarding the church—castigates Whitgift for levying accusations of heresy and schism. In his *Replye* Cartwright underscores the communal project of reform-minded brethren:

But as our knowledge and love is imperfect here in this world / so is our agreement and consent of judgment unperfect. And yet all these hard speaches of yours or uncharitable suspicions of papism, anabaptism, catharisme, donatisme etc whereby you do as much (as lieth in you) to cut us clean of from you / shal not be able so to estrange us or seperate us from you.[34]

It is a remarkable passage. The main thrust of Cartwright's argument is unmistakable—that Whitgift's "uncharitable suspicions" violate contemporary (and Christian) laws against slander—but he adds a tempering note of skepticism. He begins by invoking 1 Corinthians 13, which recognizes the fallibility of human knowledge and privileges the power of charity to "never fall away," but Cartwright modifies the scriptural passage and conflates love and judgment, suggesting that both processes can go awry despite the best intentions. There is an implicit recognition of human failure, something Piers admits as well: "So often times, when as good is meant, / Evil ensueth of wrong entent" (101–2). Finally, it offers an important reminder that Puritan dissension during Elizabeth's reign, even in its most radical form, was in fact motivated in behalf of church unity rather than religious separatism.

Despite its well-intentioned premise, the Admonition controversy remained a disappointment for Puritans, failing to initiate any immediate reform and prompting the religious establishment to entrench itself against vocal opposition. It was a rhetorical failure too, and for both sides. Despite the animadversions practiced by both Whitgift and Cartwright, a technique which placed both writers within close proximity on the page, a sense of absurd distance pervades the entire polemical exchange. Unable or unwilling to recognize the good intentions of the other side, they completely miss each other. The Puritans, keen to admonish out of charity, remained unwilling to receive their own admonishment from ecclesial superiors; and conformists, desirous of charitable interpretation that would "cover a multitude of sins," were reluctant to offer that service to dissenters. This helps situate the strange behavior of the two shepherds in Spenser's "May" eclogue, as Piers repeatedly engages Palinode in behalf of reform despite being rebuffed by the supposedly affable shepherd. Like the Admonition controversy, the shepherds' dialogue stalls on account of their limited perspectives.

"And layen her faults the world before": Charitable
Admonition in "May"

Throughout the course of the Calender's critical reception, most of the pastoral characters have acquired a personality on which readers can generally agree, which is a testament to the vivid psychological coloring of Spenser's work as well as the cooperative tendencies of the scholarly community.

So, even if readers disagree as to just how much Spenser intends to censure Palinode, there is nevertheless a consensus that he represents a kind of communal instinct, a desire for friendship, a celebration of springtime ritual, and a weakness "of fellowship" for hearing fables and tales from his companions. Piers, meanwhile, whether or not one considers him a frosty malcontent or a courageous champion of clerical piety, apparently adopts the iconoclastic pose of a solitary reformer who "list none accordaunce make" with disreputable shepherds. Note that I include quotations to support these characterizations, as the text itself repeatedly substantiates them. The narrative offers a slightly different story, however. It is Palinode who spends most of the eclogue accusing Piers of faultfinding, calling him names, and deriding his "fooles talke." Why is he, whose emblem declares "that who doth mistrust is most false," so curt, so mistrustful? What conditions his oversensitive response? And Piers, who finds no "faith in the faithlesse," who prefers a world of clear divisions between bad and good, persistently engages a companion who possesses dubious pastoral credentials and proves a recalcitrant interlocutor, even altering his tone and method halfway through the eclogue.[35] The dialogue seems unlikely from the start. But it makes more sense if we keep in mind the paradoxes evident in the Admonition controversy, and though Piers and Palinode do not serve merely as mimes for Cartwright and Whitgift, aping their exchange under a pastoral sky, the shepherds dramatize a similar conflict.

The first critical reader of "May," E.K. does not invoke the Admonition controversy in his argument but instead frames the eclogue as a debate between "two formes of pastoures or Ministers, or the protestant and the Catholique: whose chiefe talke standeth in reasoning, whether the life of the one must be like the other." It is tempting to add a qualification to E.K.'s binary, since the term "Catholic" was still contested by English Protestants who asserted the authenticity of their Christian beliefs and practices, and refused to cede to Rome all claims of catholicity (at least without the additional modifier "Romish"). But elsewhere in his glosses E.K. clearly equates the term with papism. Taken seriously, this accusation raises pragmatic issues within the eclogue.[36] Would Piers consciously fraternize with a Roman Catholic priest? Or should readers consider him more foolish than the kid in his own fable? There are other complications in casting Palinode as a Roman Catholic. Later in the Calender he appears by proxy in "June," when Thomalin (the more distinctly Protestant shepherd in this exchange) paraphrases Palinode's condemnation of Roman Catholic ecclesiology after taking a trip to Rome. Even E.K.'s attitude toward Palinode seems inconsistent, as his glosses regularly treat the shepherd as a relatively benign if misinformed figure. Obviously the paratext is dubious at best, and readers of the entire *Calender* would probably be conditioned to receive E.K.'s commentary with some degree of skepticism. But the argument also serves at least two purposes for Spenser. By identifying the exchange as a debate between Protestantism and Roman Catholicism, E.K. distances the anonymous poet from a sensitive religious controversy within the Church of England. He might be reductive, but E.K. helps defuse some of the potential hazards involved in Spenser's project, especially given its obvious topicality ("as Algrind used to say").[37] More importantly, I think, E.K.'s dichotomy introduces and reinforces the ecclesial polarities arresting contemporary religious debate. In a manner similar to the practice condemned by Elizabeth's *Injunctions*, E.K. smears Palinode with the "convicious" word of *Catholique* before the exchange is even underway, prejudicing readers against Palinode's opinions and dramatizing the problems of interpreting pastoral allegory. Thus E.K.'s argument, which prepares readers for the shepherds' failure to generate constructive dialogue, participates in the larger failures of ecclesial discourse in England.

The eclogue starts out favorably enough, in spite of E.K.'s paratext, with Palinode delivering an opening paean to the "mery moneth of May." Looking for affirmation from his companion, he asks, "Bene not thy teeth on edge, to thinke, / How great sport they gaynen with little swinck?" (89). Despite its festive spirit and colloquial irony—which might not be as innocent as it appears—Palinode's question elicits a jarring response from Piers: "Perdie so farre am I from enuie, / That their fondnesse inly I pitie. / Those faytours little regarden their charge" (37–39). Piers takes the question so seriously that he worries over the moral implications of his answer, immediately introducing the ethical conditions of his response. By insisting that his ensuing rebuke stems from a virtuous disposition, motivated by pity rather than envy, Piers intends to circumscribe his critique within the sanction of Christian admonition. Imagining a spectrum of ethical responses to the revelry (channeling his inner Aristotle), Piers introduces two important poles—"so farre am I from enuie, / That their fondnesse inly I pitie"—which help him navigate the complicated act of interpretation or judgment and likewise establish the parameters of his moral discourse. Piers is concerned about accusations of envy, a vice conventionally considered in opposition to communal fellowship because of its willfully malicious misinterpretation, and often invoked by poets like Immeritô, whose prefatory poem "To His Booke" warns the newly penned *Calender* "if that Envie barke at thee, /

As sure it will" (5–6).[38] Moreover, an envious disposition would implicitly suggest some kind of virtue among the hireling shepherds Piers derides.[39] Instead, he frames his disapproval in terms of charitable rebuke, employing pity—with all its valences of Christian love, mercy, and piety—to achieve a moral equilibrium. Piers wants his statement to fall within the purview of charitable admonition, ensuring that his critique remains focused on the communal well-being and remains distinct from mere detraction. And his actual rebuke justifies that stance to a degree; decrying the abuses of non-resident clergy with multiple benefices was a fairly moderate position of reform, one that garnered sympathy even from a number of conformists, and it was linked to the charitable imperative of poor relief.

   As a rhetorical tactic Piers's remark fails completely. Any declaration of pity typically sounds hollow and disingenuous when followed by relentless scornful derision, as it is here and throughout the eclogue when Piers hurls insults at clerics. More importantly, however, his fairly simplistic framework remains incapable of stabilizing the discourse. He claims to pity those shepherds "inly," a significant adverb which E.K. chooses to gloss as "entirely," although the word "inwardly" would be just as apt in both contemporary and archaic parlance. By pitying them "inly," Piers highlights the potential discrepancy between outward appearance and inward actuality, and suggests he might be performing his own hypocritical act, engaging in the very sin with which he smears those hireling shepherds. Moreover, his apology acknowledges the importance of intention, which, like beauty, is in the eye of the beholder. Thus the entire premise of his admonition is vulnerable to the interpretation of his interlocutor, Palinode, who promptly accuses him of envy:

> Sicker now I see thou speakest of spight,
> All for thou lackest somedele their delight.
> I (as I am) would rather be envied,
> All were it of my foe, then fonly pitied:
> And yet if neede were, pitied would be,
> Rather, then other should scorne at me:
> For pittied is misshape, that nas remedie,
> But scorned bene dedes of fond foolerie.
> (55–62)

Recent scholarship has emphasized the failures of the dialogue by diagnosing the shepherds' different poetic registers—each simply misses what the other is saying. But in this case Palinode does not retract the careful interpretive criterion employed by Piers. Instead he inflects it, filtering the spectrum of objective response through his own field of preference. There is a hypersensitivity in his reply, a tension that strains the debate, and if Piers imagines a judge of his judgment, Palinode tacitly acknowledges that his own behavior, much like those May-gaming shepherds, is under review. That self-referential position buried in a parenthesis—"I (as I am)"—might remind the reader of E.K.'s warning, that Palinode's is the voice of a self-interested and deceptive "Catholique" priest, but the statement also suggests a defensive posture: feeling the withering glance of his companion, he (as he is) "would rather be envied" by such as Piers. Lacing his response with ironic conditionals—"All were it of my foe" and "yet if neede were"—Palinode launches a complicated assault on Piers's judgment: although I suspect you are speaking out of envy, he declares, even your claims of pity are foolish ("fonly pitied") and consequently merit this scornful reply, since "scorned bene dedes of fond foolerie." Later Palinode will rebuff Piers in similar fashion, claiming his didactic carping is mere "fooles talke" (141). If Piers offers pity, Palinode wants none of it. Spenser adds to the ironic texture here, since Palinode seems to be the pastor who follows most closely the wisdom of E.K., who declares in the eclogue's argument that "it is daungerous to mainteine any felowship, or giue too much credit to their colourable and feyned goodwill."

This friction governs the entire exchange. Piers invokes the conventional nostalgia of satirists (as well as Presbyterians like Field and Wilcox), longing for a simpler society, a pastoral golden age, something akin to first-century Christianity when spiritual leadership was plainly better: "Well ywis was it with shepheardes thoe: / Nought having, nought feared they to forgoe" (109–10). Palinode might have responded with something like Mammon's pithy reply to Guyon—"Thou that doest liue in later times, must wage / Thy works for wealth" (*FQ* II.vii.18)—but he ignores the obvious counterargument. Rather than critiquing the impracticality of such pastoral idealism, Palinode chooses to attack Piers's malice, much like a conformist defending the church establishment. As opposed to deeming all things to the best, Piers "findest faulte, where nys to be found," he "buildest strong warke upon a weake ground," and he "raylest on right withouten reason" (144–46), aligning himself against truth and justice. Here Palinode combines his defense of the communal interest with something of a personal validation: "Nay sayd I thereto, by my deare borrowe, / If I may rest, I nill live in sorrowe" (150–51). This is an authentic palinode or retraction, inverting the final rhyme Piers uses earlier to express his dire view of contemporary religion: "This was the first sourse of shepheards sorowe, / That now nill be quitt with baile, nor borrowe" (130–31).[40] E.K. remarks of Palinode's "borrowe," "that is our Saviour, the commen pledge of all men's debts to death," but the word was also used to denote a loan or pledge of surety, or even an elaborate agreement among ten neighbors—a tithing—to hold themselves jointly accountable before the law (leading sixteenth-century writers to confuse "borrowe" with "borough").[41] He makes his oath in the language of economic and social community in order to dismiss Piers's troublemaking. Indeed, Palinode would later ask to "borrow" the fable for Sir John to use in kirk. The difference in attitude between the shepherds *seems* clear: whereas a suspicious Piers, worried about "wolves, full of fraud and guile," rejects the efficacy of borrowing, Palinode is more confident in the positive aspects of community:

> And sooth to sayne, nought seemeth sike strife,
> That shepheardes so witen ech others life,
> And layen her faults the world before,
> The while their foes done eache of hem scorne.
> Let none mislike of that may not be mended:
> So conteck soone by concord mought be ended.
>   (158–63)

Like Whitgift and other conformists, Palinode wants peace and concord, an end to strife, a general fellow-feeling that relies on trust, whereas Piers "list none accordaunce make / With Shepheard, that does the right way forsake" (164–65).

And yet there clearly is an ironic undercurrent, a recognizable gap between Palinode's ideals and his practice, as he himself refuses to interpret Piers's critique in a positive manner. I find myself persuaded by Patrick Cullen's suggestion that Palinode's "petulant unwillingness to accept Piers's frosty rigidity . . . represents human nature, with its natural desires and limitations," but there seems to be something more at work than mere petulance.[42] Readers genuinely sympathize with Palinode, whose springtime encomium meets a frigid reception, but one also senses that he has exploited the terms of verbal exchange in this dialogue by refusing Piers any legitimacy. He articulates communal boundaries—"by my deare borrowe"—only to stifle a contrarian perspective. He is not a stupid interlocutor but an oversensitive one who feels all too keenly the implications of Piers's remarks, and he does a masterful job of appropriating the rules of charitable interpretation in his own behalf, refusing Piers the sanction of well-meaning admonition. Such behavior declines to "touch pitch" after its own fashion.

Just when the eclogue appears to reach an impasse, Piers revises his strategy, telling the truth but telling it slant by way of beast fable: an ill-fated kid, left alone by his mother, and motivated by some combination of pity, self-love, and stupidity, opens his doors to a begging fox who destroys him. Piers's earlier discussion of irresponsible clergy becomes allegorized into a scene of actual experience. Presumably Piers intends for the fable to reiterate his earlier message and convince Palinode of the real dangers plaguing the Church of England, but the story complicates any easy dichotomy between right and wrong, importing the previous interpretive criteria of Piers and Palinode—envy and pity—into a more complex social situation. If pity worked as a corrective to envy for Piers in his criticism of absentee "shepherds," the passion remains prone to misapplication, especially in the context of foxes who disguise themselves as members of the deserving poor. The "inly" pity Piers advertises earlier will get the kid into trouble when he encounters the fox and, "pittying hys heavinesse" (259), lets in his destroyer. Piers desires a clear world reduced to binary oppositions, but the real perils of hypocrisy and misrepresentation cloud his own vision. Consequently, the stark ethical alternatives he espouses earlier feel inadequate or inhumane.

On the other hand, this shift in tactics signals a change in Piers, a recognition of rhetorical contingency that could enable him to adapt his moral to any type of audience. The sudden alteration might also suggest the impracticality of using the Admonition controversy as an analogue for the poem, but the contemporary debate does help in explaining why Piers does not merely walk home earlier after receiving abuse from Palinode. Like Cartwright and Travers and others, Piers is not simply an iconoclast—at least he does not think so—and his advocacy for more precise standards of godly conduct within the church stems from a communal imperative rather than a separatist agenda. Gregory Kneidel reminds us that Puritan reformers emphasized the importance of educating a ministry that could adapt to circumstance: "Spenser's very mode of allegorical fabulistic argumentation coyly allies his poetic project with the preaching that prudently accommodates the intellectual capacities of various audiences."[43] But the episode also provides a reminder of why fables and parables and allegories are unreliable. Piers intends for his fable to warn Palinode against prioritizing harmony before righteous conduct, but his allegory sabotages his own enterprise. That is, Piers must disguise his message in order to receive a charitable reading from Palinode, but he complicates his own lesson by dramatizing the actual dangers of a charitable act. It is impossible to know, when Palinode rebuffs his companion a final time at the eclogue's conclusion, if Piers fails outright or is merely a victim of his rhetorical success. That the fatuous and possibly papist "Sir John" will acquire the fable gives this paradox a humorous edge—now Palinode might very well ask, "Ah Piers, bene not thy teeth on edge." Spenser clearly delights in the ironic ambiguity of the moment, which shows, I think, that he remains more interested in highlighting the situation's hermeneutical instability than promoting any partisan doctrine or discipline. And by including the fable and its consequent failure, Spenser closely aligns the functions of poet and priest, dramatizing the limitations of discourses available to both pastors and pastorals.

Spenser also underscores the problematic aspects of storytelling by suggesting that Piers is complicit in the danger he describes. Much like the kid's mother, Piers abandons his own flock to potential foxes as he tells Palinode his fable. In fact, the eclogue's woodcut suggestively portrays the kid's demise occurring right under Piers's nose. This paradox bears a resemblance to the accusations Whitgift levies at Puritans, who he claims have abandoned their ministerial responsibilities because of mere *adiaphora*.[44] Moreover, Piers obviously relishes the art of entertaining. Berger is right to note the sheer poetic delight with which the shepherd describes the fox of his fable, which is "closer to the playful or impious spirit of popular beast fable than to the reform voice":[45]

> There at the dore he cast me downe hys pack,
> And layd him downe, and groned, Alack, Alack.
> Ah deare Lord, and sweete Saint Charitee,
> That some good body woulde once pitie mee.
> (238–48)

Note the elaborate alliteration and assonance, the lively sarcasm—Piers is having fun playing the poet. It is no surprise to find Piers later in "October" participating in a protracted dialogue examining the purpose and power of verse. His description of the fox suggests that he is no stranger to rhetorical disguise, that he is manipulating Palinode after his own fashion. At one point, when the anaphora and other repetitions build a momentum that culminates in that pathetic cry of the fox—"Ah dear Lord, and sweete Saint Charitee, / That some good body would once pitie mee"—the speech of Piers and the fox seem to blend together, united by a shared personal pronoun. There remains a hint of irony, a tacit acknowledgment of complicity in the deception, when Piers employs his own poetic agency to indict the fox, who "can chat, / And tell many lesings of this, and that" (284–85)—which is to say, Piers, who intends to capture Palinode's sympathies, vilifies the fox for doing just as he is. As Spenser relates how Piers describes the persuasive rhetoric of the fox, readers face an interpretive conundrum, one that demonstrates how poetry participates in the fictive spectacle that enables the fox to capture the kid.

The fable itself is a failure, of course, at least as far as Piers is concerned, and Palinode remains unconvinced. Palinode revises the performance of the kid, refusing to fall victim to the foxy rhetoric of his fellow shepherd; he seems to have grasped the fable's intended lesson but directed its force against Piers. After hearing the story to its conclusion (but not before jumping to his own conclusions about Piers's motives), he ridicules his companion—"Truly *Piers*, thou art beside thy wit, / Furthest fro the marke, weening it to hit" (306–7)—and proceeds to appropriate the story in behalf of "Sir John," precisely the type of unlearned priest Piers derides. Note that Palinode bears to his local priest the sort of interpretive posture that would facilitate a constructive dialogue with Piers: "For well he meanes" (317). At the poem's conclusion what appears to preserve the shepherds' friendship is silence, as Piers mutters to himself, before they both head back home under the evening sky, "Of their falshode more could I recount" (314). The narrative's moral works against itself, and one wonders if Piers ultimately represents the kid, fallen victim to his own conception of pastoral heroism. Indeed, Richard Chamberlain reads the poem as a commentary on the limitations of a particular brand of totalizing allegorical criticism, and instead of reinforcing the authority of E.K. or underwriting the ascetic impulse of Piers, "the work is produced by a fellowship of interpretation and text"—that is, the poem plays a joke on Piers and E.K., and supports Palinode's optimism in human fellowship.[46] Such a reading probably valorizes Palinode and his reductive notions of community more than Spenser himself intended, but it underscores the instability of allegorical interpretation as well as the eclogue's failure to provide a resolution to the conflict it dramatizes.

Perhaps the eclogue itself does not *fail* as much as circumscribe its aims. Much of this essay has labored to suggest that the Admonition controversy offered Spenser a model of unsuccessful dialogue between two irreconcilable sides, one aptly summarized by the final pair of emblems in the eclogue: "Who doth most mistrust is most false"; "What fayth then is there in the faythlesse."[47] And in terms of rhetorical success, Piers accomplishes little more than Cartwright does in the face of intractable opposition from Palinode and Whitgift. Spenser may be sympathetic to arguments for church reform—Piers is the eclogue's central speaker, after all—but he seems content merely to dramatize the mutual responsibility of both parties in the ongoing conflict. If we do not immediately implicate Palinode as a crypto-Catholic, his case for concord can be heard to echo the conformists' impatient response to Puritan arguments; and if we do not immediately congratulate Piers for a courageous satire, his rigid criteria for spiritual community embody some of the limitations inherent to the reformers' discourse. Rather than praising and blaming either Piers or Palinode, Spenser seems most interested in the dilemma itself, an immediate predicament facing the Church of England but also linked to Spenser's own vocation, with its fragile dialectic between poet and audience. The "May" eclogue provides Spenser an opportunity to stage important issues of charitable interpretation that were immediately relevant to contemporary church discipline, but these questions preoccupied him throughout his career. Even as he developed a more sophisticated allegorical poetics, Spenser continued to explore the complicated relationship between mutually competing truths and virtues—the inevitable clash of temperance and militant chastity, for example. And his paradoxical treatment of a highly charged ecclesial controversy gestures toward the rich, complex, and sometimes contradictory engagement of theology and biblical imagery in *The Faerie Queene*, which has generated fruitful readings from scholars like Carol Kaske and Darryl Gless, among many others.[48] Finally, if Spenser treats the inadequacies of polemical discourse with a delightfully ironic understanding, it was probably because he recognized the limitations of his own poetic discourse, acknowledging the likelihood that his fables would not merely meet the ridicule of Palinode but also suffer the "venomous despite" (*FQ* VI.xii.41) of the Blattant beast.

University of North Carolina at Chapel Hill

NOTES

1.   All quotations are from *The Works of Edmund Spenser: A Variorum Edition*, vol. 7, ed. Edwin A. Greenlaw, C. G. Osgood, F. M. Padelford, and Ray Heffner (Baltimore: Johns Hopkins University Press, 2002).

2.   For a hyperbolic example of this perspective, see James Jackson Higginson's declaration that "Piers manifestly expresses Spenser's own views" in *Spenser's Shepherd's Calender in Relation to Contemporary Affairs* (New York: Columbia University Press, 1912), 72. Most of these studies are more evenhanded, however, and persuasively align Spenser with the movement for continued Protestant reform. See John King, *Spenser's Poetry and the Reformation Tradition* (Princeton: Princeton University Press, 1990), 35–42; Anthea Hume, *Edmund Spenser: Protestant Poet* (Cambridge: Cambridge University Press, 1984), 15–28; Nancy Jo Hoffman, *Spenser's Pastorals* (Baltimore: Johns Hopkins University Press, 1977), 104–18; David Shore, *Spenser and the Poetics of Pastoral* (Montreal: McGill-Queen's University Press, 1985), 26–36; and Lynn Johnson, *The Shepheardes Calender: An Introduction* (University Park: Penn State University Press, 1990), 77–82. All of these readings take E.K. more or less at his word, although they disagree as to whether Piers articulates Puritan or more moderate Protestant sympathies. Two recent studies challenge E.K.'s reading of the eclogue: J. P. Conlan believes Spenser supports an Anglican ecclesiology and uses "May" as an ironic indictment of evangelical polemic in "The Anglicanism of Spenser's May Eclogue," *Reformation* 9 (2004): 205–17; Richard Chamberlain privileges Palinode's fellowship before the claims of E.K. or Piers in *Radical Spenser* (Edinburgh: Edinburgh University Press, 2005), 37–49.

3.   Harry Berger, Jr., *Revisionary Play: Studies in the Spenserian Dynamics* (Berkeley: University of California Press, 1988), 299.

4.   Berger, 294–306. Paul Alpers notes that this form of dialogue actually allows both sides to be heard. See *What is Pastoral?* (Chicago: University of Chicago Press, 1996), 178. Roland Greene suggests that the unsuccessful dialogue of "May" calls "into question the premise of dialogue itself," in "*The Shepheardes Calender*, Dialogue, and Periphrasis," *Spenser Studies* 8 (1987): 1–33. Patrick Cullen has noted the ambivalent valences of Spenser's dialogue form in *Spenser, Marvell, and Renaissance Pastoral* (Cambridge: Harvard University Press, 1970). See also Jonathan Goldberg, *Voice Terminal Echo* (New York: Methuen, 1986), 56, and Edward Armstrong, *A Ciceronian Sunburn* (Columbia: University of South Carolina Press, 2006), 82–84.

5.   Patricia Berrahou Phillippy, *Love's Remedies: Recantation and Renaissance Lyric Poetry* (Lewisburg: Bucknell University Press, 1995), 174–81.

6.   Robert Lane provides a thorough treatment of contemporary ecclesial politics and religious reform in his reading of the eclogue in *Shepheards Devises* (Athens: University of Georgia Press, 1993), 101–14, emphasizing the word and

concept of pastoral "care." Gregory Kneidel places the eclogue in the context of contemporary discussions of pastoral rhetoric in an excellent article, "'Mighty Simplenesse': Protestant Pastoral Rhetoric and Spenser's 'Shepheardes Calender,'" *Studies in Philology* 96:3 (1999): 275–312.

7.   See Jeffrey Knapp, "Spenser the Priest," *Representations* 81 (2003): 61–78.

8.   Any use of terms to distinguish between various factions within the Church of England will inevitably obscure the complexities of sixteenth-century confessional identity and church discipline, so it is with some hesitation that I employ a binary between "conformists" and "Puritans." But these labels are helpful, especially as it relates to charity in this case, if they can gesture at loosely shared church priorities and disciplinary styles. I take "Puritan" in this period to mean those who argued for more thoroughgoing ecclesial reform and supported more stringent ethical criteria for church membership, demands articulated with particular vehemence by promoters of a Presbyterian polity, and I take "conformist" to mean those who supported the ecclesiastical regulations set forth, however contentiously, by the politico-religious establishment. There was some overlap between these positions, of course. For a thoughtful consideration of these questions, see Peter Lake's and Michael Questier's introduction to *Conformity and Orthodoxy in the English Church, c. 1560–1660*, ed. Peter Lake and Michael Questier (Woodbridge, UK: Boydell Press, 2000), ix–xx, and for a helpful examination of relevant ecclesial politics during the period, see Peter Lake, *Anglicans and Puritans?: Presbyterianism and English Conformist Thought from Whitgift to Hooker* (London: Unwin Hyman, 1988).

9.   Kenneth Fincham, "Clerical Conformity from Whitgift to Laud," in *Conformity and Orthodoxy in the English Church, c. 1560–1660*, ed. Peter Lake and Michael Questier (Woodbridge, UK: Boydell Press, 2000), 127.

10.   Shuger, *Censorship and Cultural Sensibility: The Regulation of Language in Tudor-Stuart England* (Philadelphia: University of Pennsylvania Press, 2006).

11.   Ephesians 4:15–16. All biblical quotations are from *The Geneva Bible: A Facsimile of the 1560 edition* (Madison: University of Wisconsin Press, 1969). See also 1 Cor. 8:1: "knowledge puffeth up, but love edifieth," or the Geneva Bible's note to 1 Cor. 13, which claims, "Because loue is the fountaine and rule of edifying the Church, he setteth forthe the nature, office and praise thereof."

12.   John Coolidge, *The Pauline Renaissance in England* (Oxford: Clarendon Press, 1970), 23–54.

13.   *Puritan Manifestoes: A Study of the Origin of the Puritan Revolt*, ed. W. H. Frere and C. E. Douglas (London: SPCK, 1954), 35.

14.   *Puritan Manifestoes*, 51.

15.   *A replye to an answere made of M. Doctor Whitgifte* (Hemel Hempstead, 1573), 176.

16.   *A demonstration of the trueth of that discipline* (East Molesey, 1588), 90.

17.   *Puritan Manifestoes*, 60–61.

18.   See Alexandra Walsham's *Charitable Hatred* (Manchester: Manchester University Press, 2006).

19. *Puritan Manifestoes*, 69–70.

20. *Documents of the English Reformation*, ed. Gerald Bray (Cambridge: James Clarke, 1994), 345.

21. Patrick Collinson, *The Elizabethan Puritan Movement* (Berkeley: University of California Press, 1967), 346–55.

22. Claire McEachern makes a similar comment about the *Injunctions*, claiming they were based "on the premise that social order wrought through the regulation of conduct cultivated spiritual correctness, rather than the other way round." See "Spenser and Religion," *The Oxford Handbook of Edmund Spenser*, ed. Richard McCabe (Oxford: Oxford University Press, 2010), 33.

23. *The defense of the aunswere to the Admonition against the replie of T. C.* (London, 1574), 22. Cartwright uses this trope on behalf of Puritans, adding further vehemence by employing a double negative: "And then where is charitie / which covereth the multitude of faultes / especially in brethren / when you do not only not cover them / but also take away their garments / whereby they are covered." See his *Replye to an Answere*, 9.

24. *The Defense of the Ecclesiastical Regiment* (London, 1574), 40.

25. Thomas Cooper, *An admonition to the people of England* (1589), 5.

26. Michael Questier has shown that such tactics were rarely deployed in polemical disputes, although he notes that Robert Persons's *Christian Directory* was considered effective because it eschewed a polemical tone. *Conversion, Politics, and Religion in England, 1580–1625* (Cambridge: Cambridge University Press, 1996), 37–38.

27. *A defence of the gouernment established in the Church of Englande* (London, 1587), 202.

28. *A replye to an Answere made of M. Doctor W*, 68.

29. Henry Barrow, *A briefe discoverie of the false church*, 37.

30. Conformists came around to his way of thinking as well. Consider the following quote by Richard Bancroft: "Many others there be, who cover their malice more cunningly, nay more hypocritically, as though all they said proceeded of meere love and Christian charitie." *A sermon preached at Paules Crosse the 9. of Februarie 1588* (London, 1588), 92.

31. *The defense of the aunswer*, 56.

32. See Walsham, *Charitable Hatred*, 39–105.

33. *Certain Sermons or Homilies (1547)*, ed. Ronald Bond (Toronto: University of Toronto Press, 1987), 125. On account of his active role as bishop of London in eliminating heresy during the Marian years, Edmund Bonner earned a reputation among Elizabethans as a cruel persecutor.

34. *A replye to an Answere made of M. Doctor W*, 79.

35. See E.K.'s explanation of the emblems in *Variorum*, 7:58.

36. S. K. Heninger, Jr. aptly summarizes the situation: "In the Argument, E.K. oversimplifies the matter beyond recognition." See *"The Shepheardes Calender," The Spenser Encyclopedia* (Toronto: University of Toronto Press, 1990), 647.

37. Scott Lucas suggests that Spenser uses the argument of "September" as one of several protective strategies that deflect attention from his response to a volatile topical issue. See "Diggon Davie and Davy Dicar: Edmund Spenser, Thomas Churchyard, and the Poetics of Public Protest," *Spenser Studies* 16 (2002): 151–66.

38. See Lynn Johnson's note describing the political valences of Envy in *The Shepheardes Calender: An Introduction*, 30.

39. Consider, for example, Thomas Rogers, quoting Cicero: "I haue alwayes bine of this minde, that I haue thought enuie gotten by vertue, to be no obscuring of my name, but an illustrating of the same," *The anatomie of the minde* (London, 1576), 46.

40. Both Piers and Palinode repeatedly appropriate the other's diction and purposely refashion it. In this case, Palinode has echoed his companion's word "borrowe," dressing it up with the adjective "deare," which gains E.K.'s approval. But later Piers recycles "deare" for use in his fable, attaching the modifier to a "jewell" (276) that eventually proves the kid's undoing, an implicit suggestion that Piers remains skeptical of Palinode's capacity to survive the rigors of temptation. The adjectival play here is typical for Spenser. Associated with both *caritas* and *eros*, the phrase "dear love" possesses an inherent ambivalence that Spenser repeatedly exploits in *The Faerie Queene*, especially Books I and IV.

41. See *OED*, "borrow," n., 3.

42. Cullen, *Spenser, Marvell, and Renaissance Pastoral*, 49.

43. Kneidel, "'Mighty Simplenesse,'" 300.

44. Indeed, in the *Defense of the Aunswere to the Admonition*, Whitgift compares Puritans expressly to loiterers and other members of the undeserving poor, much like the Fox in Piers's fable.

45. Berger, *Revisionary Play*, 302.

46. Chamberlain, *Radical Spenser*, 49.

47. *Variorum*, 7:58.

48. See Carol Kaske, *Spenser and Biblical Poetics* (Ithaca: Cornell University Press, 1999), and Darryl Gless, *Interpretation and Theology in Spenser* (Cambridge: Cambridge University Press, 1994).

Lauren Silberman

Aesopian *Prosopopoia*: Making Faces and Playing Chicken in *Mother Hubberds Tale*

Mother Hubberds Tale locates the political engagements of the poem within a very complex Aesopian tradition. In reflecting and reflecting on this tradition, the poem registers political resentments and hostility under the cover of Aesopian deniability: generic beast fable figures can seem to conceal specific human targets while making the conclusive identification of those targets impossible. At the same time, the poem's meta-level examination of its own rhetorical tools is revealed as potentially one more defensive strategy: just as an attack on Burleigh or a critique of Elizabeth can masquerade as a fable about a fox or a lion, so sedition can purport to be discourse about sedition. Just how much Spenser might have been committed to the more radical implications of the Aesopian fictions put in play throughout *Mother Hubberds Tale* and how much he puts them in play for rhetorical effect is impossible to know for certain since Aesopian political deniability is part of the subject of the poem and cultivating political indeterminacy is an important strategy. At the same time, the way *Mother Hubberds Tale* adapts and revises its myriad subtexts hints that the political intentions of an individual poet, even if knowable, do not account for all of the political consequences of a particular poem.

Spenser Studies: A Renaissance Poetry Annual, Volume XXVII, Copyright © 2012 AMS Press, Inc. All rights reserved.   DOI: 10.7756/spst.027.010.221-247

*I*N HIS WONDERFUL EDITION of Spenser's *Complaints*, W. L. Renwick calls *Prosopopoia: Or Mother Hubberds Tale* the "only capital poem" in the volume.[1] Despite this judgment and despite new editions of Spenser's shorter poems, *Mother Hubberds Tale* has received relatively little critical attention.[2] It is best known for having caused its author political trouble.[3] Annabel Patterson has written provocatively on the poem in her *Fables of Power: Aesopian Writing and Political History* and has placed *Mother Hubberds Tale* in the Aesopian tradition of covert political engagement.[4] I should like to extend consideration of *Mother Hubberds Tale* as Aesopian fiction in a way that locates the political engagements of the poem within a very complex Aesopian tradition.[5] In reflecting and reflecting on this tradition, the poem registers political resentments and hostility under the cover of Aesopian deniability: generic beast fable figures can seem to conceal specific human targets while making the conclusive identification of those targets impossible. At the same time, the poem's meta-level examination of its own rhetorical tools is revealed as potentially one more defensive strategy: just as an attack on Burleigh or a critique of Elizabeth can masquerade as a fable about a fox or a lion, so sedition can purport to be discourse *about* sedition. Is Spenser venting his own political grudges in the course of writing *Mother Hubberds Tale*? Is he committing to print sedition against The Crown? One or both possibilities might be true, but the reciprocal reflection of politics and poetics in *Mother Hubberds Tale* makes it impossible to know for sure. At stake, I think, in the elaborate game of hide-and-seek Spenser is staging in his poem is an exploration of the political subject in relation to the multiplicity of cultural and political forces in which that subject is enmeshed.[6] Just as beast fables are ultimately about what it means to be human, so *Mother Hubberds Tale* examines what it means to be a political animal.

By framing his Aesopian *prosopopoeia* as "Mother Hubberd's tale," Spenser presents the adventures of his talking animals as the oral production of a female speaker. As Mary Ellen Lamb points out in her groundbreaking work on the fairy tale tradition in Elizabethan England, Elizabethan child-rearing practices encouraged men to associate oral fairy tales with maternal nurturance and with the pleasures of early childhood. For the first seven years of his life, an Elizabethan boy would be clothed in a dress, just like an Elizabethan girl, and brought up largely by women. At age seven, he would be allowed male clothing and taken from the company of women to be taught Latin by schoolmasters.[7] In presenting beast fables in the guise of Old Wives' Tales, Spenser follows the example of Wyatt in his second satire (entitled in Tottel's *Miscellany* "Of the Mean and Sure Estate, Written to John Poins"), which begins, "My mother's maids, when they did sew and spin." Like Wyatt, Spenser engages in strategic misdirection with this presentation.[8] In sixteenth-century English culture, Aesop's Fables belonged, not to the feminine realm of fairy tales, but to the male world of Greek and Latin study: *Aesop's Fables* would likely have been among the first Latin texts studied by a Tudor schoolboy.[9]

Mother Hubberds Tale reflects Wyatt's opening gambit of assigning an Aesopian fable to a female voice as it engages with and contests the satiric subject position Wyatt constructs in both Satire 1 ("Mine Owne John Poynz") and satire 2, ("Of the Mean and Sure Estate, written to John Poins"). In Satire 2, Wyatt's initial misdirection in presenting an Aesop Fable as a fairy tale told by "my mother's maids" signals the poet's manipulation of gender position as he claims for himself the role of self-sufficient male observer. Wyatt revises Horace's expansion of the Fable of the Town and Country Mouse.[10] In Satire 2.6, Horace transforms Aesop's straightforward parable of how it is better to live simply in security than to live luxuriously in fear into a complex meditation on point of view and the place of philosophical discussion. Horace presents himself as an urban sophisticate whose country retreat offers a venue for discussing philosophy: a guest at an informal dinner party tells a version of Aesop's fable to illuminate a discussion of the nature of the good. Not only does the tale-teller present the story in the context of abstract philosophical speculation, but the mice themselves utter philosophical talking points. In making the case for the urban good life, Horace's city mouse articulates standard Epicurean doctrine about the mortality of the soul. Wyatt's talking mice are both gendered female and neither mouse enjoys the security of a simple life on the one hand or the precarious pleasures of luxury on the other.[11] The country mouse flees a life of abject rural poverty to her sister, who lives a life of overt fear in town, Philosophical reflection is reserved for the first-person male speaker, who draws a Stoic moral significantly divergent from the fable attributed to "my mother's maids."

> Alas, my Poyntz, how men do seek the best,
> And find the worst by error as they stray!
> And no marvel: when sight is so oppressed
> And blind the guide, anon out of the way
> Goeth guide and all in seeking quiet life.
>
> . . .

Make plain thine heart, that it be not knotted
With hope or dread, and see thy will be bare
From all affects whom vice hath ever spotted;
Thyself content with that is thee assigned,
And use it well that is to thee allotted:
                                        (70–74, 92–96)

The stoic pieties offered by the speaker to his friend have little bearing on
the insecure lives of the vulnerable female mice in Wyatt's version of the
fable. In some respects, the intrusion of the first person voice at the con-
clusion of "Of the Mean and Sure Estate" serves the defensive function
Annabelle Patterson analyzes in *Fables of Power: Aesopian Writing and
Political History*. Patterson observes how the moral appended to many
Aesopian fables misrepresents the particulars of the fable in order to di-
vert attention from what is politically subversive in the fable itself. Wyatt
engages in a more complex defensive gesture. Projecting vulnerability onto
the female mice enables the detachment with which Wyatt as speaker com-
ments to his friend John Poins. He constructs verbally a place of refuge that
is something of a counterpart to Horace's country retreat.

Spenser follows Wyatt in assigning a beast fable to a female speaker as
he contests the pose of stoic detachment that Wyatt constructs for himself
through gendered voices. In his more overtly biographical satire, "Mine
Own John Poynz," Wyatt's reveals his pose of autonomy as a cultivated re-
sponse to political subjection as he creates poetically a state of liberty "in
Kent and Christendom" while under house arrest on his own estate. In
Mother Hubberds Tale, Spenser manipulates Aesopian materials in order to
destabilize and reconfigure the relationship between the poet-satirist and
the world, which is both an object of critique and a source of constraint.
Spenser systematically undermines the possibility of inhabiting a position
"in Kent and in Christendom" either as poet or as reader. In place of the
urbane exchange Wyatt stages between himself and his cultivated auditor,
Spenser takes his reader on a political and literary thrill ride.

In metaphorically displacing the poet-satirist from "Kent and
Christendom," Spenser expands the generic scope of *Mother Hubberds
Tale*. Wyatt's fable has occasional echoes of Chaucer's Aesopian "Nun's
Priest's Tale."[12] Spenser stages his own first person appearance in *Mother
Hubberds Tale* as an elaborate parody of the General Prologue to *The
Canterbury Tales* and concludes the adventures of his talking animals with
an epic descent from heaven. In place of the gender shifts Wyatt initiates

as he presents an Aesopian fable as the song of nursemaids rather than as the first work in a Tudor schoolboy's Latin curriculum, Spenser signals a pattern of temporal instability by his analogous presentation of a beast fable as a nursery tale. Where Chaucer's invocation of the sweet showers of April builds to the first-person introduction of Chaucer's pilgrim-narrator comfortably ensconced at the Tabard. Spenser describes the noisome dog days of August preparatory to evoking his first-person presence as a sick, suffering body[13]:

> It was the month, in which the righteous Maide,
> That for disdaine of sinfull worlds upbraide,
> Fled back to heaven, whence she was first conceived,
> Into her silver bowre the Sunne received;
> And the hot *Syrian* Dog on him awaiting,
> After the chafed Lyons cruell bayting,
> Corrupted had th'ayre with his noisome breath,
> And powr'd on th'earth plague, pestilence and death.
>
> . . . .
>
> My fortune was mongst manie others moe,
> To be partaker of their common woe;
> And my weake bodie set on fire with griefe,
> Was rob'd of rest, and naturall reliefe.
> In this ill plight, there came to visite mee
> Some friends, who sorie my sad case to see,
> Began to comfort me in chearfull wise,
> And meanes of gladsome solace to devise.
> (*MHT* 1–8, 13–20)[14]

These opening lines, in their blatant revision of the famous opening of *The Canterbury Tales*, invoke Spenser's great predecessor to mark a multivalent sense of decline and deterioration. The passage of time from April to August underscores the presentation of Spenser's world as a falling away from the glories of a Chaucerian springtime.[15] At the same time, presenting the Spenserian narrator as a body in pain, eventually to be comforted by Mother Hubberd and her storytelling, evokes personal longing for the comforts of a sixteenth-century childhood, comfort all the more striking since, as Mary Ellen Lamb has pointed out to me, Mother Hubberd is so much nicer than most other female narrators of the period.[16] This conflation of cosmic devolutionary history and nostalgic longing for one's own childhood puts in question the objectivity and stability of any particular, individual point of view.[17]

The descent of Mercury at the conclusion of *Mother Hubberds Tale* seems to balance the flight of Astraea that inaugurates the poem and to restore order and justice to a decadent world. Nevertheless, the apparent closure brought as Mercury rouses the Lion to restore royal justice to the animal kingdom reflects and accentuates the instabilities of the opening by alienating the reader retrospectively from the experience of reading the poem. In a final act of retribution, the Lion punishes the ape with mutilation for the crime of impersonating the king:

> But th'Apes long taile (which then he had) he quight
> Cut off, and both eares pared of their hight;
> Since which, all Apes but halfe their eares have left,
> And of their tailes are utterlie bereft.
>   (1381–84)

There is a certain poetic justice that as the Lion claims his rightful identity as king, the Ape becomes the Ape as we know it. Nevertheless, as the Ape is punished and humiliated, his story threatens to be diminished from a multivalent beast fable to a simple etiological tale: how the Ape came to look so much like a man.[18] This final transformation manifestly severs readers from the local time of the narrative—a time when Apes has tails and much larger ears. We are estranged from our own experience of reading *Mother Hubberds Tale* when the generic Ape whose adventures we imagine we are following as the narrative goes along is replaced retroactively by the exotic creature with big ears and a tail who only at the very end becomes our own image of the Ape in *Mother Hubberds Tale*.[19] At the same time that the Ape's mutilation produces a disorienting experience of Spenser's poem, it points beyond the poem to remind its readers of actual mutilations carried out in Elizabethan England in the name of public justice.

The flight of Astraea in the first lines of *Mother Hubberds Tale* opens up a poem of metamorphic change in a world of instability.[20] Mother Hubberd begins her tale by establishing a setting that is at once the distant past and the mirror of Elizabethan England.[21]

> Whilome (said she) before the world was civill,
> The Foxe and th'Ape disliking of their evill

And hard estate, determined to seeke
Their fortunes farre abroad, lyeke with his lyeke:
(*MHT* 45–48)

The world in which the Foxe and Ape practice their shape-shifting masquer-
ades evokes the Ovidian Age of Iron that follows the departure of Astraea,
in which metamorphosis and mutability underscore the absence of tran-
scendent order.[22] At the same time, the two protagonists reflect the specific
Elizabethan social problem of masterless men; their career of roguery testi-
fies to a lack of social control. The trademark Spenserian "whilome" denotes
temporal, literary and generic shifts. Mother Hubberd shares the "once-up-
on-a-time" with Chaucer's Nun's Priest, who begins his beast fable, "A povre
wyddwe, somdeel stape in age / Was whilom dwellyng in a narwe cotage."
(1–2) and with Chaucer's Knight, who begins his contribution to the epic
Matter of Thebes, "Willom, as olde stories tellen us, / Ther was a duc that
highte Theseus" (859–60).[23] In addition, *Mother Hubberds Tale* contains ele-
ments of medieval estates satire and the medieval Reynard the Fox cycle and
Renaissance picaresque as the Foxe and Ape disguise themselves as members
of the various estates in the course of their travels.[24] The poem combines the
"Mirror of Princes" tradition, in which rulers and authority figures are shown
idealized images of themselves to emulate and negative images to avoid, with
the specular dynamic of the beast fable, in which human characteristics are
projected onto animals and reflected back to the audience, as political and
social criticism is subjected to metamorphic instability.

As the Foxe and Ape undergo their transformations, how the talking
animals are being represented changes as well.[25] Let me take some modern
examples to illustrate the way modes of beast fable can shift.[26] In general,
beast fables, ancient or modern, can engage in varying degrees of anthro-
pomorphism, running the gamut from something like Richard Adams's
novel *Watership Down*, in which animals speak to one another but other-
wise act in ways consistent with what one might observe of actual animals,
to something like Kenneth Grahame's *Wind in the Willows*, in which ani-
mals wear clothes, take tea and drive motorcars. In this regard, one might
think of a variety of Disney cartoons (particularly when teaching beast
fables to undergraduates who are unfamiliar with *Wind in the Willows*
or *Watership Down*), from *Lady and the Tramp* and *101 Dalmations*, in
which dogs converse with other dogs but bark at humans, to *Robin Hood*,
in which the familiar folk characters are represented by various talking
animals in medieval dress. *The Lion King* veers very far into anthropomor-

phism, with animals performing elaborate musical numbers. One scene, however, destabilizes the mode of representation prevailing in the rest of the cartoon. The hero's wicked uncle, voiced by Jeremy Irons, torments a mute, naturalistic mouse: the anti-Mickey *mise en abyme*.

As the Fox and Ape proceed from one adventure to another and from one disguise to another, the way in which they are presented shifts along the continuum from naturalistic to anthropomorphic—from the pole of "mouse" to the pole of "Mickey," if you will. This process of morphing leads up to the politically charged masquerade of the Ape as the monarch, which scrutinizes the doctrine of the monarch's two bodies in the guise of a re-writing of the Aesopian fable of the ass in a lion's skin.[27]

The first disguises assumed by the Foxe and Ape disrupt the prevailing mode of beast fable representation in ways subtler than, but not unlike, the introduction of a naturalistic mouse into the extravagantly anthropomor-phic Disney cartoon. The opening exposition of Mother Hubberd's fable presents both protagonists as fully anthropomorphized figures. When the Foxe disguises himself as a dog, however, the rules of representation change: some animals turn out to be more human-like than others. Spenser systematically calls attention to the changes as the Foxe and Ape explicitly discuss and adjust their disguises. Initially, the Foxe envisions disguising both himself and the Ape in costumes bespeaking various human roles:

> Certes (said he) I meane me to disguize
> In some straunge habit after uncouth wize,
> Or like a Pilgrime, or a Lymiter,
> Or like a *Gipsen*, or a Juggeler,
> And so to wander to the worlds ende,
> To seeke my fortune, where I may it mend:
> For worse than that I have, I cannot meete.
> Wide is the world I wote, and everie streete
> Is full of fortunes, and adventures straunge,
> Continuallie subject unto chaunge.
> Say my faire brother now, if this device
> Doth like you, or may you to like entice
>   (*MHT* 83–94)

As the Foxe and Ape decide on a soldier's disguise to sanction a life of begging, the "likeness" of shared costume gives way to divergent physical appearance as the issue under consideration. The Foxe instructs the Ape:

Be you the Souldier, for you likest are
For manly semblance, and small skill in warre:
I will but wayte on you, and as occasion
Falls out, my selfe fit for the same will fashion.
                              (*MHT* 199–202)

The phrase "manly semblance" teasingly admits multiple understandings. If within the fiction, the Foxe deems his partner the more robust and soldier-like, in the real world, apes are more manlike in their appearance than foxes. When the masquerade becomes a full-fledged confidence game and the Ape accepts a position of shepherd from a charitable and guileless husbandman and the Foxe takes the role, not of his servant, but of his dog, the "unlikeness" between the two characters morphs into seeming differentiation of species. Although the accent on canine appearance seems to move the Foxe's disguise as a *faux* sheepdog away from the pole of anthropomorphism and toward the pole of naturalism, the apparent naturalism of this version of Beast fable representation becomes more problematic when the Foxe displays a wolf-like appetite for sheep and leads the Ape to share in the slaughter. Granted that foxes are carnivores and Spenser may not have been aware that apes are not, Aesopian fables about a wolf playing the role of a sheepdog underlies the fiction at this point and subtly destabilize it, "For that disguised Dog lov'd blood to spill, / And drew the wicked Shepheard to his will" (319–20).[28] Are we seeing a fox or a wolf or a dog in our mind's eye? Is the Foxe yielding to his canine nature as he goes after prey that, by the way, outweighs him by a considerable margin, or is he channeling his Aesopian precursor, the wolf?

    As the biblical associations of "wicked Shepheard" become concrete and visual, the beasts' masquerade modulates from shepherd and sheepdog to Pastor and Parish Clerk in the second of the four major episodes of the poem, the mode of beast fable representation shifts from the naturalistic to the anthropomorphic pole In this case, the Foxe assumes the role of Priest not because of his physical appearance, but because of his wily nature. The mirroring of human and animal that operates in the genre of beast fable shifts from primarily revealing the primitive drives humans share with other species to projecting human traits onto animals as a kind of estrangement device, so that those traits can be regarded with greater objectivity. The slaughter of the sheep by false shepherd and sheepdog reveals a viciousness shared by humans and animals. In the adventures of

Foxe and Ape as Priest and Clerk, one is invited to see clever-as-a-fox wili-
ness reflected in the sham priest and clerical duplicity shadowed by the
ecclesiastically garbed Foxe.[29]

The final two episodes bring to bear modulations from naturalistic to
anthropomorphic poles of representation in examining the Elizabethan
court. A specific focus on the element of clothing accompanies variations
in representational mode and facilitates a shift in satiric target from general
issues of status and authority to the specific political theory of the mon-
arch's two bodies. The Foxe and Ape are initially enticed to the court by a
talking Mule, "all deckt in goodly rich aray, / With bells and bosses, that full
lowdly rung, / And costly trappings, that to ground downe hung" (*MHT*
582–84). While the Mule's ornaments constitute clothing only in a meta-
phorical sense, as the third episode goes on, literal human attire becomes
a crucial issue:

> So well they shifted, that the Ape anon
> Himselfe had cloathed like a Gentleman,
> And the slie Foxe, as like to be his groome,
> That to the Court in seemly sort they come.
> Where the fond Ape himself uprearing hy
> Upon his tiptoes, stalketh stately by,
> As if he were some great *Magnifico*,
> And boldlie doth amongst the boldest go.
> And his man Reynold with fine counterfesaunce
> Supports his credite and his countenaunce.
> Then gan the Courtiers gaze on everie side,
> And stare on him, with big lookes basen wide,
> Wondering what mister wight he was, and whence:
> For he was clad in strange accoustrements,
> Fashion'd with queint devises never seene
> In Court before, yet there all fashions beene:
>   (*MHT* 659–74)

While the Mule affects courtly snobbishness in an ironic identification with
the masters who provide him with a decorative harness, the Ape insinuates
himself into the court by using opulent clothing and haughty manners to
ape a gentleman. In contrast to his earlier disguise as a shepherd, the Ape's
courtly "countenaunce" is as much a function of a superior attitude as of
manlike features.

The final masquerade, with the Ape impersonating the Lion King and the Foxe exercising the role of his chief counselor and assuming the power behind the throne, brings together the motif of clothing with the issue of how Aesopian animals mimic human beings physically and morally—in ways that are both destabilizing and unsettling. The Ape's masquerade takes the previously established movement along the continuum of Mickey to Mouse, of anthropomorphic to naturalistic representation, to a meta-level: the anthropomorphized Ape dons the natural pelt of the Lion and thereby puts in question the bond between the monarch's body natural and the monarch's body politic.[30] The image of the Lion taking off his skin to nap in comfort is both comic and creepy. At the outset of the episode, Spenser emphasizes the creepiness in the dispute between Foxe and Ape about donning the Lion's discarded skin. The Ape's reluctance, rendered all the more acute by the Foxe's urging, conflates fear of the political consequences of impersonating the monarch with the physical abhorrence of putting on the skin of another creature. This combined sense of political jeopardy and palpable contamination is intensified by the risks Spenser himself courted in allowing his satire to cleave so close to the person of the monarch. With a certain act of imaginative sympathy, even a modern reader can imagine how this *frisson* of danger might be felt by Elizabethan readers who held a copy of Spenser's audacious text in their hands.[31] The potential for comedy is realized at the close of the episode, when the Lion is awakened by Mercury, reaches for his lion-skin, and roars with indignity when he finds it missing.[32] The *Silence of the Lambs* creepiness of the detached Lion's skin has given way to the comic image of the Lion in his birthday suit, flailing angrily for his purloined gear and roaring in mock-heroic parody of Achilles *sans* armor, frightening the Greeks with his great war cry. Both the creepiness and the comedy serve to obscure the subversive political implications of the Ape's masquerade as the *frisson* of political trespass is mitigated by the variety of responses provoked in the reader.

As the Foxe and Ape go through various metamorphoses in the course of their adventures, the individual episodes that constitute those adventures alter the shape of the fables they adapt.[33] Not only do the Foxe and Ape shape-shift along a continuum from Mickey to Mouse, but the nature and extent of the engagement or detachment solicited from the reader shifts as well. By expanding the scope of Aesop's terse fables, Spenser introduces an element of suspense: how long can his rogues maintain their masquerade until they are caught at it?[34] This allows issues of authority to be explored in a context of reader engagement, as our sympathies are divided between the

Foxe and Ape, whose rogueries are entertaining, and the forces of order, which are increasingly needful as the pair pursues its depredations.

The rogues' first adventure, impersonating shepherd and sheepdog, starts out as a fairly close imitation of an Aesop fable about the wolf and the shepherd.[35] In his gullible benevolence, the husbandman who offers the Ape work caring for his sheep resembles the shepherd who commits the cardinal Aesopian sin of imprudence in leaving a seemingly tame wolf alone with his sheep. Aesop's fable moves swiftly to the familiar Aesopian insight, "It serves me right . . ." when the shepherd returns to see his sheep slaughtered. Spenser, however, extends the timeframe of Aesop's brief fable. His charitable but naive husbandman entrusts his sheep to the Ape and Foxe for half a year before he is to return for an accounting. By expanding the narrative focus, Spenser changes the way the story engages the reader emotionally. No longer does the owner of the sheep at the core of the narrative appear simply as victim of his own indiscretion; as the tale goes on, the husbandman becomes the absent authority figure whose return threatens to foreclose the story. We are invited to feel at once pity and disdain for Aesop's shepherd, who gets what he deserves for being imprudent. In Spenser's longer narrative, our feelings shift from perhaps a gentler pity than is elicited by Aesop for Spenser's exceedingly kind-hearted husbandman to a rather pleasurable anxiety about how long the Ape and Foxe can get away with it.

The second adventure of the Fox and Ape repeats the initial pattern of accumulating depredation and eventual exposure but significantly contracts the narrative scope of the masquerade:

> And craftie Reynold was a Priest ordained;
> And th'Ape his Parish Clarke procur'd to bee.
> Then made they revel route and goodly glee.
> But ere long time had passed, they so ill
> Did order their affaires, that th'evill will
> Of all their Parishners they had constrain'd;
> Who to the Ordinarie of them complain'd,
>   (*MHT* 556–62)

Compared to the first episode, with its half-year deadline and climactic escape two steps ahead of the authorities, when shepherd and dog become priest and clerk in the following episode, the familiarity of anti-clerical satire tends to replace the readerly pleasures of suspense and its resolution.

The final two episodes complicate the pleasures of the text considerably and engage the reader in more problematic fashion as they rework and expand Aesopian fables in complex ways. The talking mule that initiates the third episode recalls Aesop's fable of the Wild and the Domestic Ass, in which the wild ass envies the sleekness of the domestic ass until it observes the domestic ass being beaten by its master.[36] When the Foxe praises Spenser's mule for his sleekness and sumptuous trappings, the mule boasts of his superior condition and praises life in the court. In Aesop's fable, the contrast between wild and domestic expresses a trade-off between freedom and privation, on the one hand, and material comfort and subjection, on the other. Spenser transforms Aesop's straightforward beast fable into a dark allegory of court intrigue as the initially disdainful Mule warms to the invitation to share court gossip:

> Marie (said he) the highest now in grace,
> Be the wilde beasts, that swiftest are in chase;
> For in their speedie course and nimble flight
> The Lyon now doth take the most delight:
> But chieflie, joyes on foote them to beholde,
> Enchaste with chaine and circulet of golde:
> So wilde a beast so tame ytaught to bee,
> And buxome to his bands is joy to see.
> So well his golden Circlet him beseemeth:
> But his late chayne his Liege unmeete esteemeth;
> For so brave beasts she loveth best to see,
> In the wilde forrest raunging fresh and free.
>
> (619–30)

The Mule's speech intimates secret knowledge. In its very obscurity, the reference to "wild beasts" insinuates a determinate, but hidden, referent.[37] This gesture of blatant concealment contributes to the role of courtly insider assumed by the talking Mule; it also obscures the boundaries between inside and outside the text. The enigmatic allusion voiced by the Mule invites identification with some public figure in Spenser's own world. Contributing to the impression that the Mule's cryptic account incorporates an allegory of contemporary politics is the gender identification of the figure presiding over the court: as the focus narrows to one "wild beast," his Liege is distinguished as "she," which invites identification with Elizabeth, although not necessarily as a Lion Queen. Hitherto in Spenser's poem, the Aesopian Lion has not been assigned a gender, and later in the episode, in the digression about the ideal courtier, the generic prince is termed "he" (773–76). Spenser exploits the metamorphic quality of beast fable representation throughout his poem to slip into a potential allusion to the reigning monarch and then slip away from it. He accentuates the sense of slipperiness with characteristically Spenserian epanorthosis—or correction. First we are told that the Lion takes delight in the tameness of wild beasts and then that the liege (the same figure, presumably) loves to see beasts running wild in the forest.

Spenser's slipperiness here goes beyond teasing the reader with possible allusions to public figures. In fact, the very provocativeness of presenting a reigning queen and particular courtiers in Aesopian guise directs attention from what is arguably more subversive in Aesop's fable of the wild and the domesticated ass, namely the premise that the state of nature is to be free of political subjection. Spenser executes a rhetorical pirouette on the term "wild" as he shifts away from the generic political implication of "wild" as natural and free to use "wild" as a code word for unnamed political insiders. Just as the representation of the ass's harness as courtly trappings supersedes its original Aesopian significance as shackles, so the dangerous glamor of courtly gossip diverts attention from the far more audacious political implications of Aesop's unembellished imagery.[38]

To the extent that readers identify themselves as privileged consumers of political information, they are distracted from seeing their own political circumstances mirrored by Aesop's wild and domestic asses. The third episode of *Mother Hubberds Tale* destabilizes the subject position of the reader. Far from being "in Kent and Christendom," reflecting on the fortunes of talking animals in the company of an urbane gentleman-poet, readers experience a representation of court life that blurs distinctions between inside and outside, between the courtier-poet and the court he mirrors. The two notorious "digressions" in this episode—the encomium of the ideal courtier (717–93) and the complaint of the courtly suitor (891–14)—are significant in this process of undermining boundaries. As Kent Van den Berg has noted, both of these passages expressly represent the narrator in the process of losing control of the narrative, rather than recording unmediated personal expression.[39] Whatever personal opinions or experiences are articulated in these two passages, the digressions need also to be read as poetic constructs. Indeed, the passages may be digressions from the story of the Ape and Foxe at court, but they are salient features of the episode as an expansion and mystification of Aesop's fable of the Wild Ass and Domestic Ass. In Spenser's hands, Aesop's straightforward comparison of life inside the confines of a social structure to life in the wild becomes a complex meditation on the complex negotiations of "inside" and "outside" in the positioning of author, text and society. Although the portrait of the ideal courtier seemingly constitutes the antithesis of the Ape, that exemplary figure shares some of the Ape's metamorphic qualities. Initially the ideal courtier is described as an observer who remains aloof from the court, who "heares, and sees the follies of the rest, / And thereof gathers for himselfe the best" (725–26). By the end of the portrait, he is the ultimate political insider and advises his prince:

> For he is practiz'd well in policie,
> And thereto doth his Courting most applie:
> To learne the enterdeale of Princes strange,
> To marke th'intent of Counsells, and the change
> Of states, and eke of private men somewhile,
> Supplanted by fine falshood and faire guile;
> Of all the which he gathereth, what is fit
> T'enrich the storehouse of his powerfull wit,
> Which through wise speeches, and grave conference
> He daylie eekes, and brings to excellence.
> Such is the rightfull Courtier in his kinde:
> But unto such the Ape lent not his minde;
>   (*MHT* 783–94)

The contrary ideals of detached observer and political insider demarcate the conflicting aspirations of the humanist poet: to be at the center of power or to be at a place of vision. In principle these aspirations might be reconciled, but the multifarious encapsulated portrait allows the author to write himself into the poem, not only because the apparent digressiveness directs attention from the narrative itself to the one crafting it, but because the metamorphic quality of the portrait allows Spenser to work traces of an authorial presence into an unstable field of representation. In this third episode, negotiations between the poles of Mickey and of Mouse morph into shifting subject positions among poet, reader, and courtiers in Spenser's text and in Elizabeth's court. Spenser stages his presence as a courtier-poet in the court satire that constitutes this episode through a kind of uneasy triangulation with a dark double in the person of the Ape and with a shadowy nem-

esis whose identity is a tempting secret. Not only does the ideal court-
ier hover between insider and observer as a shifting paradigm for the
humanist poet, the figure wavers between courtly ideal and something
uncomfortably close to the poison-pen portrait in the final episode of
Mother Hubberds Tale usually identified with Burleigh.[40] When Spenser
describes the ideal courtier "[gathering] what is fit / T'enrich the store-
house of his powerfull wit" (789–90) the image looks back to the earlier
picture of the same figure as an unsullied observer who "gathers for
himselfe the best" (726) and forward to the politically-charged repre-
sentation of the Foxe who gathers for himself whatever is not nailed
down as he enriches himself in the role of chief minister.

Spenser's nemesis, as figured in the most seemingly autobiographical
line of the suitor's complaint in *Mother Hubberds Tale*, "To have thy Princes
grace, yet want her Peeres" (901), is usually identified as William Cecil,
Lord Burleigh. The story of Burleigh's antipathy for Spenser is repeated
widely and may well be true. Nevertheless, the complex relationships of
parody and opposition that link the Ape and the Peer to Spenser suggests
that in some respects the poet generates his opposite number—indeed
both opposite numbers. The narrator's hortatory exclusion of the poetic
activities of the Courtier Ape from the ranks of true poetry undercuts itself
in characteristic Spenserian fashion:

> Thereto he could fine loving verses frame,
> And play the Poet oft. But ah, for shame
> Let not sweete Poets praise, whose onely pride
> Is vertue to advaunce, and vice deride,
> Be with the worke of losels wit defamed,
> Ne let such verses Poetrie be named:
> Yet he the name on him would rashly take,
>   (809–15)

Evident in this passage is the recognition, apparent in such Spenserian
figures as Archimago and Busirane, of the fine line that separates the
craft of poetry from the perversion of poetry. More, however, than autho-
rial circumspection (and defensiveness) is at play here. The narrator goes
on to excoriate the Ape for poetic production that quite closely shadows
Spenser's own: for writing anti-clerical satire, such as could be found in
the previous episode of *Mother Hubberds Tale*, and for producing prurient
verse, to "allure / Chast Ladies eares to fantasies impure" (819–20).[41] The

latter condemnation echoes the criticism attributed metonymically in the Proem to Book IV to "the rugged forehead" that censured Spenser's 1590 *Faerie Queene*. The Ape risks being a caricature of Spenser, but Spenser's narrator comes close to reading the Ape with the taste of a Burleigh. As the poet holds up mirrors more than one to himself and his objects—now idealizing, now censuring; now conjoining, now contrasting—he releases critical energy and hits multiple targets, but in a meta-Aesopian strategy of diversion. Spenser makes it virtually impossible to isolate a discrete political attack on an identifiable object.

Accordingly, what seems to be a pointed outburst of political resentment for wrongs done the poet by a powerful enemy at court is also a supremely confident display of Spenser's poetic skill. The putative animosity between Spenser and Burleigh gets clearest allusion in *Mother Hubberds Tale* in the encapsulated complaint of the Suitor. Paradoxically, the passage stages a seeming outburst of personal grievance and loss of authorial control with the blatantly rhetorical figure of anaphora:

> To loose good dayes, that might be better spent;
> To wast long nights in pensive discontent;
> To speed to day, to be put back to morrow;
> To feed on hope, to pine with feare and sorrow;
> To have thy Princes grace, yet want her Peeres;
> To have thy asking, yet waite manie yeeres;
> To fret thy soule with crosses and with cares;
> To eate thy heart trhough comfortlesse dispaires;
> To fawne, to crowche, to waite, to ride, to ronne,
> To spend, to give to want, to be undonne.
> (897–906)

Just as the seemingly repetitive figure of anaphora becomes, in the hands of the consummate poet, the vehicle for extraordinarily subtle variations of rhythm and syntax, so the seeming loss of authorial control accompanies a skillful construction of the author's subject position as the seeming victim of neglect. The rhetorical outburst is situated between complex mirrorings. The immediate occasion for the suitor's complaint is the activity of the Foxe, who imitates the professions of various suitors, so that the Ape can "prevent" them—that is appropriate their suit and present it as his own. The complaint builds to a climactic curse that ricochets in a verbal hall of mirrors:

Who ever leaves sweete home, where meane estate
In safe assurance, without strife or hate,
Findes all things needful for contentment meeke;
And will to Court for shadowes vaine to seeke,
Or hope to gaine, himselfe will a daw trie:
That curse God send unto mine enemie.
For none but such as this bold Ape unblest,
Can ever thrive in that unluckie quest;

(909–16)

In cursing the suitor at court, Spenser is both directing the malediction
at himself and identifying himself with his enemy. His stance contrasts
pointedly with the measured disapproval with which Wyatt's first person
speaker concludes his second satire, "Of the Mean and Sure Estate, Written
to John Poins":

Henceforth, my Poynz, this shall be all and some:
These wretched fools shall have nought else of me,
But to the great God and to his high doom
None other pain pray I for them to be
But when the rage doth lead them from the right
That looking backward virtue they may see
Even as she is, so goodly fair and bright;
And whilst they clasp their lusts in arms across
Grant them, good Lord, as thou mayst of thy might,
To fret inward for losing such a loss.

(103–12)

Where Wyatt separates himself and his designated audience member
John Poins from the common rout who do not share their Stoic equanim-
ity, Spenser subverts the distinction between satirist and object of satire.
Wyatt concludes his poem, figuratively, although not literally "in Kent and
Christendom," with a restrained prayer for measured divine chastisement
of those not so philosophically privileged, Spenser moves beyond the hy-
perbolic curse of all who leave the assurance of mean estate and returns to
the narrative. The narrator's explicit statement that none but the "bold Ape
unblest," can survive in court is undercut in classic Spenserian fashion with
the immediately ensuing unmasking of the Foxe and Ape and their expul-
sion from the court.

Under the guise of writing himself into his textual house of mirrors ("To have thy Princes grace, yet want her Peeres"), Spenser establishes a distinction between the Prince, who favors her unnamed suitor, and her Peere, who does not, that becomes crucial in the last episode of *Mother Hubberds Tale*. The final masquerade of the Foxe and Ape revisits the courtly satire of the previous episode at a much higher degree of political risk. In the third episode, funhouse-mirror reflections of poet-narrator and dark double/ poetaster Ape and of poet-narrator and courtly antagonist/poet-hating peer constitute a satire that reflects criticism on the Elizabethan court while reflecting on the position of the humanist poet in Elizabethan politics. In the fourth episode, satiric representations of a monarch and a powerful minister threaten to engage the world of politics by drawing the wrath of the authorities down on the text and its author. Courting government censure, Spenser has achieved a reality effect of considerable proportions. And insofar as his readers remain responsive to a sense of jeopardy in reading an illicit text, they read themselves into a textual house of mirrors in a kind of higher-level prosopopoeia.[42]

As with previous episodes, the final masquerade begins as a revision of an Aesop fable. The Ape's donning the pelt of the sleeping Lion at the urging of the Foxe recalls Aesop's fable of the Ass clothed in the skin of the lion while amending the fable's point.[43] This fable is one of many Aesop fables that affirm essentialist identity and censure social mobility by showing animals punished or humiliated for imitating their betters. Aesop's Ass in the Lion's skin is found out as soon as he brays. In telling contrast, when Spenser's Ape replaces the rightful monarch, his subjects never see through his disguise. Like the animals in Aesop's version, which, temporarily deluded by appearances, flee the disguised Ass, a sheep and an ass run from Spenser's Ape when he dons the Lion skin. But, in contrast to Aesop, Spenser's version has speech reinforcing, rather than exposing, the masquerade. The smooth words of Spenser's Foxe persuade the animals to cease their flight from a seemingly fearsome Lion and undertake a journey to the court of the pretend Lion-king.

In doffing his skin, the Lion has effected a separation between the monarch's two bodies. In successfully masquerading in the discarded lion's skin, Spenser's Ape undermines the essential legitimacy of the monarch's body natural, that is to say, Elizabeth. Having flirted with a highly inflammatory identification of the fictional Ape and the reigning monarch, Spenser uses the prior distinction between Prince and Peere to retreat from the extremes of political danger. As the identification of the Foxe with some extra-literary figure becomes increasingly audacious, the Ape fades from view as a satiric target. The poem shifts generically from a covert critique of monarchy in the Aesopian mode to an Elizabethan poem of personal destruction in the manner of, say, *Leicester's Commonwealth*. Although the charges that the Foxe plundered the kingdom to "fe[e]d his cubs" (1151) invites identification with Burleigh, who was frequently accused of using his office to enrich his relatives, other self-serving politicians, either of the court of Elizabeth or of earlier monarchs, fit the description well enough. Indeed, just about any politician with relatives is open to the accusation.[44] As in the previous episode, hints of personal attack on a specific contemporary political figure function as a diversionary strategy: the seeming specificity and genuine indeterminacy of the poison pen portrait grafted onto the Foxe shifts focus from the critique of the Lion, which need not be very pointed to be read as Elizabeth in Elizabethan England.

If the third episode of *Mother Hubberds Tale* destabilizes the rhetorical from which Wyatt and his intimate audience John Poins reflect on the fable of Town and Country Mouse, in the fourth and final episode the Aesopian fiction threatens to usurp any position outside itself. In the previous episodes, the Lion and Fox pursue their rogueries until caught at it by the authorities. In the rogues' impersonation of Lion King and his sly minister the pair has gained control of the institutions of authority.[45] Accordingly, the final episode of the poem closes with a double set-piece: a formal trial within the beast fable that abets the corrupt rule of the Foxe and Ape and a deus ex machina intervention that concludes the poem by radically disrupting the boundaries of genre. The trial is a revised version of the well-known Aesop fable of the Wolf and the Lamb, which enters Spenser's text as the sequel of an earlier encounter.[46] The Sheep who was placated by the Foxe as she fled the imitation Lion and invited to court turns up with a legal complaint: she is the mother of the Lamb of the well-known fable and is bringing a law case against the Wolf. In response, the Foxe accuses the hapless Sheep of slandering his cousin the Wolf and dismisses her. The Foxe's claim of family ties to the Wolf both satirizes political corruption and recalls the initial masquerade, in which the Foxe played the role of the Aesopian Wolf set to guard the sheepfold. The Aesopian world, in which raw power overrides the discourse of justice and the fate of the powerless is to be eaten, gives way to a more sophisticated polity, in which the capacity of power to control the judicial discourse has been institutionalized and speech is rendered powerless by being termed slander. In this world, individual Aesopian fables are connected one to another generationally, rather than by iteration of Aesopian types, so that the sheep from one fable becomes the mother of the lamb from another and the shared rapaciousness of Wolf and Fox becomes the corruption of family connections. The regime of the Ape and Foxe threatens to become a nightmare image of the political world inhabited by the reader, rather than a terse comment on that world.

Mother Hubberds Tale opens with the flight of Astraea, goddess of justice, from the corrupt and decadent world, but the programmatic injustice represented by the Aesopian-fable-turned-courtroom drama heralds a counter movement in the descent of Mercury. The arrival of Mercury seems to reestablish the pattern established in the first episode of increasing suspense—as the rogues continue their depredations—followed by resolution—as the authorities restore order. In fact, this conclusion of *Mother Hubberds Tale* complicates the sense of an ending. Although in *Mother Hubberds Tale,* the descent of Mercury functions as a deus ex machina in bringing the poem closure not generated by the foregoing narrative, this is not its traditional function. In the epic tradition, the descent from heaven serves to move the plot forward, not bring it to a close. Conventionally, what Mercury and his avatars terminate is the truancy of the epic hero from his epic quest.[47] In a sense, Spenser's Mercury does rouse the sleeping Lion—to a mock-heroic parody of Achilles—but once the true king is awakened, the Ape's masquerade is as good as over. Although the aim of Mercury is to restore the Lion to his rightful place of authority, the language with which he rouses the Lion directs an extremely harsh verbal attack in the general direction of a monarch:

> Arise (said *Mercurie*) thou sluggish beast,
> That here liest senseless, like the corpse deceast,
> The whilste thy kingdome from thy head is rent,
> And thy throne royall with dishonour blent:
> Arise, and doo thy selfe redeeme from shame,
> And be aveng'd on those that breed thy blame.
> (1327–32)

Nevertheless, at the same time that the Lion is castigated verbally by Mercury, he is significantly exculpated by a narrative detail: Mercury removes a hitherto unmentioned sleep-inducing weed that, we are now told, the Foxe had placed under the Lion's head. The detail partly

justifies the Lion's truancy, but the last-minute retrojection of the ex-
culpatory detail compromises the integrity of the narrative, just as the
mutilation of the Ape destabilizes readers' ongoing experience of the
fiction while reminding them of the potential real-world consequences
of defaming the reigning monarch.

The temerity of the reproach directed to the Lion is one more of the
poem's defensive gestures. In bidding him to redeem himself and his
honor, Mercurie confirms the essential royalty of the Lion. The criti-
cism voiced by Mercurie is in the traditional mirror of princes mode
as it posits distance between individual monarch and the ideal of mon-
archy in order to offer the monarch an image of his (or her) ideal self
and effaces more subversive understandings of how the monarch's two
bodies are figured by Spenser's Lion and his detachable skin. Just how
much Spenser might have been committed to the more radical implica-
tions of the Aesopian fictions put in play throughout *Mother Hubberds
Tale* and how much he puts them in play for rhetorical effect is impos-
sible to know for certain since Aesopian political deniability is part of
the subject of the poem and cultivating political indeterminacy is an
important strategy. At the same time, the way *Mother Hubberds Tale*
adapts and revises its myriad subtexts hints that the political intentions
of an individual poet, even if knowable, do not account for all of the
political consequences of a particular poem. In his important study
Shakespeare and Republicanism, Andrew Hadfield traces what he terms
"forms of republican culture" through a very wide range of Elizabethan
writing, much not explicit in its advocacy of a form of government that
one might technically term "republican."[48] It was the great intuition of
Sir Isaac Newton that the planets in their motions are *falling*. When
Newton articulated that insight, earlier studies of falling bodies became
part of Newtonian mechanics. Spenser manipulates Aesopian imagery
and tropes with conscious, indisputable skill and makes them more
fully available to anyone who would use them as an instrument of po-
litical thought. As *Mother Hubberds Tale* enmeshes poet and reader in
a metamorphic world of Aesopian political discourse, it intervenes in
the political conversation of the English-speaking world and beyond in
ways that are unpredictable but genuine.

Baruch College

NOTES

1. W. L. Renwick, *Complaints by Edmund Spenser* (London: Scholartis Press, 1928), 179.

2. In "Still Reading Spenser after All These Years," *ELR* 25 (1995): 432–44, Annabel Patterson aptly characterizes *Mother Hubberds Tale* as "An extremely peculiar poem, which has . . . been assiduously avoided by literary scholars" (436) and then goes on to comment perceptively about the ways in which *Mother Hubberds Tale* presents poetry as a safe-conduct passport for satire. On the esoteric quality of the *Complaints* volume in general, see Katherine A. Craik, "Spenser's 'Complaints' and the New Poet," *HLQ* 64 (2001): 63–79. For a summary of earlier criticism of the poem, see Kenneth John Atchity, "Spenser's *Mother Hubberds Tale*: Three Themes of Order," *PQ* 52 (1973): 161–72.

3. Richard S. Peterson has discovered a contemporary reference to the calling-in of Spenser's *Complaints*. See Richard S. Peterson, "Laurel Crown and Ape's Tail: New Light on Spenser's Career from Sir Thomas Tresham," *Spenser Studies* 12 (1991): 16. See also H. S. V. Jones, *A Spenser Handbook* (New York: Appleton-Century-Crofts, 1930), 74–75; and Harold Stein, *Studies in Spenser's Complaints* (New York: Oxford University Press, 1934), 81–83.

4. Annabel Patterson, *Fables of Power: Aesopian Writing and Political History* (Durham: Duke University Press, 1991).

5. For a discussion of how the medieval Renard the Fox material underlies the anti-court satire in the poem, see Edwin Greenlaw, "The Sources of Spenser's 'Mother Hubberd's Tale,'" *Modern Philology* 2 (1905): 411–32.

6. In many respects, I am taking the argument by Kent Van den Berg, in "The Counterfeit in Personation: Spenser's *Prosopopoia, or Mother Hubberds Tale*," in *The Author in His Work: Essays on a Problem in Criticism*, ed. Louis Martz and Aubrey Williams (New Haven: Yale University Press, 1978), 85–102, that in *Mother Hubberds Tale*, Spenser "sets the poet's power to personify against his disdain for the counterfeit self, and thereby exemplifies his struggle to maintain moral and aesthetic integrity in the face of a fragmented and deceptive world" (86) and suggesting that Spenser is engaging in a much more risk-taking, metamorphic performance. For an illuminating study of how literature of the period can explore political subjecthood in the guise of treating erotic subject matter, see Melissa E. Sanchez, *Erotic Subjects: The Sexuality of Politics in Early Modern English Literature*, (New York: Oxford University Press, 2011.

7. Mary Ellen Lamb, "Gloriana, Acrasia, and the House of Busirane: Gendered Fictions in *The Faerie Queene* as Fairy Tale," in *Worldmaking Spenser: Explorations in the Early Modern Age*, ed. Patrick Cheney and Lauren Silberman (Lexington: University Press of Kentucky, 2000), 81–100.

8.   Quotations from Wyatt taken from Joost Daalder, ed., *Sir Thomas Wyatt: Collected Poems* (London: Oxford University Press, 1975).

9.   T. W. Baldwin, *William Shakespere's Small Latine and Lesse Greeke* (Urbana, University of Illinois Press, 1944), 1:607; Patterson, 52.

10.   In Spenser's time, there were multiple collections of fables, printed in England and on the continent attributed to Aesop. The question of what edition or editions Spenser might have consulted is a vexed one, to say the least. For a sense of how difficult it is to determine what, exactly, an Elizabethan poet might have used as a source, see Baldwin, 1:610–16. Very briefly, Tudor schoolboys would use a Greek/Latin collection of prose fables by Aesop and verse fables by Babrius, geared toward the study of grammar, imitation, and paraphrase (correspondence, William P. Weaver). An English translation was done by Caxton of (a French translation of) the German version by Steinhowel. In 1585, there was another English version by William Bullokar. For more information on collections of Aesopian fables, see Paul Thoen, "Les grands recueils ésopiques des XVe et XVIe siècles et leur importance pour les littératures des temps modernes," *Acta Conventus Neo-Latini Lovaniensis: Proceedings of the First International Congress of Neo-Latin Studies, Louvain 23–28 August 1971*, ed. J. Ijsewijn and E. Kessler (Louvain: Leuven University Press, 1971), 659–79. See also, *Caxton's* Aesop, ed. with introduction and notes R. T. Lenaghan (Cambridge: Harvard University Press, 1967). Also of interest is the extensive introduction to Ben Edwin Perry's edition and translation of *Babrius and Phaedrus* (Cambridge: Harvard University Press, 1965). I shall be citing tale numbers and any English translations from the edition by Laura Gibbs, *Aesop's Fables* (New York: Oxford University Press, 2002), as well as the numbers given in Gibbs's edition from the monumental modern edition by Perry entitled, *Aesopica* as well as the other editions cited by Gibbs. A complete listing of the numbers, along with the Greek and Latin texts may be found at <http://www.aesopica.net>. In Gibbs, the Fable of the Town and Country Mouse is number 408, and Fable 352 in the modern edition by Perry, and Fable 13 in the medieval Ademar of Chabannes.

11.   In his satire, Horace refers to the beast fable as an old woman's tale. In Wyatt's time, however, Aesop's Fables were assigned to schoolboys newly liberated from the world of female storytelling. In "My Mother's Maids," gender reversals accompany Wyatt's rather artful identification of an Aesopian Fable as an old wives' tale.

12.   Compare Satire 2, lines 50–58 with "The Nun's Priest's Tale," lines B 4394–405.

13.   In the nursery rhyme, Mother Hubbard goes to the cupboard to get her poor dog a bone. To my knowledge, there are no printed versions of the nursery rhyme that predate the nineteenth century, but it would be nice to imagine it as part of Spenser's oral heritage.

14.   Quotations are taken from *The Yale Edition of the Shorter Poems of Edmund Spenser*, ed. William Oram et al. (New Haven: Yale University Press, 1989).

15. Complicating the revision of Chaucer is allusion to Horace's satire 2.6, in which the Dog Star figures the sufferings of the poet who must summer in the city for want of patronage.

16. Personal correspondence. For the classic study of the body in pain, see Elaine Scarry, *The Body in Pain: The Making and Unmaking of the World* (Oxford: Oxford University Press, 1985).

17. The classic study of devolutionary and evolutionary theories of history in Western Culture is Eric Havelock, *The Liberal Temper in Greek Politics* (2nd ed. New Haven: Yale University Press, 1964). Fascinating here are suggestions of nostalgia for a specifically Roman Catholic past, when the cult of the saints was a source of comfort not conspicuously present in the cultural dog days of Elizabethan England. This is not to suggest a revisionary reading of Spenser as crypto-Catholic (although it might be fun to do so just to watch the reaction). Rather, Spenser seems to be making use of the tradition of satire as *lanx satura*— a generic combination platter, a plate metaphorically filled with a wide variety of literary elements—as he allows his poem to register some sense of England's lost medieval past. One might pause here to remark how grievous and wrenching must have been Elizabethan England's unavoidable alienation from its medieval Catholic past that even so staunch a Protestant as Spenser acknowledges the loss.

18. The sixteenth-century Sir Thomas Tresham disparages readers of *Mother Hubberds Tale* who "thus desire to be resolved howe apes did first forgoe their tayles." See Peterson, 8.

19. A similar shift in which readers must revise significantly their mental picture occurs in Apuleius's *Metamorphoses (The Golden Ass)*. A character named Thelyphron tells a first-person story which culminates in his realization that his own ears and nose have been stolen by witches and replaced with wax substitutes (2.20-31). The audience within the work, fellow guests at a dinner party, laugh cruelly when Thelyphron describes first discovering his deformity, while the audience of the work learns for the first time that the narrator has a piece of linen glued where his nose once was. Apuleius, *Metamorphoses*, ed. and trans. J. Arthur Hanson (Cambridge: Harvard University Press, 1989), 98-121.

20. For a reading of the poem that focuses on order and harmony, see Atchity.

21. See the *Yale Edition of the Shorter Poems of Edmund Spenser*, note to line 45, p. 336.

22. For a reading of how the Protean nature of the Foxe and Ape figures engages the role of the poet in the world, see Harry Berger, Jr. "The Prospect of Imagination: Spenser and the Limits of Poetry," *SEL* 1 (1961): 93-120.

23. Quotations from Chaucer are from F. N. Robinson, ed., *The Works of Geoffrey Chaucer*, 2nd ed. Boston: Houghton Mifflin, 1957.

24. See the introduction to *Mother Hubberds Tale* in *The Yale Edition of the Shorter Poems of Edmund Spenser*, 327-30.

25. Stein observes the shift but ascribes it to Spenser's carelessness, 56-62. In "Poets, Poetry and Mercury in Spenser's *Prosopopoia: Mother Hubberds Tale*,"

Costerus 5 (1972): 27–33, Robert Bryan argues more judiciously that a shift from the world of men to the world of animals organizes the poem in a devolutionary pattern. See also Van den Berg, 91. I will argue that these transformations are very radical and highly intentional.

26. Ursula K. Le Guin has an interesting account of the variety of animal personification in *Cheek by Jowl* (Seattle: Aqueduct Press, 2009), 44–108.

27. Gibbs, 322 and 323; Perry, 188 and 358. The first, in which the donkey reveals itself when it brays is found in Chambry's 1925–26 edition of anonymous Greek fables as number 267. The second, in which a wind reveals the disguised donkey is Aphthonius 10. See also Erasmus, *Adages* 1.7.12 and 1.3.66, which cites Lucian's *Fisherman.*

28. Gibbs, 38; Chambry, 229; Perry, 234; Gibbs, 36; Chambry, 314; Perry, 366.

29. On the relationship of the rogues' second masquerade to the first, see Van den Berg, 88–90.

30. The classic study of the doctrine of the monarch's two bodies is Ernst Hartwig Kantorowicz, *The King's Two Bodies; A Study in Mediaeval Political Theology* (Princeton: Princeton University Press, 1957).

31. Compare the narrator's interjected comment "(Let none them read)" when describing the spell with which Archimago calls forth Gorgon as he fashions the false Una (*FQ* I.i.37.2).

32. To continue the popular culture analogy, Walt Disney is giving way to Tex Avery as the Aesopian counterpart.

33. See particularly Van den Berg.

34. As William P. Weaver points out in his "Marlowe's Fable: *Hero and Leander* and the Rudiments of Eloquence," *Studies in Philology* 105 (2008): 388–408, taking Aesop's fables and expanding them was a standard grammar school exercise in imitation recommended by Quintilian. Weaver describes how Marlowe expands on this rhetorical exercise as he revises Musaeus in his *Hero and Leander*, particularly in amplifying the descriptions of the lovers. Spenser may well be doing something analogous in expanding the narrative scope of the fables.

35. Gibbs, 38; Chambry, 229; Perry, 234.

36. Gibbs 4 (entitled "The Onager, the Donkey and the Driver,") Chambry 264, Perry 183.

37. On this point, see Richard Rambuss, *Spenser's Secret Career* (New York: Cambridge University Press, 1993).

38. In making the word "wild" a focus of politically charged ambiguity, Spenser echoes a crux in Wyatt that he fascinatingly revisits in *Amoretti* 67. Although one can take the wild beast that provokes his Liege's displeasure with "his late chayne" as a reference to any number of courtiers who displeased Elizabeth by marrying, the coded language of "wild" and "tame" and the image of the chain recalls the sonnet by Sir Thomas Wyatt "Who so list to hunt," a poem from which has been read veiled allusion to sexual politics of an earlier Tudor court. The conclusion of *Amoretti* 67, "Strange thing me seemd to see a beast so wyld, / so goodly wonne

with her owne will beguyld" recalls the inscription worn around the neck of Wyatt's anthropomorphic deer, "*Noli me tangere*, for Cæsar's I am, / And wild for to hold, though I seem tame" and transforms the play of female chastity and political subjecthood in Wyatt's poem to a private interplay between courting lovers.

39.   Van den Berg, 93.

40.   Bryan has a useful survey of roman-à-clef readings of *Mother Hubberds Tale*. See also Thomas Herron, "Exotic Beasts: The Earl of Ormond and Nicholas Dawtry in *Mother Hubberds* Tale?" *Spenser Studies* 19 (2004): 245–51. On this point, Renwick's comments in his 1928 edition of the poem hold up beautifully:

> Men naturally seek for allegory in the works of a professed allegorist, but those who have attempted of late years to unravel the complicated meanings of these poems have more rigidly systematic minds that I believe Spenser had; certainly narrower minds. It is easy to press too closely this one point of personal allusion, to find Burghley and that unlucky pension at every turn, forgetting that there may have been other men in England whom Spenser may have disliked, and forgetting—what is more important—that Spenser was a professed philosopher and moralist. The *Complaints* do contain allusions to persons and events. What poem does not? (183)

41   For another view of the Ape as sorcerer-poet played against the ideal courtier as true reader, see David Lee Miller, "Spenser's Vocation, Spenser's Career" *ELH* 50 (1983), 204. On the Foxe and Ape as poet figures, see also Brown, 184–212. Lady Ralegh seems to have identified the Foxe as Burleigh and the Ape as his son, Robert Cecil, in the family copy of Spenser. See Walter Oakeshott, "Carew Ralegh's Copy of Spenser," *The Library*, 5th ser. 26 (1971): 1–21. As Oakeshott points out, Lady Ralegh had her own reasons for hostility to the Cecils (8).

42   Richard Rambuss astutely analyzes the paradoxes of Spenser's conspicuous display of secrecy in *Spenser's Secret Career* (Cambridge: Cambridge University Press, 1993).

43   Gibbs, 322; Chambry, 267; Perry, 188.

44   See Renwick, 231.

45   Nelson notes how Spenser echoes in this, not only contemporary attacks on Burleigh but also Aristotle, Erasmus, and Skelton (81).

46   Gibbs 130, Babrius 89, Perry 155.

47   See Thomas M. Greene, *The Descent From Heaven: A Study in Epic Continuity* (New Haven: Yale University Press, 1963), esp. 301–4; and Brown, 205–7.

48   Andrew Hadfield, *Shakespeare and Republicanism* (Cambridge: Cambridge University Press, 2005). See also the exchange between Hadfield and David Scott Wilson-Okamura in *Spenser Studies* 17 (2003): 253–92.

DEBRA RIENSTRA

"Disorder Best Fit": Henry Lok and Holy Disorder in Devotional Lyric

Henry Lok's devotional sonnets, printed in 1593 and 1597, combine the emerging patterns of English Petrarchism with postures, emotive contours, and readerly habits associated with the Psalms, creating a coherent blend of Calvinist-inflected devotion and artful lyric sequence. Lok's figuring of disorder in particular presents workable solutions to problems that will occupy later English devotional poets. In the first century of sonnets, Lok problematizes sincerity through disordered speech, transposing the Petrarchan drama of unfulfilled desire into a devotional mode. Subsuming the speaker into biblical personae reflects the layering of speakers associated with the Psalms, while the "parabolic puzzle" of each poem involves the reader in constructing a redeemed subjectivity. In the second century, Lok explores the aesthetics of praise, creating a pleasing lack of resolution and proposing a role for grace in poetic style. For Lok, the performed/disordered speech in a given poem, along with sequential disorder, enables a vital exchange wherein the reader displaces the speaker/author and the Holy Spirit activates disorder toward a devotionally edifying result.

*I*N THE BUSY 1590s, Henry Lok wrote almost 400 sonnets, a major corpus that has been largely overlooked in favor of his more famous contemporaries. Both Barbara Lewalski and Thomas Roche have sug-

Spenser Studies: A Renaissance Poetry Annual, Volume XXVII, Copyright © 2012 AMS Press, Inc. All rights reserved.   DOI: 10.7756/spst.027.011.249-287

gested that Lok's contribution to the early development of English devotional lyric offers numerous treasures, though in each case their broader, encyclopedic agendas prevented a further cataloguing of those treasures.[1] Lewalski observes briefly in *Protestant Poetics* that Lok "pioneered strategies which were to be refined and perfected in the seventeenth century." Roche, writing ten years later in *Petrarch and the English Sonnet Sequences*, spends a few pages on Lok's sonnets before turning to the two "elaborately numerological" dedicatory poems that preface Lok's second volume. Still, Roche notes that at a grand total of 388 sonnets, "Lok's is the second most extensive collection of sonnets in English, exceeded only by the cumulative collections of Wordsworth and Merrill Moore."[2]

Quantity is not necessarily quality, of course, and Lok's work in the sonnet form rightly bows before the achievements of Sidney, Daniel, Spenser, Shakespeare, Donne, and Milton. Nevertheless, Lok's sonnets deserve greater attention; they qualify him not only as a skilled, innovative practitioner of English devotional verse, but also as a theoretician of the genre. Lok meditated thoughtfully in verse and prose on problems inherent to the devotional lyric, problems that would later fruitfully (and more famously) preoccupy Donne and Herbert. I will consider in particular Lok's concern with certain manifestations of disorder—to adopt a term he uses—as both artistic and spiritual phenomena. Focusing on the way in which Lok figures disorder, both in the performance of a poem and in the structure of a sequence, brings into relief vital features Lok borrowed from his two main source traditions: the love lyric, especially the Petrarchan sonnet sequence, and the devotional tradition, especially the metrical psalm. The Petrarchan tradition lends Lok the drama of unfulfilled desire and sophisticated attention to the problem of the speaker's sincerity, while the metrical psalm tradition offers Lok a reading methodology, a complex layering of speakers, and a useful conversation about the role of artfulness in devotional verse. Lok appears to be drawing on both traditions in order to explore in a sustained way and at a key moment what it means to be a Calvinist devotional poet, and his ambitious project may have suggested workable and appealing solutions to the English devotional poets who follow him.

Henry Lok seems to have come by his interest in devotional poetry through his mother, Anne Lock,[3] the presumed author of the first sonnet sequence in English, printed in 1560. This sequence of 26 sonnets meditates on the verses of Psalm 51 and represents a "maternal inheritance" upon which Henry would later draw.[4] As Susan Felch has established, Anne was a capable scholar and an "active advocate for Protestantism" throughout her adult life. Born and married into the successful Protestant merchant class,[5] she hosted, corresponded with, and mediated for John Knox in the early years of her first marriage, even fleeing for a time to Geneva (1557–59) when Henry, born in 1553, was still a small child. Through two later marriages Anne remained prominent among Calvinist, nonconformist circles as a translator and personal influence. Her son Henry may have received some of his education at the home of William Cecil and his wife Mildred Cooke, and by the age of eighteen, young Henry had entered the service of Edward de Vere, earl of Oxford, who later became Cecil's son-in-law. Henry himself was well connected not only with the Cecils and Cookes, but also with Henry Carey, Lord Hunsdon.[6]

From about 1590 to 1595, Lok worked as an "agent, messenger and intelligencer" for Queen Elizabeth, primarily reporting to her on her lords' efforts to quell Catholic influence at James's court in Scotland.[7] The first of Lok's two volumes appeared during this period. The 1593 *Sundry Christian Passions*, printed by Richard Field, featured 204 devotional sonnets prefaced by a dedication to the queen. The sonnets are divided into two centuries, plus a prefatory and concluding sonnet for each set: part 1 is presented as sonnets of "meditation, humiliation, and prayer," while part 2 is presented as sonnets of "comfort, joy, and thanksgiving." James Doelman notes that by 1597 Lok was seeking patronage with some urgency, which may explain the publication of a second volume in that year, also printed by Richard Field, titled *Ecclesiastes, otherwise called The preacher*. This volume contains different dedicatory material to the queen, a verse paraphrase of the book of Ecclesiastes, several metrical psalms, and the previously published 204 sonnets lightly edited.[8] In this edition, Lok adds to the sonnet collection another century of sonnets—"sonets of a feeling conscience"— also with framing sonnets, plus twenty sonnets titled "Peculiar Prayers." These latter are numbered continuously with the previous hundred but accompanied by their own framing sonnets. Finally, Lok adds sixty dedicatory sonnets in 1597, covering a full range of possible patrons: members of the Privy Council, ladies of the chamber, and other influential figures.

While Anne Lock's poetic endeavors surely influenced her son, as is often true in this period, unemployment—or at least underemployment— was for Henry the figurative mother of the sonnet sequence.[9] His multigenerational connections to powerful families with reformist leanings may have created opportunities for him, but his professional life was mostly disappointing. The intelligence work he performed in Scotland was risky and volatile, and Lok seems not to have been particularly suited to it. Doelman describes an early 1596 letter from Lok to the queen, requesting a fifty-pound pension and implying that he desired a more secure and honorable post. On the back of the letter, Lord Hunsdon wrote a recommendation addressed to Robert Cecil. But in July of 1596, Hunsdon died, leaving Lok bereft of his most amenable senior patron. The barrage of dedicatory sonnets appended to the 1597 volume may have been a scattershot, perhaps indecorous effort to find support somewhere, anywhere, but it appears that Lok never did find satisfactory employment. He continued to work for Robert Cecil as an intelligencer on the Continent for few years, struggling with debt until his death in 1611. His books were never reprinted. Doelman writes, "In this disappointment with the patronage system, Lok was certainly not alone. . . . But in few [other cases] was the attempt so broad and the failure so marked as in the case of Henry Lok" (11).

Artistically, at least considering the matter in retrospect, Lok did accomplish some significant things. Like his mother, Lok experimented with combining the sonnet form and the psalmic mode.[10] Lok was born into the "psalm culture" of mid-century reformist circles and would have known the Geneva Bible psalms and the Coverdale translations in the Book of Common Prayer, the metrical versions in the *Whole Booke of Psalmes*, Latin and French metrical versions including the Geneva Psalter and perhaps Buchanan's Latin paraphrases, and probably other versions.[11] Moreover, Lok's close connections with the Cecils and his dedicatory sonnet to the Countess of Pembroke suggest that he may have had access to Philip and Mary Sidney's *Psalmes* in manuscript.[12] His sonnet to the countess is unlike others in the set in its attention to the poetic work of his dedicatee. Lok praises the late Philip as a "Lampe of heavenly light . . . Whose share in this my worke, hath greatest place"; he praises Mary as one who has earned "equall honour" with her brother by her own "pregnancie of spright" (sig. Yi^v).[13] In the sonnet category, by 1593 Lok would have had access to the printed first editions of Watson's *Hekatompathia*, Sidney's *Astrophil and Stella*, Constable's *Diana*, and Daniel's *Delia*, to mention only a few printed English sequences.[14] Like others of his class and generation, he may have read French and Italian sonnets as well.[15] Lok deserves credit at least, then, for catching the English sonnet craze on its ascent and for combining, in an extensive and thoughtful body of work, the emerging patterns of English Petrarchism with postures, emotive contours, and readerly habits associated with that ancient lyric sequence, the Psalms.

The combination of "secular" poetic modes and biblical modes was not new, of course, and the Petrarchan tradition was entangled from the beginning with Christian devotion, haunted by it both earnestly and ironically.[16] However, Lok entered the scene in the 1590s at an especially fruitful moment. English poetry in the Petrarchan tradition, with its many source streams in Ovidean and other classical modes, had been generating increasing interest and work among English poets for several decades, catalyzed by Tottel's Miscellany among other works in print and manuscript. Meanwhile, Protestant devotional writing in many forms, including metrical Psalm translation, had also been developing steadily for several decades.[17] The thoroughgoing Reformation effort to "denizen" the Psalms into English and the flowering of English sonnet sequences occurred side by side, and their boundaries were not absolute. The time was ripe to ask, How might these traditions be combined *now*? Answering the question required attending to numerous issues currently under discussion, perhaps most urgently the question of whether or not poetry had a legitimate place in the Christian life. "Light" verse was frequently cited as a threat to public devotion, while prefaces to metrical psalms and other devotional writings typically included careful defenses of the author's plain style, lest the elaborate "clothing" distract from the beauty and truth of the scriptural matter. More broadly, as both Elizabeth Clarke and Kimberly Anne Coles have argued, prominent voices, especially in Calvinist and then Puritan circles, perceived human rhetoric, invention, and art as raising thorny problems— for instance, whether it was possible to mitigate factors such as the corrupt nature of human imagination, the potential of art to incite lust or otherwise deceive, and the assertion of human technique over the "motions" of the Holy Spirit.[18] Sir Philip Sidney's *Defence of Poesy* provided a brilliant and authoritative, if playful, reply to some of these concerns, and the Countess of Pembroke presided over an influential circle in which devotional poetry was encouraged and exchanged—along with other kinds of writing. The Sidney *Psalmes*, the most magnificent product of the Sidneys' effort to reconcile art and devotion, exemplify and subtly justify the use of "utmost skill" in devotional verse.[19] Nevertheless, concerns about "secular" verse and about the use of verse for devotional purposes persist throughout and beyond the sixteenth century.

Even so, many English poets—including Wyatt, Surrey, Gascoigne, Sidney, Spenser, Drayton, and Barnes—wrote verse psalms (or biblical verse) as well as various kinds of lyrics based on classical and medieval models, including sets based on Petrarchan sonnets. These poets must have heard, but evidently chose not to heed complaints about the impiety of love lyric. After all, the sonnet craze of the 1590s occurred well after Coverdale, John Hall, and others had made their cases for replacing impious verse with biblical verse.[20] Poets might preface their work with ritual apologies, but they went right on printing their "light" verse and Petrarchan sequences anyway.[21] Gascoigne, for instance, as early as 1575 provides elaborate justification for his racier lyrics, claiming them as medicinal weeds and placing the moral burden on readers, exhorting them that "the industrious Bee may gather honie out of the most stinking weede."[22] Daniel in 1592 prefaces the first edition of his sonnets to Delia with a request to the Countess of Pembroke for protection, claiming that these sonnets are "the private passions of my youth" and explaining that he was "betraide by the indiscretion of a greedie Printer," just as Philip Sidney was, alas. Such prefatory statements ought to be read with the same sense of irony and wry humor as the poems themselves. Despite continued anxiety—sincere and posed—over the idolatry and impiety of Petrarchan lyrics and other secular verse, the English printing presses busily produced multiple volumes of love sonnet sequences right into the 1630s.[23]

English metrical psalms and Petrarchan sonnets existed, then, in tight proximity in the imaginations and often the work of Tudor and early Stuart poets, a fact whose implications modern scholarship has not much explored.[24] In fact, reading them as intertwined traditions of lyric sequences helps reveal the sometimes poignant, sometimes deliciously ironic resonances between them. In Philip Sidney's Psalm 7, for example, the psalmist's enemy du jour sounds vaguely familiar:

> Lo, he that first conceived a wretched thought,
>   And great with child of mischief travailed long,
> Now brought abed, hath brought naught forth but naught.
>   (lines 37–39)[25]

Sidney must have been aware that this eloquent judgment on the enemy's vanity suggests that Astrophil, "great with child to speak," might have brought forth 108 variations on nought (not to mention the songs). Meanwhile, Daniel throughout his *Delia* sequence makes the speaker's idolatry painfully, even laughably evident, as when he protests in Sonnet 11 that his "Teares, vowes and prayers" do not seem to be working to soften up his goddess, and how can this be, since "So rare a faith ought better be rewarded"? Daniel writes for readers who could be expected to recognize the particular pattern of the psalms, in which the psalmist cries out and the Lord faithfully hears his cry. Such an audience would comprehend the subtle joke—a speaker who has trouble imagining why this same pattern does not work so well with the ladies.

Henry Lok was also attentive to the resonances between devotional literature, especially Psalms, and the Petrarchan tradition as it was developing in English. The idea of a coherent, meaningfully structured lyric sequence clearly appealed to him, and Lok attempted to create such a sequence combining the strengths of the sonnet form with postures and reading practices associated with the Bible and devotional literature. He was not the only person to write a set of devotional sonnets in English, but his sequence was earlier than Barnabe Barnes's or Fulke Greville's sequences, and far more extensive and probably earlier than Henry Constable's short and distinctly Roman Catholic sequence.[26] His sonnets are neither psalm translations nor pastiches nor translations of biblical canticles, but poems drenched in the whole of Scripture and addressing a huge range of concerns in the Christian life. With a few rare exceptions, they eschew mythological or classical allusion and in that sense take a strong turn away from Petrarchism. Like the Sidney *Psalmes*, however, Lok 's sonnets combine scriptural modes with technical innovation. Each of his four main groupings of sonnets—the three centuries plus the "Peculiar Prayers"—experiments with a different sonnet rhyme scheme, with all four schemes distinct from what we now refer to as the English and Italian forms. The first century is almost entirely in the Spenserian sonnet form, although Spenser had only written a dozen or so sonnets in this form by early 1593—instead Lok may have been imitating James VI's little 1585 sonnet sequence.[27]

Lok's body of work appealingly combines devotional material with technical accomplishment, but he is also concerned with larger issues of theology and aesthetics. Certainly, particularly in the second century of sonnets, Lok engages in the usual polemic against deploying poetic skill in the pursuit of earthly love—a standard Petrarchan counterdiscourse and practically a required *topos* for any English poet in the 1590s. But beyond that, both the poems themselves and his prefatory comments indicate that Lok was thinking carefully about what we might call theoretical concerns from a Calvinist point of view. How does a person obtain "grace to begin" the process of penitence, and how might a poet represent that dilemma in a poem or sequence? What is the status of the poem's art in the devotional act? Does the sonnet have particular usefulness in devotion? How does a poet follow the Protestant exhortation to read Scripture as written "for us," mapping an individual's experience onto the narratives of the Bible? How might poems depict the paradox of imputed justification and not-yet-fulfilled sanctification, the already/not yet problem? (This last has intriguing resonance with the unfulfilled desire of Petrarchan sonnets.) The result of Lok's grappling with such problems is an extensive and coherent blend of Calvinist-inflected devotion and artful lyric sequence, appearing at a moment just before Donne and later Herbert and others would be concerned with the same challenges.

The sincerity of the devotional speaker is one of the salient concerns in Lok's first century of sonnets, those focused primarily on repentance. In a fashion similar to typical love sonneteers, Lok both represents and problematizes sincerity through the creation of what we might term distressed or disordered speech.[28] Sidney's *Astrophil and Stella* lays out the analogous issues in the Petrarchan tradition beginning with the first sonnets. For the lover-speaker, sorting out truth from feigning or blending feeling and skill are never simple matters, all the worse in the throes of desire. A speaker experiencing inner contradictions and protesting the difficulty of speech are hardly themes unique to Petrarchan sequences, but these issues do constitute a persistent area of vexing concern in the tradition.[29] In many love sonnet sequences, the beloved's disregard or refusal (for whatever reason) leads to interesting fragmentations and refractions of the speaking self and to forms of speech which, however skillfully they fit the meter, claim to be diminished, fragmentary, inadequate—in one or several ways, the performed speech is something less than the controlled expression of a centered self. An unstable, dis-integrated subjectivity in turn vexes the question of genuineness. How can a lover-speaker love in truth, how can he look in his heart and write, when the possibility of any kind of unified, genuine self is already destabilized? "I am not I, pity the tale of me," proposes Astrophil. Meanwhile, readers are expected to perceive that this self-in-dissolution is all the while achieving a glittering, intricately ordered performance in the sonnet form. Astrophil, the speaker of *Delia,* and other lover-speakers worry this enigma by riffing on the theme of performance and in some cases training anger on the beloved.[30] In late-Elizabethan sonnet sequences, speakers *perform* even as fragmented selves, claiming their distressed speech as evidence of their sincerity while foregrounding the irony of simultaneous performance. Moreover, their disordered/ordered/sincere/contrived speech is typically presented as amusingly, poignantly ineffective in gaining the desired outcome: the beloved's favor—commonly rendered with the wonderfully ironic term "grace," with all its theological resonance.[31]

Lok seems to have this sincerity problem in mind, even as he transposes it in the context of divine sonnets by taking his cues from the Psalms. For the psalmist, the fragmentation of the subject is a consequence of sin. The paradox of the diminished or disintegrating speaker—who is nevertheless still speaking—is a commonplace especially of the penitential psalms: "But I am a worme, & not a man," "My strength is dryed up like a potsheard, and my tongue cleveth to my jawes," says the psalmist in Psalm 22 (Geneva Bible, vss. 6, 15). Or in Psalm 102: "Mine heart is smitten and withereth like grasse, because I forgate to eat my bread. . . . I am like a pelicane of the wildernes: I am like an owle of the deserts" (vss. 4, 6).[32] Similarly, Anne Lock's sonnets on Psalm 51 depict a blind and groveling speaker who sighs, wails, and groans, who with "fainting breath" and "shrieking crye" "brayest forth [a] bootlesse noyse."[33] Sir Philip Sidney's metrical version of Psalm 38 draws the paradox of the disintegrating/performing speaker into sharp outline. The speaker laments to God that "thy shafts have pierc't me sore" (line 4), and almost seems to lose consciousness altogether:

> But I like a man become,
>   Deaf and dumb,
>   Little hearing, speaking less;
> I ev'n as such kind of wight,
>   Senseless quite,
> Word with word do not repress.
>   (lines 37–42)

Nevertheless, the speaker "roars" in this psalm and declares that God will "hear my voice." Lok takes up this same strategy immediately in his sequence; the speaker in sonnet 1.4 is "Wounded so deepe with deadly poysned dart/ Of serpents sting."[34] Here Lok broadens the literal/symbolic physical suffering of the psalmist, apparently wounded by God, into a metaphor for sin in general: the serpent's originary, Genesis sting, "which did from parents grow," is the source of the problem. Lok's speaker, too, professes a "feeble minde" and eyes pressed down "on earth so low,/ As dares not search the heavens, true helpe to finde." In no condition to speak, the poet still manages an utterance.

Can one speak truly and genuinely from such a state, however? Or, alternatively, is the diminished speech itself a mark of genuine contrition? Is the self in dissolution the only honest self? Mary Sidney's Psalm 77 poses this problem as well:

> So lay I all oppressed,
> My heart in office lame,
> My tongue as lamely fares,
> No part his part supplies.
>   (lines 21–24)

Both Sidneys perceive and highlight the Psalms' ample demonstrations that, because of sin, whatever utterance arises from "inward touch" is bound to be unreliable, inelegant, inarticulate, fragmented—in short, disordered; the heart is lame and thus so is the tongue. Meanwhile, the divine Beloved sees right through the speaker; there is no point in contriving a glittering performance. God will not "pity the tale" of the speaker, because God—as Lok's prefatory sonnet bluntly points out—"doest hearts intent bewray,/ For from thy sight Lord nothing is conceald." One must strive for sincerity before the all-knowing God, but what can sincerity even mean, coming from a creature so fraught with confusion, rebellion, suffering, and self-deception?

Lisa Freinkel, in accounting for an Augustinian approach to sacred text, describes how the book of Psalms models a "deflected structure of address" which "centers on the exemplary status of the 'I.'"[35] "David" functions in the Psalm both as speaker, seemingly issuing an utterance in the moment, and as author, reflecting on that speaking moment, structuring it in retrospect. Similarly, readers are split into two roles, both "interlocutor" with the speaker-in-the-moment and "witness" to the performance of that moment (65).[36] A Psalm from sacred scripture, then, in the Augustinian economy of reading, "transpires as a performance conducted for another's benefit. . . . A purely inward colloquy is hence enacted for an outward show" (65). Freinkel emphasizes the consequent disappearance of the author in this rendering of the reading act: the reader recognizes the originary "I" only as a placeholder; when the reader enters that "I" for herself, the author is—momentarily, at least—displaced: "Hence, on a variety of fronts, the psalm's relation to its audience is no simple matter: simultaneously literal and figural, within and without the psalm, present and absent, affirmed and denied, the third-person witness disrupts discourse's symmetry and linearity on both sides, disturbing both the 'I' and the 'you'" (66). A further complication here is that, especially for certain psalms such as Psalm 22,

"David" as speaker stood not only for a historic figure but for a prophetic voice, prefiguring Christ—thereby placing the voice of Christ as an additional layer in the multi-layered "I." Moreover, all the Psalms were considered to be composed ultimately by the Holy Spirit.[37] Freinkel's account of Augustinian reading, as well as her later contrast with Petrarch's adaptation of Augustine's ideas, decants these complications to offer useful terms for Lok's strategies in his devotional sonnets. The simultaneous speaker/author phenomenon provides a way through the sincerity dilemma. The disordered speech is at once a genuine utterance of a fallen, suffering speaker *and* a crafted performance of the author—or even Author. The love sonnet's potential ironic collapse into disingenuous performance need not apply here. At the same time, the ready displacement of the author prepares the way for one of Lok's most distinctive strategies, particularly characteristic of the first hundred sonnets.

In his first century of "meditation, humiliation, and prayer," Lok negotiates the dilemma of the fallen, dis-integrating speaker by emphatically disappearing the author—in other words, by further subsuming the speaker in other voices. In the course of the first hundred sonnets, Lok dissolves the speaking self in a kaleidoscopic series of biblical personae. In a quest for sincere speech, this would seem to make matters worse, but the idea, I think, is to remake the self through identification with the whole of salvation history, detail by detail.[38] This process is enabled by a typological approach to Scripture adapted from the medieval four-fold theory of scriptural interpretation and still alive to the Reformers, including Calvin. Scripture is a seamless garment, a consistent and unified account of God's encounter with human history. Moreover, biblical characters and events are not only themselves but can also be read as types, ultimately fulfilled in Christ, but proximately fulfilled in the church and even in the individual believer.[39] This is, of course, the broad theological basis of the Augustinian reading Freinkel examines, and English devotional literature commonly uses the strategy of comparing the author's situation to a biblical story or character, thus modeling this process for the reader.[40] However, Lok uses the particular strengths of the sonnet form to develop this strategy into much more than a quick simile or passing comparison. His speakers enter into scriptural stories and act out spiritual dramas in the personae of biblical characters: Noah, Samson, Jacob, the wandering Israelites, the one-talent man of the parable, a hungry sheep, a wedding guest in need of a garment. Sonnet 1.2 merges the speaker with the figure of Jonah—"Fro out the darknesse of this sea of feare,/ Where I in whale remaine devourd of sin"—so that the speaker can "confesse my fault, who did begin/ To flie from thee, ô Lord, and leave undone/ Thy service." In sonnet 1.7, the speaker becomes the lame man from John 5:2: "Lame of my limmes, and sencelesse of my state,/ Neere fortie yeares Lord have I groveling line." Here the speaker asks not for forgiveness, but—as the fellow in the biblical story implies but does not state—for aid: "Vouchsafe thou then me to this bath to beare,/ By the assistance of thy heavenly grace." Interestingly, perhaps because of his associations with powerful female readers—including his mother, the Cooke women, Lady Carey, and the twenty-one female addressees of his dedicatory sonnets—Lok is not at all shy about adopting female personae, examples of which will be examined below.

This method of subsuming the self in biblical personae is not only a fitting response to patterns of traditional biblical hermeneutics, but also an inventive way of coping with the paradox of the disintegrated speaker speaking. No doubt, these poems present speakers-in-performance much as in Petrarchan sonnets, but these performances are designed not to impress a beloved (or an overhearing reader) but to school the self (and the overhearing reader) through text and tradition. "Oft turning others' leaves"—the leaves of the Bible—is precisely the method Lok proposes on the way toward genuine utterance.[41] However, to constitute the steps in this process, Lok follows the model of the Petrarchan tradition more than the model of the Psalms. The moment of "unfulfilled desire" and resulting distressed speech in the Psalms, typically, is resolved within a single poem. Or, more precisely, a distressed lyric self is typically embedded in a memory. The Geneva Bible's Psalm 30, for example, declares in verse 2, "O Lord my God, I cryed unto thee, and thou hast restored me." The psalmist then recalls a time when "thou didest hide thy face and I was troubled." The moment of trouble and disorder is safely rendered in the past; the moment of utterance occurs in a secure and reassuring present. Alternatively, the moment of trouble is followed by powerful recollections of God's saving mercies on some other occasion, with explicit or implicit expectations that God will do the same for the present trouble. As poems, then, these prayers contain—or are embedded in—their own answers. This pattern serves a teaching function for the reader by demonstrating, in compact space, that faithfulness is rewarded through the grace of God. Lok apparently recognized, however, that embedding the moment of disorder in this way does tend to dilute its dramatic power. Thus, in his devotional sonnets he follows more closely the Petrarchan model by distilling, in poem after poem, the moment of unfulfilled desire, not-yet-answered prayer.

Freinkel's account of the Petrarchan lyric posits that Petrarch's departure from Augustine is precisely in his habit of figuring the erotics of desire and loss, in keeping the moment of the poem "unconverted" (102). That suspension of resolution drives many love sonnet sequences, often to the bitter end. Resolutions, if they come, depend on transcending the original object of desire for a higher, divine object; forcing an unsavory consummation, as in Barnes's sequence; settling for the consolations of fame and the laurel; or deflecting resolution through a switch in voice and genre.[42] In any case, the speaker does not get what he or she originally desired in the sonnets themselves—even Spenser needs the *Epithalamion* to provide resolution for the *Amoretti*. By contrast, Lok's dwelling in the moment of desire seems to be precisely the means through which a distressed speaker can begin to offer reordered and effective speech—effective in the sense of preparing for the delivery of the grace requested. In the course of the first hundred sonnets, Lok's speakers move from that opening position of sin-induced unconsciousness, through a dizzying tour of the biblical figures and stories that compose salvation history, finally arriving at the concluding sonnet:

> Mourne thou no more my soule, thy plaint is heard,
>   The bill is canseld of the debt it owes,
>   The vaile is rent, which thee before debard,
> And Christ his righteousnesse on thee bestowes.
> (lines 1–4)

As an understanding of typology and the theology of imputation would predict, the speaker is eventually reconstituted only through Christ, or more precisely, the imputation of Christ's righteousness. In terms of how this century is structured, then, the process of repentance does not proceed through a linear series of steps endeavored through human effort; rather, repentance remains perpetually cyclical until, by grace, Christ intervenes. It is Christ, this sonnet continues, who "turnes our plaints into more pleasant song," restoring the possiblity of ordered speech (line 12). Near the end of the second century of sonnets, the speaker will explicitly "wish to be *dissolv'd* with Christ to dwell" (2.98.6) (emphasis added). The idea that the voice of Christ himself shimmers behind the layered voices of David and every subsequent speaker of the Psalms here finds its ultimate expression. Decades before Herbert was invoking altars of unhewn stone or associating his speaker with the thief on the cross, Lok was working typologically through the Scriptures, taking the long road to the destination that "all things"—especially matters of the earnest human will and utterance—"were more ours by being his."

Lok manages to have his drama and a theologically fitting resolution, too. However, there's more to Lok's strategy even than this. Lok's best poems settle into a methodology that might be described as "the parabolic puzzle." Reading through Lok's first century of sonnets is like solving a series of riddles.[43] As we face each new poem in the sequence, we wonder, "Who is the speaker this time?" The complex layering and shifting of speakers, taken for granted when reading Psalms, becomes the basis for an intriguing game in Lok's sequence. Lok does not always make the references immediately obvious, nor do his speakers always slip straightforwardly into the role of a particular biblical figure. Each poem must be "solved" and then reread against the full force of the biblical allusions—and Lok's transformations of them. Moreover, Lok's poems do not always align precisely with the biblical story or stories to which they allude, and those misalignments are also meaningful. For the reader, the simultaneous pleasure, frustration, and enlightenment of this deciphering process may be exactly what Lok intended.

Sonnet 1.19 will demonstrate the technique:

A Wicked soule sold to all fleshly sin,
  Lord here I prostrate at thy feete do lie,
  To gather crummes of grace, soules health to win,
  Which Lord to give me do thou not denie:
The precious oyle of penitence will I
  Powre forth with teares, fro out my melting eyes
  To bath thy feete, and after will I drie
  Them with my haires (which balms no treasure bies)
Though worldly love (when he my fact espies)
  Repine to see my soule so well inclind:
  To my defence o Lord vouchsafe to rise,
  And fructifie this first frute of my minde;
    Vouchsafe to sup with humble servant thine,
    And that of service, better choyse be mine.

In this sonnet, the first distinct clue to the speaker's identity appears in line 3 with the word "crummes." This immediately suggests the Canaanite woman of Matthew 15. In the biblical account, she convinces an initially reluctant Jesus to heal her daughter of demon-possession. Jesus accedes to her request apparently because she accepts his metaphorical association of her and her people with dogs, then turns that metaphor to her advantage by claiming that even dogs eat the crumbs that fall from the master's table. In the poem, the speaker's soul might be both the woman, prostrate and begging, but also the daughter, desperate for "soules health." In the second quatrain, though, the reference shifts. "Precious oyle" and "teares" signal that the speaker has transformed into Mary of Bethany, bathing Jesus' feet and drying them with her hair in John 12; or perhaps she is the unnamed woman (or women) in parallel stories in Luke 7, Matthew 26, and Mark 14.[44] Judas, who accuses Mary of Bethany in the John account, or the Pharisee who plays the same role in the Luke account, or the disciples in the Matthew account, merge in the poem and become the allegorized "worldly love." The couplet moves to yet another story, that of Mary of Bethany and her sister Martha hosting Jesus in Luke 10:38–42. The speaker, who now seems to be both Mary and Martha at once, prays that the Lord will "Vouchsafe to sup with humble servant thine" and assist the speaker in making the "better choyse" of service.

Once the references have been identified, one can reread the poem and notice how Lok has adapted the biblical stories. This shifting of personae in the poem captures each of these characters at precisely the most concentrated moment of possibility: the Canaanite woman before the healing, the foot-bathing woman before Jesus' defense of her, and Mary/Martha before Jesus' pronouncement on who has chosen the better part. Lok's speaker enters each story at the point of need, the prayer before the answer to the prayer. Moreover, the proposed outcome in the poem is not necessarily the same as the outcome in the biblical story. In the couplet, for instance, the speaker wishes to choose "service" as the better part, while in the Luke story Jesus commends Mary, the one who sat contemplatively at his feet, over Martha, who busied herself serving and worrying. A subtle Protestant revision in order to reject the contemplative life? Perhaps. But the methodological payoff here is that in the performance of the poem, the outcome of each biblical model-story is still open-ended. The speaker can propose a different ending to the story, and that possibility is neither sustained nor denied by the poem. It remains open, still a prayer.

Another fine example of Lok's purposeful calibrations occurs in Sonnet 1.87:

THe talent which thou pleasedst Lord to give,
  To me thy servant that I should bestow,

Whilst in thy service on the earth I live,
My diligent increase thereof to show,
I have abused Lord (too long) I know,
    And feare thy comming to be nigh at hand,
    I see for breach of dutie what I owe,
    And of thy judgments do in terror stand:
Thy grace hath left me in a forreine land,
    Where unexpert of virtue I do straie,
    I shall be throwne to Satans thralfull band,
    Voyd of thy heavenly joy and blisse for aye,
        Unlesse thou helpe, for thou doest use to give,
        Grace unto grace, and faith from faithlesse drive.

Here we have the familiar parable of the talents, and the speaker is the servant with the one talent—the one talent, as Milton will later put it in his own sonnet, "which is death to hide." The speaker knows very well what will happen when the master returns: he will be "throwne to Satans thralfull band." But the poem captures that moment before the return, before the outcome of judgment for the poor one-talent fellow is sure. In the couplet, there's still the possibility, still the "Unlesse." This master, unlike the one in the parable, is not always and necessarily a "hard man." He could go either way; he "doest use to give,/ Grace unto grace, and faith from faithlesse drive." With such a master, a different outcome is possible. If he will take the servant/speaker's implied request for help as a moment of faith, a gesture of grace—then the speaker has half a chance of receiving mercy.

Sonnet 1.78—which I believe is a previously unnoted prototype for Herbert's "Redemption"—further demonstrates Lok's keen eye for that moment of greatest dramatic tension.[45]

A Wicked theefe that oft have robd and slaine,
    Thy graces of their frute, my selfe of blisse,
    Now on the crosse of conscience I remaine,
    To die the death the which eternall is:
I see no way to quit my selfe of this,
    Unlesse thou Lord whose kingdome is above,
    Remember me, and cansell life amisse
    Out of thy memorie, through Christ thy love:
Who in my flesh with me like death did prove,
    That guiltlesse he, might guilties ransome bee,

Love to my soule it was, that did him move,
The bands of death to bide to make us free:
　　Blesse thou my tong, increase thou faith in mee,
　　This night to be in paradise with thee.

In this sonnet, the thief on the cross next to Jesus becomes that part of the speaker's self that robs another part of "blisse" and now hangs on the "crosse of conscience." Here the speaker is in a hopeless bind, divided against himself, "Unlesse"—and this is the key word in Lok's first century— the Lord remembers him. But the poem remains at that point of possibility. The speaker does not, in the poem, call out for mercy as the thief on the cross manages to do in Luke 23. Nor does the poem resolve with "Your suit is granted," as Herbert's version does. Instead, the speaker waits for that blessing of the "tong," that increased faith from Christ which will enable him to call out.

Both the puzzle-like construction and the open-ended nature of these poems strike me as significant for what Lok is trying to do with devotional verse. When reading Scripture, especially the Psalms, readers were accustomed to knowing who had occupied the "I" before them—they could imagine David as the speaker, most commonly. The marginalia and headnotes to the Psalms in the Geneva Bible, for example, frequently suggest a narrative framework from David's life. Sometimes they suggest a more porous narrative framework, referring to David or another named psalmist as "the Prophet," mapping the psalm to events in Israel's history or describing an occasion in more general terms that could easily be applied to sixteenth-century England. Lok plays with this process of speaker-displacement, familiar to Psalm readers, by keeping the identity of the original "I" in his poems a matter of clues and hints. In terms of Roland Greene's distinction between the "ritual" and "fictional" elements of the lyric, Lok keeps the reader dancing in the middle: the poems at once activate "fictional" speakers from biblical narratives and invite the reader to enter, in "ritual" fashion, into a re-performance of the poem.[46] For Lok, this has two purposes that I can surmise. First, it creates an experience for the reader analogous to the puzzles of the spiritual life. We first read the poem not knowing who occupied the "I" before the poet or before ourselves as readers. Once we figure out the clues in each poem, we can read it again, understanding the implications more fully. In similar fashion, as Lok's preface to the reader suggests, humans do not always understand the actions of God upon them while in the midst of those actions. Only when we apprehend some clue, some key to the mystery, Lok implies, can we go back and read the meaning of our own lives, seeing God's action in it. Thus the importance in the spiritual life of arousing the memory, which is exactly what Lok seeks to do, for himself and the reader, through these poems:

> I having (through gods great goodnes) felt in the direction and protection of my unstable youth, a plentifull portion of the wonderfull care he hath over us, and of the unspeakable force of praier and thanksgiving in all extremities: the more to stirre up my selfe to a memorie thereof, have thought good to set downe these abrupt passions of my passed afflictions, as witnesses of the impediments most stopping me in my Christian pilgrimage, and testimonies of the meanes of my evasion hitherto, which may serve for presidents for my selfe in the like future occasions: and not be altogither unprofitable for others to imitate.[47]

The purposes of God become discernible in retrospect, just as the full force of the poem emerges only after a full reading and further contemplation backward into the poem.

The open-ended nature of these first hundred poems also goes beyond straightforward typological readings. Its second purpose is to draw the reader into involvement in the poem and thereby emphasize the engagement of the individual in the spiritual life. The reader must actively participate in the exemplarity of the biblical type(s), through the poem's mediation. We capture the fellow with the one talent in a significant, highly fraught moment, and from there we may be like but also unlike him. We can go to school on him, under the tutelage of the poet, who has re-performed his story in order that the outcome of the story might be different for the reader than for the character in the parable.

All of this creates an experience for the reader of the devotional sonnet that contrasts with that of the love sonnet reader. Lok cleverly recaptured and sustained, in a devotional context, the most dramatic feature of the love sonnet sequence: the moment of unfulfilled desire. However, in many cases—certainly with Sidney and Daniel, Lok's immediate English predecessors—love sonnet readers were expected to experience a tension between sympathy for the speaker and their perception of the lover's foolishness. This is exactly what Petrarch requests, in fact, in his first sonnet: "I hope to find pity, not only pardon" for my "error."[48] If a reader were to follow the example of these love sonnet speakers, he would be "oft turning others' leaves" to no avail. Alternatively, he could learn from love sonnet speakers what *not* to do, and perhaps imagine a shortcut around frustration, distraction, pain, futility. Lok, on the other hand, recognized that readers of devotional verse might well take a different stance toward the poems: his readers are invited to fall into the poems, eliding rather than sustaining the distance between themselves and the speaker. Even when recognizing the speaker's shortcomings or errors, the reader is not to relish his or her readerly superiority. Rather, the potential ironic distance evokes humility and prompts another loop of self-examination—as would reading Psalms—in light of ultimate spiritual stakes. In this way, the experience of reading the poems has a dynamic exemplarity for the reader; the parabolic puzzles in these sonnets indicate that Lok has given some thought to that key word: "profitable." Late Elizabethan title pages frequently claimed that the contents of the volume to follow would be *profitable* for readers, or at least *not unprofitable*. Lok evidently took this term seriously and considered its particular operations in his own work. Exactly how might reading a devotional sonnet be profitable for a reader?

Lok's poems show evidence that he has considered this question, but the preface, "To the Christian Reader," is even more direct. As suggested in the excerpt above, Lok figures the spiritual life most dominantly using the standard trope of the pilgrimage. This pilgrimage is full of "afflictions of the minde, frailties of the flesh, bayts of the world, and snares of Satan," and those are merely the spiritual perils. God has, however, in his grace provided "a direction and ready way of safetie," which is prayer. Thus Lok figures the poems as exemplary prayers, placing them in the mainstream of devotional works being printed at this time. However, Lok also wishes to give meaning to the structure of the sequence—or, as he puts it, "the confused placing of them [the poems] without speciall titles"—and the choice of the sonnet form. Poetry has the ability to "pearce and penetrate affections of men, with the aptnesse thereof, for helpe of memorie," but the sonnet form in particular, Lok proposes, is especially mimetic of experience and suited to readerly habits: ". . . for my deducing these passions and affections into Sonnets, it answereth best for the shortnesse, to the nature, and common humor of men, who are either not long touched with so good motions, or by their worldly affaires not permitted to continue much reading." People have short attention spans (or short good-intention spans) and they lead busy lives—perhaps one of the more curious defenses of the sonnet in all of literature. The next sentence considers why a sonnet sequence is a fitting way to depict the spiritual life:

To the cause of my so preposterous placing of [the poems], and divi-
sion onely into three [1593: two] sorts, I confesse indeed I am per-
swaded their disorder doth best fit the nature of mankind, who com-
monly is delighted with contraries, and exercised with extreames;
and also as they were by God ministred unto my mind to set downe
by sundrie Accidents: so I suppose my providence could not (by a
formall placing of them) so soone hit the affection of every reader,
as Gods direction (by that which men call chance) might often do.
As they are therefore, I recommend them to thy courtesie in reading,
and thee to Gods holy spirit in the perusing of them. If they have the
same working in thee, that I praise God some of them had in me, they
shall be not utterly unprofitable. (sigs. lviii^{r-v})

The apparent disorder of the sequence is thus defended as appealing to
intellectual tastes, reflective of the compositional process (divinely assist-
ed), and helpful in promoting "profitable" reading practices. The random
shuffle, as it were, makes the sonnets more amenable to "Gods direction," a
necessary element, according to Lok, in the economy of reading them. This
disorder becomes holy through the particular workings of the Holy Spirit
in the individual reader's experience of the poems.[49]

   Thus Lok essentially argues in the preface for the spiritual benefits of
two registers of what might be called disorder. On the level of the indi-
vidual sonnet, Lok champions the lyric's salient aesthetic feature, which
Teodolinda Barolini has described as the "paradox of mobile fixity."[50] Each
poem in a sequence represents a moment of tension, dramatized through
various intensities of disordered speech; this moment is stilled (rather than
resolved) for the observation of the reader, its formal resolution a beauti-
ful illusion. On the macro-level, Lok posits that a nonsequential assembly
of poems accords more readily to the vicissitudes and particularities of
each reader's spiritual pilgrimage, more flexible in its exemplarity insofar
as it arises out of and represents life's dynamic disorder. If lyric functions
in a dialectic between ritual and fictional, Lok is here leaning away from
the pressure toward resolution and narrative arc that the fictional element
implies. Although Lok might gesture toward the conventional narrative
of "pilgrimage" and draw frequently on the narratives of Scripture, he is
essentially acknowledging the mimetic weight of disorder for devotional
lyric. The narrative arc of the spiritual life is necessarily loose and elusive. A
sequence of moments, their resolution and ordering left undefined, is "best
fit," not only as representation but as edification.

Lok is applying to the devotional sonnet sequence ideas readily derived from Psalm commentary well known in the period, drawing on discussions of disorder, mimesis, and exemplarity with regard to the Psalms. While the Psalms were constantly praised for their beauties and adornments, another, quieter thread of commentary acknowledges that the Psalms can be "doubtfull and obscure," as Francis Seager observed.[51] This was not merely a translation issue. Arthur Golding, in his preface to the 1571 translation of Calvin's commentary on the Psalms, acknowledges a number of potentially confusing features of the Psalms—types and figures, changes in tense, and "borowed personages" for example. He further admits that the Psalms do not always represent elegant, sensible, ordered speech. Yet this is a result of their nature as prayers, he argues, because naturally, in such earnest communication with God

there be many unperfect sentences, many broken speeches, and many displaced words: according as the voice of the partie that prayed, was eyther prevented with the swiftnesse of his thoughtes, or interrupted with vehemency of joy or greef, or forced to surcease through infirmitie, that hee might recover newe strength and cheerfulnesse, by interminding Gods former promises and benefites.[52]

Thus the messiness of Psalms is the very mark of their genuineness as representations of spiritual struggle. Here the disordered speech within a particular psalm is attributable to suffering and powerful passions rather than to a fallen nature per se, and Golding makes no reference to performativity—in this account, in other words, Golding is focused on the speaker in the author/speaker dialectic. Moreover, the compendious nature of the entire lyric group—with abrupt changes of mood and kind from psalm to psalm, and no particular narrative throughline—was also to be understood as fitting and salutary.[53] In his epistle to the reader, Calvin acknowledges the Psalms as compendious assortment, famously remarking that they are an "anatomie of the soul." He then proceeds to outline the appropriate method for reading this anatomy: "But in this booke, the Prophets themselves talking with God, bycause they discover all the inner thoughts, do call or drawe every one of us to the peculiar examination of himself, so as no whit of all the infirmities to which wee are subject, and of so many vyces wherwith we are fraughted, may abyde hidden" (sig. *vi^v). Calvin moves swiftly from mimesis—the apparent randomness of the sequence as mimetic of spiritual life—to exemplarity.

The disorderly qualities of the Psalms serve to reveal the disorder within the reader. Because the speakers of the Psalms expose through unperfect sentences and misplaced words their own inner secrets—guilty truths and innocent sufferings alike—readers "discover" all *their* inner secrets as well, and are called to examine themselves in response to their reading. The psalmic speaker's sincerity may be messy and puzzling and compromised by sin, but meanwhile, with appropriate readerly attention, the reader's sincere self-examination is effectively enabled.

The comments of the fourth-century church father Athanasius on the connection between the Psalms' rough emotional terrain and their exemplarity were also well known. Archbishop Matthew Parker included the little treatise "Athanasius in Psalmos" in his 1567 metrical psalter, for example, in which Athanasius remarks that in the emotional churnings of the Psalms, we see

the motions, the mutations, the alterations of every mans hart and conscience described and lively paynted to his owne sight, so that if a man list, he might easely gather out thereof certaine considerations of himselfe as out of a bright glasse and playne paterne set before his face, so therby to refourme himselfe as he red therin. (sig. Biv^v)

The exhortation to the reader is to recognize the reflections of his own unstable spiritual states in the Psalms, then advance to the next step: reform. The reader can learn from the Psalms "how he may heale these his affections and passions, by worde and by deede" (sig. Ci^r).[54] The means to reform is also contained in the texts themselves; the Psalms are, to recall that common medicinal trope, both diagnosis and remedy. However, precisely because the Psalms are compendious in their representation of spiritual states, finding the particular diagnosis and remedy for a particular reader's particular malady in a given moment of reading—this requires some assistance, both human and divine. To help provide the former, Athanasius produced a table of recommendations for using the Psalms. The table lists a variety of occasions along with a few Psalms that are appropriate to each. For example, "If thou feelest the threatninges of God, and thereby perceyvest thy selfe to be dismaied," Athanasius's schematic recommends Psalms 6 and 37.[55] This table was printed with the 1562 *Whole Booke of Psalmes* and in several subsequent editions, making it a familiar resource for Elizabethans.[56] Athanasius intended his table to help a reader determine "with what forme of woordes he may amend himself."[57] The translators of the 1559 Geneva Psalms were cautious about daily reading schedules for the Psalms, such as were common in popular primers designed for private use, on the grounds that tedious, inattentive repetition does no one any good.[58] Instead, they advocated knowing the Psalms well enough to choose one that suited the occasion, reading it with full attention. They exhort the reader

> not unadvisedly to read whatsoever Psalme cometh first to hand, or that which is appointed for this day or that day, but diligently to marke, what maketh to the pourpose & present necessitie. For except we understand that, which we speake, we can not pray in faith, and that which we fele not in our selves, and to the which our heartes consent not, is done without understanding, and so is not available.[59]

Tables such as Athanasius's were designed to develop the kind of occasional savvy with the Psalms and the attentive reading that the Geneva translators recommend. For Lok and his contemporaries, using such a table was meant not to repair the sequential disorder of the Psalms but to activate it in the devotion of each reader.

Thus Lok's particular combination of the sonnet and psalm traditions, along with his comments upon it, can be seen as constituting a theory of devotional verse in terms of form, structure, construction of the speaker, and reading methods. From the sonnet tradition, Lok borrows the practice of distilling the moment of unfulfilled desire and problematizing the question of sincerity in the speaker's complaint from that position. From the psalm tradition, Lok borrows a reading methodology in which a poem is expected to provide a locus of exchange wherein the reader displaces the speaker/author, creating a shifting layering of selves that activates exemplarity. The performed/disordered speech in a given poem, as well as the sequential disorder, are what enable this vital exchange, holding up a mirror to the reader's experience and simultaneously instructing the reader's devotional response to that reflection. The way in which Herbert will later offer an "account of spiritual conflicts" and invite the reader to "thrust himself into the lines," therefore, was presented and to some extent explained, with skill and attention, by Henry Lok, three decades before.

Lok's first century of sonnets, I have suggested, repeatedly captures that moment of desperation, poised between the need and the answer to that need. The inherent tension of that moment, as Petrachan poets knew, makes for interesting poetry. What might the poem of answered prayer look like? Is it possible to create a devotional poem of "healed disorder" and still create a good poem? What are the aesthetics, in other words, of answered desire? Lok's second hundred sonnets of "comfort, joy, and thanksgiving" shift the focus to this surprisingly difficult question. Some poems in the second century find the speaker once again placing himself into biblical stories, but we also see a new attention to the "others" around the speaker, particularly the unrighteous or indifferent. Lok's second century coalesces thematically around the many poems exploring the moment in which the speaker, whose troubled speech has been graciously heard by the Divine Beloved, now seeks to return fitting praise for that rescue. In the biblical Psalms, these two key moments in the psalmic economy—desperate plea and praise—are usually combined in a single poem, but Lok divides them in his volume into two broad, separate fields of meditation. If the first century finds an apt prototype in Sidney's Psalm 38, the second century might be exemplified by Sidney's Psalm 43:

> Then, lo, then I will
> With sweet music's skill
>   Grateful meaning show thee:
> Then, God, yea, my God,
> I will sing abroad
> What great thanks I owe thee.
>   (lines 25–30)

As in Sidney's version of this psalm, Lok's solution to the problem of resolution aesthetics is to create a new moment of pleasingly unfulfilled expectation. The speaker, having been rescued from a state of disintegration, speaks the *intention* to praise. Praise is both posited as a future act and performed in the words of the poem. This simultaneous performance and promise reflects the fact that the pattern of plea, rescue, and praise in the Psalms is both pleasingly linear—a problem and resolution—but paradoxically cyclical. From the point of view of Christian devotion, one is never rescued once and for all, not in this life. One is at once saved, but still a sinner, *simul justus et peccator*, safe but always in peril, already there but not yet there. So in order for Lok's second theme also to be exemplary (and interesting) for the reader, he must acknowledge that the moment of comfort and praise is tricky both to achieve and sustain. Thus, the resolution to praise opens out into another version of the unresolved, and we enjoy again the "paradox of mobile fixity" as Lok captures for our examination an alternative version of unfulfilled desire.[60]

In this century of sonnets, Lok addresses the sonnet tradition more directly, this time as a foil for the devotional poem of praise. In this way, Lok participates in a prominent "counterdiscourse," as Heather Dubrow terms it, within the Petrarchan tradition.[61] Sonnet 2.31 opens a subsequence in which the speaker criticizes those who waste their time praising earthly beloveds:

> WHo so beholds with constant fixed eye,
> The favour and perfection of my choyce,
> He cannot chuse but must in heart rejoyce,
> That mortall sight may heavenly blisse espie,
> All earthly beautie he will straight defie,
> As thing too base to occupie his braine,
> Whose fading pleasures so are payd with paine,
> That they true tast of pleasure do denie:
> But who so can this perfect sight attaine,
> Cannot containe, but yeeld with cheerfull voyce,
> An Eccho to the Angels heavenly noyse,
> Who to his praise do singing still remaine:
> They then are vaine Who fix their sight so low,
> That such a glorious God they will not know.

The octave, by referring to God, evokes the ironic idolatries of the love sonnets that speak in nearly identical, apotheosizing terms about one earthly goddess as compared to other, rival beloveds. Lok's sonnet 2.46, continuing this same line of criticism, seems to refer directly to *Astrophil & Stella* sonnet 1:

> HOw fond a thing it is which men do use,
> To beat their braines, and so torment their hart,
> In compassing the thing which breeds their smart,
> And do not know what is the thing they chuse.
>
> (lines 1–4)

The sonnet then observes that such brain-beaters "childishly" abuse the name of love, defining its nature "By passions which belong to hatreds name,/ Wherein to pine with pleasure they do chuse" (lines 7–8). In a few words, Lok offers a stinging analysis of the pleasure-in-pain convention frequently deployed in the Petrarchan tradition. Such lovers choose their suffering, Lok's speaker insists, emphasizing the word "choose" twice in the poem. And their artifice is apparent: they "frame" their passions "With judgment lame." By way of contrast, Lok's sonnet concludes: "Love is a heavenly thing,/ Where being plast, it perfect love doth bring."

In love sonnets, praising the beloved requires delicate poise because the act of skilled praise tends to aggrandize the poet and eclipse the beloved. This does not seem to be Lok's dilemma in praising the Divine. Instead, we find the familiar terms of the inexpressibility topos: "WHere shall I find fit words or proper phrase,/ Wherewith to witnesse all the love I owe?" (2.7.1–2). Or "So farre I runne In seeking to begin,/ I cannot write, such maze my muse is in" (2.8.13–14). In seeking fit words to paint, not the blackest face of woe, but the incomparable beauties of God, Lok's speakers often use a familiar love sonnet trope: they seek the salutary effect of the beloved's gaze: "My eyes no beautie but in thee shall see, / And thy regard my wandring will shall tame" (2.39.11–12). A sonnet beloved's gaze may turn away or register scorn, but this divine gaze reliably assists the lover in all his inadequacies and doubts. "I Will not feare with fervency of zeale,/ To follow forth this faire affect of mine," declares the speaker of 2.38, because one who "Bestows his love so well" can expect that his "hope is payd with pleasures that excell." Despite confidence in this benevolent regard, the in-expressibility problem remains. How even to begin praising God?

The solution to the dilemma of praise is grace, the grace to begin (as Donne might say) but more than that, the grace to speak in answerable style (to bring Milton into it). Thus we find in the second century an explicit involvement of the Divine in problems of poetic style. In his dedicatory poem to "Gentlemen Courtiers in generall," Lok evokes the modesty topos and describes his "rude lines" as wearing "plaine array" and "home-woven robes," suggesting that his poems are like a combination of plain clothes and a "wholesome dyet," which might present a wise choice even for grand people (Xviii^v). However, the poems present a somewhat more complicated theology of style, as we might call it. Much as Sidney renders it so significantly in his Psalm 32, the speaker rescued from sin—and its concomitant disordered pleas—is saved "to songs." Lok first sounds this theme, as previously noted, at the end of the first century with the declaration that the Savior "turnes our plaints into more pleasant song" (1.C). In the second century, Lok expands on the theme beginning with sonnet 2.4:

> SInce to so holy use I consecrate
> The silly talent Lord thou lentst to me,

That it a trumpe unto thy praise might be,
And witnesse of their woe that thou doest hate.
Doe thou ô Lord forget the abject state
  Of flesh and bloud, base mettle of my frame,
  And since that thou hast sanctified the same,
  Vouchsafe thy grace my weaknesse may abate:
Thou that my former wandring will didst tame,
  And me prepare in minde to honour thee,
  Canst give me gifts the which thereto agree,
  How ere my proper power be weake and lame,
    So shall thy name Be precious in my sight
    And in thy praise shall be my whole delight.

The term "frame," so often used in this sequence and elsewhere to refer to the made-ness of a poem, here gathers into itself both the speaker's sin-tainted body and his poem.[62] Both have been "sanctified," and their weakness ameliorated by grace, hence the further request for gifts agreeing to the task of honoring God. "Proper power" in the next line suggests both the power belonging to the particular speaker, his own powers, but also, perhaps, the conventionality of the potential utterance, "weake and lame" without divine assistance. However, "lame" is quickly covered over by the holy "name" in the promised intention/performance of grace-assisted praise.

Sonnet 2.20 develops this line of thinking further:

NO recompence ô Lord is fit for thee,
  If duly thy desert we do regard,
  Ne hast thou want or need of mans reward,
  At whose command all creatures readie bee:
Yet if our thankfull minds thy goodnesse see,
  Confessing whence to us these blessings flow,
  And in the use of them obedience show,
  Although alas it be in meane degree,
Thou yet doest frame thy love to ours below,
  And as thou findst the givers heart preparde,
  (Who to his power his present hath sparde)
  So doest thou cansell debt which he did owe,
    And doest bestow More graces then we crave,
    For which naught els but thanks thou lokst to have.

Lines 3–4 immediately bring to mind the lines from Milton's Sonnet XIX: "God doth not need / Either man's work or his own gifts; . . . / / . . . Thousands at his bidding speed/ And post o'er Land and Ocean without rest."[63] I also see in Lok's lines 9–14 a prototype of Herbert's "A True Hymn." Even when our responses to God's goodness remain, necessarily, "in meane degree," the speaker declares that "Thou yet doest frame thy love to ours below." The final line reiterates that all God looks to have is our thanks. However meanly we offer those thanks, as Herbert might put it, "if th' heart be moved,/ Although the verse be somewhat scant,/ God doth supply the want."[64] The secret is whether or not the giver's heart is "preparde"—or as Herbert would say, whether "the soul unto the lines accords." And of course, what's happening here is that Lok is framing a crafted poem that disowns its own craft and credits divine intervention for its efficacy. God meets the poet halfway—or more—and stoops to ensure the efficacy of an utterance that would otherwise, by definition, fail. God writeth loved.

Sonnet 2.77 is perhaps Lok's most confident and finished declaration of divinely enhanced poetic style.

> FOr common matter common speech may serve,
> But for this theame both wit and words do want,
> For he that heaven and earth and all did plant,
> The frutes of all he justly doth deserve:
> No marvell then though oft my pen do swarve,
> In middle of the matter I intend,
> Since oft so high, my thoughts seeke to ascend,
> As want of wisedome makes my will to starve:
> But thou ô Lord who cloven tongs didst send,
> Unto thy servants, when their skills were scant,
> And such a zeale unto thy praise that brant,
> As made them fearelesse speake, and never bend,
> Unto the end,   One jot from thy behest,
> Shall guide my stile, as fits thy glory best.

The poem begins with the standard observation that no common style is fitting to a divine theme ("Nothing could seem too rich to clothe the sun"). This leaves the poet understandably dazed, his pen swerving, his will starving. We are back to the opening poem of the second century. The sestet, however, brings a direct reference to the story of Pentecost, when the Holy Spirit came in "cloven tongs" upon the Apostles and enabled their miraculous utterance when their skills were—and here's that word again—"scant." The speaker is bold enough to suggest that if God were to dole out even a drop, a "jot" of such power, such a jot "Shall guide my stile, as fits thy glory best." The syntax of the lines does not rise even to the level of request; we remain in the realm of suggestion. *If* you were to do this, God, my style would obtain to its glorious subject. So even in this bold moment, invoking the most powerful event of Spirit-filled utterance in Scripture, we are left, as in the love sonnet sequences, as in the first century, still poised in unfulfilled desire, unconsummated possibility.

Between 1593 and 1597, Lok seems to have lost some steam. The third century, "sonets of a feeling conscience," is concerned with the ethical challenges of daily life, faith in action. Unfortunately, these poems mostly lack the lyric intensity and inventiveness of the earlier sonnets, lapsing into a more conventional hortatory mode, philosophical without the interior drama of the 1593 poems. But in those first two centuries, in individual poems as well as in the sequence as a whole, Lok seeks to release a kind of holy disorder. Innovatively combining the formal parameters, the sincerity/performance dilemma, and especially the "mobile fixity" of the Petrarchan sequence with familiar postures and reading practices associated with the Psalms, Lok sought to reintegrate a speaking self and represent a move from disordered speech to a "framing" of suitable praise. Moreover, Lok moves outward from issues of poetic utterance in the devotional lyric to questions of exemplarity, as raised by habits of biblical reading. His volume of work thus presents a substantial, largely underappreciated field of exploration for the theory and practice of the devotional lyric, in which Lok provided compelling English models for working through what happens when a poet restores the energy of divine grace to the vibrant poetic world of the love lyric sequence.

Calvin College

NOTES

My sincere thanks to Prof. Hannibal Hamlin and to the anonymous reviewers at *Spenser Studies* for reading earlier drafts of this article and offering many excellent and transformative suggestions.

1.   Barbara Kiefer Lewalski, *Protestant Poetics and the Seventeenth-Century Religious Lyric* (Princeton: Princeton University Press, 1979), and Thomas P. Roche, Jr., *Petrarch and the English Sonnet Sequences* (New York: AMS Press, 1989). Other previous treatments of Lok are very few: Lily V. Campbell includes a few pages on Lok in *Divine Poetry and Drama in Sixteenth-Century England* (Berkeley: University of California Press, 1959). James Scanlon's "Henry Lok's Sundry Christian Passions: A Critical Edition" (PhD diss., Brown University, 1971), which includes only the first two centuries of sonnets, is the only edition after Alexander Grosart's. Articles specifically on Lok include: James Doelman, "Seeking 'The Fruit of Favour': The Dedicatory Sonnets of Henry Lok's *Ecclesiastes,*" *ELH* 60:1 (1993): 1–15; John H. Ottenhoff, "The Shadow and the Real: Typology and the Religious Sonnet," *University of Hartford Studies in Literature* 15–16 (1983–84), 43–59; and Michael G. Brennan's article on Lok in the Oxford *Dictionary of National Biography* (2004). Kimberly Anne Coles places Lok helpfully in the context of his mother's work and his peers' work in the chapter on Anne Lock in *Religion, Reform, and Women's Writing in Early Modern England* (Cambridge: Cambridge University Press, 2008), 141–48. See also reference to Christopher Warley, below. William Stull mentions Lok's sonnets in two articles on the origins of devotional poetry. In both cases, Stull dismisses Lok's work as "ponderous" or dull. See "'Why Are Not "Sonnets" Made of Thee?' A New Context for the 'Holy Sonnets' of Donne, Herbert, and Milton," *Modern Philology* 80:2 (1982): 129–35, and "Sacred Sonnets in Three Styles," *Studies in Philology* 79:1 (Winter 1982): 78–99. Some sources with briefer mentions of Lok will appear in references below.

2.   Lewalski, 239; Roche, 157. There is one additional sonnet by Lok that Roche is not counting here: the prefatory sonnet addressed to James VI, printed in *His Majesties poeticall exercises at vacant hours* (Edinburgh, 1591).

3.   The spelling of the name Lock is problematic. Lok is the usual spelling associated with Henry Lok, the subject of this essay. His mother's name has been spelled various ways. Here I follow the practice of Susan Felch, editor of *The Collected Works of Anne Vaughan Lock* (Tempe: University of Arizona Press, 1999), xxxvi.

4.   Coles, 144.

5.   For an extensive analysis of class position in relation to Anne Lock and her sonnets, see Christopher Warley, *Sonnet Sequences and Social Distinction in Renaissance England* (Cambridge: Cambridge University Press, 2005). Warley's argument that sonnets both responded to and were influential upon the negotiating of social distinction has interesting implications for Henry Lok's work, and Warley does briefly consider Lok's attention to disorder. However, he does not further analyze the class implications of Lok's devotional verse, nor is that my focus here.

6.   The brief summary of Lok's life here is based on the introduction to Felch's *Collected Works*, xv–lxvii.

7.   Doelman, 5.

8.   The metrical psalms, all in 14-syllable couplets, include 27, 71, 119 (in 22 parts), 121, and 130, plus a version of the Lord's Prayer in the same meter. They

seem to form a short bridge from the Ecclesiastes verse paraphrase to the sonnets. The paraphrase is immediately followed by one sonnet titled "Adue to worlds vaine delight," very much in the standard mode of turning from the pursuit of earthly pleasures to heavenly bliss. The following psalms are prefaced with a brief comment: "Sundry Psalmes of David translated into verse, as briefly and significantly as the scope of the text will suffer; by the same Author."

9. Henry's sister, Anne Lock Moyle, was also an admired scholar and part of an active circle of women writer/scholars. See Micheline White, "Women Writers and Literary-Religious Circles in the Elizabethan West Country: Anne Dowriche, Anne Lock Prowse, Anne Lock Moyle, Ursula Fulford, and Elizabeth Rous," *Modern Philology* 103:2 (2005): 187–214.

10. Anne Lock may have been consciously adapting French lyric biblical meditation for a Reformist audience, creating a poetic rendition of Scripture for meditation. See Catherine A. Carsley, "Biblical Versification and French Religious Paraphrase in Anne Lock's "A Meditation of a Penitent Sinner," *ANQ* 24:1–2 (2011): 42–50.

11. For an overview of metrical psalms in English, Rivkah Zim's appendix, listing printed English psalms from 1530–1601, is still an indispensable resource, although Hannibal Hamlin's more recent book gives an extensive overview of the development of metrical psalms and their uses in early modern England, including a persuasive explanation for the popularity of the *Whole Booke of Psalmes.* Zim, *English Metrical Psalms: Poetry as Praise and Prayer, 1535–1601* (Cambridge: Cambridge University Press, 1987); Hamlin, *Psalm Culture and Early Modern English Literature* (Cambridge: Cambridge University Press, 2004). More recently, Beth Quitslund's *The Reformation in Rhyme: Sternhold, Hopkins and the English Metrical Psalter, 1547–1603* (Burlington, VT: Ashgate, 2008), has contributed a much-needed study of this psalter to the literature.

12. William Herbert (Mary Sidney's father-in-law), Robert Dudley (Philip's and Mary's uncle), and William Cecil were allies in the 1560s in the effort to nudge "the reluctant Elizabeth toward the role of Protestant champion." See Margaret P. Hannay, *Philip's Phoenix: Mary Sidney, Countess of Pembroke* (New York: Oxford University Press, 1990), 37. In 1597, a match was almost negotiated between Mary Sidney's son William and William Cecil's granddaughter Bridget. Later, her son Philip married Susan de Vere, Bridget's younger sister (Hannay, *Philip's Phoenix*, 159–62). These are only two examples of interconnections that were—as usual in matters of powerful early modern families—complex, ranging from harmony to bitter rivalry. Nevertheless, Lok's connection with the Cecils would have placed him in a circle that included Mary Sidney and her relations.

13. Quotations from Lok are taken from the 1597 version unless otherwise indicated.

14. Thomas Watson, *The Hekatompathia or Passionate Centurie of Love* (London, 1582); Sir Philip Sidney, *Sir P. S. his Astrophel and Stella* (London, 1591); Samuel Daniel, *Delia . . . with the complaint of Rosamond* (London, 1592); Henry

Constable, *Diana* (London, 1592). The first edition of Sidney's sonnets, printed by Thomas Newman, was problematic probably because of a preface by Thomas Nashe and a dedication that Sidney's family, especially his sister Mary, evidently considered inappropriate. The first printing was called in, amended, and reissued that same year. (See Hannay, *Philip's Phoenix*, 69.) Watson, though his volume is usually listed among sonnet sequences, wrote in an eighteen-line, expanded-sonnet form. For a useful listing of sonnet sequences in English, in date order, see Appendix A of Roche, *Petrarch and the English Sonnet Sequences*, 518ff.

15. On the Continental sonnet tradition, see Gordon Braden, *Petrarchan Love and the Continental Renaissance* (New Haven: Yale University Press, 1999).

16. Petrarch's Latin prose poems, the *Psalmi penitentiales,* are not paraphrases of the biblical Penitential Psalms. They are a set of freely composed poems loosely based on the penitential mode but full of allusions to classical and Christian sources and tangled enough in matters of love to prompt a critical debate: "Is it a set of love poems or a religious work in the penitential mode? Could it be both at once?" See E. Ann Matter, "Petrarch's Personal Psalms: *Psalmi penitentiales,*" in *Petrarch: A Critical Guide to the Complete Works,* ed. Victoria Kirkham and Armando Maggi (Chicago: University of Chicago Press, 2009), 219–27.

17. The scholarship on both Petrarchism and devotional writing in sixteenth-century England is, of course, extensive. Especially useful introductions to English Petrarchism are Michael R. G. Spiller, *The Development of the Sonnet: An Introduction* (London: Routledge, 1992) and Heather Dubrow, *Echoes of Desire: English Petrarchism and its Counterdiscourses* (Ithaca: Cornell University Press, 1995). For devotional writing, in addition to works mentioned elsewhere in this essay, Ian Green's *Print and Protestantism in Early Modern England* (New York: Oxford University Press, 2000) provides a perspective focused on the publishing business. Much current work in sixteenth-century devotional writing is related to women's work in that genre. For useful overviews, see Susan M. Felch, "English Women's Devotional Writing: Surveying the Scene," *ANQ* 24:1–2 (2011): 118–30 and Micheline White, ed., *English Women, Religion, and Textual Production, 1500–1625* (Burlington, VT: Ashgate, 2011).

18. See Elizabeth Clarke, *Theory and Theology in George Herbert's Poetry: 'Divinitie, and Poesie, Met'* (Oxford: Oxford University Press, 1997) and Coles's chapter on the Sidney-Pembroke Psalter in *Religion, Reform, and Women's Writing,* 75–112.

19. Coles argues that "Rather than the publication of *L'Uranie,* the watershed event for devotional lyric in England was the concurrent circulation of the Sidney-Pembroke Psalter and the published *Defence*" (100). This may be too large a claim for these two works; however, for a complementary account of the Sidney-Pembroke Psalter as an influential argument against suspicion of pleasure and poetic skill, see Debra Rienstra, "The Countess of Pembroke and the Problem of Skill in Devotional Writing," *Sidney Journal* 23:1–2 (2005): 37–60.

20. In the section "Miles Coverdale unto the Christen Reader," Coverdale laments the public fancy for light verse and wishes people would sing Psalms instead

(*Goostly psalmes* +ii^v). John Hall's *Courte of Vertue*, printed in 1565, purports to offer a pious counterbalance to the *Courte of Venus* as well as to Tottel's Miscellany. Curiously, printer Thomas Marshe published both *Courtes*, and they came out looking very similar in appearance. So while Hall may have been sincere in his rampage against vice, it's not entirely certain that Thomas Marshe was. See Russell Fraser's introduction, *The Court of Virtue 1565*, ed. Russell A. Fraser (London: Routledge and Kegan Paul, 1961). In his 1619 *A preparation to the Psalter*, George Wither is still complaining that people prefer popular ballads, which he compares to "puddle water," instead of the psalms' "living streames of his [God's] owne pure fountaine" (5 [sig. Biii^r]).

21. Daniel revised the *Delia* sequence several times, from 1592 through 1601, and continued to print the sequence in editions of his work, alongside his later historical writings. Michael Drayton printed a religious work first, *The harmonie of the church* (London, 1591), and then his Petrarchan sequence, *Idea* (London, 1593). Both volumes were reprinted several times before Drayton's death in 1631, though his sonnets far more frequently than the religious verse. Barnabe Barnes printed the frankly sexual *Parthenophil and Parthenophe* in 1593, then turned to *A divine centurie of spirituall sonnets* in 1595. Heather Dubrow, *Echoes of Desire*, is especially helpful in assessing the contradictions and contentions within the tradition, including religious sonnets as a form of anti-Petrarchism. See esp. 57–64, 226ff.

22. *The Posies of George Gascoigne, Esquire* (London, 1575), "To al yong Gentlemen," sig. Ppiii^v. This image is used also in the epistle "To the reverende Divines" in this edition and in "'The Printer to the Reader" in an earlier volume of Gascoigne's works, *A hundreth sundrie flowres* (London, 1573). Felicity Hughes argues that Gascoigne issued *Posies* in order to "brazen it out with the censors," and that his piety is indeed a pose—that in fact Gascoigne was an adept at poses even after he turned to more sober subjects. See Felicity A. Hughes, "Gascoigne's Poses," *SEL* 37:1 (1997): 1–19.

23. The sonnet-sequence fashion subsided by the 1630s, but anthologies of secular verse continued to be printed and collected in manuscript throughout the seventeenth century. See Michael R. G. Spiller, *The Development of the Sonnet*. For an account of the continued importance of manuscript anthologies of verse, see Arthur F. Marotti, *Manuscript, Print, and the English Renaissance Lyric* (Ithaca: Cornell University Press, 1995).

24. Hannibal Hamlin succinctly summarizes the close coexistence of psalms and secular lyric poetry in *Psalm Culture*, 1–16. An important early effort to grapple with the interconnections in English between traditions is Roland Greene, "Sir Philip Sidney's Psalms, the Sixteenth-Century Psalter, and the Nature of Lyric," *SEL* 30 (1990): 19–40. Other suggestive works, even if this is not their main topic, are Carol Kaske, "Spenser's *Amoretti and Epithalamion*: A Psalter of Love," in *Centered on the Word: Literature, Scripture, and the Tudor-Stuart Middle Way*, ed. Daniel W. Doerksen and Christopher Hodgkins (Newark: University of Delware Press, 2004), 28–49; and Heather Dubrow, *Echoes of Desire*.

25. Quotations from the Sidneys' psalms are taken from *The Sidney Psalter: The Psalms of Sir Philip and Mary Sidney*, ed. Hannibal Hamlin, Michael G. Brennan, Margaret P. Hannay, and Noel J. Kinnamon (Oxford: Oxford University Press, 2009).

26. Constable completed an unpublished religious sequence in a blatantly Catholic mode; Joan Grundy dates it 1593 or later. See *The Poems of Henry Constable*, ed. Joan Grundy (Liverpool: Liverpool University Press, 1960), 59. Barnabe Barnes's 1595 sequence deserves its own essay; it is also deeply engaged with the Psalms, but Barnes was clearly taken by Du Bartas's idea of the muse Urania. For him, sacred poetry is often figured as arising from states of spiritual ecstasy. Fulke Greville's sequence *Caelica* (London, 1633) is another interesting case. Greville began the sequence in the 1580s, but never printed it. He combines the two kinds of love—amatory and divine—in one sequence: sonnets 1–84 follow Petrarchan models, then 25 additional sonnets make a turn toward more general religious and philosophical musings. Roche discusses the sequence at length in chap. 5 (294–317). See also Gavin Alexander, "Fulke Greville and the Afterlife," *Huntington Library Quaterly* 62:3/4 (1999): 203–31. For comments on this impulse within Petrarchism on the Continent, see Braden, *Petrarchan Love and the Continental Renaissance*, esp. 99–101.

27. James VI, *Twelf Sonnets of Invocations to the Goddis*, printed in *The essayes of a prentise, in the diuine art of poesie* (Edinburgh, 1585), described in Spiller, *Development*, 103–4. For the dating of Spenser's *Amoretti*, see *The Yale Edition of the Shorter Poems of Edmund Spenser*, ed. William A. Oram (New Haven: Yale University Press, 1989), 583. Spenser's *Visions of the worlds vanitie*, a set of twelve sonnets in the Spenserian pattern, was printed in 1591 in *Complaints*. Lok's rhyme schemes are as follows:

First century: abab bcbc cdcd ee; five sonnets are exceptions with slight variations.

Second century: abba acca cbbc dd, plus internal c rhyme in line 13; nine exceptions with slight variations.

Third century: abba cdcd dbbd aa; eleven exceptions comprising five slight variations.

Peculiar Prayers: abbaab cddccd ee, with the end of line 6 rhyming with the middle of line 7, connecting the first two groups of six lines, and the end of line 12 rhyming with the middle of line 13, connecting the second group of six with the couplet; four exceptions including three slight variations and the concluding sonnet in the form used in the first century.

Dedicatory sonnets: these match the form used in the first century with three exceptions.

Special thanks to Alex Westenbroek for analyzing the rhyme schemes in the 1597 version and compiling the data for this summary.

28. For an extensive examination of inwardness in this period, including a consideration of how the word "sincere" was understood, see Anne Ferry, *The "Inward"*

Language: Sonnets of Wyatt, Sidney, Shakespeare, and Donne (Chicago: University of Chicago Press, 1983), esp. 22 and 247.

29. On Petrarch's representations of a divided self, Michael Spiller remarks, "This is what Italian critics call Petrarch's *dissidio* ('variance', 'contradiction'), and it is the first time in European literature that such instability, both psychic and rhetorical, is announced as the principle of a work of poesis. Dante's *Vita Nuova*, Augustine's *Confessions* and Boethius's *Consolation of Philosophy* may deal with unstable states of mind, but the texts themselves do not proclaim it as a principle of style and construction" (*Development*, 49).

30. For an influential though controversial exploration of dismemberment in love sonnets, both of the beloved and the speaker, see Nancy J. Vickers, "Diana Described: Scattered Woman and Scattered Rhyme," *Critical Inquiry* 8:2 (1981): 265–79. While the speaker's rage (and even, in Vickers's approach, violence) is not an element in Petrarch's originary *Rime sparse*, Gordon Braden notes that Petrarchan sequences do contain a stronger element of anger over time: "The longterm history of the topic [pride] in Petrarchan imitation is one of escalating rage." See "Pride, Humility, and the Petrarchan Happy Ending," *Spenser Studies* 18 (2003): 128. Also Heather Dubrow notes the strength of the "misogynistic hostility and anger" in Petrarchan sequences (*Echoes of Desire*, 12), though she offers throughout her study a subtle and extensive analysis of the gender politics involved.

31. For an analysis of how Spenser manages to alter the convention of ending in unfulfilled desire, see Braden, "Pride, Humility, and the Petrarchan Happy Ending."

32. Besides Anne Lock's version of Psalm 51, Sir Thomas Wyatt's *Certayne psalmes* (1549) is perhaps the most famous example of this phenomenon, and the complex interiority of Wyatt's metrical translation of Psalm 51 is the subject of a chapter in Stephen Greenblatt's *Renaissance Self-Fashioning: From More to Shakespeare* (Chicago: University of Chicago Press, 1980), 115–56. For a treatment of Wyatt in the context of other translators of Psalm 51, see Hamlin, *Psalm Culture*, 173–217. On the prevalence of the penitential Psalms in English devotion, see Clare Costley King'oo, *Miserere Mei: The Penitential Psalms in Late Medieval and Early Modern England* (Notre Dame: University of Notre Dame Press, 2012).

33. *The Collected Works of Anne Vaughan Lock*, sonnets 2 and 3 (62–63). As part of her larger argument about the concept of sacrifice in Lock's sonnets, Mary Trull briefly argues that Anne Lock chose the sonnet form in part because certain Petrarchan features—volatile emotion, the speaker's powerlessness and the addressee's mastery, and the speaker's gratitude for attention, for example—fit with the psalmic material. However, this may reflect the way in which the Petrarchan tradition was itself interrelated with Psalms. Mary Trull, "Petrarchism and the Gift: The Sacrifice of Praise in Anne Lock's 'A Meditation of a Penitent Sinner,'" *Religion and Literature* 41:3 (2009): 1–25.

34. To identify Lok's sonnets, I use a numbering system in which the century and the sonnet are each given. Thus sonnet 1.4 is the sonnet numbered 4 in the first century of sonnets.

35. Lisa Freinkel, *Reading Shakespeare's Will: The Theology of Figure from Augustine to the Sonnets* (New York: Columbia University Press, 2002), 63.

36. Readers of Roland Greene will recognize that Freinkel's analysis somewhat resembles Greene's distinction between the "ritual" and "fictional" elements, as described in "Sir Philip Sidney's Psalms, the Sixteenth-Century Psalter, and the Nature of Lyric" as well as *Post-Petrarchism* (Princeton: Princeton University Press, 1991). Freinkel offers, in my view, a finer-grained approach more amenable to issues raised by psalm reading.

37. Discussing congregational singing in 1542, Calvin wrote, "Look where we may, we will never find songs better, nor more suited to the purpose, than the Psalms of David; which the Holy Ghost himself composed." Quoted in Nicholas Temperley, *The Music of the English Parish Church* (Cambridge: Cambridge University Press, 1979), 1:20. Also quoted in the introduction to *Psalms in the Early Modern World*, ed. Linda Phyllis Austern, Kari Boyd McBride, and David L. Orvis (Burlington, VT: Ashgate, 2011), 20.

38. Kimberly Coles argues that Anne Lock creates a collective voice in her sonnets, and that her "principal innovation is the inscription of polyphonic subjectivity—a multiplication of voices that allegorises the Presbyterian congregation" (*Religion, Reform, and Women's Writing*, 136). I would argue that polyphonic subjectivities were characteristic of sonnet sequences from the beginning (though not as allegories of Presbyterian congregations, of course). At any rate, I see Henry Lok's process here as quite different, but interestingly related. Perhaps Lok is creating serial subjectivities in order to arrive at a cumulative subjectivity rather than a collective one.

39. Though Calvin and Luther both claimed to reject the allegorical interpretation of Scripture in favor of a "plain sense," in fact the habits of typology persist in their commentary. Lewalski's chapter is one useful summary of typology: *Protestant Poetics*, 111–44. For a more nuanced account of Reformation hermeneutics, see Debora Shuger, *The Renaissance Bible: Scholarship, Sacrifice, and Subjectivity* (Berkeley: University of California Press, 1994), particularly chapters 1 and 3. Shuger argues intriguingly that the "de-centered" subject is characteristic of Calvinist piety and is modeled on Erasmian and Calvinist Christology (100–107).

40. For a helpful and brief summary, see Kate Narveson, "Assistances and Encouragements in the Ways of Piety: Conceptions of Private Devotion in Early Modern England," *ANQ* 24:1–2 (2011): 1–10.

41. Kate Narveson makes a similar argument for the formative rather than expressive purpose of devotional writing in "Profession or Performance? Religion in Early Modern Literary Study," in *Fault Lines and Controversies in the Study of Seventeenth-Century English Literature*, ed. Claude J. Summers and Ted-Larry Pebworth (Columbia: University of Missouri Press, 2002), 111–29.

42. For matters of resolution in Petrarchan sequences, see Gordon Braden, "Beyond Frustration: Petrarchan Laurels in the Seventeenth Century," *SEL* 26:1 (Winter 1986): 5–23, and "Pride, Humility, and the Petrarchan Happy Ending";

Heather Dubrow, *Echoes of Desire* on genre, 75–81; and Carol Thomas Neely, "The Structure of English Renaissance Sonnet Sequences," *ELH* 45:3 (Autumn 1978): 359–89.

43. Lok's fondness for puzzles is evidenced by the prefatory "A Square in verse of a hundred monasillables only" (sig. Ivii^r), a complex sudoku-like structure examined in Roche's chapter on Lok (164–66 and 549–52).

44. The shift to the foot-bathing story in the second quatrain suggests that the first line could be read as a reference to Mary Magdelene, who was traditionally supposed to have been a prostitute. In fact, dating back to Gregory the Great, the foot-bathing episode in all four gospels was attributed to Mary Magdelene, thus conflating two Marys and the unnamed woman into a "composite Mary." However, as David Urban explains, Reformed and Puritan comentators, beginning in the mid-sixteenth century, flatly and persistently rejected both these conflations as biblically inaccurate and associated with Roman Catholic practice and tradition. Thus, it is doubtful that the strongly Protestant Lok would wish to evoke a "popish" reading of the foot-bathing stories. Moreover, the term "crummes" remains a significant reference to the Matthew 15 story of the Canaanite woman and suggests that Lok is intentionally creating his own conflation of female figures for the purposes of the poem. Intriguingly, there is no mention in any of the referenced biblical accounts of the women in question evidencing penitence. See David V. Urban, "The Lady of Christ's College, Himself a 'Virgin Wise and Pure': Parabolic Self-Reference in John Milton's *Sonnet IX*," *Milton Studies* 47 (2007): 10–12.

45. Roche examines Lok's sonnet 1.50 at length as a prototype for "Redemption," arguing that the use of the term "tenant" in Herbert's poem alluding to this same parable did not come from any contemporary biblical translations, and thus may have come from Tyndale through Lok. I would suggest that Herbert may well have combined features of both sonnets, 1.50 and 1.78, for his poem. See Roche, 158–63.

46. Roland Greene, "Sir Philip Sidney's Psalms, the Sixteenth-Century Psalter, and the Nature of Lyric." See note 36 above.

47. The passage is quoted from the 1597 volume, Iviii^r. Lok added only very minor edits from the 1593 version.

48. *Petrarch's Lyric Poems: The Rime Sparse and Other Lyrics*, trans. and ed. by Robert M. Durling (Cambridge: Harvard University Press, 1976), 36.

49. Christopher Warley uses this same passage as a kind of answer to the lack of a preface in Drayton's *Idea* sequence. Warley's interest is in the way sonnet sequences both imagine and undermine a social ideal. In Lok's case, according to Warley, a "preposterous" placing of things "similarly disrupts order, but in that disruption it also seeks to create a new order, 'another world.'" Lok turns the unruliness of spiritual life into a pilgrimage, a progress. Warley, *Sonnet Sequences and Social Distinction*, 15.

50. Teodolinda Barolini, "The Making of a Lyric Sequence: Time and Narrative in Petrarch's *Rerum vulgarium fragmenta*," *Modern Language Notes* 104:1 (1989): 5. Qtd. in Freinkel, 92.

51. Francis Seager, *Certayne Psalmes select out of the Psalter of David* (London, 1553), Aiii[r].

52. John Calvin, *The Psalmes of Dauid and others. With M. Iohn Caluins commentaries*, trans. Arthur Golding (London, 1571), sig. *iv[v].

53. Although headnotes and commentaries encouraged the reading of the Psalms in terms of David's (auto)biography, this hardly yields an orderly narrative if the Psalms are read in sequence.

54. The translation of Athanasius is from Matthew Parker, *The whole Psalter translated into English Metre* (London, 1567). Anne Prescott notes from this same passage in Athanasius one source of the common idea in the period of the Psalms as an image of the reader's soul: her interest is in Sidney's use of this idea in developing the notion of the "right poet." The mirror and painting were among the many tropes derived from the fathers (Athanasius and Basil especially) and frequently drawn upon by Reformation commentators to describe how the Psalms effected the edification of readers. See "King David as a 'Right Poet': Sidney and the Psalmist," *ELR* 19:3 (Spring 1989): 131–51.

55. *The whole booke of Psalmes collected into Englysh metre by T. Sternhold, I. Hopkins, & others*, (London, John Day, 1562), sig. vii[v].

56. Hannibal Hamlin gives a brief account of appearances of Athanasius's treatise, 29–30. The 1562 edition of the *Whole Book of Psalmes* also printed an addendum to Athanasius's suggestions, "a set of applications particularly suitable to Englishmen in the 1560s" (29). This addendum was not reprinted in subsequent editions. For a more detailed account, see also Beth Quitslund, *The Reformation in Rhyme*, 193–238.

57. Matthew Parker's translation of Athanasius, sig. Cii[v].

58. For a concise summary of sixteenth-century prayer books, see the introduction to Susan Felch, ed., *Elizabeth Tyrwhit's Morning and Evening Prayers* (Burlington, VT: Ashgate, 2007), 19–32.

59. *The Boke of Psalmes* (Geneva, 1559), sig. Bbviii[r]. In his consideration of the devotional "steady sellers" in early modern New England, Matthew Brown argues that the reader's active engagement with devotional texts—which includes intentional, nonlinear reference to texts of multivalent meaning—was heavily advocated and practiced in Protestant devotion. He terms this nexus of textual qualities and reading practices "thick style." See Matthew Brown, "Thick Style: Steady Sellers, Textual Aesthetics, and Early Modern Devotional Reading," *PMLA* 121:1 (2006): 67–86.

60. Heather Dubrow makes a similar observation: "Thus spiritual sonnets like Henry Lok's eschew the failure implicit in writing love poems by not writing them and even, as in Barnes's opening poem, by openly rejecting such poems and renouncing one's own earlier involvement with them. Yet, as we observed earlier, the reader sometimes questions whether the spiritual vision in such poems represents a final, secure position or merely a moment on a giddy merry-go-round, one more continuing struggle between desire and its renunciation." I would add

that the spiritual sonnets do not necessarily return to the erotic sonnets in an alternating cycle, but rather that spiritual sonnets have their own unresolving merry-go-round of the already-but-not-yet. The difference for Lok and other devotional writers is that the spiritual merry-go-round is the right one to be on. *Echoes of Desire*, 85ff.

61. Dubrow, *Echoes of Desire*, 62–75.

62. According to Herbert S. Donow, *A Concordance to the Sonnet Sequences of Daniel, Drayton, Shakespeare, Sidney, and Spenser* (Carbondale: University of Southern Illinois Press, 1969), 229–30, all of the included poets except Drayton use the term "frame" or "framed" to refer to the made-ness of poems. Another relevant example would be the lines in Herbert's "The Altar": "Wherefore each part/ Of my hard heart/ Meets in this frame/ To praise thy name." For a further examination of this term and its uses among seventeenth-century religious lyricists, see Helen Wilcox, "'Curious Frame': The Seventeenth-Century Religious Lyric as Genre," in *New Perspectives on the Seventeenth-Century English Religious Lyric*, ed. John R. Roberts (Columbia: University of Missouri Press, 1994), 9–27.

63. John Milton, *Complete Poems and Major Prose*, ed. Merritt Y. Hughes (New York: Prentice Hall, 1957), 168.

64. George Herbert, *George Herbert: The Complete English Poems*, ed. John Tobin (New York: Penguin, 2004), 158–59.

RACHEL E. HILE

Spenserianism and Satire before and after the Bishops' Ban: Evidence from Thomas Middleton

This article[1] examines the "Spenserianism" of two early satires of Thomas Middleton to make the argument that two incidents of censorship in the 1590s—the 1592 censoring of Spenser's *Complaints* (which included *Mother Hubberds Tale*) and the 1599 "Bishops' Ban" on satire—affected the reception of Edmund Spenser as a satirist and his influence on satires written during this time period. I find debts to Spenser in both Middleton's *Micro-Cynicon* (1599), which was named in the text of the Bishops' Ban and burned on June 4, 1599, and his *Father Hubburds Tales* (1604), although the form of *Micro-Cynicon*— Juvenalian verse satire—makes it appear un-Spenserian. Middleton's allusions to Spenser's methods of satirizing William and Robert Cecil served to teach contemporary readers how to understand the satire by suggesting that Middleton shared the political and religious ideas associated in the public mind with Spenser. Five years later, Middleton blunts the force of the satire of *Father Hubburds Tales* by making it quite different in form from the verse satires of the 1590s and by creating extremely general satiric targets. At the same time, though, he calls attention to the presence of a satirical message by repeated references and allusions to Spenser. Identifying the Spenserianism in these early satires of Middleton is important for what it tells

Spenser Studies: A Renaissance Poetry Annual, Volume XXVII, Copyright © 2012 AMS Press, Inc. All rights reserved. DOI: 10.7756/spst.027.012.289-311

us about Middleton's politics and also for what it tells us about Spenserianism as a tool for satirical meaning-making during this period of harsh and often capricious censorship. I argue that writers in the 1590s saw Spenser's *Mother Hubberds Tale* as an unsafe stylistic model for satire, but that the Bishops' Ban, by censoring primarily works modeled on Juvenal, made Spenser seem a more acceptable model for satires written afterward.

*T*WO IMPORTANT CENSORSHIP EVENTS in the 1590s affected the reception of Edmund Spenser as a satirist and his influence on satires written in the decades after the censoring of his *Complaints* volume. At the beginning of the decade, Spenser's poetry collection *Complaints* (1591) was "called in" by the government in response to criticisms of Lord Treasurer William Cecil, Lord Burghley, and his son, Secretary of State Robert Cecil, in poems in the volume, especially *Prosopopoia; or, Mother Hubberds Tale,* a beast fable and estates satire that featured a fox and an ape as the villains, with the fox character and his broken-backed cubs widely understood as referring to the Cecils.[2] At the end of the decade, on June 1, 1599, the "Bishops' Ban" on satire, promulgated by John Whitgift, Archbishop of Canterbury, and Richard Bancroft, bishop of London, identified particular books to be called in and burned as well as specifying "That noe Satyres or Epigramms be printed hereafter," thus bringing a premature end to the immense popularity during the late 1590s of the formal verse satires modeled on those of the Roman poet Juvenal.[3] Much work has explored the impact on satire of government censorship in the Marprelate controversy and the Bishops' Ban, but the importance of Spenser's influence on satires written in the 1590s and early 1600s, and how the censorship of *Mother Hubberds Tale* affected this influence, remain relatively obscure. The calling in of *Mother Hubberds Tale* had a chilling effect on beast fables; although some beast fables appeared in print in the 1590s, satirical writers mostly channeled their energies into formal verse satires.[4] In response to the Bishops' Ban, poets reversed this strategy, so that overtly Spenserian beast fables began to appear in print following 1599. In this article, I will analyze the change in how satirists responded to and used Spenserian satire as a model by discussing Thomas Middleton's *Micro-Cynicon* (1599), which was named in the text of the Bishops' Ban and burned on June 4, 1599, and *Father Hubburds Tales* (1604).

SPENSERIAN POLITICAL CRITIQUES IN
MIDDLETON'S JUVENALIAN *MICRO-CYNICON*

The limited critical attention to *Micro-Cynicon* has tended to assess it as a mostly unremarkable iteration of Juvenalian verse satire, notable for the ways in which the future dramatist sometimes shifts from the discursive satirical approach characteristic of the genre to semi-dramatic character sketches that aim for more realism than one generally finds in formal verse satires.[5] Numerous critics have offered hypotheses for what led to the Bishops' Ban, with some asserting that the bishops were motivated by moral concerns, others arguing that politics drove the decision to ban these books, and still others seeking ways around the erotica/politics dichotomy created by earlier scholars.[6] I believe that *Micro-Cynicon* was singled out to be among the satires specifically named in the Bishops' Ban and burned because the offense it gave was clearer and more specific than has been recognized. In the literary-political climate of 1599, because the genre of formal verse satire cued readers to look for topical, political allusions, the apparently general nature of Middleton's satire in *Micro-Cynicon* was not enough to spare it from scrutiny. The first two satires in the collection, focusing on "Insatiate Cron" and his son, "Prodigal Zodon," were likely read as referring to William and Robert Cecil. Middleton's use of imagery and ideas associated with Lord Burghley, most notably by Spenser in *Mother Hubberds Tale*, increases the likelihood that contemporary readers would read Cron as a satire on the Lord Treasurer. Given this association, the repeated references to Cron's death (and the unflattering observation that Cron has "fled to hell") would presumably be particularly offensive, given that Lord Burghley had died less than a year earlier.

The general obscurity in which *Micro-Cynicon* languishes means that few critics who have considered the Bishops' Ban have paid specific attention to what Middleton's work might have done to merit being recalled and burned, but the two hypotheses that have been put forth address both sides of the erotica/politics split in critical opinion regarding the motivations of the ban. John Peter, arguing that *Micro-Cynicon* offended the morals of the censors, calls the author "deliberately offensive" and notes that "in the fifth satire, 'Ingling Pyander,' besides what appear to be dark references to pederasty, there are several touches of unpleasantness where Marston's influence may be suspected."[7] Peter's allusions to "dark references to pederasty" are of a piece with his own moral repugnance at the style and method of the satirists who followed Marston's lead, but he is certainly correct that Middleton's fifth satire contains a titillating situation that leads to moral corruption of the satiric speaker—and thus perhaps of the reader as well. The speaker "loved Pyander well" before he realized that Pyander, "Whose rolling eye sets gazers' hearts on fire, / Whose cherry lip, black brow and smiles procure / Lust-burning buzzards to the tempting lure," was in fact "a pale chequered black hermaphrodite" (5.42, 5.36–38, 5.24).[8] Proving the relevance of Bruce Smith's assertion that with late-Elizabethan verse satire, "scourgers could be seduced by their sexual subjects and . . . the seducers could turn into scourgers of moral authority,"[9] part of the speaker's desire to expose Pyander stems from his own shame at being deceived ("shall I then procure eternal blame / By secret cloaking of Pyander's shame, / And he not blush?" [5.53–55]) and the rest from his vexation that he spent his money in vain ("Fair words I had, for store of coin I gave, / But not enjoyed the fruit I thought to have" [5.82–83]).

Cyndia Clegg, on the other hand, explains *Micro-Cynicon*'s inclusion in the named works of the Bishops' Ban as stemming from political, not moral, offensiveness in its second satire, which mocks "Prodigal Zodon." According to Clegg, because of the heightened political tensions in England at the time of publication surrounding the earl of Essex's Irish expedition and concerns regarding his loyalty to the queen, instead of appearing to be "a general satire of pretension and vanity," "Zodon looks like Essex, a man who indulged in luxuries though beset by debts."[10] She comments that phrases such as "glorious on his progress day" and "Two days encaged at least in strongest hold" (2.26, 2.29) might have seemed extremely topical if the book were published after Essex's departure for Ireland. Clegg does not argue strenuously for Middleton's authorial intention to criticize Essex (Middleton's dedication of *The Wisdom of Solomon, Paraphrased* [1597] to Essex only two years earlier would make this a problematic assertion). Instead, she believes that Whitgift, because of his warm friendship with Essex, responded to Essex's concerns about John Hayward's *The First Part of the Life and Raigne of King Henrie the IIII* (1599) with such zeal that he also identified and banned several other books that he saw as giving bad press to Essex, including *Micro-Cynicon*.

The bishops' silence regarding their motivations, coupled with the varied and complex cultural and political meanings of the genre of verse satire in the late 1590s, mean that we cannot definitively identify a single unifying offense committed by all of the named works, or even by Middleton's *Micro-Cynicon* alone. Instead, we can look at the ways that a single work may have given offense for multiple reasons, which, taken together, constituted grounds for censorship. As religious leaders, the bishops may have been shocked not only by Pyander's cross-dressing, but also by the speaker's frank desire for Pyander. As a friend of Essex, Whitgift may have zealously attempted to protect his friend's political interests. Likewise, however, Whitgift and Bancroft, as part of what was after all a *state* church, may have taken action on behalf of both Robert Cecil and the memory of his recently deceased father, William Cecil, Lord Burghley, both extremely high-ranking advisors to Queen Elizabeth. Richard McCabe notes that both Whitgift and Bancroft "were in constant correspondence with Robert Cecil on the issue of the press" and that their letters indicate a commitment to politically motivated censorship.[11]

In *Micro-Cynicon*, Middleton uses facts and images strongly associated with the Cecils and with Spenser's satire on them: calling Cron a fox; emphasizing the father-son relationship between these two satirical characters (and emphasizing their power by making this dyad's initials correspond to that other rapacious and power-hungry father and son, Chronos and Zeus[12]); referring to a "fardel at his [Cron's] back" in the satire on Zodon; and creating the name Zodon itself, which derives from the Greek *zodion* for "little animal."

As Anthony Petti has shown, there was a general identification of Lord Burghley with fox imagery within Elizabethan culture; additionally, we know that Spenser's particular fox references were interpreted as referring to Burghley because of Richard Peterson's discovery of a letter from Thomas Tresham regarding the "calling in" of the *Complaints* volume and by Bruce Danner's careful cataloguing of numerous sixteenth- and seventeenth-century readers' identification of the fox in *Mother Hubberds Tale* with Burghley.[13] Although Thomas Herron has complicated our understanding of the topical references in Spenser's satire by reminding us of the need to consider Irish readings and identifications of the Fox and other characters, for the English audience analyzed here, fox imagery strongly represents Lord Burghley.[14]

In Spenser's satire, although the fox shows his corruption throughout the poem, he becomes most similar to Lord Burghley in the fourth episode, in which the Ape impersonates the king and the Fox serves as his second-in-command. The narration of the Fox's crimes allegorizes the litany of complaints leveled against Burghley: he is greedy (nothing "that might him profit bring, / But he the same did to his purpose wring" [1141–42]); he wields disproportionate influence with the monarch ("Nought suffered he

the Ape to give or graunt, / But through his hand must passe the Fiaunt"
[1143–44]); he does not support learning and the arts ("For men of learn-
ing little he esteemed; / His wisedome he above their learning deemed"
[1191–92]); and his ostentatious building projects show his pride and self-
ishness ("But his owne treasure he encreased more / And lifted up his loftie
towers thereby" [1171–72]).[15]

We would not expect Middleton's Juvenalian satire to include this degree
of allegorized critique—it is not, after all, a beast fable. Middleton refers to
a fox only once, in a dense passage (editor Wendy Wall calls it "obscure")
that seems allusive in part because the nature and animal images seem in-
congruous with the rest of the poem. The overall message of the passage
seems to be that desire (presumably lascivious) would be preferable to the
"gain insatiate" that "this hoar-agèd peasant deems his bliss":

> O that desire might hunt amongst that fur!
> It should go hard but he would loose a cur
> To rouse the fox hid in a bramble bush,
> Who frighteth conscience with a wry-mouthed "Push!"
> (1.17–22)

The image of desire using a dog to hunt for a fox hidden, confusingly, in
both fur and in a bramble bush—shifting the poem temporarily to al-
legory and beast fable—surely would remind a sixteenth-century reader
of Spenser's known satirical methods. Additionally, though, this difficult
passage becomes much more comprehensible if we read it with the popu-
lar image of the aged, censorious Burghley in mind. Though none of the
words in this passage describes an old man, the fur suggests someone
wealthy, especially in proximity to the word "fox," as fox fur served in lit-
erature to identify usurers.[16] Further, the descriptor "wry-mouthed" calls
to mind an old man expressing his disdain with the interjection "push"
(obsolete, now "pish"); ingenious readers might find support for import-
ing the idea of Burghley through the similarity of a "bramble" to a "burr."
This passage, which differs in tone from the rest of the satire, calls atten-
tion to the possibility of a reading influenced by the concerns of *Mother
Hubberds Tale*, as does Middleton's emphasis on the father-son relation-
ship between Cron and Zodon.

One way that Spenser identified Lord Burghley as a target of the satire
in *Mother Hubberds Tale* was by criticizing the Fox's preferential treat-
ment of his cubs:

He fed his cubs with fat of all the soyle,

....

And loded them with lordships and with might,
So much as they were able well to beare,
That with the weight their backs nigh broken were.[17]

Significantly, Catholic apologist Richard Verstegan, in an unlicensed tract against Lord Burghley smuggled into England, describes *Mother Hubberds Tale* using only the detail that it concerns "the false fox and his crooked cubbes," indicating that contemporary readers saw the father-son(s) relationship as crucial in identifying the real-world targets of Spenser's satire.[18]

Clegg's argument identifying Zodon with Essex fails to convince not only because of Middleton's public warmth for Essex in his dedication of *Solomon Paraphrased,* but also because it doesn't take account of the significance of the father-son dyad in Middleton's creation of these characters. Numerous details of Cron and Zodon line up neatly with the biographical details of Cecil *père et fils,* who were without a doubt the most hated and powerful father-son dyad of late Elizabethan England. Like Lord Burghley, Cron has recently died, bequeathing his fabulous wealth to his corrupt son: "And scraping Cron hath got a world of wealth. / Now what of that? Cron's dead. Where's all his pelf? / Bequeathèd to young Prodigal. That's well: / His god hath left him, and he's fled to hell" (2.49–52). Lord Burghley had died August 4, 1598, ten months before the burning of *Micro-Cynicon.*[19] Additionally, the satire's references to Cron's base birth and facetious references to London as "Troynovant" call to mind widespread mockery of Lord Burghley's pretensions in claiming ancient genealogical connections, which appears most freely in unlicensed pro-Catholic propaganda tracts. The Catholic apologist Robert Parsons in 1592, for example, notes that Burghley first claimed descent from the Caecilius Claudius described by Pliny, before later connecting himself with the ancient Welsh Sitsilt family. Parsons asks, if this were true, if it were likely that Burghley's grandfather

would keepe an Inne in Sta[m]ford as diuers vvorshipfull yet aliue or lately dead haue affirmed to haue layen in the same; also how it is possible that his sonne the Treasures father, named also Dauid Cecil (if I forget not) should be onely groome of the vvardrobe, & so plaine, and meane a man, as thousandes yet can testifie that he was? & how finally VVilliam Cecil their child now Treasurer could be so poore, and

meanely brought vp, as to get parte of his mayntenance by ringing the
morning bel at his beginning in S. Ihons colledge in Cambridge as
commonly yet in that vniuersitie is reported.[20]

Parsons closes his withering analysis of Burghley's pretensions to status
by noting that, instead of lions for his coat of arms, "a good fatt capon, or
a rosted pigg seemeth a fitter cognisaunce for an Inneholders grandchild
as this man affirmeth, seing that those things are more commonly to be
founde in Innes, and Osteries then are Lyons."[21] Verstegan also makes ref-
erence to Burghley's father's relatively low-ranking post of groom of the
wardrobe, noting that to Burghley's "wylinesse was joined a wonderfull
ambition," even though he was "by birth but of meane degree," and warn-
ing of the possibility "whereby England may happen to haue a King *Cecill*
the first, that is suddainly metamorphosed from a grome of the wardrobe,
to the wearing of the best robe within the wardrobe."[22]

Middleton, of course, is more circumspect than these illicit publica-
tions, but Cron's exaggeratedly abject poverty in his youth, coupled with
the references to Troynovant, which facetiously implies how very, very far
back Cron's pedigree extends, echo the criticisms made of Burghley in un-
licensed works and in works such as Spenser's that were censored. Cron's
son Zodon is a "mounted beggar" (2.31),

> A base-born issue of a baser sire,
> Bred in a cottage, wand'ring in the mire
> With nailèd shoes and whipstaff in his hand,
> Who with a 'hey and ree' the beasts command,
> And being seven years practiced in that trade,
> At seven years' end by Tom a journey's made
> Unto the city of fair Troynovant,
> Where through extremity of need and want
> He's forced to trot with fardel at his back
> From house to house, demanding if they lack
> A poor young man that's willing to take pain
> And mickle labour, though for little gain.
>   (2.33–44)

The narrative of these two satires together—the story of a poor young man
who becomes wealthy and powerful, hoards his wealth, and then bequeaths
it at his death to his undeserving and corrupt son—allegorizes (and exag-

gerates) the actual biographies of the two most powerful men in England in the 1590s. Middleton emphasizes the connection with the reference to the "fardel at [Cron's] back" (2.41); although it seems to refer to the father, not the son (though the syntax is cloudy, and it could be either), anything reminiscent of a hunchback at this time served to point the allusion to Robert Cecil, whose back was crooked.

The "fardel" calls to mind Spenser's fox cubs with backs "nigh broken" (1158), and both are part of the mean-spirited shorthand from the 1590s up to Robert Cecil's death in 1612 and beyond that used language of deformity and subhumanness to refer to Cecil, because of his crooked back and short stature. Pauline Croft has analyzed Cecil's reputation by studying the libels written against him both after the fall of the earl of Essex and following Cecil's death, finding that "The themes which emerged most insistently and savagely were those of [Robert Cecil, earl of] Salisbury's crooked back and his sexual appetites."[23] Animal imagery abounds to highlight these themes, with fox, ape, dolphin, and spider imagery used to refer to him.[24] Middleton's sly use of a fardel on a back to allude to Cecil's crooked back is echoed by other anti-Cecil writers. Writing in 1592, Verstegan jests that Robert Cecil's father should have helped him to a job as "writer vnder some clerck or officier of the courte," because "he was fittest for such purpose, for that he caried his deske on his back."[25] Twenty years later, following the Earl of Salisbury's death in 1612, a libelist describes him as "a Ciciliane monster beegott of a fox / some caulde him crookebacke & some litle Robbin / hee bore on his backe a packe like ower Dobbin."[26] Although Middleton creates deniability for his satire by placing the fardel on *Cron's* back, not Zodon's, this narration of Cron's youth appears in the second satire, on Zodon, thus connecting the image of deformity to the son.

Another way that Middleton subtly connects this satire to Spenser's work is through the unusual name of Zodon. A search of Early English Books Online for the word "Zodon" yields only Middleton's *Micro-Cynicon*, but a search for "zodion" indicates that the etymological connection between this word and the English "zodiac" (which tangentially connects Zodon's name to Zeus through the mythological reference) was well known. All occurrences of the word "zodion" appear in the context of providing an etymology for "zodiac." In three instances (Richard Eden's translation of Martín Cortés, 1589; Thomas Blundeville, 1594; and Thomas Hill, 1599), the author translates *zodion* simply as "beast," but Philemon Holland's 1609 translation of Ammianus Marcellinus retains the sense of the word as a diminutive (especially fitting for the short and hunchbacked Robert Cecil):

"*Zodiak,* of *Zodion* in Greeke, a little living creature."[27] As I have argued, the beast fable was in the 1590s the satire that dared not speak its name, but Middleton finds ingenious ways of referring to animal satire in general and to Spenser's infamous *Mother Hubberds Tale* in particular.

These allusions to Spenser's methods of satirizing William and Robert Cecil—reference to a fox, emphasis on a corrupt father-son dynasty, subtle allusions to physical deformity, and an animal reference in Zodon's name— served to teach contemporary readers how to understand the satire by suggesting the likelihood that Middleton shared the political and religious ideas associated in the public mind with Spenser. Identifying the nature of Middleton's offense in this work is important for what it tells us about Middleton—about his politics in the late 1590s, for example, and also his ideological alignment with Edmund Spenser and others whose satirical toolboxes the young poet raided to create this early work. Identifying the possible source of the decision to censor Middleton's work is also important for what it tells us about the political significance of the genre of formal verse satire in the 1590s. To a present-day reader, the references to the Cecils in the first two satires of *Micro-Cynicon* may appear tenuous and circuitous. And yet the reader of a formal verse satire in the 1590s came to the text not only with a wealth of contextual information about animal nicknames, popular criticisms of leading political figures, and the like, but also with a desire, inspired by the social meaning of the genre itself, to find secrets hidden within the text. In this rhetorical situation, authorial intention joined with readerly ingenuity to create topical, and potentially dangerous, interpretations.

SPENSER'S SATIRIC INFLUENCE ON
MIDDLETON'S *FATHER HUBBURDS TALES*

Being an oppositional writer in a time of repressive censorship is a dangerous business; having learned his lesson in 1599, Middleton in *Father Hubburds Tales* (1604) aimed to convey a satirical message, but more safely. He blunts the force of the satire by making *Father Hubburds Tales* quite different in form from the verse satires of the 1590s and by creating extremely general satiric targets. At the same time, he calls attention to the fact that there is indeed a satirical message by making insistent reference to Spenser.

Andrew McRae argues that, rather than forcing satire "underground," the Bishops' Ban instead "contributed to a dispersal or diffusion of the mode, which subsequently informed a wide range of texts."[28] Middleton, because of the 1599 burning of *Micro-Cynicon*, was presumably highly motivated in 1604 to vent his satirical ire in non-incendiary ways. In *Father Hubburds Tales; or, The Ant and the Nightingale*, Middleton responds to the danger of censorship and/or punishment by hiding his meanings in typically Spenserian fashion.[29] As Spenser did in his *Complaints* volume, Middleton creates formal and stylistic parallels with the medieval complaints tradition, thus distancing himself from the problematic, classically inspired formal verse satire even as he deploys nostalgia as a tool for political critique of Jacobean England. Second, in creating an "insect fable" akin to Spenser's *Virgils Gnat* and *Muiopotmos*, Middleton invites readers to use the same interpretive strategies they had applied to Spenser's *Prosopopoia; or, Mother Hubberds Tale* and to the fox imagery in *Micro-Cynicon* to understand the satirical message. By adapting these strategies from Spenser, and by insistently reminding readers of Spenser's infamous satire, Middleton places himself both politically and artistically within the camp of the Spenserian poets of the early seventeenth century.

Father Hubburds Tales, differentiated in multiple ways from *Micro-Cynicon*, appears innocuous. Ovid's Philomel, in her nightingale form, catches an ant, but he persuades her not to eat him. Instead, he tells of his past—like her, he used to be a human, and he reports his experiences as a ploughman, as a soldier, and as a scholar. Middleton distinguishes this satire formally from the clearly Juvenalian mode of *Micro-Cynicon* by using the mixed verse and prose associated with Menippean satire (the ant's stories are in prose, whereas the conversations between the ant and Philomel are in verse) and thematically by means of the fable-like use of animals as characters. To complicate these classical satiric models with reference to the native English tradition, we might also say that the plot and concerns of *Father Hubburds Tales*—the unfair treatment of ploughmen by rack-renting aristocrats, the lack of public care for a soldier wounded in battle, and the declining appreciation of poets and scholars—seem more akin to the medieval complaint than to early modern satire per se.[30] Additionally, the work engages with the estates satire tradition, but Middleton modifies Chaucer's inclusive estates satire in the General Prologue by focusing *only* on poor characters. The work thus references an entirely different literary genealogy than *Micro-Cynicon* and the other verse satires of the 1590s, with debts to Ovid, Menippus, Chaucer, and English complaint in sharp contrast to the 1590s poems' allegiance to Juvenal. Yet whereas Middleton in *Micro-Cynicon* makes no overt reference to Spenser and does not model the form on Spenser but uses Spenser's satirical strategies to criticize the Cecils, in *Father Hubburds Tales* he references Spenser insistently, both explicitly and through formal and stylistic parallels.

Presumably these references to Spenser serve to counteract the danger that, because of the vagueness regarding specific targets in *Father Hubburds Tales,* Middleton risks blunting entirely the satiric force of his work. Calling attention repeatedly to Spenser's *Mother Hubberds Tale* reminds Middleton's audience to read carefully to interpret his meaning. Whereas the first edition uses "Father Hubburd's Tales" as the subtitle, the second edition foregrounds the allusion by making that the main title of the work. Middleton alludes to Spenser's work again in the address to the reader: "Why I call these *Father Hubburd's Tales* is not to have them called in again, as the *Tale of Mother Hubburd*: the world would show little judgment in that, i'faith, and I should say then *plena stultorum omnia,* for I entreat here neither of ragged bears or apes, no, nor the lamentable downfall of the old wife's platters" (166). Of course, *Mother Hubberds Tale* does not include an old wife's platters; perhaps Middleton had not read Spenser's controversial satire, or perhaps he purposefully introduced an erroneous plot point in order to imply his own lack of familiarity with Spenser's work, given that it was a banned book. Despite this effort at deniability, Middleton's reference to the title reminds his audience of it, and the reference to animals would call to many readers' minds the fact that topical interpretations of the animal characters in that work had led to its censoring.

This reminder to read attentively, and especially to think about the cultural meanings of the animal characters, would prime Middleton's audience to read this work with the same searching ingenuity that they brought to Spenser's *Mother Hubberds Tale* and to the formal verse satires of the 1590s. The work repays such a reading. Plot parallels with Spenser's translation of the pseudo-Virgilian *Culex,* titled *Virgils Gnat,* remind readers of Spenser's ideal of poetry as a guide and teacher for those in political power. References to monkey and marmoset characters and the frequent description of the ant-ploughman's young lord as an ape or baboon echo the fox and ape villains in the beast fable of *Mother Hubberds Tale,* as does the use of estates satire. Additionally, the use of a passage from Proverbs and a tale from Ovid as intertexts for the work suggests Middleton's reasons for using an ant as the protagonist and leads to a potentially anti-royalist interpretation of the satire.

The use of an insect protagonist would surely call to readers' minds Spenser's use of a gnat character in *Virgils Gnat* and a butterfly in *Muiopotmos; or, The Fate of the Butterflie* (both published in 1591 in *Complaints*) or the bumblebee protagonist of Cutwode's very Spenserian *Caltha Poetarum*, one of the poems named in the 1599 Bishops' Ban. Confirmation of contemporary understanding that *Virgils Gnat* refers to poets' attempts to reform their social superiors appears in Thomas Scot's 1616 comment that "If *Spencer* now were liuing," "The Ghost of *Virgils Gnat* would now sting so, / That great Men durst not in the Citie goe."[31] As Spenser does in *Virgils Gnat*, Middleton plays up the contrast between his insect protagonist and the more powerful figure he seeks to influence. The ant tells Philomel, "I am a little emmet [ant] born to work" and "Why seeks your gentleness a poor worm's end? / . . . . / I come to wonder, not to work offence: / There is no glory to spoil innocence."[32] The subtly anti-Jacobean didactic focus of *Father Hubburds Tales* appears in Philomel's merciful response to the ant. Philomel, presumably a type of Queen Elizabeth, models the kindness to inferiors presented as proper to royalty; she releases the ant from her hold, saying, "I give thee life and way. / The worthy will not prey on yielding things. / Pity's enfeoffed to the blood of kings!" (167; lines 183–85). The use of "enfeoff," a feudal term, further emphasizes the sense of nostalgia, as Elizabeth through Philomel becomes associated with an idealized view of the feudal ties that connected people in earlier days.

As a satirist, Spenser was best known for his *Mother Hubberds Tale*, and Middleton, as he had done in *Micro-Cynicon*, uses beast fable imagery in "The Ant's Tale when he was a Ploughman" to connect this work to Spenser's famous satire. Each of the ant's tales focuses on the unfair treatment that a poor man endures at the hands of the wealthy and powerful, but the first tale, that of the ant-ploughman, is by far the longest and most thoroughly developed. The ant tells what happened to him and his fellow ploughmen when his wise, prudent, and hospitable landlord died, leaving the estate to his son, who was "accustomed to wild and unfruitful company about the court and London" (169–70). After his father's death, the son engages a monkey and a marmoset as servants, further identified as a "French page and Italianate servingman," respectively, and then himself becomes "so metamorphosed into the shape of a French puppet that, at the first, we [i.e., the ploughmen] started and thought one of the baboons had marched in in man's apparel" (170). References to these animals abound in the rest of the tale. The son quickly signs away his patrimony to a merchant and a mercer in order to have ready cash. The ant-ploughman describes the son's profligacy in detail, but he also pays brief attention to how life changed for the ploughmen: "what a sad Christmas we all kept in the country without either carols, wassail-bowls, dancing of Sellinger's Round in moonshine nights about maypoles, shoeing the mare, hoodman-blind, hot-cockles, or any of our old Christmas gambols; no, not so much as choosing king and queen on Twelfth Night" (174). Again, we here see nostalgia for an earlier era, when landlords understood that their social position conferred upon them the obligation of hospitality, especially at Christmas-time, toward social inferiors.[33]

The wide variety of animal characters hearkens to *Virgils Gnat*, *Muiopotmos*, and *Mother Hubberds Tale*; in addition, Middleton's unusual use of the ant alludes to both Proverbs and to Ovid's *Metamorphoses* 7, creating an intertextual web of ideas about ants that coalesces into a message against the oppression of the poor. Ants' industriousness is, quite literally, proverbial, appearing notably in Proverbs 6:6–8, which Middleton paraphrases in *Father Hubburds Tales* just before Philomel catches the ant:

> There was a bed of busy, toiling ants,
> That in their summer, winter's comfort got,
> Teaching poor men how to shun after-wants;
>   Whose rules if sluggards could be learned to keep,
>   They should not starve awake, lie cold asleep.
>   (167)

Using an ant to represent the lives of a ploughman, a soldier, and a scholar reminds the reader of the laboriousness of all of these endeavors, and lends them as well the aura of virtue that attaches to the ant's work in cultural references to the ant's industry. Dignifying the work of these unglamorous characters certainly serves a polemical purpose, but I believe the work supports an even more radical interpretation.

Let us compare Middleton's paraphrase of the passage from Proverbs with the Geneva Bible version:

> 6 Go to the pismire [ant], O sluggard: behold her ways, and be wise.
> 7 For she having no guide, governor, nor ruler,
> 8 Prepareth her meat in the summer, and gathereth her food in harvest.
> 9 How long wilt thou sleep, O sluggard? when wilt thou arise out of thy sleep?[34]

We see that Middleton left out one verse: Proverbs 6:7, about how the ant has "no guide, governor, nor ruler." One can certainly read the Proverbs passage as favoring political hierarchy, as William Burton does in a 1595 sermon:

And what a shame is this to the slouthful person (if he be not past shame) that hath both guides, and gouernours, and rulers, both to teach him, and keep him in order, besides the benefite of reason and vnderstanding: and yet for all these meanes and helpes, which the Pismire wanteth, is carelesse of his owne good?[35]

In Burton's reading, guides, governors, and rulers are unambiguously good. Yet, Middleton's ant-ploughman, ant-soldier, and ant-scholar are human laborers who would be better off *without* the oppression and corruption of their "natural betters." In this regard, both the missing Proverbs 6:7 and the plot points—such as, for example, the unfair treatment of the ploughmen through the legal machinations of the young heir to the estate and the disregard of needs of the disabled soldier, whose captain and commanders cheat him of his pay, granting him only "a passport to beg in all countries" (178)—will remind the audience that, to the extent they buy the connection between English laborers and the virtuous, foresightful, and industrious ant, perhaps those ant-people would also be better off without the guides, governors, and rulers who oppress them.

The industrious ants of Proverbs, of course, remain ants; but Middleton surely had in mind as well a tale in which ants crawling up and down the length of a tree *do* become human. In book 7 of *Metamorphoses,* King Aeacus, heartbroken over the death of his subjects from a plague, prays to Jupiter to have his city filled with people again. Aeacus relates, "And Jupiter sent omens—lightning followed by confirming thunder .... I happened to be standing beside an oak .... On this tree we saw a long line of ants carrying bits of grain, huge burdens for their tiny mouths .... Marveling at how many there were, I said, 'Father, highest of the gods, grant to me the same number of citizens to fill my empty city!'"[36] He sleeps and dreams of the ants, who "appeared to grow and to become larger and to raise themselves from the ground, stand upright, shed their thin bodies, their many legs, and their black color, and take on human form" (122–23). He wakes and goes outside to find the ant-men of his dream, whom he names the Myrmidons, hailing him as king. He notes to his companion that "they still have the character they had before: a frugal, hardworking race, holding on to what they've acquired and storing it up for the future. All the same age and equal in courage, they will go off to war with you as soon as the wind blowing from the east . . . changes around to the south" (123).

Middleton's Philomel sings not in an oak tree, but "On a green hawthorn, from the thunder blest" (166; line 109); the thunder blessing may connect this tree to Jupiter's blessing in *Metamorphoses*. Although an oak tree would connect these images more firmly to the Ovidean text, the hawthorn in the early seventeenth century served as the usual perch for the nightingale.[37] Additionally, the use of the hawthorn tree, traditionally associated with fairies, serves to connect Philomel to Queen Elizabeth, the "Faery Queen" of early modern English literature.[38] Of the "bed of busy, toiling ants" in *Father Hubburds Tale,* only one actually transforms to a human, but the allusions to the tale of King Aeacus serve to remind the reader that those who look like ants—ploughmen, poor soldiers, and scholars— might rise up and become, like the Myrmidons, a warlike people.

Nostalgia for the past permeates this satire, from the black-letter type used for the ant's tales, to the use of the medieval forms of beast fable and estates satire, to the insistent references to Edmund Spenser's satirical work.[39] Middleton uses this nostalgia to imply—circuitously, of course— that England under James was in decline from an idealized time represented by Elizabeth. Some references to James seem laudatory, such as "there's a manly lion now can roar, / Thunder more dreaded than the lioness; / Of him let simple beasts his aid implore, / For he conceives more than they can express" (168; lines 222–25). In the same section, however, he implies that the English have already forgotten Elizabeth ("They that forget a queen, soothe with a king" [168; line 200]) and that even more "curs . . . fawn" over Robert Cecil under James's rule than flattered his father in Elizabeth's time ("Else would not soothing glossers oil the son, / Who, while his father lived, his acts did hate" [168; lines 214, 216–17]).[40] In this way, Middleton seems strongly to suggest that James—and his luxury-seeking, spendthrift ways—bears some responsibility for the decline in care for the poor evidenced in the ant's tales.

CONCLUSION: OR, SO WHAT?

Under conditions of censorship both violent and capricious, authors had to consider the possibility of offending not only with *what* they said but also with *how they said it*. I believe that writers in the 1590s saw Spenser's *Mother Hubberds Tale* as an unsafe stylistic model for satire, but that the Bishops' Ban, by censoring primarily works modeled on either Juvenal or the railing satirical style popularized by the Marprelate tracts and Thomas Nashe, made Spenser seem a more acceptable model for satires written afterward. These stylistic tendencies were strong enough to constitute a trend, as we can see from comparing Middleton's work in satire during this time period with that of John Donne, that is, his *Satires* of the 1590s and his *Metempsychosis; Poêma Satyricon* (1601; published 1633).

These two writers came to satire after 1599 from very different positions, in terms of both censorship risk and ideology. Middleton, who printed his works and whose *Micro-Cynicon* was named and burned, had much more to fear from government oversight after 1599 than did Donne, whose poetry circulated only in manuscript. Thus, in Middleton we must read the poetry as the author's negotiation between what he wants to say and what he can safely say; for this reason, the pervasive Spenserianism of his satires, whether he writes in the Juvenalian vein before the ban, as in *Micro-Cynicon,* or the Menippean after the ban, as in *Father Hubburds Tales,* suggests an ideological commitment to the religious and political ideas associated by him and his contemporaries with Spenser, and this fits with what we know of Middleton's lifelong sympathy for the reform-minded Protestantism associated with the Leicester faction and celebrated by Spenser.[41]

On the other hand, we would not expect the sometimes Catholic, sometimes Anglican Donne to use Spenserianism as a covert means of signaling Puritan dissent. Unconcerned with outright censorship, the manuscript poet Donne has the freedom simply to explore contemporary trends in satirical writing; the Spenserianism of *Metempsychosis,* coupled with its absence from his *Satires* of the 1590s, suggests that he may simply be following a fad.[42] In the supposedly unfinished *Metempsychosis,* Donne narrates the transmigration of a single soul from the apple that Adam and Eve ate to a mandrake, a sparrow, two fishes, a whale, a mouse, a wolf, the wolf's half-wolf/half-dog offspring, an ape, and finally, at the point where the poem ends, a human: Themech, the wife of Cain. Donne never arrives at the revelation he promises in the "Epistle," that he will "deliver you by her relation all her passages from her first making when she was that apple which Eve eat, to this time when she is he, whose life you shall find in the end of this book."[43] Probably intentionally, however, the apparently unfinished state of the poem has not prevented efforts to identify the target of the satire, with, for example, M. van Wyk Smith arguing that the poem satirizes Robert Cecil.[44]

Donne's subtitle, *Poêma Satyricon,* tells us how to approach reading, but the poem clearly differs substantially from the satires of the 1590s. Janel Mueller, arguing against reading *Metempsychosis* as a satire, succeeds in describing, though not explaining, the important shift that took place in satirical writing in England after the Bishops' Ban. She writes:

> [T]he prosodic, thematic, and tonal differences between the *Metempsychosis* and Donne's undoubted five satires have been almost entirely lost to view. The *Metempsychosis* confronts the scholar and critic with a number of distinctive characteristics—a rapid and continuous narrative sequence, a commitment to myth, the dominant themes of change and gradation into evil rather than achieved and assailable vice, a strong narrative presence which is subject to wide variations of tone and mood, and a full-blown epic framework. None of these can be matched, except intermittently, by Donne's satires.[45]

Despite the stylistic and generic differences, the *Satires* and *Metempsychosis* are both satires, and I believe that closer attention to the government's relatively minor intervention into the literary field in 1591 can help to explain the differences in works of satire by Middleton, Donne, and others before and after the Bishops' Ban.

I call the censorship of Spenser's *Complaints* relatively minor because Spenser didn't lose a hand or his life (the fates, respectively, of John Stubbs for publishing his opposition to Elizabeth's Anjou marriage negotiations and of John Penry for publishing the Marprelate tracts). Further, the controversy appears to have blown over rather quickly.[46] Although the censorship apparently did not damage Spenser physically or professionally, it contributed to Spenser's contemporary reputation as a satirist while at the same time dissuading poets immediately afterward from modeling their own work too closely on his. Despite the sense that it was dangerous to write too much in the vein of Mother Hubbard, Spenser and Spenserianism clearly served as important inspirations for reformist Protestant authors such as the young Thomas Middleton.

Indiana University-Purdue University Fort Wayne

NOTES

1.   Portions of this article were presented at the 39th Annual Meeting of the Shakespeare Association of America, Chicago, IL, April 1–3, 2010, and the 45th International Congress on Medieval Studies, Kalamazoo, MI, May 13–16, 2010. I am grateful to David Bergeron, Anne Lake Prescott, John Staines, and two anonymous reviewers for their attentive readings of earlier drafts and to Jean Goodrich for her knowledge of fairy lore.

2.   For more details on the censorship of *Mother Hubberds Tale* and its connection to the Cecils, see Richard S. Peterson, "Laurel Crown and Ape's Tail: New Light on Spenser's Career from Sir Thomas Tresham," *Spenser Studies* 12 (1998): 1–35. Bruce Danner discusses critiques of the Cecils in other poems in the collection in *Edmund Spenser's War on Lord Burghley* (Basingstoke: Palgrave Macmillan, 2011).

3.   Richard A. McCabe provides this quotation from the text of the ban in "Elizabethan Satire and the Bishops' Ban of 1599," *The Yearbook of English Studies* 11 (1981): 188–93, at 188.

4.   Some published examples of animal fables in the 1590s include an interpolated beast allegory in Thomas Nashe's *Pierce Penniless, His Supplication to the Devil* (1592) and Thomas Cutwode's (pseud. Tailboys Dymoke) *Caltha Poetarum* (1599).

5.   See, for example, Genevra Lee McCaw, "Middleton's Protest against Deceit and Luxury in His Time: An Examination of Six Satiric Plays" (PhD diss., Columbia University, 1950), 10–12; Richard Hindry Barker, *Thomas Middleton* (New York: Columbia University Press, 1958), 30; David M. Holmes, *The Art of Thomas Middleton: A Critical Study* (Oxford: Clarendon Press, 1970), 7.

6.   Those arguing for moral motivations for the ban include John Peter, *Complaint and Satire in Early English Literature* (Oxford: Clarendon Press, 1956), 149; Bruce R. Smith, *Homosexual Desire in Shakespeare's England: A Cultural Poetics* (Chicago: University of Chicago Press, 1991), 164; and Lynda E. Boose, "The 1599 Bishops' Ban, Elizabethan Pornography, and the Sexualization of the Jacobean Stage," in *Enclosure Acts: Sexuality, Property, and Culture in Early Modern England*, ed. Richard Burt and John Michael Archer (Ithaca: Cornell University Press, 1994), 185–200, at 196. Arguments for political causes for the ban appear in the following works: McCabe; Annabel Patterson, *Censorship and Interpretation: The Conditions of Writing and Reading in Early Modern England* (Madison: University of Wisconsin Press, 1984), 47; Cyndia Susan Clegg, *Press Censorship in Elizabethan England* (Cambridge: Cambridge University Press, 1997), 198–217. Given the generic diversity of the texts included in the ban, recent critics have looked for overarching themes that can help to explain the collective offensiveness of the named works. According to Douglas Bruster, the named works' "embodied writing" offended because they "took liberties

with bodies considered either above mention or above certain kinds of mention"; "The Structural Transformation of Print in Late Elizabethan England," in *Print, Manuscript, & Performance: The Changing Relations of the Media in Early Modern England,* ed. Arthur F. Marotti and Michael D. Bristol (Columbus: Ohio State University Press, 2000), 49–89, at 50, 53. William R. Jones avoids genre-based interpretations by arguing that the ban attempted to address a concern about ideology, specifically the Juvenalian mode as "a tangible threat to the ideological stability of the English nation"; "The Bishops' Ban of 1599 and the Ideology of English Satire," *Literature Compass* 7:5 (2010): 332–46, at 332.

7.	Peter, 147.

8.	All references to *Micro-Cynicon* are from *Microcynicon: Six Snarling Satires,* ed. Wendy Wall, in *Thomas Middleton: The Collected Works,* ed. Gary Taylor and John Lavagnino (Oxford: Clarendon Press, 2007), 1970–84; hereafter cited parenthetically by satire and line numbers.

9.	Smith, 164.

10.	Clegg, 213.

11.	McCabe, 189.

12.	I am indebted to Anne Lake Prescott for this observation. Larry Wayne Irwin, in "A Critical Edition of Thomas Middleton's *Micro-Cynicon, Father Hubburds Tales,* and *The Blacke Booke*" (PhD diss., University of Wisconsin, 1969) connects Cron to "Cronus" and his pride and rebellion (124).

13.	Anthony G. Petti, "Beast and Politics in Elizabethan Literature," *Essays and Studies* 16 (1963): 68–90; Peterson; Danner, chap. 5.

14.	Thomas Herron, "Reforming the Fox: Spenser's 'Mother Hubberds Tale,' the Beast Fables of Barnabe Riche, and Adam Loftus, Archbishop of Dublin," *Studies in Philology* 105:3 (2008): 336–87.

15.	See Danner, chap. 5, for a thorough analysis of the historical context of Burghley's building projects.

16.	Irwin, 125. An anti-Cecilian libel written after the fall of Essex refers to either Robert Cecil or his brother Thomas (Lord Burghley after the death of William Cecil) as wearing a fox-furred cloak: "Little Cecil trips up and down / He rules both court and crown / With his brother Burghley clown / In his great fox furred gown." Quoted in Pauline Croft, "The Reputation of Robert Cecil: Libels, Political Opinion and Popular Awareness in the Early Seventeenth Century," *Transactions of the Royal Historical Society,* 6th series, 1 (1991): 43–69, at 47.

17.	Edmund Spenser, *Prosopopoia; or, Mother Hubberds Tale,* in *The Yale Edition of the Shorter Poems of Edmund Spenser,* ed. William A. Oram et al. (New Haven: Yale University Press, 1989), 327–79, lines 1151, 1156–58. Future quotations will refer to the line number parenthetically in the text.

18.	Richard Verstegan, *A Declaration of the True Causes of the Great Troubles...* (Antwerp, 1592), 68. Accessed through Early English Books Online.

19.	*Micro-Cynicon* was not entered into the Stationers' Register (see Clegg, 286n52), so the *terminus a quo* for the book's publication is January 1, 1599.

20. Robert Parsons, *An Aduertisement Written to a Secretarie of My L. Treasurers of Ingland* . . . (Antwerp, 1592), 39–40. Accessed through Early English Books Online.

21. Parsons, 40.

22. Verstegan, 9, 55–56.

23. Croft, 54.

24. See Alastair Bellany and Andrew McRae, eds., "Early Stuart Libels: An Edition of Poetry from Manuscript Sources." *Early Modern Literary Studies*, Text Series I (2005). Available at <http://purl.oclc.org/emls/texts/libels/>.

25. Verstegan, 71.

26. Anonymous libel, 1612. *Newsletters from the Archpresbyterate of George Birkhead* 193 (from Archives of the Archdiocese of Westminster, Series A, AAW A XI, no. 136, pp. 369–72). Available at <http://www.earlystuartlibels.net/htdocs/cecil_section/D16.html>.

27. Ammianus Marcellinus, *The Roman Historie*, trans. Philemon Holland (London: Adam Jslip, 1609), c4v of the appended *Annotations and Conjectures*. Accessed through Early English Books Online.

28. Andrew McRae, *Literature, Satire and the Early Stuart State* (Cambridge: Cambridge University Press, 2004), 90.

29. The first edition of the work was titled *The Ant, and the Nightingale, or Father Hubburds Tales*; the second edition, which like the first appeared in 1604, was titled *Father Hubburd's Tales, or the Ant, and the Nightingale*. See M. A. Shaaber, "The Ant and the Nightingale and Father Hubburds Tales," *Library Chronicle* 14:2 (1947): 13–16; and Joel H. Kaplan, "Printer's Copy for Thomas Middleton's *The Ant and the Nightingale*," *Papers of the Bibliographical Society of America* 81 (1987): 173–75, for a more detailed explication of bibliographic issues related to the two editions of the work.

30. John Peter, in *Complaint and Satire in Early English Literature*, contrasts complaint and satire concisely: "while Complaint is usually conceptual, and often allegorical, Satire tends rather to work in the concrete particularity of real life. Secondly, Complaint is impersonal, Satire personal" (9).

31. Thomas Scot, *Philomythologie* (London, 1616), B1r,v; accessed through Early English Books Online.

32. Thomas Middleton, *The Nightingale and the Ant* and *Father Hubburd's Tales*, ed. Adrian Weiss, in *Thomas Middleton: The Collected Works*, ed. Gary Taylor and John Lavagnino (Oxford: Clarendon Press, 2007), 149–82, at 167, lines 174, 164, 166–67. Hereafter cited parenthetically by page number and by line numbers where relevant.

33. See Felicity Heal, *Hospitality in Early Modern England* (Oxford: Clarendon Press, 1990); Daryl W. Palmer, *Hospitable Performances: Dramatic Genre and Cultural Practices in Early Modern England* (West Lafayette, IN: Purdue University Press, 1992), 27–31.

34. *The Proverbs of Solomon* [Geneva Bible]. Accessed March 11, 2010 <http://www.genevabible.org/files/Geneva_Bible/Old_Testament/Proverbs.pdf>.

35. William Burton, *The Rowsing of the Sluggard, in 7. sermons* (London, 1595), 10–11. Accessed through Early English Books Online.

36. Ovid, *The Metamorphoses of Ovid*, trans. Michael Simpson (Amherst: University of Massachusetts Press, 2001), 122. Hereafter cited parenthetically.

37. For example, "the Nightingale vpon the hawthoren singeth" (Richard Carlton, *Madrigals to Fiue Voyces* [London, 1601], accessed through Early English Books Online) and "The Nitingale vpon the hawthorne brire / And all the wingd Musitions in a Quire, / Do with their notes rebuke dull lazie men" (Henry Chettle, *Englands Mourning Garment* [London, 1603], accessed through Early English Books Online).

38. Lewis Spence, *The Fairy Tradition in Britain* (London: Rider, 1948), 321–22; Lizanne Henderson and Edward J. Cowan, *Scottish Fairy Belief: A History* (East Linton, Scotland: Tuckwell Press, 2001).

39. According to Zachary Lesser, "one of the dominant meanings of black letter in this period . . . was the powerful combination of Englishness (the 'English letter') and past-ness (the 'antiquated' appearance of black letter by the seventeenth century) that I call typographic nostalgia. It is this combination that allows black letter to evoke the traditional English community"; "Typographic Nostalgia: Play-Reading, Popularity, and the Meanings of Black Letter," in *The Book of the Play: Playwrights, Stationers, and Readers in Early Modern England*, ed. Marta Straznicky (Amherst: University of Massachusetts Press, 2006), 99–126, at 107. Note that Spenser himself had used black-letter type to activate both nostalgic and nationalistic feelings in his *Shepheardes Calender*; see Steven K. Galbraith, "'English' Black-Letter Type and Spenser's *Shepheardes Calender*," *Spenser Studies* 23 (2008): 13–40.

40. Although Perry argues in "The Citizen Politics of Nostalgia" that Elizabethanism was not a fully developed rhetorical strategy of protest during the first decade of James's reign, his discussion of Dekker's use in *The Whore of Babylon* (1607) of explicit praise of James coupled with implicit critique seems germane to the similar strategy discussed here.

41. See, for example, Margot Heinemann, *Puritanism and Theatre: Thomas Middleton and Opposition Drama under the Early Stuarts* (Cambridge: Cambridge University Press, 1980), especially the lengthy appendix on "Middleton's Parliamentary Puritan Patrons."

42. For critical comments noting Spenserian elements in Donne's *Metempsychosis*, see M. van Wyk Smith, "John Donne's *Metempsychosis* (Concluded)," *Review of English Studies* n.s. 24:94 (1973): 141–52; Ronald J. Corthell, "Donne's *Metempsychosis*: An 'Alarum to Truth,'" *SEL: Studies in English Literature* 21 (1981): 97–110, at 98–99.

43. John Donne, *The Progress of the Soul (Metempsychosis)*, in *John Donne: The Complete English Poems*, ed. A. J. Smith (Harmondsworth, UK: Penguin Books, 1971), 176–93, at 177.

44. Smith, 142–43.

45. Janel M. Mueller, "Donne's Epic Venture in the *Metempsychosis*," *Modern Philology* 70:2 (1972): 109–37, at 113.

46. Thomas Tresham's letter was dated 19 March 1591 (i.e., 1592) and describes the scandal, with Spenser recently having returned to Ireland, authorities trying to collect all copies of the offending book, and booksellers profiting by selling the book at inflated prices (Peterson). In *Foure Letters*, Gabriel Harvey criticized Spenser for writing the work, because "Mother-Hubbard in heat of choller, forgetting the pure sanguine of her sweete Faery Queene, wilfully over-shott her malcontented self"; this work was entered in the Stationers' Register on 4 December 1592. In Thomas Nashe's response to Harvey's criticism in *Strange News* ("Immortall *Spencer*, no frailtie hath thy fame, but the imputation of this Idiots friendship"), he charges that "If any man were vndeseruedly toucht in it, thou hast reuiued his disgrace that was so toucht in it, by renaming it, when it was worn out of al mens mouths and minds." This work was entered in the Stationers' Register 12 January 1592 (i.e., 1593), and thus we learn that the scandal, at least as it touched Spenser, was of short duration.

GLEANINGS

Joe Moshenska

"Spencerus isthic conditur": Kenelm Digby's Transcription of William Alabaster

Kenelm Digby, perhaps the most significant early critic of *The Faerie Queene*, copied a four-line Latin epigram by William Alabaster onto the flyleaf of his own copy of Spenser's work. In this article I place his decision to do so in context, and suggest that Digby's choice of these verses may have been informed by his uncertainty surrounding his own confessional identity. Alabaster had converted to Catholicism in 1597, before rejoining the English church in 1611: Digby, born into a disgraced Catholic family, sought to understand his own religious allegiance in the late 1620s, and his reading of Spenser and broader engagement with Renaissance romance was one dimension of this attempt. I therefore suggest that a surprising strand of the afterlife of Spenser's poem was located amidst the complications of English Catholic conversion and reconversion.

S IR KENELM DIGBY set sail from the port of Deal in Kent on January 6, 1627/28, crossed the Mediterranean after several arduous months and a six week sojourn in Algiers, and eventually arrived at the port of Scanderoon in Asia Minor (now Iskanderun, formerly Alexandretta). He fought a sea battle with the Venetian galleasses guarding the port, and commandeered several French vessels with which he returned to England.[1] Digby

Spenser Studies: A Renaissance Poetry Annual, Volume XXVII, Copyright © 2012 AMS Press, Inc. All rights reserved.   DOI: 10.7756/spst.027.013.315-328

took his copy of *The Faerie Queene* with him on these adventures. A 1617 edition of Spenser's poetic works printed by Matthew Lownes, with Digby's name on the title page, is currently held in the library of Wellesley College in Massachusetts, and is presumably the very same volume which accompanied him on his voyage, its peregrinations and final resting place making it surely one of the best travelled copies of Spenser's poem. While aboard ship, Digby made good use of this edition, and took the time to pen his *Observations on the 22. Stanza in the 9th. Canto of the 2d. book of Spencers Faery Queen*, addressed to his vice-admiral on the voyage, the Glamorgan gentleman Sir Edward Stradling, and eventually published in 1644. The modern academic, tapping away before a computer screen in an office or library, can only fantasize of writing literary criticism under conditions as swashbuckling as these. For Digby, it seems, his daring and much discussed sea-voyage and his careful reading of Spenser went hand in hand.

While Digby's importance as an early respondent to Spenser has periodically been noted—he also wrote *A Discourse Concerning Edmund Spenser*, several pages long and now preserved in the British Library—both his readings and the context in which he produced them merit further consideration, which I hope to offer at a later date.[2] In this article, however, I propose to discuss not Digby's reading of this copy of *The Faerie Queene* on his voyage, but what he wrote in it. Sadly, there are no marginalia in the book, no evidence of the meticulous teasing out of Spenser's densely geometrical description of the human body which Digby was later to publish. In addition to Digby's signature and the standard motto "Vindica te tibi" on the title page [fig. 1], there are, however, four lines of Latin verse written on the flyleaf in his lustrously swooping hand [fig. 2].[3] In what follows, I offer some tentative interpretations of Digby's decision to copy these particular lines into the flyleaf of his book, and, in doing so, I put his reading of Spenser on this voyage in the context of Digby's complex personal and confessional identity. Interpreting Digby's transcription of these lines, we not only witness the development of attempts to establish Spenser as a preeminent English poet following his death, but encounter one writer whose relationship with his own Catholic heritage was fraught citing the lines of another vexed onetime Catholic, all while reading a poem seemingly written in support of militant English Protestantism.

The lines in question read:

> Hoc qui sepulchro conditur, si quis fuit
> Quaeris viator, Dignus es qui rescias:

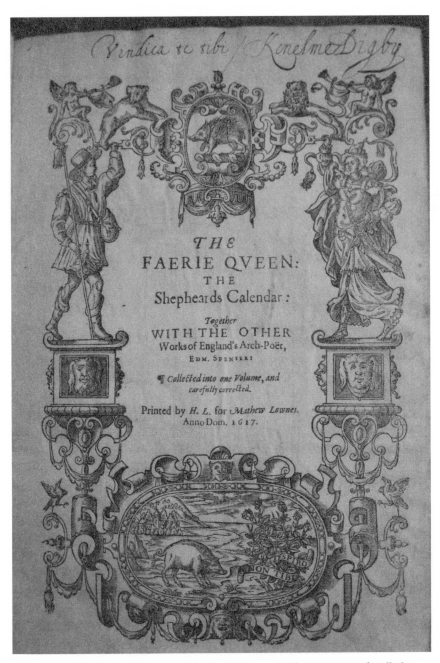

Fig. 1: Sir Kenelm Digby's copy of *The Faerie Queene*. With permission of Wellesley College, Margaret Clapp Library, Special Collections.

Spencerus isthic conditur. Si quis fuit
Rogare pergis, Dignus es qui nescias.

If you inquire who he was who is preserved in this tomb, traveler,
you are worthy of finding out: Spenser is preserved there. If you con-
tinue to ask who he was, you are worthy of remaining ignorant. (My
translation)

The epigram is witty enough: such is Spenser's renown, that a person igno-
rant of his name would probably be unable to comprehend his greatness
even if he or she were informed of it, and therefore may as well remain
in the dark. The pun on *rescias/nescias*, contrasting the worthy and the
foolish questioner, makes the point neatly. According to this poem, mere
knowledge of Spenser's greatness is a litmus test of sorts—a way of divid-
ing its readers (and Spenser's) into haves and have-nots. So great a poet

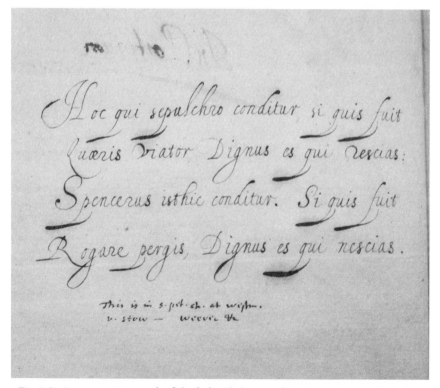

Fig. 2: Latin verse written on the flyleaf of Digby's copy of *The Faerie Queene*. With per-
mission of Wellesley College, Margaret Clapp Library, Special Collections.

was he, that it is impossible to come to understand his greatness, or to
have it explained, illustrated, or justified—you appreciate him either in-
stantly and intuitively, or not at all. The epigram, we might say, is as neatly
self-contained as the community of knowing readers that it describes. It
does not say very much, because there is little to say; it makes no case,
because no case needs to be made. These knowing lines, though, are not
Digby's own creation, but were written by the poet William Alabaster in his
Epigrammata (1600).[4]

It is difficult to know how much to read into Digby's decision to tran-
scribe these lines. At the very least, they tell us something about ongoing
attempts to secure Spenser's poetic reputation in the seventeenth century
and the role that Alabaster's epigram played in this process. Later in the
seventeenth century, "Edward Fuscus" (a probable pseudonym) published
an epitaph on Thomas Beal which closely echoes Alabaster's on Spenser,
beginning "Who lieth here? If any ask, 'tis one/Whose very nam's enough
to make him known."[5] This suggests that Alabaster's epigram was suffi-
ciently widely known to serve as a model for later declamations concern-
ing the inevitability of posthumous fame. Digby, searching for some verses
with which to adorn his copy of Spenser's work, might simply have been
attracted by the crisp wit of these lines, and deemed them suitable for his
purpose, without giving much thought to their source. As the study of texts
as material objects has gathered momentum, however, we are more in-
clined to see even the most casual marks left by an early modern reader in
a text as significant, and I believe that it is worth speculating further about
the meaning of Digby's transcription of Alabaster. If we understand some-
thing of the lives of both men, and the context in which Digby transcribed
Alabaster's verses, we can appreciate that various tangles of confessional
identity lay behind this act of copying.

After being somewhat neglected, Alabaster has recently received con-
certed attention as part of a generally resurgent interest in early modern
English Catholicism. His religious conversions were in fact among the most
prominent and notorious of the age.[6] Alabaster was a contemporary and
friend of Spenser at Cambridge: they were probably introduced by John
Still, later bishop of Bath and Wells and a significant figure in Alabaster's
life. Still, who was master of Trinity College, married Alabaster's cousin
and probably influenced his entry to Westminster in 1578 and his subse-
quent admission to Trinity in 1583. Spenser had left Cambridge several
years before, proceeding MA in 1576, but it is likely that he visited the
town in 1591, when he was introduced to Alabaster by Still. The young-

er man showed Spenser his *Elisaeis*, a Latin poem in praise of Elizabeth which he never finished.[7] Michael O'Connell, who has edited and translated Alabaster's poem, doubts that it influenced Spenser directly as he continued writing the second installment of *The Faerie Queene*, though its fierily militant Protestantism and historical specificity are certainly redolent of some of the starker passages from Spenser's Book of Justice.[8] What is certain, however, is that the most famous praise of Alabaster's poem issued from Spenser's pen. In *Colin Clouts Come Home Againe*, praising the virtues of various poet-singers, Spenser writes:

> And there is ALABASTER throughly taught
> In all his skill, though knowen yet to few:
> Yet were he knowne to CYNTHIA as he ought,
> His Eliseïs would be redde anew.
> Who liues that can match that heroïck song,
> Which he hath of that mightie Princess made?
> (400–405)[9]

When Spenser wrote these lines, in 1591, he had only recently met Alabaster in Cambridge, and had encountered him as an ally in constructing a Protestant poetics centered on the figure of the queen. They were published in 1595, and Spenser died in 1599, soon after which Alabaster wrote his epigram. In the years separating the publication of Spenser's poem and his death, however, Alabaster underwent a startling and very public transformation. In 1597 he met the Catholic priest Thomas Wright in London, who was being held under house arrest. Despite widespread hope that Alabaster might convert Wright, as Francis J. Bremer notes, "the reverse appears to have happened."[10] Alabaster began to speak openly of his newfound Catholicism upon his return to Cambridge, and it was then that he wrote the tortured sonnets which may have influenced those later written by John Donne. His conversion was brought to the attention of Bishop Richard Bancroft, scourge of papists and puritans alike, who intercepted letters from Wright. Alabaster was imprisoned, and withstood various attempts to win him back to the fold by Bancroft, Still, and another Cambridge contemporary and acquaintance of Spenser's, Lancelot Andrewes. Alabaster fled to the Continent, eventually taking up residence in the English College in Rome, where he wrote a narrative of his conversion.[11] He travelled again to England in 1599, where he was arrested and spent time in the Tower, although he was pardoned upon the accession of

James I. It was presumably during this time, at the height of his newfound fervor and persecution, that he wrote his epigram on Spenser. Returning to the English College in Rome by 1609, he fell out with Robert Persons, head of the College; brought before the Inquisition, he fled to England in 1611. There, astonishingly, he returned to the bosom of the national Church, was absolved of past wrongdoing by James I, and granted a living in Hertfordshire. He went on to preach before the king at Whitehall and at St. Paul's, devoting much of his time to producing hermetical and cabbalistic writings until his death in 1640.

When Digby wrote Alabaster's verses into his copy of Spenser's work, then, he appropriated not only the lines of a fellow admirer of this great poet but also those of a man who had not only sensationally abandoned the English Church but, equally sensationally, rejoined it, apparently cleansing himself of his besmirched past while attaining royal favor and public acclaim. There is good reason for such a man's example to weigh heavily on Digby's mind during his earlier years, especially as he set out on his voyage to Scanderoon. Digby himself had grown up under the shadow of his family's scandalous Catholicism: his father, Everard, had been publically and gruesomely executed as one of the ringleaders of the Gunpowder Plot. Much of Digby's younger life was spent dealing with this fact and attempting to rebuild his family's decimated reputation.[12] A major step had been taken in 1623 when he was knighted by James I upon his return to England from several years on the Continent, a success which had resulted from his involvement with the negotiations over the proposed marriage of Prince Charles to the Spanish Infanta. The need remained, however, for him to assert his loyalty to the new king, Charles, and to the country which his father had betrayed, so as to silence any continuing doubts concerning his allegiance and worth. The voyage to Scanderoon provided a perfect opportunity to do so: England was not only at war with France and Spain at the time, but reeling from a series of naval embarrassments, so Digby's capture of the French ships was a prominent and crowd-pleasing act.[13] The ploy seemed to work: despite his attack causing a minor diplomatic crisis with Venice and threatening to disrupt the lucrative Levant trade, Digby returned a hero in courtly circles, and was made surveyor general of the navy.

This was also a period in which Digby's own religious allegiance was in flux and in question. Despite her husband's disgrace, Digby's mother, Mary, raised her children in the family's old faith: he and his brothers were taught by Jesuits in their youth, and Kenelm then proceeded to Gloucester Hall at Oxford, something of a recusant enclave. There he was placed under the care of the eminent and respected Catholic don Thomas Allen, who would later bequeath to his former pupil his extraordinary collection of medieval manuscripts.[14] Digby's youthful beloved and then wife, Venetia, was from another old Catholic family, the Stanleys. It was therefore as the son of a disgraced and treasonous Catholic, raised and educated as a Catholic, that Digby embarked upon his Mediterranean expedition; Alabaster, whose lines he copied, was a man who had successfully overcome his dubious past and been welcomed into the fold of orthodoxy. Confirmation that Digby's religion mattered to his contemporaries and informed the way in which they judged his attack on Scanderoon is provided by a letter written by Thomas Roe, who was then coming to the end of an eventful tenure as English ambassador to Constantinople. Roe was a better travelled man even than Digby, but a man of a different sort: having sailed up the Amazon in 1610–11, he then spent 1615–19 as James's ambassador to the Mughal court in India before coming to Constantinople in 1621.[15] Roe deftly navigated the choppy waters of Ottoman politics, but the diplomatic tensions caused by Digby's actions at Scanderoon were a late irritation prior to his return to England. Writing in July 1628 to Edward Stringer, treasurer of the Levant Company at Constantinople, Roe stated that

> Whatsoeuer Sir Kenelm Digbyes commission be, Scandaron was no fitt place wherein to execute yt, to disturbe the quiet trade of merchants that pay better tenths then any rouer, and to give attention to the greedy and needy Turke to prey vpon us. The company must be sensible of this at home. And for myne owne part, I doe not like the libertye and trust giuen to any of that religion; for howsoeuer they may be honest and braue morall men, yet eyther they, or some that looke farther than they, may haue other and vaster dessignes then only punishing the foolish French, or enriching the admiraltye, to cast *petram scandali*, a rocke into our best trades, and, if possible, to worke a breach with this rash state. I remember, that in queen Elisabeth's time, *beatissimae memoriae*, no papist in England could preuayle for a letter of mart; not that some might not be trusted, but that euery such trust was a breach of that rule, by which the state was constantly gouerned: it was grace enough for them to keepe their defensiue armes in their owne houses, and not to arme them abroad.[16]

Roe sees the potential for a Catholic plot, some "vaster dessignes," lurking behind Digby's actions, and recalls the Elizabethan age nostalgically as one in which Catholics knew their place, and were kept there. The fact that a "papist" could roam the seas bearing with him official dispensation from the state was a sign, for Roe, of the inexorable decline of his times.[17] This was the sort of judgment that Digby undertook his voyage in order ultimately to overcome, proving to the world that he was far from a mere opportunist or a dangerous papist, but a loyal servant of the state.

The process by which Digby created and presented a new religious identity for himself involved not only his voyage to Scanderoon, but his protracted encounter with the materials of sixteenth-century romance, including his careful reading of Spenser. Stopping on the island of Milos on his return, Digby took a week to begin an extraordinary (if never published) autobiographical romance, while he also produced a translation of Torquato Tasso's pastoral drama *Aminta*, now lost.[18] His wrestling with the question of who he was at this stage in his life involved, for Digby, not only a confrontation with his own shameful past, but an intense engagement with Spenser and other renaissance romances. The upshot of Digby's voyage and this process of self-interpretation was made clear in a report by the Venetian ambassador to England to the Doge and Senate on 27 December 1630. There had been talk of sending an ordinary ambassador to Spain, he claims, "and many mention the name of Sir Kenelm Digby, who was at one time a pirate in the Mediterranean, and who let your Serenity's subjects feel the unlawful effects of his robberies. Moved by ambition he has recently abandoned the Catholic Faith and become a Protestant."[19] Like Alabaster, then, Digby returned to the fold of the English church, publically distancing himself from the Catholicism which he had not chosen but inherited.

Unlike Alabaster, who retained the faith that he rejoined until his death, this was far from the end of Digby's religious vacillations: he returned to the Catholic fold after Venetia's death, and his later philosophical and alchemical writings have been interpreted as justifications of his religious stance, although he continued to lean toward the English church at various moments, being forcefully wooed in this direction by Archbishop Laud.[20] The story of Digby's later life, however, takes us beyond the bounds of this article. We cannot know what was in Digby's mind when he chose to transcribe Alabaster's epigram into the copy of Spenser's works that accompanied him on his travels; the decision, as I have acknowledged, may have been unthinking, with Alabaster's poem chosen as a pleasingly feuilletonistic piece of wit, rather than for any deeper meaning.[21] Even if the poem itself does not explicitly concern questions of religious identity, however, it does posit the existence of a coherent community, comprised of those who admire Spenser's work—a community to which even Catholics such as Alabaster and Digby might belong, rather than being excluded in advance. I have presented some of the most significant events in both Alabaster and Digby's lives because I think that this context must at least cause us seriously to ask just how unthinking Digby's act of transcription might have been. There were plenty of other poetic paeans to the deceased Spenser that Digby could have chosen. At a crucial juncture in his life, however, as he struggled with his own religious inheritance and allegiance before publically disavowing it and converting, he chose lines by another writer who had prominently embraced before later repudiating the Catholic church.

The records of Digby's Mediterranean voyage, I have suggested, show that he addressed his personal dilemmas in part through an encounter with the materials of romance, and especially with Spenser's *Faerie Queene*. His quotation of Alabaster, a man whose tortured relationship with his own Catholicism rivaled and echoed Digby's own, can be read as a continuation of this encounter, a point at which the praise of Spenser and the vexations of religious identity and conversion collided. Recent work on *The Faerie Queene* has emphasized that this assertively Protestant poem nonetheless features characteristics which could be interpreted by its earliest readers as residually Catholic, for Spenser's allegory committed him to the ambiguous investment of material objects with immanent significance.[22] Digby's transcription of Alabaster at least suggests that one of the poem's many afterlives brought it into contact with the vicissitudes of English Catholic conversion and reconversion.

Trinity College, University of Cambridge

NOTES

I would like to thank Ruth Rogers for her help in accessing the Special Collections at the Margaret Clapp Library, Wellesley; Anne Prescott for her gently constructive criticism and advice; and Rosa Andujar for assistance with Latin detective work.

1.   The fullest account of this voyage is by Kenneth R. Andrews, *Ships, Money and Politics: Seafaring and Naval Enterprise in the Reign of Charles I* (Cambridge: Cambridge University Press, 1991), chap. 5.

2.   The most extended consideration of Digby's *Observations* is by Alastair Fowler, *Spenser and the Numbers of Time* (London: Routledge & K. Paul, 1964), 260–88. For brief accounts of Digby as a Spenser critic see Jewel Wurtsbaugh, "Digby's Criticism of Spenser," *The Review of English Studies* 11 (1935): 192–95, and Arlene Stiebel, "Digby, Kenelme," in *The Spenser Encyclopedia*, ed. A. C. Hamilton (Toronto: University of Toronto Press, 1990), 219–20. There is a brief recent discussion of the argument of the *Observations* by Elizabeth D. Harvey, who calls Digby "Spenser's first psychological critic": "Psychoanalytical Criticism," in *The Oxford Handbook of Edmund Spenser*, ed. Richard McCabe (Oxford: Oxford University Press, 2010), 775–91, 778.

3.   The same motto is copied into many of the books that Digby owned. Drawn from the very first of Seneca's *Epistulae Morales*, where it appears as advice to Lucilius, it might be translated "claim yourself for yourself." It is tempting, given the argument concerning Digby's unstable identity at this point in his life that I will be making, to read some significance into this choice of motto—a felt need on his part to grasp precisely who he was. Digby, however, scribbled the same words in many of his books: several of the volumes that he bequeathed to the Bodleian in the 1630s, for example, bear the same motto with his signature, such as Digby MSS 145 and 181. This was not his only motto of choice—Digby MS 9, for example, a small and pleasingly chunky illuminated bible, bears the inscription "Vacate et videte" (often translated "be still and know," more literally "be empty and see") which is from Psalm 45: the nature of the volume in question seemingly demanded this more pious citation. It is surely "Vindica te tibi" to which Digby was referring in a letter of November 7, 1654 to Gerard Langbaine, master of Queen's College, Oxford, in which he discussed his preferred borrowing policies for his donated books and enquired after the fate of some volumes in Arabic that he had also given. These, he mentioned, contained "my ordinary motto and name written att length in my owne hand" (Bodleian MS Ballard 11, fol. 21ʳ). We cannot, then, read much into the same transcription in his edition of Spenser, though it does make his unusual decision to transcribe further poetic lines onto the flyleaf all the more notable.

4.   Alabaster's *Epigrammata* can be found in Bodleian MS Rawlinson D.293: this epigram at fol. 19ᵛ. The lines are reprinted, with a slightly less literal translation, by R. M. Cummings in *Spenser: The Critical Heritage* (London: Routledge, 1971), 101. Cummings also prints Digby's two discussions of Spenser and briefly mentions his transcription of Alabaster's poem, though without comment (147): this is the only mention of these lines' presence on the flyleaf that I have encountered. In Digby's edition, a later hand had added the words "This is s. pet. ch. at. westm. v. stow—weever etc." This presumably refers to Westminster Abbey (officially the Collegiate Church of St. Peter) and to two antiquarian works—John Stowe's *The Annales of England* (1592) and John Weever's *Ancient Funeral Monuments* (1631). The reference is, however, somewhat confusing: Alabaster's lines bear no relation to the inscription on Nicholas Stone's 1620 monument to Spenser in the Abbey (though

it is possible that Alabaster, who was on the Continent at the time of Spenser's death, intended the lines to adorn or to be added to a funeral monument), they postdate Stowe, and are not to be found in Weever. Some of the inscriptions in Weever bear a passing resemblance to Alabaster's, notably an epitaph for Chaucer beginning "Qui fuit Anglorum vates ter maximus olim/Galfridus Chaucer conditur hoc tumulo . . ." (*Ancient funerall monuments within the vnited monarchie of Great Britaine, Ireland* [London, 1631], 490). Two possibilities suggest themselves. Either the person who wrote this note was merely pointing out the general resemblance between Alabaster's lines and other posthumous testimonies to great poets, rather than suggesting their specific provenance; or this person actually thought that Alabaster's poem was to be found in these other locations, and failed to check before writing this note. I am very grateful to Roger Kuin for his thoughts on the significance of these words, and for this latter suggestion.

5.   Edward Fuscus, *Ovids Ghost: or, Venus overthrown by the Nasonian Polititian. With A remedy for Love-Sick Gallants. In a Poem. On the dispraise of all sorts of Wives* (1657), sig. G3ᵛ. Cited in "Spenser Allusions in the Sixteenth and Seventeenth Centuries, Part II: 1626–1700," ed. William Wells, *Studies in Philology* 69:5 (1972): 173–351, 244. I found this later example in David Hill Radcliffe's on-line archive, "Spenser and the Tradition: English Poetry 1579–1830."

6.   See Alison Shell, *Catholicism, Controversy and the English Literary Imagination, 1558–1660* (Cambridge: Cambridge University Press, 1999), 88–94; Arthur F. Marotti, *Religious Ideology and Cultural Fantasy: Catholic and Anti-Catholic Discourses in Early Modern England* (Notre Dame: University of Notre Dame Press, 2005), 98–109; Molly Murray, ""Nowe I ame a Catholique": William Alabaster and the Early Modern Catholic Conversion Narrative," in *Catholic Culture in Early Modern England*, ed. Ronald Corthell, Frances E. Dolan, Christopher Highley, and Arthur F. Marotti (Notre Dame: University of Notre Dame Press, 2007), 427–49; Murray, *The Poetics of Conversion in Early Modern English Literature: Verse and Change from Donne to Dryden* (Cambridge: Cambridge University Press, 2009), chap. 2: "William Alabaster's Lyric Turn."

7.   See the ODNB entries for Alabaster and Still, and R. V. Caro, "William Alabaster: Rhetor, Meditator, Devotional Poet," *Recusant History* 19 (1988): 62–79, 155–70.

8.   "*The Elisaeis* of William Alabaster," ed. & trans. Michael O'Connell, *Studies in Philology* 76 (1979): 1–77, 8–9. O'Connell argues that the most significant poetic impact of Alabaster's poem was on the young Milton, and can be seen in his "In Quintum Novembris."

9.   I cite these lines as they appear in Digby's edition of Spenser's poems.

10.   Francis J. Bremer, "Alabaster, William," ODNB.

11.   See Louis L. Martz, *The Poetry of Meditation* (New Haven: Yale University Press, 1974), preface to the 2nd edition, for Alabaster's influence on Donne, and also the above references to Shell, Marotti, and Murray for accounts of this poetry and his conversion narrative.

12. The existing biographies of Digby are not entirely reliable: the best over-views of his life are Michael Foster's article for the ODNB, and his "Sir Kenelm Digby (1603–65) as Man of Religion and Thinker I: Intellectual Formation," *The Downside Review* (1988): 35–58; "Sir Kenelm Digby (1603–65) as Man of Religion and Thinker II," *The Downside Review* (1988): 101–25. For Everard Digby's role in the Plot and his subsequent execution see Mark Nicholls, *Investigating Gunpowder Plot* (Manchester: Manchester University Press, 1991), 34, 42, 52–57.

13. These included the ill-fated voyage to Cadiz orchestrated by Buckingham, which ended in a drunken debacle, and the Earl of Warwick's equally unsuccessful attack on the Iberian coast. For contemporary accounts of these voyages see *The Voyage to Cadiz in 1625, Being a journal written by John Glanville, secretary to the lord admiral of the fleet*, ed. Alexander B. Grosart (Westminster: Camden Society, 1883) and "The Earl of Warwick's Voyage of 1627," ed. Nelson P. Bard, *The Naval Miscellany V*, ed. N. A. M. Rodger (Hemel Hempstead: George Allen & Unwin, 1984), 15–93. On Digby's voyage in the context of these other disasters see N. A. M Rodger, *The Safeguard of the Sea: A Naval History of Britain, 660–1649* (London: Penguin, 2004), 357–60.

14. Michael Foster, "Thomas Allen (1540–1632), Gloucester Hall and the Survival of Catholicism in Post-Reformation Oxford," *Oxoniensia* 46 (1982): 99–128.

15. See Michael Strachan, *Sir Thomas Roe, 1581–1644: A Life* (Salisbury: Michael Russell, 1989).

16. *The negotiations of Sir Thomas Roe, in his embassy to the Ottoman porte, from the year 1621 to 1628 inclusive, containing a great variety of curious and important matters, relating not only to the affairs of the Turkish Empire, but also to those of the others states of Europe, in that period* (London, 1740), 821.

17. Despite their vast religious differences—Roe was a staunch Protestant, who would be influential in convincing King Gustavus Adolphus to join combat in the Thirty Years War on his next diplomatic assignment—Digby and Roe would, oddly enough, end up as colleagues in naval administration. In 1631, the two men were among those whom Charles I instructed to investigate the best means by which English subjects held captive by pirates might be redeemed, and such attacks best stopped. Roe's extensive experience in Ottoman lands, and Digby's liberation of captives from Algiers on his Mediterranean voyage, might have recommended them, but it is a delicious coincidence that they should end up as allies, seeking to regulate the seas. See David Hebb, *Piracy and the English Government, 1616–1642* (Aldershot: Scolar, 1994), 213.

18. The earliest version of this text is in the British Library, MS Harley 6758. A modern edition, with excellent notes, is Kenelm Digby, *Loose Fantasies*, ed. Vittorio Gabrieli (Rome: Edizioni di Storia e Letteratura, 1968). I argue in work currently in progress that Digby selected a romance as the form in which to cast his life precisely because it offered an opportunity to present his youthful stumbles and interruptions as generically apt, echoing the discontinuities of romance

narrative. On Digby's enduring interest in the tropes of the genre see Elizabeth Hedrick, "Romancing the Salve: Sir Kenelm Digby and the Powder of Sympathy," *British Journal for the History of Science* 41:2 (2008): 161–85.

19. Giovanni Soranzo to the Doge and Senate of Venice, 27 December 1630 in *Calendar of State Papers and Manuscripts Relating to English Affairs Existing in the Archives and Collections of Venice, vol. 22: 1629–32*, ed. Allen B. Hinds (London: His Majesty's Stationery Office, 1919), 452.

20. For Laud's letter to Digby trying to win him back to the church see *The History of the Troubles and Tryal of the most Reverent Father in God, and Blessed Martyr, Archbishop William Laud* (London, 1695), 610–16. For interpretations of Digby's later alchemical and philosophical interests as justifications of his Catholicism see Bruce Janacek, "Catholic Natural Philosophy: Alchemy and the Revivification of Sir Kenelm Digby," in *Rethinking the Scientific Revolution*, ed. Margaret J. Osler (Cambridge: Cambridge University Press, 2000), 89–118, and John Henry, "Sir Kenelm Digby, Recusant Philosopher," in *Insiders and Outsiders in Seventeenth-Century Philosophy*, ed. G. A. J. Rogers, Tom Sorrell, and Jill Kraye (New York: Routledge, 2010), 43–75.

21. In his *Observations*, Digby cites several lines from *Colin Clouts Come Home Againe* as a gloss on the Spenserian stanza that he is discussing (*Observations on the 22. stanza in the 9th canto of the 2d book of Spencers Faery queen, full of excellent notions concerning the frame of man, and his rationall soul*, [London, 1645], 18). Clearly, then, when he undertook this work he had recently read the very poem in which Spenser had praised Alabaster. His citation is significant because it is a relatively rare reference to a poem which "inspired only sporadic comment" in the century following Spenser's death: see Patrick Cheney, "*Colin Clouts Come Home Againe, Astrophel*, and *The Doleful Lay of Clorinda* (1595)," in *The Oxford Handbook of Edmund Spenser*, ed. Richard McCabe (Oxford: Oxford University Press, 2010), 237–55, 239–40.

22. For a fascinating account of how an early Puritan reader criticized what he perceived as the Catholicism of Spenser's poem see Stephen Orgel, "Margins of Truth," in *The Renaissance Text: Theory, Editing, Textuality*, ed. Andrew Murphy (Manchester: Manchester University Press, 2000), 91–107. See also H. L. Weatherby, "Holy Things," *English Literary Renaissance* 29:3 (1999): 422–42, and James Kearney, *The Incarnate Text: Imagining the Book in Reformation England* (Philadelphia: University of Pennsylvania Press, 2009), chap. 2.

ANDREW HADFIELD

A Mortgage Agreement of Hugolin Spenser, Edmund Spenser's Grandson

This gleaning presents and interprets the mortgage agreement between Edmund Spenser's grandson, Hugolin Spenser, and Pierce Power on 9 August 1673, conveying a number of lands in Renny, County Cork, to Pierce Power, after Hugolin's daughter, Dorothy, had married Pierce in 1673. The lands may constitute Dorothy's dowry.

*I*N THE NATIONAL ARCHIVES of Ireland in Dublin, several large folio volumes survive, the results of the Royal Commission inspections of material in the nineteenth century. One of these, "Transcripts of Deeds and Wills recited in Inquisitions (Chancery)" (RC 5), is a collection of miscellaneous documents, mainly from the seventeenth and early eighteenth centuries. One of these is an indenture produced on behalf of Hugolin Spenser, Edmund's grandson, on 9 August 1673, passing over a number of lands to Pierce Power in return for various sums of money.[1]

The survival of this document is somewhat fortuitous as the original was destroyed during the Irish Civil War when the Public Record Office was destroyed in the fire that consumed the Irish Public Record Office in Dublin on 30 June 1922, during the Irish Civil War, hours before the surrender of the anti-treaty I.R.A.[2] As the great Spenser genealogist W. H. Welply, who was responsible for recovering most of the documents relating to Spenser's life, notes at the end of one of his early articles, "Most,

Spenser Studies: A Renaissance Poetry Annual, Volume XXVII, Copyright © 2012 AMS Press, Inc. All rights reserved.   DOI: 10.7756/spst.027.014.329-335

if not all, of the documents cited as being in the Public Record Office, Dublin, no longer exist, having been burned in the recent destruction of the Four Courts."[3] This document was known to some early Spenser scholars and was consulted by Welply in the early twentieth century and, earlier, by James Ferguson in the 1850s.[4] Both would have seen the original and not the copy (fig. 1). However, the indenture has never been produced in full, has been somewhat under-interpreted, and, perhaps, even misinterpreted, which makes it worth reproducing now.

The indenture was drawn up after Hugolin's daughter, Dorothy, married Pierce Power in 1673. It states that Hugolin conveys the estates at Rinny (Renny) to Pierce Power, in what looks like her dowry. When the lands became forfeit as a result of Hugolin's siding with James in the Williamite Wars (1689–91), Pierce Power sought to have them returned and it was agreed that Nathaniel Spenser, Sylvanus's grandson, was liable for the estate and had to pay Pierce Power the agreed value of £500.[5] This suggests that, certainly by the end of the seventeenth century, the Spensers and their extended family did not live in Renny. The castle and lands at Renny had originally been bought by Edmund in 1597 for £200, for his infant son, Peregrine, Hugolin's father.[6] The castle, now demolished, was a prime site on the Blackwater, about fifteen miles south-east of Kilcolman, and on the way to Youghal, a further thirty-five miles down the river. It was an ideal place for Spenser to acquire, and it is not surprising that anecdotes have developed suggesting that Spenser lived there and wrote parts of *The Faerie Queene* under a tree—"Spenser's oak"—overlooking the river.[7] Of course, they are unlikely to be true.[8] Opposite the castle was the magnificent Augustinian foundation, Bridgetown Priory, the most significant religious foundation in the area, dating back to the early thirteenth century, which had become the chief burial place of its founders, Spenser's bitter rivals for the land beneath the Ballyhoura Hills, the Roches of Fermoy.[9] This had become the property of Sir Henry Sidney in 1576, and had then been passed on to Lodowick Bryskett, showing how closely New English settlers stayed together and how they undoubtedly made land deals that advantaged them all.[10]

It is likely that Hugolin was doing what most fathers in this period did, which was dividing the lands among his dependants and making sure that estates remained within the family. Indeed, this is exactly what Edmund did when buying the property in 1597. The indenture also tells us that Hugolin was living, or claimed to be living, a long way to the East of the Kilcolman and Renny estates, in Knockananig, about ten miles

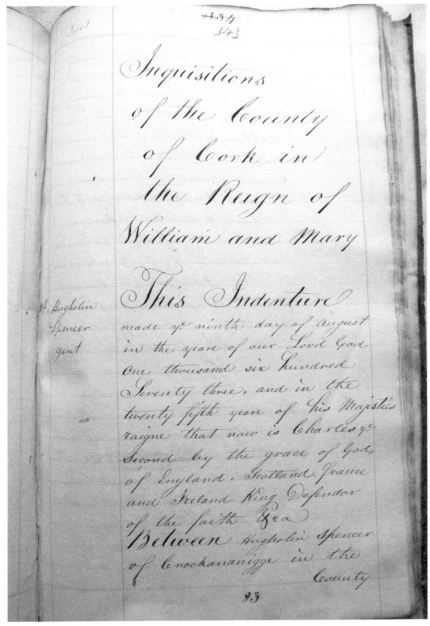

Fig. 1: The first page of Hugolin Spenser's mortgage agreement, as copied out in the
nineteenth century. "Transcripts of Deeds and Wills recited in Inquisitions (Chancery),"
National Archives of Ireland (Dublin).

southeast of Castletownroche, suggesting that he was using his inher-
itance as an investment property not a home. Pierce Power was from
Clonmult, a further twenty miles south-east, from a family who rose to
local prominence in this period.[11] All surviving evidence shows that both
of Spenser's sons, Sylvanus and Peregrine, married into local families and
became Catholic, Hugolin probably being the clearest example of this
trend.[12] This document provides further evidence of the interrelation-
ships between planters and natives in seventeenth-century Ireland, and
that Peregrine's son had moved a considerable distance from the family
estates and deeper into Catholic Ireland.

Inquisitions of the County of Cork in the Reigne of William and Mary

Hugolin Spencer gent.

This Indenture made ye ninth day of august in the yeare of our Lord God
One thousand six hundred Seventy Three, and in the twenty fifth yeare of
his Majistie's raigne that now is Charles ye Second by the grace of God, of
England, Scotland, France and Ireland King Defender of the faith yea
    Between Hugholin Spencer of Cnocthananigge in the County of
Coorke Gent. of y^e. one parte and Pierce Power of Clonmult in y^e. said
County Gent. of the other parte, **Wittnesseth** that the said Hugholin
Spencer for and in Consideration of the same of three hundred pounds
to him in hand before the Sealing and Delivery of these presents well and
truely paid wherewith he doth acknowledge himself fully satisfied and
paid, and whereof and of every parte and parcel thereof doe clearly ac-
quit. and discharge the said Pierce Power his Heires. Executors adminis-
trators and assignees and every of these by these presents. **Have bargaine**
sold graunted aliened and Confirmed and by these presents doe bargaine
sell graunt alien and confirme unto the said Pierce Power his heires, and
assignes, for ever all that the towne and Landes of Rinny Conteineing by
estimation one plowland Scituate in the Barrony of Farmoy and County
aforesaid with all and Singular the Houses, Edifices, buildings, Gardens,
Orchards, Woods, Underwoods, profits, Comodities and Hereditaments
whatsoever to the said towne and Lands belonging or in any wise ap-
perteyning or now accepted, reputed, accepted, taken, used, or knowne,
parte, or parcel or Member, of the same, and all the the [*sic*] estate,

right, little interest, use, possession, remainder inheritance, claime and Demand, whatsoever of the said Hugholin Spencer of in and to the said towne, and lands, and of every parte and parcel thereof. **To have and to hold**, the said towne and lands called Rinny and all other the premises, with all and Singular the appertenaunces, before by these presents bargained and sold, or mentioned or intended to be bargained and sold, and every parte and parcel thereof unto the said Pierce Power, his heires and assignees for ever, to the onely proper use, and behoofe of the said Pierce Power his heires and assignees for ever and the said Hugholine Spencer for him his heires Executors and administrators and of every of them, Doth Covenant and graunt by these presents to and with the said Pierce Power his heires Executors and administrators, and every of them in forme ensueing, that is to say that the said Hugholine Spencer for and notwithstanding, any fact or thing by him done, or perceived by him to be done, Caused, or perceived to be done, is and att the execution of the first Estate to be had, and made of and in the premisses, to the said Pierce Power, and his heires according to the true Intent, and meaning of these presents, shall then be solely seised of the premisses, before by these present bargained, and sold, or mentioned, or Intended, to be bargained, and sold, of a good lawfull, and Indefeazeable, estate in fee simple, without any manner of Condition or Limitation, of any use, or uses, and now hath all the Execution of the said Estate and shall and then have good right full power, and lawfull, and absolute authority to graunt bargaine, and sell, all and Singular the premisses, and that the said Towne and Lands, and all other Premisses with theire and every of their appurtanances, now are, and soe shall and may for ever hereafter remaine, Continue, and be unto the said Pierce Power, his heires and assignees, free and freely and Clearely acquitted, Exonerated, or discharged of and from, all and all manner of former and other gifts, Grants, Joyntures, Dowers, Uses, Wills, Intailes, Annuityes, Statutes, Merchant and of the Staple, Bills, Recognizances, Bonds, Judgements, Executions, Extents, Seizures, Rents, services, Arrearages of rents, forfeitures, Mortgages, Debts, of Record or any other Charges, or Incumbrances, whatsoever (omitted, [*sic*] Done or Suffered, or Permitted by the said Hugholine Spencer or by his Consent, Act, Meanes, or procurement, **Provided** always, and it is Covenanted, Concluded and agreed, upon by and betweene, the said parties, to these presents, that the said Pierce Power his heires and assignees, shall be contented with twenty pounds per anume as Interest out of the said Hugholine Spencer, the said twenty pounds accreweing, and payable

out of the said lands of Rinny yearly att all Hollantide, and May Day
and the payment of the first ten pounds, to be on the first of November
next Insewing the Date hereof and that after his Death the said Interest
to be thirty pounds per annum and the said Hugholine Spencer Doth
for himself his heires and assignees Covenant and agree to and with the
said Pierce Power his heires and assignees, that if the said Hugholine
Spencer Dies without issue male that then the said Pierce Power his
heires and assignees shall enjoy all and Singular the Premisses until he
shall be fully satisfied and payed, of five hundred pounds sterl. and it
is further covenanted **betweene** the said parties that if Dorothy Power,
after Spencer's wife to the said Pierce Power, and Daughter to the said
Hugholine Spencer shall survive the said Pierce Power, that then she shall
enjoy the use of such mortgage, Dureing her Life, as alsoe a third parte
of what reall and personall Estate the said Pierce Power shall Dye seased
and possessed of, and if the said Dorathie's happens to Dye without issue
by the said Pierce Power, the same to reverte unto the said Hugholine
Spencer or his heires. It is also agreed **between** the said parties that if
the said Hugholine Spencer, or such his issue male of his lady shall be
pleased to redeeme the said mortgage of three hundred pounds that the
said Pierce Power is nott to accept lesse then Fifty Pounds in each pay-
ment, and that the alone yearly interest, of twenty pounds, be fully paid,
and Satisfied unto thee said Pierce Power his heires and assignees yearely
and of the premisses, until the one Moyety of the three hundred pounds,
be fully satisfied and paied unto the said Pierce Power his heires and as-
signees, and then the said Interest to fall agreeable with the payment of
the said other Remaineing Moyety and it is Lastly agreed betweene the
said parties and the said Hugholine Spencer, Doth for himself, his heires
and assignees, Covenant, to and with the said Pierce Power his heires
and assignees that for the further, better, and more assurance, and sure
Makeing and Conveying, of all and Singular the Premisses and every part
and parcel thereof, that the said Hugholine Spencer his hieres or assign-
ees will make such assurance and Assurances in the Lawe, as shall be
Advised or devised by the said Pierce Power his Councill learned in the
Law, **In Witness** whereof the said parties first above named have unto
these presents Interchangeably sett their hands and seales the day and
yeare above written.

University of Sussex

NOTES

1. Indenture between Hugolin Spenser and Pierce Power, NAI RC5, "Transcripts of Deeds and Wills recited in Inquisitions (Chancery)," 19:343–53.

2. Calton Younger, *Ireland's Civil War* (London: Muller, 1968), 321–26. ("The Family and Descendants of Edmund Spenser," *Journal of the Cork Historical and Archaeological Society* 2nd ser., 28 (1922): 22–34, 49–61, at 59.)

3. W. H. Welply, "The Family and Descendants of Edmund Spenser," *Journal of the Cork Historical and Archaeological Society* 2nd ser., 28 (1922): 22–34, 49–61, at 59.

4. James F. Ferguson, "Memorials of Edmund Spenser the Poet, and His Descendants, from the Public Records of Ireland," *Gentleman's Magazine* 44 (1855): 605–9, at 608.

5. W. H. Welply, "Edmund Spenser: Being an Account of Some Recent Researches into His Life and Lineage, with Some Notice of His Family and Descendants," *Notes and Queries* 162 (1932): 128–32, 146–50, 165–69, 182–27, 202–6, 220–24, 239–42, 256–60, at 240. Hugolin died without a male heir or the cost would have been £300.

6. Welply, "Edmund Spenser: Account," 169; Ferguson, "Memorials of Spenser," 607. The original document was also destroyed in 1622.

7. J. R. O'Flanagan, *The Blackwater in Munster* (London, 1844), 118. Colonel James Grove White, *Historical and Topographical Notes, etc, on Buttevant, Castletownroche, Doneraile, Mallow, and Places in Their Vicinity*, 4 vols. (Cork: Guy, 1905–25), 3:172–73, shows that the tree was still standing in the early twentieth century, "situated in the S. W. of the townland of Renny Lower, on the bank of the River Blackwater, about 10 chains S. of the road leading from Fermoy to Castletownroche."

8. I spent some time trying to locate the oak or, at least, its site but was unsuccessful, despite the best efforts of Andrew King.

9. Aubrey Gwynn and R. Neville Hadcock, *Medieval Religious Houses: Ireland* (Dublin: Blackrock, 1970), 161–62.

10. Gwynn and Hadcock, *Medieval Religious Houses: Ireland*, 161–62.

11. See estate record Power (Clonmult) <http://www.landedestates.ie/LandedEstates/jsp/estate-show.jsp?id=2967> (accessed 1 July 2011).

12. David Edwards, "A Haven of Popery: English Catholic Migration to Ireland in the Age of Plantations," in *The Origins of Sectarianism in Early Modern Ireland*, ed. Alan Ford and John McCafferty (Cambridge: Cambridge University Press, 2005), 95–126, at 117.

Index

(Page numbers in italics represent illustrations)